INDIA:
A LOVE STORY

INDIA:
A LOVE STORY

Robert McGahey

Dancing Elk Press
Burnsville, North Carolina

Robert McGahey/Dancing Elk Press
300 Dharma Way
Burnsville, NC 28714
ecospirit.blogspot.com

Cover and text design by Robert McGahey
Cover photo: Sri Ramanasramam, January 1974. Photo is in the collection of the author.

Publisher's Note: This is a memoir. Names, characters, places, and incidents are factual, to the best of the author's memory, with the exception of occasional names.

Ordering Information:
Quantity sales. Special discounts are available on quantity purchases by corporations, associations, and others. For details, contact the publisher at the address above.

All rights reserved. No part of this publication may be reproduced, distributed or transmitted in any form or by any means, including photocopying, recording, or other electronic or mechanical methods, without the prior written permission of the publisher, except in the case of brief quotations embodied in critical reviews and certain other noncommercial uses permitted by copyright law. For permission requests, write to the publisher at the address below.

Copyright © 2020 by Robert McGahey
First edition 2021

ISBN 978-1-7346200-0-9

For Geeta Jyothi: life-partner, trusted advisor, beloved mother of Jacob and Jesse, revered *dadiji* to our grandkids.

Contents

Acknowledgments	ix
Prologue	x

PART ONE: PUER'S PROGRESS

1	Gateway to India	3
2	Malwa and the College	13
3	Meeting a Guru	21
4	Encounter with the Goddess	30
5	Kumar Gandharva: God-Musician	39
6	Struggle	48
7	High Noon in Goa	52
8	Indore: Retrenchment	60
9	Spinout on the Malwa Plain	66
10	Puer's Endgame	70
11	Apprentice Teacher	84

PART TWO: KRISHNA AND RADHA

12	Trouble at Springs	95
13	Kudzoo Kastle and a Wedding	101
14	Inauspicious Honeymoon	106
15	India: Dragged Across the Threshold	120
16	Sivananda Ashram	131
17	Morris and Little Atman	143
18	Tiruvanamalai and Ramana Maharshi	147
19	Mary and Joseph in the Deep South	157
20	Bombay: Death and a Blast from Morris	163

21	Dewas: a Trial Apprenticeship	168
22	Crisscrossing North India in Hot Season	181

PART THREE: RETURN TO INDIA

23	The Siren's Call	195
24	Reconnected with Sunderlal	200
25	Old Man of the River	210
26	End of the Road	218
27	Urban Adventures	223
28	Kodaikanal	231
29	Return to Malwa	243
30	Bombay Farewell	256
31	Another Sabbath, Another Passage	262
32	Return to Arunachala	268
33	Sunderlal's Challenge	273

PART FOUR: THE TABLES TURN

	Dance of the Gods	281
34	"Shiva Has Stolen My Heart"	283
35	Geeta of Garhwal	290
36	Turn and Turn Again	304

CODA: The Platform of the Heart	324
Glossary	335
About the Author	339

Acknowledgments

This book has been a long time coming, beginning the summer before my return to India, fall 1996. My first readers were colleagues at Moorhead State University (MN), who provided initial encouragement. I want to especially thank Lin Enger, whose response was "I believe in your book." During subsequent moments of doubt, that sentence has been my ballast.

I also want to thank my editors, without whom I would probably still be floundering with a "promising" but ungainly manuscript. Abigail DeWitt taught me scenic writing, noting that a memoir was more like a novel than a long personal essay. Susan Monsky taught me the crucial difference between myself as a character and as narrator. Reynolds Smith pushed me to explore underlying metaphors and cut parts that were not central to my story, while reaffirming the value of what I had labored with for so long. Catherine Reid led me to understand the difference between autobiography and memoir. This was decisive in giving the text its final form. Diana Donovan rescued me in the final stages of book design. Finally, I thank my life partner Geeta Jyothi (Judith Goldman) for her patience during this long ordeal. I release it to the world with her blessing, though it reveals almost as much about her as it does about me.

Prologue

India. My mother Virginia, my closest companion for decades, was captivated by the place ever since her Aunt Lucille visited on a steamer in the 1920s. She told Virginia all about it, but what the little girl remembered best was the set of colored plastic bangles Aunt Lucille wore on her wrist. What struck Virginia was not only the rainbow hues, but the tinkling sound they made whenever she moved her forearm. She was infected with a longing to go to India someday herself.

So when I was granted a Fulbright tutorship there after college graduation, Mother was mesmerized. Halfway across the world from each other, I couldn't share my latest excitement seated on her bed each afternoon over what I had learned at prep school that day, about Plato, Oedipus, Jung, or the liberal politics I first absorbed from her. But I wrote long, detailed letters, at least until I came under the spell of Kumar Gandharva, the legendary North Indian vocal teacher I was lucky enough to study with. His inspiration was so profound that I considered staying after the Fulbright year to be his *shishya*, sitting at his feet in Dewas and living in his household, just like legions of aspiring musicians within the *gurukela* tradition over millennia. As this scenario unfolded, I stopped writing, because I didn't want to say I wouldn't be coming home until I was sure.

We were a family of musicians. Mother had gone to Julliard to study voice right out of Converse College at age 20. Singing was a delight for me which began with church children's choir, and progressed through opera choruses and men's glee clubs through my career at Harvard. Being a Hindustani vocalist would be another thing entirely, especially since I would need to train in India and refrain from listening to Western classical music, which we both adored.

Then, scarcely a month after settling into life as a Fulbright tutor, I met Maurice Frydman in Bombay, who would launch me on the spiritual path I had sought since age 15. The Episcopal Church in Birmingham had introduced me to social gospel. Now this wiry little Polish Jew invited me into the path of Advaita Vedanta, illuminated by his master the sage Ramana Maharshi. Exploring the depths of this self-inquiry was like peeling back the layers of an onion.

PART ONE
PUER'S PROGRESS

1 Gateway to India

August 1967

Arriving late at night, the chorus, men dressed in summer jackets and glee club ties with musical staves on crimson background, women in sensible blue skirts with floral blouses to match, drifted out the doors of Bombay's Santa Cruz airport, stale and humid, our clothes smelly and crumpled, as if sleep-walking. The air smelled vaguely tropical, an odd mixture of fresh and rotten fruit. Downtown the full complement of smells arrived: fresh mango, ripe banana, green coriander, feces, urine, rotten vegetables, incense, *bedi* fumes and sweat, all suffused by the penetrating reek of diesel. As I floated into this miasma of smells, which both attracted and repelled me, I found myself stuffed into a tank-like black and yellow Ambassador cab with my roommate Sean. The windows were up, so the smells retreated, but now the streets of Bombay presented themselves, cows and bullocks at almost every turn, a few scruffy pigs and skinny mongrel dogs rooting and snuffling through the piles of garbage everywhere. Then came the bodies.

I was dead tired. But I began to notice that we were threading our way through thousands of bodies scattered along the sidewalks, sometimes in the gutters. The driver casually drove on, oblivious to the horror. I turned to Sean, who was asleep, slumped heavily against the cab door. Now I was bolt upright, dumbfounded by the raggedly clad bodies of men and women, children, old people, flung everywhere along our route. I had seen dead bodies before, a couple of times amidst highway carnage on family trips and Grandpa McGahey lying stiff and formal in his coffin when I was twelve. This was eerily different. We had entered a city beset by the Plague, and nobody had told us. The bodies began to thin out, disappearing by the time we reached our hosts' beachfront home in fashionable Breach Candy. Was this a dream? By the gray sea, the tips of the waves curled successively into the dull light, high walls, steel gates, the trailing branches of bougainvillea.

Our host, a wealthy industrialist in coat and tie, greeted us stiffly and quickly excused himself. He reminded me of Mountain Brook Country Club types from Birmingham in my teen years. His wife, resplendent in her silk sari, stayed to show us our room.

"You have had a pleasant journey?"

Sean looked as if he were still asleep, managing a wan smile. The driver brought in our bags as I answered, "Yes, thank you. I am sorry to have kept you up so late."

"Oh, that is no problem at all. My little boy will want to meet you in the morning. Now we shall all take rest."

"Certainly," I answered. "But excuse me. On the way here I saw bodies everywhere along the road. Is there a problem?"

Mrs. Mehta laughed. "Those are the homeless. They are simply *sleeping.*"

The Asian Tour segment in Malaysia had been canceled due to civil strife there, so we had spent quite a long time in the Philippines—long enough to encounter their civil war in Mindanao. Our bus was commandeered one evening by government troops, and the walls of the brothel where Sean and I were accidentally bivouacked were peppered with rebel machine-gun fire in the middle of the night. Unable to awaken Sean, I dove under my bed and waited for quiet to return. The world was a dangerous place, and music was a form of peace diplomacy. Our country was at war, the longest and most costly since World War Two. I had been spared, but those bodies were my introduction to war of another kind, an underworld descent that turned my comfortable world upside down.

I finished the choral tour, returning to complete my senior year. We were in the midst of the Vietnam war, but I focused more on escaping jockish Winthrop House and writing my thesis on Poe and Mallarmé than in joining the mounting protests. House Master Chalmers was confused and hurt by the request of the editor and two of his staff from *The Lion Rampant*, Winthrop's literary rag, to move off-campus, but granted it nevertheless. Central Square was my first working-class neighborhood. It felt liberating, an escape from the pretensions of the Yard, just as the Yard had afforded an escape from the suffocating classism and racism of Birmingham. I commuted to classes through alternately icy and slushy streets on a rusty old woman's bike I bought for ten dollars.

But the biggest development my senior year was Kathy. She came to Cambridge to visit her sister Susan, my Jay Street housemate. We hit it off instantly. Kathy was a playful, invitingly plump, pigtailed California free spirit, immature for a college freshman, but liberating for me. She was studying Carnatic flute, and planned to go to India to deepen her musical studies as soon as she finished Oberlin—three more years. After an evening nuzzling on the rug, she blurted, "We could get along."

So my first serious love affair was with a fellow *India-freak*. I celebrated the loss of my virginity with Kathy on a couch in Greenwich Village over Thanksgiving, embarrassed that her friend's mother walked in the next morning, condom lying in full view on the floor by the couch. We continued our relationship by long distance. Kathy was already working on her plan to go to India after graduation. We vaguely fantasized about my joining her there.

In my Jay Street back bedroom later that year, Kathy read my psych composition analyzing a dream about intercourse, diving into channels embedded in underwater mud, accompanied by a confession of virginal fears and Mother-fantasies.

"I doubt I would have slept with you if I had known how sexually hung up you were."

As for a return passage to India, I had never been very adventurous, but the memory of bodies lining the midnight streets of Bombay had unsettled me. I longed to experience more of this underworld place, the mirror opposite of my world. I was awarded a Fulbright to India, then dismayed to find my Pittsburgh draft board refusing to let me leave the country before my birthday physical on Bastille Day, 1968. Vietnam was heating up, and they would not make it easy to escape military service. Then I remembered the EKG.

Studying one night in my favorite lounge chair in the Lamont Poetry Room, I noticed the pencil in my pocket bobbing rapidly. I calmly walked down to the Health Center, where they took an EKG and gave me an interview with the attending doc. He listened carefully to my heart, then penned a letter about the seriousness of this episode of ventricular tachycardia. I carefully filed both EKG and letter.

I planned to circumvent my draft board by volunteering and flunking the army physical. As I left for the physical in downtown Pittsburgh, Mother was in tears. Daddy was in his cubicle high in the nearby US Steel Building, having accepted my decision the night before with his usual fatalism. I was confident I would flunk.

Stripped to our underwear, my induction-mates and I shuffled lemming-like through the physical. The sergeant barked at the slouches around me: "Stand up straight like this soldier here," pointing to me. Where was the doctor whose job was to save me? What if I were mistaken about the EKG?

"Does anyone have anything to tell the doctor?" the sergeant muttered routinely. Raising my hand, I produced the letter I clutched tightly.

So now it became clear why the Harvard senior, almost a grad, wanted to abandon the ladder of privilege to fight for his country. The attending doc read the letter, glanced at the long roll of film, and granted me a 1-Y. When I reached the stairs outside, I bounded down, leaping towards the road, hurtling onto the sidewalk. I was free, and India awaited me.

I graduated that summer, magna cum laude, Phi Beta Kappa. With my beard and scarlet armband, I looked like "The Graduate" on the June 1968 cover of *Time*, as the scrapbook Mother proudly assembled clearly shows. In addition to my family, Kathy attended in pigtails, wearing a simple printed frock. She called my father "Daddy," hugging him affectionately, to his obvious discomfort.

Martin Luther King was invited to speak at our commencement, but after his assassination, the Shah of Iran was chosen to speak in his stead. The choice was unfathomable. When Reverend King was shot, I was visiting Kathy at Oberlin. She bore me the message in the language dorm cafeteria. Shocked, I simply couldn't absorb the news. My enormous sadness was regularly invaded by angry thoughts about the *white trash* who shot him, though I dimly sensed I was just perpetuating the kind of prejudice King himself had fought so hard against. In the Yard, we listened blithely to the Shah's peroration to the Dream of Progress in modernist Iran, wearing our scarlet armbands protesting the American presence in Vietnam. At the rear of the assembly, I noticed Iranian students picketing and leafleting, feeling to us like an impolite little rabble, Islamist provincials who were ignorant of truly global issues like *our* War. Three days later, I was on a plane back to India as a Fulbright tutor.

Landing in Delhi after an interminable flight, I peered out at the dry, parched ground and saw the morning sun through dust and haze so thick I could directly observe its silver disk. It looked more like the moon. Though apprehensive, I was mostly excited. When we disembarked, I experienced a *feeling of finality*. It felt like I had come home, truly home for the first time in my life. I had a crazy impulse to kiss the earth.

The last flight that day was to Srinagar, Kashmir's summer capital. Some of us had found each other on the flight from New York, but lining up for this final leg we discovered our full complement. I met an attractive fellow Fulbright tutor, Carolyn, and we agreed to sit together.

The plane was a four-prop, buzzy, but otherwise comfortable. Tired though I was, being near this bright Carleton grad woke me up. She was blonde, blue-eyed, about five-four, svelte, well-formed. We fell into animated conversation. She was interested in music, as was I, and planned to study classical South Indian dance, Bharat Natyam. We were both liberals. I was enthusiastic about "T-groups."

Carolyn looked puzzled, and asked with a direct, earnest look which I found disarming, "What does that mean, T-groups?"

"Self-analytic groups. The 'T' stands for "training." They're small groups whose main purpose is to observe their own functioning, figure out the social dynamics, you know, the effect of different personalities on the group."

Carolyn nodded and leaned closer, listening intently.

"The leaders—the trainers—are usually silent, but intervene from time to time to draw attention to some dynamic—or just draw a reaction. A one-way mirror faced one end of the room. Grad students watched from in there. We could go watch too."

"So if you weren't there the others in the group wouldn't know whether you were observing them or simply absent."

"Exactly, Carolyn." This lass was sharp. I had heard that Carleton was a good school, and here was living proof. I smiled at her, feeling lucky I was getting on with the most attractive girl of the lot.

"Self-analytic groups have tremendous possibilities. They're being tapped by the human potential movement."

She was pretty, and I loved her serious look. "Really?" she asked.

I found myself looking at the top button of her V-necked blouse.

I went on to talk about T-groups leading to social transformation and the possibility of going into graduate work in social psych, becoming a trainer myself.

"What about you?"

"I majored in political science, and I might be interested in politics, though I'll probably work with a social service or development agency—after I get my PhD."

"In what?"

"I'm not sure. Political Science. Economics. Maybe Social Psych. I'm really interested in this T-group stuff. I want to hear more. It's so good we're going to be together in Kashmir."

Contented and cozy, I dropped back for a nap.

A few minutes later, Carolyn grabbed my arm. ... "Bob, look." I awakened to see range upon range of Himalayas. Heads scrunched together at the window, we watched, mostly in silence, occasionally pointing to a distant peak. Neither of us had ever seen anything like it. Then, spread before us was the vast Kashmiri Valley, the "Vale" much-contested by India and Pakistan: huge green swards, patched with forests, crisscrossed by rivers, all surrounded by a bowl of snow-capped mountains. I was entering Eden, Eve at my side.

When we disembarked, a brass band played, bass drum thumping. Amazed, I looked out at the crowd of perhaps a hundred on the tarmac below us, exchanging wondering glances with Carolyn. Were we that important? But then the object of this display stepped forward to be garlanded with about three hundred tightly sewn marigolds. Various officials bowed, touched hands together in *namaste* and garlanded each other, bobbing heads and pumping hands. We had been on the same plane as the Interior Minister from Delhi, come to lead the National Integration Conference in Srinagar.

As the gaggle of politicians moved on, a tall, balding, fairly distinguished looking man with military bearing made his way to our little group. Holmes, the Fulbright Director, an ex-pat missionaries' son, greeted us: "Kids, you don't know how lucky you are." Looking around at the beckoning Vale and the faces of the other tutors around me—especially Carolyn's—I suspected I did. We were in India, starting at the summit, the jewel in her crown.

We jounced through a breathtaking traverse of the Vale to orientation camp, passing temples and mosques, mountains and fields of lush vegetation, little groups of smiling school children uniformed in blue. We crossed rushing streams, skirted lakes bounding large conifer forests, fertile cropland blanketing their interstices. Everywhere flowers: roses and cosmos, fields of yellow-flowering grain. We stopped at a cooling waterfall for soft drinks, poor Indian imitations of Coke, and *chai*: a slurry of supersaturated sugar tanned by a healthy dose of black tea leaves thickened by full-fat milk, all brewed together. Handsome Muslim women with high cheekbones and proud eyes sat by the falls with their smutchfaced kids, all dressed in rich rainbow hues. They wore veils daringly pulled back behind their ears to trail down their backs—more like headdresses than veils.

After traversing the Vale, the bus pulled into the front of a canopied area on a broad, idyllic body of water, Nagin Lake. We got down and dispersed into five long, sleek houseboats, where we paired with our roommates for the year. In my case, it was Stuart, a Colgate activist from Brooklyn. His father was a "plummah"; mine worked for US Steel marketing. "You're from the South? I'd nevud'uv guessed. A Dixiecrat, then. Did you ever get to shake hands with Guvnuh Warless?" he added with a huge, sadistic grin, a twinkle in his energetic hazel eyes.

I wasn't really sure what Dixiecrat meant, but it didn't sound good. I explained that I was a good liberal, and would never consort with the likes of George Wallace.

"We'll wait and see about that." Stuart was brash, energetic, almost handsome with his delicately arched nose and strong white teeth. He had extremely long fingers, with which he caressed any object momentarily dear to him—a pencil, an apple, a woman. I marveled at these delicate hands, like a pianist's or surgeon's, decisively contrasting with his brash accent and sarcasm. They hinted of another side.

So our Fulbright tutor group began a two-week period of orientation at our Kashmiri base camp. We studied Hindi, intently followed cultural lessons, visited some local schools and lived as bourgeois tourists on our tethered houseboats. Except for the four-hour language and culture sessions each morning, it was mostly casual. Our linguistic and cultural preparations were much less thorough than those of Peace Corps Volunteers I later met. Stuart and I misjudged just how casual things were when we slept in during an early morning Hindi lesson. Looking from one lump to the other in disbelief, Director Holmes had barked, "Unprofessional, gentlemen!"

In the late afternoons small boys dove for algae, piling it high on their shell-like craft to take ashore and dry for fuel. Merchants sailed up bearing wares: enameled brass, woodcarvings, including chessboards inlaid with semiprecious stones, carved ivory, and piles of carpets and shawls handmade from Kashmiri wool. They didn't seem to understand that we were poor students. But I bought two woolen shawls, one for my grandmother, one for my "future wife." I don't remember writing Kathy during base camp.

At Nagin Lake, the tutors' group secured merciful protection from the last weeks of the North Indian plain's searing heat; it was in the eighties and low nineties and not too humid, cooling every night. Meanwhile, we slowly heated up our palates, graduating from western to Indian food by degrees, meals served under a brightly colored central canopy that reminded me of a circus tent. I foolishly entered a green chili-eating contest with a Kashmiri man one evening, for which I paid the next day with a second burning orifice.

One day an early rain came, big heavy drops soaking my wavy hair. I celebrated by dancing wildly in the central grassy area in my Bermuda shorts and bush shirt, Balkan leaps with hangtime—or so I imagined—having learned folk dancing at Carnegie Tech during Pittsburgh summers. The children gathered in the field watched incredulously.

Romances sprouted, a marriage started to unravel, and I had my first chance in India for romantic involvement. Though I had hit it off with Carolyn on the plane, she was reserved in the group and I was interested in getting to know the others. Stuart was omnipresent, and it was primarily because of him that I dined some with Carolyn, since he was courting her roommate Lynn. I liked Lynn. In fact, sitting across the table from the two women, I found myself wishing I was the one paired with Lynn. There was a mystery behind those grey long-lidded eyes, a depth I missed in Carolyn.

One night after dinner, Carolyn asked if we could talk. We walked by the lake, watching the little boats piled high with the day's harvest of slick brownish-green algae framed by pink evening monsoon clouds. We smiled at the ragtag kids who came up, saying, "Goodah evuhning, surrh" and "goodah evuhning, madam," running away giggling. As we wound our way towards my houseboat and up the wooden ramp to the deck, she reached for my hand. Natural enough, but it felt awkward. We went into Stuart's and my room and sat on my saggy bed piled with Kashmiri spreads of the sort the merchants tried to sell us each afternoon.

"We're leaving here in a week," Carolyn began.

"I know, I can hardly wait." I was going to Madhya Pradesh and she was going much farther south, to Tirupathi, near the big Vishnu Temple where they shaved devotees' heads and made wigs.

"Stuart and Lynn are planning to spend the Dussehra-Diwali holiday together."

"Stuart was telling me—that's neat."

"What about us? When do you think we'll see each other again?"

I was surprised. We had eagerly shared our life-hopes on the plane, the way you do sometimes with an interesting stranger in transit. Then you don't see that person again. We kept sliding together on the soft bed, touching thighs. It felt awkward.

"Oh, I don't know. ... I'll have to see what Indore has in store. I just got here. It feels too soon to make travel plans. Besides, we have nine months."

She looked more thoughtful than disappointed, with a serious, little-girl look on her face. She seemed to be thinking, hard. "Don't you think it would be fun to travel together, the four of us?"

Having spent the last week with Stuart, that didn't sound so inviting, though Carolyn certainly *looked* inviting. "Uh, yes, I mean maybe. I'd love to see you some more. But the *four* of us? I've been thinking of going to Benares and then to Calcutta for Durga Puja with Jon and Loren." This was starting to feel lonely and sad, like I'd already said all the wrong things, and we were soon going to be strangers again.

"I think we need to make plans soon. Maybe you could spend some time with me—and Stuart and Lynn—then head to the North. You know the South is supposed to be really beautiful, very traditional. You would like it."

"I'm sure I would, but like I said I feel a need to settle into Indore." "Do you think we should sleep together?"

I looked at her—then quickly dropped my gaze. "No." I hadn't meant to speak so quickly, so firmly. I was shocked, not having many such opportunities, but Carolyn gave no look, no declaration of desire, no gesture or touch, just that verb, *should.*

Carolyn nodded, accepting my refusal. It was as if her father or elder brother had spoken. Her earnest look, so serious, so touchingly winsome—gave me a pang of instant regret, but something wasn't right here.

It was to be a wild, but celibate year, and I suspect there was a deeper reason for my hesitancy. India was evocative, but also strange and threatening. Even as others instinctively moved to emotionally protect themselves from her, I, Puer, was being saved for an encounter with Mother-India. Though I was aware of a *giant emptiness* which awaited me, I wrote it was something *I don't fear ... and accept in a strange way.* To fill this emptiness I told myself, *Fill yourself with yourself.* It became a refrain.

Puer would learn soon enough from a little humpbacked Polish Jew in Bombay that he didn't understand very well what this self was. He found himself singing another refrain that accompanied the clacking wheels during frequent lone rail travels, watching the live cinders from the steam engines shooting by, fly-ash streaking his new white kurta: *Just a tiny incandescent spark on the sea of time.*

2 Malwa and the College

July 1968

Stuart and I were assigned to Indore in the large central state of Madhya Pradesh for our nine months' tutorship. Our assignment was half teaching college English, half pursuing an elective project. Since I had edited the *Lion Rampant* at Harvard, I chose something suitable and defensible: interviewing Hindi poets on the influence of the Raj upon their tradition. The trouble was, I had never read any Hindi poets. So when Holmes told us one fine morning that we were free to do anything we wanted, I switched my proposal to studying North Indian classical singing. But my prospects for vocal training seemed uncertain. The Fulbright bureaucrats in Delhi told me there were no vocal teachers in Indore. They advised me to commute to Bombay for lessons, over three hundred miles and fourteen hours by train.

New Delhi Station is a miniature of India herself, full of extremes of wealth and poverty, legions of beggars and pickpockets complemented by corpulent wealthy men and women actually being carried in litters. The noise was deafening: honks of traffic, people shouting, film tunes blaring at ear-splitting decibels—the high-pitched girlish voice of Lata Mandeshkar or one of her imitators offset by the high baritone of the male responding like a maddened dove. The love-duet blares in some places twenty-four hours a day. *These* are the latter-day gods and goddesses for the masses.

The Janata ("People's") Express left at two-thirty in the afternoon, scheduled to reach Indore after seventeen hours. As we spotted our train, several porters rushed around us, reaching for our bags. I continually shook my head, pushing the closest away as gently as I could: "Nahin, babuji." They persisted, so finally Stuart stood up straight, flashed his eyes, cocked his arm, then extended it as far as he could to the end of his long finger: "Go! We don't want any porters. Scram! Vamos! Jao!" They cowered, muttering, and left us alone. Our third-class reserved car was not very crowded, half-filled with pleasant middle-class people—mostly businessmen, a few families, and an elderly lady traveling with her daughter and two adolescent girls.

The train was propelled by a steam engine, a classic black beauty, starting to be replaced by diesels. When she fired up, it immediately conjured images of early childhood: the huge cloud of sighing steam, the slow turning of the wheels, mechanical arms attached to pistons configuring their gracefully roundabout arcs, gradually building to the chugging rhythm of the pistons. Mother, Eleanor Barry and I used to take the train from Birmingham to Kinston in eastern North Carolina during the summer, but those were sleek diesels. My image is a palimpsest of old newsreel footage and children's books, clouds of steam encircling my delighted face.

The car was pretty basic: single facing wooden seats on one side of the aisle, benches for four with sleeper berths doubling as baggage racks on the other. The berths hung from steel rods suspending platforms of wooden slats. Third class reserved was by far the best way to travel. You paid for a third-class ticket, but for pennies you could reserve a seat; for a little more, a berth. The only problem was booking them, since they were scarce. Most train travelers either buy third class simple tickets, or ride gratis. Cheaters are rarely caught since most third-class cars are so packed the conductor cannot even enter—though I was surprised at their ability to negotiate seemingly impassable knots of human flesh.

By early evening we were already nearly two hours late, but nobody seemed concerned. Indian trains have no dining cars, so at a longish stop in Bharatpur we descended and bought a supper of potato *puris*. I looked forward to station stops. Vendors would rush at the train, hawking their wares, the chai-wallah always in the forefront: "*Chai! Garam garam chai!*"

It was comforting to have the steel train wall with barred windows between us and these potential assailants, though I soon learned that they could board us, as would beggars and saddhus. The Fulbright folk told us to avoid street-foods, but I usually ate them if they seemed fresh and not black with flies. The *puris* were always a treat, as were *samosas* and *pakoras*. But the mainstays of rail travel were sweet biscuits and bananas, which India has in abundance: little ones, big ones, green ones, reddish ones more like plantains—always cheap. Since you peeled before eating, you avoided the lurking threat of disease in every unpeeled vegetable and fruit.

As we pulled away from Bharatpur, a man with one scarified eye, its mate rolled upward, leaving white marble, approached through the aisle. He propelled himself with his arms, having only stumps for legs. The man's face was covered with flies, and he had dried mucous on his upper lip. My fellow passengers studiously avoided his eyeless gaze as he paused between each tier of seats, bracing himself with one arm while extending the other, piteously repeating the cry for alms, "Baksheesh, baksheesh."

Stuart avoided his blank gaze, burying himself in a book, but, sensing I was looking at him, the man dragged himself over, sweeping banana peels, bedi butts and other refuse with his foul shirttail. He came right up to me, extended his arm, and as I hesitated, grabbed the tail of my kurta, then my hand, which I failed to retract soon enough. I looked up to see the other passengers watching all this, and reached for a fifty-paisa piece in my other pocket. I gave it to him and he repeatedly namaste'd with one hand, bowing his head slightly each time, then whirled to move on through the train. Stuart watched all this and remarked, "You shouldn't have done that." It would be a long time before I was socialized into the stone-faced avoidance my compartment mates had mastered as children.

An Indian family boarded. They seemed to be carrying their entire earthly possessions. With a porter's help, three generations of men passed up huge khaki bedrolls, large sacks and baskets tied neatly with twine. Then the mother and grandmother followed with two towering stacked *talis* of food tins. Before bed, I watched them as they unstacked the *tali*-towers to reveal multiple delicacies and fifty chapathis, with which they fed the family of twelve. I soon learned that both the massive bedrolls and the food-towers were standard for train travel. The main class differences (between upper and lower middle) are whether the *talis* are of tin or steel, and whether or not pillows accompany the bedrolls.

It was a long train ride, mercifully broken by over eight hours' sleep. I have always slept well on the train, the rhythmic clacking of her mechanical heart soothing me like a babe. By morning we were in the farming belt of the Madhya Pradesh plains—not as productive as the Gangetic Plain, but rolling grain fields nonetheless. Mothers looked out the windows as they held nursing babies under their saris. They would walk through the aisles, their hands under soft naked-bottomed babies in tiny t-shirts. I observed one woman wiping a tiny rump with the end of her sari. Only the rich had diapers, and a sari measured six meters—plenty of toilet paper.

The next morning a little after ten-thirty Stuart and I arrived at Indore. A pleasant, very light-skinned man with a tidy moustache was there to meet us with a big smile. He had intelligent eyes and wore the usual grey slacks and immaculately pressed white bush shirt. It was Munshee, our department liaison at Government Arts and Commerce College. Putting us in one autorickshaw, he jumped into a second along with our baggage, and we headed to our flat.

Indore is right in the middle of the subcontinent, a textile center and marketplace for Central India sitting at two thousand feet on the Malwa Plateau, creating a merciful, even idyllic, climate. In 1968, it was a city of 500,000. When we arrived in early July, the hottest part of the summer was over, soon to be followed by the monsoon, which I loved, at least while it remained a novelty.

The Fulbright flat came equipped with Salim, our Muslim cook. Salim was around fifty, balding, with long fleshy hound dog ears and habitually sad eyes which, when provoked, brightened with childlike glee into a wide, beautiful smile. He wore a faded old black hat in the Muslim style, a threadbare jacket in winter. Trained as a British army chef from age ten, Salim prepared the same food we'd had in Kashmir, including clumsily spiced biryanis, and many meat stews—especially mutton, which he rarely succeeded in disguising. Even my favorite tomato soup disappointed; the croutons tasted of kerosene. In a country graced with what became my favorite cuisine, eating Salim's fare was purgatory.

Stuart was a sociologist. Indian society was new to him, something he rectified by reading the huge India volume of Gunnar Myrdal's *Asian Drama*. This impressed me, but I had a different take on this vast, contradictory subcontinent. *The mystic bag is one I think I want to climb into for a long time.* Stuart was agnostic, a realist: "So you really believe that some of these saddhus, these jerks who've deserted their families and don't work, are for real?"

Our flat was on the second floor in a modest neighborhood built after

Independence. Our neighbor was one Swami Satchidananda, a member of Ananda Marga who ran a nursery school in which he taught four- and five-year-olds to "meditate"—or rather sit still and quiet with straight backs and unwavering gaze. It felt like Nazi youth training. The Swami was a large, well-built man who breathed *rajas*. He wore a bright scarlet robe, black-rimmed glasses, his tousled black mane greased like the ladies' with coconut oil.

Our first morning at the flat I smelled the neighborhood garbage, for all the housewives dumped it outside their front door. The night before, I took in a rich mixture of dung cakes and charcoal fires burning from the poorer section a couple of blocks away, plus the nearer odors from propane burners of popping mustard seeds and hot chilis, frying onions, cumin and coriander. And *hing*—the Brits call it asafoetida—the most overpowering of them all. Now the dominant smell was the rot from the previous night, mostly vegetable leavings, tea leaves, and butter solids left over from making ghee. Rankness prevailed, for few people had refrigeration: onions that were too far gone to be in last night's curry base, yogurt that had gone way too far, soured milk, overripe fruits, everything covered with flies. I went outside that first morning to check out the neighborhood, and almost stepped in our own garbage. I soon met our loyal garbage-dog, a tricolored mutt who Salim loved to feed, snuffling through our leavings. I went down the landing and around the corner to the street, where a few cows were grazing, scouring the alleyways and drives for garbage. Along the way I passed spent marigolds in little strewn piles, dirt, dung, patches of blood-red betel-juice, and endured the acrid stench of urine.

Despite the olfactory challenge, ours was a quiet, pleasant neighborhood, solidly middle-class, the kind of place I felt I belonged. I settled in rapidly, and grew to love the little daily routine. In the mornings, I would awaken to Salim's flat, insistent "Baab-Saab, Baab-Saab, B-bbuh-Brrrakefust." I would lurch sleepily into my pants, struggling like Pavlov's dog to get my bellyful of lumpy cereal with slightly rancid ghee, chai, and fruit, usually papaya, which I found unappealing unless bathed in lime juice. The sounds of birds sometimes penetrated our concrete walls. From the other side of the table, I was assaulted by jocular Brooklynese. "Another day in India—oh boy! Wonder what Bharti Solanki will have to say today. She's sharp, she's good-looking, she's my girl!" I didn't have any students like her. I was jealous.

At night I could hear the sound of crickets, the barking of dogs, and during the early part of the evening, the sounds of vendors: "*luckarri*," "*chai!* ... *garam dood*," echoing through the gentle Malwan atmosphere. Locals call it *shabe Malwa*—the nights of Malwa. From the four directions, I would hear sounds of soft voices in houses, the baritone or tenor of the father, the soprano of the mother, then the varied trebles of the kids. Occasionally I would hear the dull tinkling of cowbells, as the Hindu mascot made her rounds through the streets, scavenging for leaves, paper, bits of vegetable matter. Sometimes housewives would come out their back doors to give the cows kitchen leavings directly from their hands. On special occasions, this would be sweets, made from slowly cooking milk down to its essence: sweets to the sweet, essence to essence. You could hear the cows' wide, sober molars mashing the fiber, jaws rotating.

Before classes began, I made a quick trip to Bombay, where it all started the summer before. I stayed with my friend Udayan on Bhulabhai Desai Road—old Warden Road. I had met him at a party for Asian Tour members the previous year. Udayan's apartment was on the ninth floor, which you reached by one of those tiny little black open-grill steel elevators; it felt like traveling up the center of a miniature Eiffel Tower. The apartment was capacious by Indian standards, with a huge master bedroom, a large dining-living area, a small kitchen where the servants worked and slept, and Udayan's room, an only child. Balconies opened to splendid views of the Arabian Sea.

The sea, gray and sullen, was my constant companion in Bombay, and I often walked across the busy road to climb the black rocks and watch the breakers. Women did the same, pulling up their saris to escape the seafoam from breakers crashing around them. From Udayan's balcony, you had a broad view not only of the sea, but of street activity below. Hawkers pushed big carts propelled on bicycle wheels laden with fruits or vegetables, or attended little stands of fried snacks. Tank-like Ambassador cabs plied the crowded street, with an occasional double-decker Leyland bus, many mid-sized trucks and a few bicycles—not nearly as many as in provincial Indore. Just around the corner were poor women with matted hair, deeply lined faces, and soiled half-saris sitting on the sidewalk selling the catch of the day, which withered fast in the heat, contributing a ripe fishy odor to the briny air. One was attached to an aging toddler swirling playfully at her breast. Nearby, little kids played with pieces of junk, perhaps future inventors. On Saturdays, a man brought in a pony for which the upper-class kids of the neighborhood queued up to ride, attended by their mommies or nannies, girls with fresh dresses and ribbons in their hair. One boy wore a little sailor suit, like Puer when he was four.

Udayan was training to be a psychoanalyst. His father Ramanlal was one of India's prominent Freudians, Bombay's first. His mother Padmaben spoke no English, but she was a superb cook and full of heart. "Mother was one of Gandhiji's lieutenants. She headed a whole brigade of women freedom fighters. She was jailed by the Raj," Udayan noted with pride.

Ramanlal and Padmaben were both quite portly—a sign of status. Matrimonial ads often list weight—more kilos equaled more wealth. But who could resist? The Gujarati cuisine that Padmaben supervised was the most delicious food I had ever eaten. The range of flavors augmented in the sour direction particularly, especially through judicious use of tamarind. Here I had my first charred eggplant, a simple yet regal delicacy made into two or three different dishes, and the homemade chutneys were beyond my culinary imagination. The whole experience was like being in food heaven.

Every time I glanced in Padmaben's direction she was looking at me, watching my various states of delectation with a huge smile that radiated through her whole ample girth. The affection I felt from her seemed unlimited, a quality I rarely experienced so richly, except from my grandmother McGahey's black cook Melissa. I also appreciated these times at table with Ramanlal, who watched me with a bemused smile on his face. "So what draws you to India, Robert?"

"Spirit. The spirituality you feel everywhere. And the way everything happens out in the open—the animals wandering freely, seeing dead bodies. We hide death in our culture."

"I see. And is this quality of spirituality something that is lacking in America?"

"I'm afraid so. We are empiricists and materialists. For most people, Spirit is at best a hypothesis, not a lived truth. People just go through the motions in case there is something to it all. They're hypocrites."

Ramanlal smiled. "I'm no hypocrite, Robert. I don't believe in God. Religion is, after all, the opiate of the people—though Padmaben would disagree with me." He glanced at Padmaben, who nodded and beamed her gat-toothed smile.

"But there are higher realms of thought, and we in India always love discussing metaphysics, isn't it, Udayan?" With Ramanlal, everything was always being weighed and measured. I began to realize that some of his questions were merely means of testing me, finding out what made me tick.

Like his father, Udayan loved to observe people. He was the leader of a sizable group of young wealthy brahmins, the center of a whole web of relationships, which he relished. At the Breach Candy party for the Asian Tour, he had been the pivot. And there was his lifelong friend Roshan, who had beguiled me with her big dark eyes and palm-reading. The parlor game was a ploy for holding hands, but I got to touch an Indian girl! Glee Club friends teased me that this "Indian Princess" was the *real* reason for my return to India. She was definitely in the mix. Since her family lived directly upstairs, a rendezvous was easy for my friend to arrange.

Roshan's father and mother received me. They were charming, cultured, prosperous people, their flat filled with tasteful, sumptuous art, reminding me of Birmingham society. When Roshan floated into the parlor, they discretely took their leave. She wore a lavender pastel salwar chemise—Bombay girls only wore saris to formal events—which highlighted her dark, round, direct eyes above a gleaming white smile. It wasn't long before she again held my hand *to check the glories in my lines,* looking at me dreamily through those smoky eyes as we sat on the ample family divan, surrounded by sumptuous rugs and fabrics, sculptures, paintings and friezes. She delicately traced the various crossings and deltas, then moved to the plump highland mound by my thumb.

"So you have again come to see us. You are staying with Udayan?"

"Yes. I have a few days before college classes start in Indore."

"You are a professor there?"

"Not exactly. I am what they call a lecturer. The Fulbright people call us tutors. I also plan to learn Hindustani singing."

"Oh really? I love classical music. What *gharana* will you learn? Who will teach you?"

"I'm really not sure. I might study with a Maharashtrian who works for All-India Radio."

Roshan smiled and looked straight at me. I was afraid she would see my knees starting to shake. "You really should see about finding a teacher here in Bombay. That would be much more satisfactory, I think."

"I'm afraid I wouldn't be able to do that. I can't afford a plane commute, and the train takes forever."

"Of course. Still, I hope you will come visit us often. There are so many wonderful classical concerts here. Perhaps I—Udayan and I—could accompany you. Come, give me your hand so I can study this music." She drew her knees together and pulled my right hand to rest upon them. Glory. Perhaps *Roshan* was going to be my Gateway to India.

3 Meeting a Guru

"Would you like to join the fellowship of the undeceived?"
—Maurice Frydman

The heart of my life in Indore was the Government Arts and Commerce College of Indore University, where Stuart and I were English lecturers. We bicycled there a brisk four miles each morning, usually running slightly late. The wide roads carried bicycles, motor scooters, and autorickshaws, in that order, with some animal carts, lorries, buses and a few private cars rounding out the traffic. After skirting downtown, with its mild cacophony of three-wheeled autorickshaw Clarabell honks and occasional deeper truck-blasts, the principal sound was a concert of tinkling bells as riders signaled one another of their mutual approach on the wide boulevard to the college south of town. They sounded like the tiniest brass cymbals you could buy in the marketplace.

The program for an "arts" college in India was a huge shock for someone trained in critical thinking since ninth grade prep school. Basically, the idea was to read ("lecture") from a pony, diluted passages hemmed in by a lot of stilted, third-hand critical commentary. The students took all this down verbatim. I remember in particular the wreck the editors made of Melville, and I realized with deep regret that none of these students would ever encounter his prose—or that of any other great writer in English. They had huge difficulty understanding my American accent, which compounded the fact that many of them had minimal English skills. Since I wasn't really trained to teach English as a second language, I took to entertaining them with songs. At the second college assembly I sang "Shenandoah," aiming at the very top of the four-story classroom on the back of the quad, where students lined the corridors in unusually respectful silence.

Stuart and I quickly learned that it was going to be a long year in the classroom. On the first exam, three boys in the back row were blatantly copying each other's bluebooks. Irate, I marched back, snatched their papers and demanded they leave. I was forthwith summoned by the Principal, who promptly relieved me of proctoring future exams. He explained that Indian students were *allowed* to cheat, and that it was typically American of me to be so moralistic. I soon learned that students were courted by politicians, the rank-and-file with free cigarettes, the bosses with more substantial lucre. They basically ran the college, and the Principal was their stooge.

The Principal was a Yale Law graduate and his wife had a master's in public health from the same place. He was a short, plump man whose buttons strained to hold his shirtfront together. Occasionally one fell off, a permanent loss since his wife was proud to be a professional woman and would not sew. He was inevitably tousled, even at his finest, usually with a pleasant smile on his face. Stuart and I took chai with the Principal and his Queen a few times, and his conversation was intelligent, though he doted too much on news from *Time* magazine and memories of the Good Old Days in the US. His Keralite wife had huge buck teeth, and she, too, preferred to talk about news from the US. I was often distracted by food running down his chin, and the stains on his white shirt. I was amazed that a college president could be not only casual, but downright slovenly. But ours was an arts college in provincial India.

We settled into the monsoon, which lent itself to reading, writing long letters, and to moments of extraordinary joy when the sunshine broke through. I began an evening habit of feeding moths to the chameleons who patrolled our veranda walls by flipping the light off and on, momentarily halting the poor creatures' journey towards light, making them easy prey. *I feel little urgency, pressure to do anything now. Let things happen. I feel quiet, gentle, comfortable, and also pregnant with many things.*

After a fitful beginning of only ten days, classes were delayed by a clerical workers' strike, soon joined by the students in a show of solidarity. The school calendar was already shot through with three months of holiday; now the schedule became even more porous. Encouraged by my opportunistic housemate, I informed our chair that I was going to Bombay, and to please telegram if the strike terminated before my projected return. Our departmental colleagues were shocked at the speed with which the brazen Amreekans seized their opening. As luck would have it, Sharma, the program director in New Delhi, made a site visit while we were absent, much to his consternation. Our poor colleague Munshee felt particularly awkward. We were bad boys.

I took the first train I could get. I relished being back on these amazing trains, which seemed to have the capacity to carry all of India. This one was packed, and as we neared Bombay, more people got on, clinging increasingly to the *outside* of the train as well as cramming shoulder-to-shoulder inside. The fly-ash from the steam engine streaked my white shirt, and my white face as well.

For the first time, I wore my pyjama-kurta on the rails, whites the first day, changing kurtas the second day to an un-Indian deep blue. Like my hippy cousins, I started wearing a necklace of *rudraksha* seeds. Stuart and I had grown beards since arriving in Kashmir, to the disapproval of the Fulbright hierarchy. I was beginning to take on the characteristic mask of Puer's early twenties, though my hair still was a long way from reaching its shoulder-length curls. Then I would look like the photo of myself at two, spongy curls, wide smile, fingering a set of keys. Now that I was hairier and had swapped the bush shirt and khakis for North Indian garb, my fellow passengers took even more interest. As we headed out of Ratlam junction, the man on the facing bench asked me, "Exx-uh-scuse me sirruh ... are you Amreekan hippy-saddhu please?"

"You have the 'Amreekan' right. But no, I'm professor of English at Indore University."

My interlocuter had been leaning far forward, almost in my face. He backed off sharply, in perfect sync with the four men who had leaned with him, a dance ensemble. They looked at each other, puzzled. The ensemble leaned into me again, and another man persisted: "But sirrh, you must be being hippy-saddhu. See how you dress."

Towards evening, we stopped at a few remote stations. I began to enjoy the slow pace, to notice the subtle change in the landscape from central to coastal plain as we crept southwest towards Bombay. The call of the chai-wallahs at each stop became the *muezzin's* call to evening prayers at the mosque—my own private one where I worshiped the Indian landscape.

Now the train was traveling slower and slower, stopping more frequently. Finally, right at dusk she gave a steamy sigh which felt all but terminal. Heads of families got down and walked forward. I leaned as far out on the running bar as I could and saw a small gaggle of men speaking with the conductor. They soon dispersed and returned to their carriages. Then, as if on cue, a thousand passengers got down, carrying precipitously leaning piles of food tins, in some cases bedrolls. The assembled company evenly filled a broad rolling field on the western side of the train (seaward), backed by a small forest. Older children went to gather kindling, and fires started to appear.

As night fell, I could see the campfires spreading across the field. Then, as the onions started to fry and the chapathis developed their characteristic black welts in the open flames, thousands of fireflies appeared about our heads and up into those bordering trees, answering the campfires. I had totally stopped worrying about when the train might rumble again, and after finishing supper I leaned back on my bedroll to join the others in the most civilized response to a train breakdown I had ever witnessed. The stars twinkled their blessings above our field, reflecting its own dance of a myriad lights. When the engine repair was completed and we resumed our journey two hours later, I joined the other passengers, boarding with a twinge of regret.

At the main station in Bombay the next morning, I fairly skipped to the taxi-stand, free at last to explore India on my own terms. Again I stayed with Udayan, again regaled with superb food. The little dalliance with Roshan had faded, but Udayan had someone else he wanted me to meet. One morning at a fine breakfast of eggs scrambled with tomatoes, onions, chilies, and fresh coriander, Udayan turned to me with the usual self-assured expression conveyed by his whole body.

"You must meet Morris."

"Who is Morris?" I wondered at the un-Indian name.

"Morris is my friend, and the most interesting person I could introduce you to in Bombay. He would be perfect for you. He is a Jew, born in Poland, who came here in the Thirties. He must have been fleeing Hitler. He worked with Gandhi and is a close friend of J. Krishnamurthi. They have the best arguments."

Maurice Frydman was indeed a Polish Jew, but left long before Hitler overran his country. Graduating first in the country in engineering, he spent his youth in Paris, then came to work with Gandhi in the Thirties, hoping to persuade him to set aside the spinning wheel and adopt small scale machining skills as the basis for village industry. After spending some time at Gandhi's ashram Sevagram and failing to convince him, Maurice had lived at the ashram of Ramana Maharshi, one of the great sages of modern India, in Tiruvannamalai, an ancient temple town in South India. In Bombay, Maurice hung out with Krishnamurthi's circle. He had befriended the young teacher when K first moved to Bangalore and was a virtual prisoner in the house of a wealthy devotee; the wily Maurice helped arrange an escape.

So Udayan arranged a meeting. I remember the expectant sense with which I climbed the three stories to the entrance of his flat on Nepean Sea Rd, near a small upscale bazaar. A sign on the door read "Indo-Tibetan Library and Refugee Centre."

Maurice greeted me at the door, a humpbacked elfin little man wearing khadicloth, white pyjamas and a coffee kurta, probably in his late sixties, with keen grey eyes which I would learn held equal capacity to pierce or twinkle. Because of his back, he always held his head at a tilt, a little to the right. I remember my surprise the first time the tilt grew into the South Asian lantern-nod of agreement. Maurice Frydman had lived here a long time.

"Morris" received me in the comfortably cluttered dining area at the center of the flat. It led to the piano studio, which was silent today, but where I would later hear a student plunking away under the hugely watchful eyes of Miss Petit, who wore the most powerful magnifying lenses I had ever seen. Hilla Petit was a Parsee with whom, I imagined, Maurice lived chastely. I later learned they had married. The room was framed with faded old lace curtains, and an assortment of photos and a few nondescript prints hung on the wall. The photos were of historical figures, some European, some Parsee (the Petits were quite a prominent family), some Indian, representing the combined interests of the two inhabitants: a cultured widow and a spiritual teacher. I was particularly drawn to a man's face with short cropped white hair, chiseled features and penetrating eyes. A linen tablecloth covered the table, same faded white as the curtains, and bore several piles of books and papers. The room had a decidedly musty odor.

We had tea and Maurice asked how I had come to India. Then he got down to business. Putting down his teacup, he rather abruptly asked in his reedy voice, "Tell me, what is the self?

"You mean *my* self?"

"Yes, if that's how you experience it."

After an initial hesitation, I launched into a detailed response, summing up a lifetime's experience of thinking about the matter; this was not a new thought. After all I had gone to an innovative prep school where we were introduced as freshmen to the core curriculum under the heading, "Search for Self." "The self is the part of me which remains the same even when everything else changes. I remember the time when I was eleven or twelve years old when I seemed to become *me*. I was walking along the road and suddenly realized that I was acutely aware of a consciousness which was right behind the face I could never see, intensely *me*, taking in the world at each moment as I strode through it. This "me" hasn't changed, though I've grown and gone through a lot of life changes." I looked at the faded lace tablecloth, then over at the Victorian photos on the wall. I did not look at Maurice.

"Sure, there are masks you wear in certain circumstances, and I seem to behave somewhat differently around different people, but I also think I'm truer to my self than most people … very honest, and honest about myself. The self, my self, is an inner core, an essence that is absolutely me, and I am confident that it will remain so throughout the rest of my life."

This is essentially what I said, though it seemed to me that I had spoken for an uncomfortably long time. At the end, I found myself looking into the dregs of the teacup. When I summoned the courage to meet Maurice's gaze, his steel-grey eyes were no longer twinkling, and with a stern look he shook his head continuously, jaw jutting forward. I expected some fine-tuning from this wise, tough old bird of a man, but was shocked at his wholesale rejection of my response.

"What you are describing is the ego, your own ego-sense. Beyond this self as you call it is a deeper unfathomable Self, the very source of I-consciousness. You need to learn to experience that Self, not identify with this possessive little king you are so dearly attached to."

I was stunned, confused and defensive, thinking I had given a very good answer. Still, I was intrigued, sensing that this little man knew something I did not. Maurice went on to delineate a whole process of inquiry, simply trying doggedly to answer the question, "Who am I?" in the unflinchingly honest way that his master, Ramana Maharshi, had demonstrated. Finally Maurice queried, "Would you like to join the fellowship of the undeceived?"

"Yes. I would." This sounded like an elite group, and I was accustomed to belonging to elites. And I was interested in finding out what was wrong with my thinking, which had felt reasonably clear just a few moments before. Maurice asked me to return on Thursday, when he regularly baked black Polish bread: "They don't know how to bake good bread here, so I must do it myself."

I left, feeling embarrassed and chastened like a child, but eager to pursue his "fellowship." After all, wasn't one of my highest values absolute honesty? I saw Maurice several times during my ten days in Bombay. He became the focus of my life. This work seemed to be at the very heart of the mysterious quality that had drawn me back to India. The unformulated question was now given form, and the guidance I so sorely needed was embodied in the figure of this grey-eyed little elfin man.

At my next visit, Maurice confounded me by reciting the essentials of my dream of Mother in the interim. How did he know? He calmly explained that mind was present everywhere, not imprisoned in our separate craniums, as most of us experienced it. If one lived in the Self, letting go of the little "i" to be absorbed in the ocean of Brahman, then Mind would eclipse "minds" and such feats as knowing others dreams or thoughts would be commonplace. Though his facile penetration of my thought processes seemed god-like, I had an inkling this was not the point. Mind was Mind, not the Mind of God or the mind of man.

Now the room was lit with wonder. Maurice approached a black-and-white photograph framed on the wall—the one that had attracted me my first visit—then turned to me. "Do you want this?" It was Ramana Maharshi. I was disappointed he didn't take it down and hand it to me on the spot. Instead, he opened to a copy of the same photo in a book. He said he would give it to me on condition that I commit myself to spending half an hour observing that face every day. I pondered a moment, mind racing forward into my unfathomable lifespan, and agreed. Maurice cut the photo from the book with a pen knife and presented it to me in a little grey pebbled canvas notebook cover to protect it. My instructions were simply to watch carefully and observe what occurred, not trying to make anything happen.

Alone back in Udayan's room, where I slept on a floor pallet, I watched as the face crawled, turning into devilish figures. The right eye was hard, cold, impassive, whereas the left was warm, loving, glowing, ready to laugh. These eyes penetrated my very core, and I was scared. Ramana's face seemed like some kind of superego watching me. It turned me back on myself, making this an arduous, uncomfortable exercise. "So what now?" I asked the figure as I ended the exercise. I kept up this practice of meditating on the face for several days, but then it lapsed into intermittent observance, dying out entirely after a few years.

Near Udayan's was a park overlooking the sea and the arm of the Malabar coast with the modern city behind it, a lovely spot full of tall palms, flowering shrubs, and grass, a rarity in this country. It was a fine place for a picnic. It was also site of the twin Towers of Silence, where the Parsees placed their dead to be picked clean by carrion birds: ravens and vultures. So efficient were the birds that I never smelled rotten flesh. Since this experience I am often reminded of death when I hear their call, or see a raven fly overhead.

"Would you like to meet a sage, an enlightened being?" Maurice asked one day.

"Of course I would."

"Good. We'll go tomorrow evening."

Nisargadatta Maharaj lived in another quarter of the megapolis, much poorer, which we reached by city bus, then walking several blocks. Maurice prepped me. "Remember to be open-minded and observe everything that happens—both what this man says and does and what happens *within you.*"

I nodded gravely. But I was obsessed with avoiding the cowshit, the red betel spit, the human excrement and rotting vegetable matter strewn all over the street. I didn't want to soil my new chappals.

Noticing my hesitation Maurice upbraided me. "Hold your head up and pay attention to the world."

It was late afternoon as we wedged our way into the back of a shop in a densely populated street, little kids observing me with mild curiosity. We climbed a ladder into the loft where Nisargadatta awaited us, quietly smoking a *bedi*. He was big and fleshy, clad in a dhoti like Gandhi and Ramana, but without their cultivated brahmin air. This guy was more like a butcher or a cabdriver—very earthy, a chain smoker, a distinct, strong smell. Folks called him "Bedi-Wallah Baba," since he supported himself rolling *bedis* on his thigh.

Maurice greeted him in Marahti and they had a short conversation. He was working on a translation of the sage's sayings. Then my teacher turned to me and said, "Do you have a question for this saddhu?" I should have been prepared for this, but having been told to come and observe, my mind was empty, just observing, more anthropologist than seeker. I remember the mind racing, coming up with a generic "spiritual" question. But I recall neither the question nor the man's answer. I remember his face, big, kind but piercing eyes, and a hawk-like nose hooking all errancy and bullshit.

"Remember to pay attention to what happens within you," Maurice had advised. All I remember is my anxiety over being put on the spot. I remember the adventure of it, the joy of going to see a secret master who Maurice had discovered. But I did not *feel* the presence of a master, only a balanced, tough, streetwise man who I figured had to be at least in a league with Maurice. Within, I was inert. The lingering memories are sensory: the man's rubbery flesh,, his barnyard odor, his striking face, and the somewhat claustrophobic, musty dimness of the shop, all infused with the pungent smell of *bedis*. As we descended the ladder and went back out into the gathering twilight, I was relieved to escape the dingy confines. But I quickly wished I could do it all over again.

The last time we were together that Bombay sojourn, Maurice shocked me during a discussion of romance and sexuality: "To young men your age, a woman is just a seminal spittoon." I started to object, but quickly realized the accuracy of the remark, while mentally noting I seemed to be rather careful in my choice of spittoons.

I returned to Indore with a day or two to spare for class preps, having missed no teaching assignments, but losing nonetheless the respect of Munshi in particular. We were not to be counted on; what if the strike had resolved itself quickly? Most importantly, we had shamed our colleagues when Sharma made his unannounced site visit. At the flat, I was greeted with a sick roommate, an overstuffed, clogged, stinking toilet, a whimpering landlord (he thought we'd never return), and total monsoon. To humor him, I played chess with Stuart, losing again. At least Salim shuffled on: steady, smiling, dependable.

4 Encounter with the Goddess

After Durga drowned, Calcutta was all dark, rain, and winds, a lot of sleeping. ... My body and soul suddenly slept.

The encounter with Maurice in Bombay unhinged me, weakening the bonds between the separate parts of a self I had heretofore experienced as singular. Following the trail of shock and wonder after that first night's ride through the corpse-ridden streets of Bombay, I had returned to enter a dream-reality. Though I sometimes stepped back to take stock, marking plateaus in the descent, the dream continued to lurk, leading me further and further into its depths.

The clerical strike which opened the way for meeting Maurice in Bombay had barely ended before it was time for the long fall break, the Dussehra and Diwali holidays. Stuart was heading south to be with Lynn, while I made plans for a northern itinerary to include Delhi, Benares, Allahabad, Calcutta—essentially crossing the Gangetic Plain, then back to Jaipur via Agra and the Taj. My girl Fulbright colleagues in Jaipur and Allahabad would host me, but most important was the plan to be in Calcutta for Durga Puja, celebrating the martial goddess especially dear to

Bengalis with my Fulbright mates Jon and Loren at their tiny college on the outskirts of the megapolis.

The Batgods

On my way northeast, I visited the remote, beautifully preserved Buddhist site at Sanchi, which I shared with one lone student in his underwear, his clothes neatly hanging on a neem branch. The idyll ended when some boys threw firecrackers at me on my descent.

The next day, with my canteen of boiled water, I set out by horse-tonga for the nearby Udaigiri Caves at two in the afternoon. It was hot, incredibly still. The ride was rough, the board seat very hard. We soon left the little town far in the distance. The only sounds were the horse's hooves striking the hard sun-baked clay road surface and the occasional gentle clucking of the driver as the horse backed a little on steeper grades. We entered a canyon with steep sheer walls, and the little village and its museum disappeared. Above, the sky was blue, eternal. Below, the horse toiled in the sun, shaking her head and whisking her tail in futile gestures against the flies. We arrived at the entrance to the caves. After motioning me towards it, the driver lay down in the shade of the mountain for an afternoon nap.

Inside the caves, I wandered from chamber to chamber. It was extremely quiet and still. This was unlike previous spelunking, comfortably enfolded within a chatty group with my parents and little sister within the Luray Caverns along the Skyline Drive in Virginia. I sought the expected religious images. None. Then I entered a large cave and was instantly overcome by the acrid smell of guano. I studied the expanse of the cave floor, which was thick with droppings. For a moment, I feared I would retch. My gaze climbed the cavern walls until I caught sight of a few bats, hanging in a clump near the edge of the chamber. Then, with a shudder I discovered that the entire ceiling was covered with hundreds of them. I imagined they were looking at me, but studying them, I saw that all but a few were sleeping.

It seems to me that what seized Puer in India was not only the inescapable *spiritual trip*, but more immediately the moods, tones, and textures of experience. The yogi's ideal of a crystal-clear subtle body with no *samskaras*, the colorings or stains left by experiences governed by desire and fear, was Puer's as well. To be an unconditioned man, that was it. Yet the desire for experience—and a romantic fascination with death—ruled him. *Just a tiny incandescent spark on the sea of time.*

Sure, Maurice had introduced him to bedrock Advaita, the yoga of discriminating real from unreal. And liberation from the ego's petty concerns, the final Vedic ideal of *moksha*, was what ultimately drew all of us Western "hippy-saddhus." But in those caves, Puer did not experience transcendence, rather the uncanny, the Other.

Puer was searching for the Nameless God behind the moment's fleeting experience, behind the implacable azure sky on the afternoon's journey, but here was something else: a god-in-the-moment, a priceless treasure to be noticed, feared—above all, valued. In that upward glance, he was not grasped by an Eternity oblivious to the evanescence of the moment, standing before and after time, but a momentary god whose nature could *only* be expressed in that particular moment.

The god of that moment as Puer looked overhead at the vast canopy of dark brown winged flesh covering the cavernous ceiling was those bats. Their presence in the shrine was sacred, more immediate than the images produced by the exquisite religious imagination of Medieval sculptors, east or west. He was their guest. This was the pilgrim's lesson for the day.

But the heart of Puer's pilgrimage still lay ahead of him: Durga Puja in Calcutta. Once again he would be a guest, and a marked man.

I boarded the train for Calcutta at Old Delhi station, which was absolutely jammed. I would guess four or five thousand souls milled about, carrying carts of baggage, thoroughly plied by hawkers weaving their way through the crowd. Though I had a reservation, I saw with alarm that my car was bulging with people, and pushed my way in. I never got used to the experience of a crushing crowd in India, and constantly marveled at natives' ability to shove through with ease, like invertebrates.

The train was a modern diesel express, hewing to its schedule more closely than most. But in the middle of the Gangetic Plain the train hit something and screeched to a halt. I joined the group of men who disembarked. I immediately smelled the carnage, an odd intermixture of raw and cooked meat. Before me was the severed head of a bull, staring back huge-eyed, impassive, an image right out of Guernica. The whole front of the train was splattered with blood, entrails, limbs, and blobs of cattle flesh. A herd had wandered into the path of the hurtling train at a crossing, and fifteen or twenty animals had been killed. Some of the animals had been caught, dragged, and partially roasted under the train's wheels. The farmer, who sat in shock and disbelief by the side of the train in a tattered turban, was ruined. We watched silently while members of the crew cleaned away the disemboweled kine.

Once the tracks were cleared our pilgrim-train again headed to Calcutta. Durga, the goddess whose festival we were steadily approaching is one of several variants of Devi, the Hindu Ur-Goddess. Unlike other goddesses, she is never shown with a consort. Even Kali, the powerful goddess of destruction, is depicted dancing on Shiva's ecstatic body. As I read in his biography, the great saint Ramakrishna had been Durga's disciple, re-infusing a torrent of devotion into her temple at Dakshineshwar. She visited him there one day while he meditated at the delta where the Hoogly River empties into the Bay of Bengal, appearing as a lovely young mother holding a baby in tender embrace. But suddenly, transformed into the blazing-eyed All-Devourer, she crushed the infant's head between her jaws and disappeared beneath the waves. Reading this right after my return, I shivered with fear and recognition like a child hearing a dark fairy tale, imagining the very spot where it happened, off the finger of land where the temple sits.

Ramakrishna's vision is the aspect that Bengalis worship at Durga's puja. Her wooden-framed papier-mache statue is a ten-armed terror riding on a lion's back, weapons in each hand, stabbing to death a rather pitiful looking buffalo, the demon Mahishta, who once drove the gods out of the celestial kingdom.

My Fulbright buddy Jon was waiting at busy Howra Station when I arrived, looking the all-American boy with his solid frame and ruddy cheeks—despite the flowing whites he wore. The huge station was wrapped in bridges and overpasses everywhere I looked. Seeing him, I ignored the coolies and the crush of people. We hugged in the midst of the crowd. I shouldered my "Bombay-pack," a World War II US Army copy, and followed him to his motorcycle.

It was about twenty-five miles to the little college where he and Loren taught. The streets were packed: *ten million people* dancing, howling, milling in the streets along with the cows and goats *and 800,000 taxicabs, pedicabs, bicycle rickshaws, battered double decker buses and 100,000 motorcycles.* Thousands of images of Durga were erected all over Calcutta. Drums beat incessantly, smoke billowing from massive incense-logs, while priests sat rapt in ecstasy.

I roared around the mobbed, wild city behind Jon on his motorcycle. In the traffic and crush, I think we were almost killed three times. I felt such abandon I didn't care. We watched a beautiful sunset down by the

Hoogly and listened as the boatmen sang hauntingly sad songs--the time had come for daughters who had spent the Puja with their parents to return to their taskmasters.

At the end of a carnivalesque day, we went to Jon's favorite restaurant, the Olympia, for dinner. We both ordered the Chateaubriand, at the incredibly low price of Rs. 5.50 (seventy cents). It felt like enjoying contraband (though it was buffalo, not beef). Afterwards, he drove me to the relative quiet of the sleepy college in the countryside, moonlit with an occasional illuminated cloud, through coconut palms and lush paddies. Even in that remote place, I could occasionally hear bands of villagers singing and yelling as they accompanied Durga-carts down little muddy lanes.

At sundown the following day, Durga's festival would come to an end, marked by the ritual drowning of the terrible Goddess. We rose at five a.m. to visit a neighboring village, paying our respects while drinking endless cups of chai and eating *barfi*. Some villagers Jon knew invited us to accompany them for Durga-ma's final ride to the nearby creek for immolation. A man carefully explained that this drowning was for the purpose of reminding devotees that the image, so adored for ten days, was but an idol, to be cast aside for another year, while the spirit behind it was eternal and constant. It also seemed to me that it was necessary to quench the Dionysian fires which had been lit at this crazy festival, a religious carnival which seemed to have possessed an entire modern city. *Several people will drown in the excitement. They do every year.*

Late that afternoon, we mounted the bed of an old truck, along with the Goddess. I held onto the hooped frame, the skeletal structure which bounded and supported the ten-armed creature, chanting, along with the crew of young men and boys, Bengali cries of "long live Durga" and "long live Durgapur." When it started to rain, I abandoned myself to the spirit of the occasion. Soaked and wildly happy, we cheered lustily as Durga was dumped off the rear of the truck. She sank slowly into the little creek. The water barely covered her hoop. They would know where to find her next year.

On the trip back to the village I stood behind the cab on the spot where Durga had rested, a throng of young men holding me—hanging onto my arms, legs, and fingers—as the truck lurched through muddy traces. They formed a human chain to keep from falling, and I felt like a colossus of sorts. The villagers complimented my steadiness.

"Sirrh, you very good," said one boy about twelve, gesturing with his legs braced and arms outstretched, holding his head high. Others in the company laughed, and many of the boys still clung to me. A boy in his late teens added, "Yes, you are being strong for us. I think you are feeling jolly and liking this place?" I smiled. "Yes, I like it here very much. It is peaceful and lush. You are a happy village."

A young boy blurted out, "Will you stay, sahib?" Others nodded their heads in unison, and the oldest man there, probably about thirty, gave me a formal invitation. "Yes, Robert, you must stay with us. We would be most honored."

I shot a look at Jon, who was beaming, a little awed by all this. "But I must return to Indore and teach. Very soon."

"Then come back," said the first boy. "Yes, yes, yes," they chanted. "You stay here, you part of *our* village" he added.

As Jon and I headed for the Harley, some of the smaller boys clung to my feet, while others pulled at my hands, each holding onto a finger like so many cow's teats, which made it difficult for me to disengage. I felt like Gulliver. When we finally mounted the motorcycle, Jon turned to me.

"You know, Bob, they were kissing your feet."

I must have looked quizzical.

"They were kissing your feet. It's a gesture of extreme respect."

We roared off as the deepening colors shaded into darkness. The rain had ceased, twilight had turned to evening, and the moon shone on our faces as we rode through the fragrant Bengali countryside, tall palms etched blackly against the night sky. I felt enormously blessed, and a little like a god myself.

But from the dreamside of the little stream, one might see Puer differently. Not a god, more like the eunuchs who still inhabit Durga's temple in Calcutta, serving as her priests. Or the sacrificial bull Mahishta, entwined in Durga's multiple arms.

After Durga drowned, Calcutta was all dark, rain, and winds, a lot of sleeping. My body and soul suddenly slept.

Up until the ritual drowning of the Goddess, events had moved at a frenzied pace. The ecstatic crowds and Jon's Harley propelled me, but I had also been driven by a necessity to experience where all this led. That drive consummated, I now slept.

The next evening, sitting around the parlor of their thatched quarters amid the rice fields, Jon, Loren, and I smoked some harsh Orissan ganja.

"This shit is terrible," Loren said. Jon and I agreed, coughing violently. But its hallucinatory effects were powerful. That night, I dreamt:

The universe, the night-sky filled with stars. Overtones of a droning tanpura ascending, descending, then re-ascending again to higher and higher tonal realms. Stretching my range of hearing. I wonder each time if I can bear hearing pitches that go any higher. This isn't a matter of aural pain, but rather of being stretched, becoming airier and airier. The essences of the tones emerge in richly colored geometrical shapes, outlined against the vast blackness. A sense of timelessness. I am alone and helpless. I become a grain of sand, then observe this grain lying among all the others, and this grainy self is marked, transformed: changing from black to gray to white. The beauty of it all is inexpressible. But also, Death comes several times, white-hot molten rods driving through my heart, over and over again.

Then, I have intercourse with hard, rasping drainpipes, ridged steel culverts, extremely unpleasant. But they change to Mother, and this intercourse is pleasurable at last.

Now I catapult through the vast, starry realm. I see a rag doll flying far into space, past the stars. The doll lands limp and akimbo, skirt flopping, on a braided rug before a warm, blazing hearth-fire, next to a large easy chair. The chair is empty, but next to it lies a pair of slippers, awaiting their Master. There is an awesome sense of Presence. I, the rag doll, feel incredibly comfortable and safe.

I awoke in the middle of the night and sensed that the place this doll had been flung was the Hearth of God. Actually, upon reflection it looked suspiciously like the rug, hearth, and chair in the "sun porch" at Gran Howard's in Eastern North Carolina. This was Granddaddy's chair by rights, and I remember him leaning forward, patiently shifting lumps of coal in the grate. But I was never around him as much as I would have wished, and the palimpsest of experience and dream are of an empty chair. The rag doll reminds me of the curly-headed two-year-old holding a pair of keys—their beloved Puer—in the photo on my parents' bedroom bureau. And I was sure that when death came, it would be a heart attack—those molten rods.

I continued to lie awake under mosquito netting in the dark Bengali countryside, a rag doll totally amazed at this dream, still clinging to me. I drifted back into sleep for a few hours, but when I awoke the next morning, it enshrouded me like another layer of clothing.

Ever since awakening from that dream, with its uncanny sense of presence, Puer accepted it as an experience of God as an ultimate safe haven. It became a mythic marker in his life journey, the secret cairn he would return to and bless, laying before it stones of memory. In doing so, he remembered the ending, the rag doll flying through the black universe, landing at the hearth, bouncing, then realizing it was at the Hearth. But Puer ignored all the rest: the passages up and down the *tanpura*'s overtones, purifying the sand-grains of self. He especially repressed the intercourse with Mother.

The experience of India, and the sense of necessity which drove him to it, seemed to be about transcendence. Puer always saw the core experience as the encounter with Maurice Frydman in Bombay, stripping away the ego's sense of importance, pointing instead to the immutable Self. It was a drive for purity and for union with the Absolute; here, the hidden occupant of the empty chair and the pair of slippers.

But the other part of the dream-image is union with Mother—in the nocturnal dream, Puer's biological mother, Virginia; in his Hindu waking dream, the Goddess. While Puer was in India, and for many years afterwards, he experienced what felt like a reawakening of spiritual life, a quickening of something which had drawn him from an early age. What Puer missed until much later was the corresponding awakening of a murkier desire for the birth canal.

The year before, in Greenwich Village, that initiation with Kathy was not a simple matter, for as I approached penetration I suddenly felt Mother's presence between us, her face hovering in the darkness, this huge face framed by salt-and-pepper hair, neither threatening nor inviting. No wonder I had avoided sex so long. But years of sexual frustration had proved stronger than their dam. I thrust past her guardian image and entered, triumphant. Lord, how deliciously hot it was in that slippery oven-pouch! I was enveloped, enfolded, contained, no more worries about "fitting."

Spiritual awareness awoke with Maurice's direct, jolting confrontation of the ego's confused identity with the Self. Wearing the mantle of Spirit—the great masquerade Maurice had identified—Puer entirely missed the rapid descent into the Underworld, spinning in Durga's vortex. While spirit was being consciously tuned through meditation, soul was being fashioned in the dark dreamplace which had clutched Puer's subtle body ever since that first night in the Sleeping City, Bombay's

Gateway. This union with the Goddess was a nocturnal affair, secretly cloaking Puer's life well into his thirties.

That Goddess had the local name Durga. But let's call her Mother India: the Ground of all the Hindu gods. The Brahmanists, emerging from the domination of the petty sky-god Indra, had said, "Thou art That." And That was what India was all about: realizing the priority of Brahman, the self's anamnesis of Self, peeling back the onion. The Dark Goddess, though, entering in oedipal fashion through the place which gave me birth, was the absolute blackness out of which light appears, ground to the bright figure. She was the pitch-black sky through which Puer's rag doll flew: the Greeks' Nyx, formless bird-mother preceding all of creation. This was the unnamed deity he worshipped as Mother India.

A giant wave flooded my heart, and having felt nothing like it before, I was unmoored. This upwelling washed aside my Apollo, the stance nurtured through years of rigorous intellectual training. The train hurtling into the cattle, the days in the crowd at Calcutta, abandoning myself into its surge as I sped around on the back of Jon's Harley, and finally, immersed in chant with the villagers as we carried Durga back to her river; all these prefigured my response to her call, her rhythm.

Enmeshed in that lunar tide at last, amid the chanting of adoring villagers, I went down with Durga, the limbs of my psychic body enmeshed in her multiple arms. Raindrops dotted the surface of the little creek that barely covered us.

After the first few days in Kashmir, I knew I loved India. But then, I was giving reasons. Because of this or that beautiful sight, this particular weather, that particular band of children. I can no longer enumerate. A giant wave has washed over and into me. The love I feel for India fills every little nook and cranny of my heart. It's hard to explain anymore except as a total, massive phenomenon. At first, my acceptance of the "bad" sides: the delays, probability of illness, unmotivated students, etc. was a conscious effort. Now, acceptance has become a kind of love. Love for the "bad" smells, the cows everywhere, the lepers, the dung, the flies, the heat, the mosquito-bites, even my raging, scalding fever. It all is part of a profound and beautiful experience.

5 Kumar Gandharva: God Musician

When I sit with him between the droning tanpuras I feel humbled ... as if I were in the presence of divinity.

The Dussehra-Diwali voyage was an unforgettable adventure and an initiation. I had gone to Durga Puja as a tourist and morphed into an unwitting participant in her rite. Whether I was suffocating in the goddess's womb-culvert or prancing as an infant god at the Hearth was unclear, but it was time to don the Fulbright lecturer mask again. Returning to Indore, I struggled to readjust to life with Stuart and the renewed rigors of teaching at the college. I completely reorganized my classes, and accepted a request to coach the Indore University basketball team, hosting the fledgling All-India university tournament in early spring.

A new Peace Corps girl had arrived, Leah, an attractive mellow blonde acidhead from Colorado who was interested in Buddhist yoga, Indian music, and stargazing. She was also interested in me. Through Stuart's doings, we broke our lease at the customary Fulbright flat and rented a brand-new house on the edge of town (and got into our biggest trouble yet with the Fulbright authorities). It had stairs to the flat cement roof, a great place for stargazing. We invited friends over for a rooftop housewarming. The stars were bountiful, filling the midnight sky above the Malwa plain more densely than any sky I had ever seen. The Milky Way was thick cream, and the heavenly fireworks mocked those at the Ganesha festival put on by the wealthy Indore mill-owners in late summer. One November night during the Leonid shower I counted over a hundred meteors.

We built a fire up there, smearing the newly minted gray concrete finish with charcoal. The fire, the ganja, the stars, and our moving apparitions induced hallucinatory visions. Marilyn, high school daughter of some Canadian OXFAM workers, big blue bloodshot eyes and pronounced blonde bangs, was sure she saw a large dying bird in the corner. I looked over and thought I saw it too. But searching the next morning I found no sign, only ash and charcoal stains. Perhaps a failed Phoenix.

Large ravens flew over one evening. They felt like omens. Then several bats got caught in the flat, circling desperately round and round as I ducked my head, feeling the adrenalin rush of fear at each pass. Revenants of the Udaigiri bat-gods, they seemed to weave me more tightly into a fate-web.

Riding home on my bike after dinner at some PCV girls' flat, I was chased under a dark moonless sky by a pack of dogs. They yelped and snarled as I pedaled until I thought my lungs would burst. Then it grew quiet again, and I relaxed. Turning to check the pack's progress, I was horrified to find them right on my heels, still silently pursuing their quarry. I felt like Actaeon, pursued by his own hounds when he had accidentally glimpsed Artemis at her bath—an echo of the youthful bull-calf Mahishta, Durga's quarry. Maybe Puer was still entwined with Durga, that other great hunter-goddess ranging a little Bengali village at a rainy twilight.

Sargams

But November back in Indore was focused upon Hindustani vocal music. Before the fall holiday, I had met Chandu at a Peace Corps friends' house. Chandu was a small, bespectacled Maharashtrian who made his rounds on a pastel green Vespa. We hit it off right away, and within a week he invited Stuart and me to dinner. This was a pivotal occasion, for not only was I delighted with both Chandu and his beautiful graygreen-eyed wife

Sulu, I was introduced to true Malwan homestyle cuisine, which I sought to ingest as often as possible thereafter. Salim was not happy. With his raggedy old black hat in his hands, he stood before me, putting on his most lugubrious look, every line in his face sagging, "Bob-Saab is not liking my cooking." Being able to go home early to his wife and children was nothing compared to the shame he felt upon sensing that we preferred cooking other than his. The next week, he tried cooking "Indian-style" (Muslim) food, but he was a British army chef to the core.

Chandu and Sulu were a Maharashtrian couple who had lived together in considerable sin for well over a year before marrying, a "love-marriage" in a land where arranged marriage is the norm. They had been art students, free spirits who felt right at home with the hip western youth filtering into their world. Chandu held a master's degree in philosophy, and was quite interested in both western culture and modernist architecture and design. He was an interior designer, producing Scandinavian-style furniture with a small crew in a shop behind his house. Chandu found work wherever the money and taste sent him: Bombay, Baroda, Bhopal, and Delhi, as well as the homes of Indore industrialists. Sulu taught art in their home. They had one son, Milind, who was eight. Milind delighted in my fractured, inventive Hindi. I became "Uncle."

Chandu had introduced me to my first vocal teacher, his friend Vishnu, a Hindustani classical DJ and vocalist with All India Radio who trained me to sing raga patterns, or *sargams*—"sa re ga ma pa dha ni sa," Hindustani solfege—as well as a couple of simple *bhajans* (devotional hymns). Vishnu was a small man, very precise in his motions and speech. The careful way he moved the pencil, lips puckered, invariably sent chills up my spine. He loved to joke and pun, animating these forays with wonderfully buggy eyes which he rolled to exaggeration.

My friend was part of a tight-knit community of Maharashtrian artists in Indore. One member of this lively group, a Hindustani vocalist named Kumar Gandharva, lived in nearby Dewas. Many considered Kumarji to be the greatest contemporary North Indian singer, certainly the most innovative. He hosted a series of musical events at the Dewas concert hall every fall, and when Chandu learned I was interested in Hindustani classical music, he suggested I come along.

My introduction to Kumarji's gift came after a concert he sponsored in Dewas before I went to Calcutta. We went by train—Chandu, Sulu, Milind, Vishnu, and Puer. The scenery was beautiful: a marvelous sunset, lush, green, monsoon-fed fields, little green hillocks, large spreading trees, cows everywhere, and, as we neared Dewas, several outlying temples. From the station we took a horse tonga to a drop-spot near Kumar's, and walked from there. Having become accustomed to the auto-rickshaw and its stomach-turning careens and sudden stops, the sedate tonga was a delight.

The guest artist was Kumar's colleague, the acclaimed vocalist Bhimsen Joshi. Before Joshi's concert, Chandu introduced me to Kumar in the big music den at Banukhul. Kumar had a high, round forehead, with squirrel-cheeks, a round belly, and quick, shining eyes. I later learned the puffed cheeks were the effect of his beloved betel nut, packed in each gum. He smiled warmly, saying he was honored to meet me, having heard much about me and my lessons from Vishnu. I was embarrassed at the compliment from such a great musician, and demurred that the honor was mine.

Soon Joshi was warming up in his underwear, attended by a small group of men sitting on the mattressed floor in the den, which was the heart of the vocalist's world. As he stretched his vocal cords from the slow *alap* to the fast moving *taana* at the end of the session, he frequently sipped from a bottle of Indian whiskey. I was told this was his custom; he claimed it helped loosen up his voice. It certainly made him loose, for his subsequent concert, which was magnificent, was punctuated with dramatic affects, including a couple of histrionic arm-swoops betraying his partially inebriated state. By night's end, Joshi had polished off an entire fifth.

Returning to Banukhul after the performance, we enjoyed a "snack" consisting of a superb Malwan meal, served by Kumar's attentive wife Vasundhara Komkali, a former student and fellow vocalist who frequently accompanied him in concert. Soon afterwards—it must have been after three a.m.—the singing resumed. Now Kumar Gandharva joined Joshi in the music den, grunting and wagging his head at his colleague's acrobatics between mouthfuls of *paan* which reddened his gleaming lips. I never witnessed anything like the musical joust which followed. This demonstration was an intimate affair, the men sitting around (where were the women?) on the floor clad in spotless white cotton, most in their underwear, sipping whiskey, emitting little cries and exchanging amazed glances as the vocalists lifted us to more and more ecstatic heights. Now I was grunting with them.

Chandu had told me how Shivputra Komkali received his name, meaning "boy wonder" or wood-sprite (gandharvas were magical forest beings from Vedic tradition). At age twelve he asked to take the platform at a competition in Bombay's storied Jinnah Hall after one of the country's greatest had finished performing a composition. The lad had taken the stage, promptly reproducing the entire composition flawlessly. The audience was spellbound. So this night I felt like I was witnessing a repeat of the founding event of this legendary musician's career. Joshi and Kumar spontaneously jousted, each trying to outdo the other. Though Joshi had a stronger voice—Kumar had one collapsed lung since a bout of TB from 1947 to 1952—Kumar had more genius, and could easily reproduce anything Joshi threw at him. I don't think Joshi would've attempted this mad joust if he hadn't been drinking since early evening. Here were two of the greatest North Indian classical vocalists on the same platform, at ease in their underwear, playfully trading riffs. It was a once-in-a-lifetime experience, and the air was crackling with excitement. This second, impromptu concert ended at 6:30 am. I slept for fifteen minutes before heading through the cool, quiet early morning to the waiting minivan.

Chandu's plan was for me to learn the basics with Vishnu, then, if we were lucky, move on to something grander. So when I returned from the long fall vacation *the sweetest news, and cause for immense jubilation,* making November the fulcrum of the year, was Chandu's report—delivered with his huge, warm twinkly smile, "Kumarji would be happy to have you as his student. Lessons begin next week."

When asked to sing at my audition, I said, "I have two voices; which one?" A fairly high tenor himself, he was not particularly interested in my countertenor, which I had maintained since my boy soprano days as a hedge against fully joining the adult male world. Listening, he quickly decided. "For Indian music, you use the low voice." After ascertaining my range he ordered a *tanpura* to be crafted for my voice range in Miraj, where the best sitars and *tanpuras* in the country were hand crafted from gourds, teak, and magnificent inlaid ivory by what Kumarji termed the "Indian Stradivarius family," Abdul Sattar. The instrument cost around sixty-five dollars, delivered a month after my lessons began.

Lessons were twice a week. Since Kumarji spoke little English, (he understood much more), Chandu accompanied me, serving as interpreter. We took the bus, which was the fastest way to reach Dewas. The first couple of weeks the lessons directly followed basketball practice, and we returned at eleven or eleven-thirty each night. These were long days, but I was enthusiastic. Kumarji's creativity inspired the idea of becoming an Indian musician.

From the bus depot we walked a few short blocks to Kumarji's house.

Within half a block we left the aura of electric lights for a world of kerosene lanterns and wood-fired clay cookstoves. Children appeared at doors to stare at us. Occasionally I glimpsed adults within, the men lying at ease in their pyjamas or squatting on the floor with their evening meal. After walking through narrow alleyways, the air hearty with wood smoke and pungent with burning dung, we turned into the avenue leading to the Hill of Devi and Banukhul, with its welcoming porch light.

The Komkali home had a spacious front porch with a wide swing, flanked by large pink oleanders in bloom, and a garden in the rear, which we would pass to climb up to Mataji, the tiny goddess who presided over the Hill of Devi and the town itself. In fact, the postal address reads Banukhul, "Mataji ke rasta." I took my lessons in the front lounge where I first heard Kumarji sing with Bhimsen Joshi. The process was immemorial: the guru sang a line, and the diksha reproduced it until he got it right. No notational system has ever been developed other than writing out the *sargam* syllables, with rhythmic markings underneath the line.

After Thai served tea and sweet biscuits, Kumarji would explain the composition, including the meaning of the words (*bandish*), as well as invaluable remarks on music theory. Chandu translated. Sometimes the master interspersed remarks on his philosophy of life. Vasuthai instructed me directly in English. Kumarji's son by his first marriage, Mukhul, sometimes played the tanpura—later, a tabla accompaniment—nodding respectfully when I reproduced a line fairly accurately. Though Vasuthai became my immediate teacher, Kumarji would break in to correct me by re-singing the line, often with his impish little smile. The lessons usually lasted two hours, and I would protest at the end when Kumarji would say *bus hain*. I learned two compositions while working in this way, one in praise of Shiva in Bhairav (*Shobhe jata*), the other on "going home" (*Jawa hun desa*) in Bhimpalassee. Kumarji thought this would be appropriate for my concert at the final gathering of our tutor group in the northern hill station at Mussoorie in March. I also learned a couple of *bhajans* composed by the medieval Muslim weaver-saint, Kabir. I especially identified with Kumarji's hit single, *Naia mori nike nike chalana lagi*: "my new little boat is just getting underway." Indeed, it felt like Kabir had named my experience.

One particularly memorable time, Chandu and I stayed for dinner after my lesson. Everyone retired to the kitchen and proceeded to cut vegetables. Kumarji pointed with his knife as he spoke: "Always eat vegetables and fruits in season ... like performing ragas at correct times, isn't it?" He looked from Mukhul to Vasuthai, who nodded, smiling broadly. He then proceeded to musically coach each member of his family, correcting them with punctuations of squash, beans and his knife blade. It was at times like these that I realized the man truly lived and breathed music. It never stopped running through his head, and if you lived with him, you bathed in its rushing stream.

I was always eager for the next lesson, but practicing was a problem. Since the method was one of close repetition, Kumarji recorded the compositions line by line, with spaces for me to repeat in rhythm, the *tanpura* drone in the background. So it was necessary to have a tape recorder, which I did not procure until December, borrowing it from a wealthy acquaintance, Ranju. But during the two weeks or so that I had the machine, I spent as much time playing with it as I did practicing. I was contemplating staying in India, continuing lessons with Kumarji and "becoming an Indian musician." At lessons I was very focused and attentive, and picked up the music fairly quickly. But the reality was that I actually only practiced at home a handful of times during the first month and a half.

When I arrived for my lesson in mid-December, Kumarji met me at the door with a big smile. "Your tanpura has arrived," he said in his halting English. I followed him into the music den. There it was, standing on its solid gourd foundation, lacquered to a glowing orange, its neck and front made from teak or rosewood, burnished to a deep reddish color. It was inlaid with ivory, and as I ran my fingers over it, I felt and saw the tiny holes that must have provided blood to the living tusk. I was immediately smitten with this glorious instrument, and couldn't keep my hands from stroking it. The different textures, shifting from smooth wood to the ever so slightly rough ivory, to the delicate polished surface of the gourd, which I just touched with the ends of my fingers. I didn't want to break the thin shell. (Years later, I would put my whole hand under it, like feeling a woman's rump, every surface of my hand in contact.)

Kumarji had shown me how to play the tanpura before, thumb on the neck as a fulcrum, index finger firmly stroking the bass sa, Shiva's universe-creating sound—the *aum* of string instruments. Then the middle finger on the pa, the fifth, followed by the index finger flopping from string to string for the high sa's in the middle, returning to the bass sa to end the circle. Over and over, stroking the strings evenly, creating the foundation for the sound-universe of the raga system. It was like a basso continuo. Tuned properly, these notes would create a frame for raga compositions, as well as all the overtones needed to elicit and underscore the melody.

It didn't take long to get the feel of it. I loved the sensation of touch, which was even more sensual than playing the piano, where being in touch with the finger pads was sufficient to properly address the keys. Now Kumarji taught me tuning, finding the bass sa by simply hearing the note as my own vocal foundation, then carefully listening for the overtone beats, slowly turning the black, swirled wooden pegs attached to the top of each string. When all the overtones sounded clearly, ringing out their beat, you had it. The vibrations were key, and when you had adjusted the strings as much as you could, you then moved to the ivory bridge, where Kumarji had attached thread beneath each string. By delicately adjusting the thread with the tiniest of movements, you could enhance the vibration. On the high sa's, the effect could be striking, the sound suddenly ringing and twanging when the thread found its sweet spot. I have never had such an exquisite conjunction of ear and touch. Kumarji was pleased at the demonstration of my ear.

Having my own tanpura made a difference in my practicing, because I loved to touch it, and tune it. As I began to memorize the music, I was able to sing without a tape recorder, accompanying myself on the *tanpura*. But I still lacked rhythmic accompaniment, which would cause problems later on.

Kumarji had a large collection of *tanpuras* in the living room, lined up on the back wall. They were all different sizes, necessary to match the varied voice ranges of students and sundry family members. Among them was a strange little one-stringed instrument. One day I asked, "How can I order one of those?"

My teacher laughed heartily, explaining that I would have to make my own, for that was the way it was done. There were no fabricators of this simple instrument. He explained that this was an *ektara*, "one-string," the instrument used by the *nirguni bhajan wallahs*, holy singers who praised the divine without attribute, *nirgun*. The singer uses the *ektara* both to play the one note metonymic of the *nirgun* over and over, as well as to strum out the rhythm, a singularly simple arrangement, convenient for an itinerant singer to carry. Most westerners think of Hindus as polytheistic, a welter of gods in the pantheon. But the Advaitan approach avoids all this, and the *nirguni* tradition is a particularly effective way of cutting through "names and forms" to the Absolute, Brahman.

Dewas was a *nirguni* town. In his early years there, Kumarji met a holy singer authentic to this tradition and asked to learn some songs. The man obliged, and in the process, showed Kumar how to fashion an *ektara*. This entailed growing a gourd in his garden, cutting a sapling and carving the single tuning peg, hollowing out the gourd, and stringing the *nirgun*. Kumarji later popularized some of these bhajans.

Meanwhile, I was a plant growing in Kumarji's garden, carefully tended under his watchful tutelage. These lessons, crown of a young life of privilege and good fortune, rapidly led to a Great Plan.

6 Struggle

December 1968

I have consciously decided to let Indian society shape me as it will, to take it as far as it wants to go ... I have become an eternal youth. —Puer

The real test of ego-strength is the ability to tolerate ambiguity.
—Saul Bellow, *Herzog*

There were two widely different paths to an ecstatic life which could prolong the India Moratorium indefinitely. One was classical music, which centered and positively altered my consciousness much more readily and frequently than my irregular spurts of meditation, primarily contemplating the face of Ramana Maharshi, as Maurice had instructed. The buzz came both from listening intently to live classical music—especially Kumarji's— and singing, notably the transformative period of *alap*: warm-up with tanpura, entering into the raga by slow, meditative musical probing. This process emptied my mind of everything else. I was enveloped in the sound, the oceanic surround of the *tanpura*'s vibration wedded to my own vocalization, navigating the steady waves of that sea.

The other path was the yoga of smoking ganja. But in both paths I wavered: the quavering vibrato—so pleasing to our western ears—which carried me either side of the perfect center of pitch, and the vacillation of the mind which I mistook for ecstatic play while inebriated with good grass, transporting me everywhere but the center of a steady mind.

On occasion I tried to combine the two. Once when I arrived recognizably stoned for a session, Kumarji gave me a firm look and said, "Ganja not good for singers—bad for throat." At the concerts, I found that listening intently, entering into the stream of music and losing the subjective sense of a separate self was as effective as listening stoned, and less energy-sapping.

The Plan was to stay in India another year, giving the notion of becoming a North Indian singer a chance to put down roots. I would again defer matriculating at Harvard Ed School. When I shared this with my parents, they had doubts. My father had conventional fears, concerned that I would miss my place on the job-ladder. This held little weight for me. Mother was open-minded about India, had in fact been living the experience through me, ever since being entranced by Aunt Lucille's multicolored glass bangles. She was delighted by my love for India, but not with my notion of staying indefinitely. Her concerns were deeper than my father's, focused on turning my back upon the West. A trained musician, it particularly concerned her that I thought it necessary to cloister myself away from western music. And then there was all the rest the West had to offer. Threatened by the clear and strongly felt argument set forth in her letter, I reacted angrily, trying to smother self-doubt.

Dec. 1. *The wildest odyssey of my spirit has rushed through five hectic days of the largest sheer volume of thoughts per minute my mind has ever produced. ... The turmoil is probably the greatest I have ever felt, because the impending decision is the most radical aberration yet in a life of expecteds. It will be a lonely excursion into the heart of myself, of a civilization, potentially the universe and God-Mind. It kills me that I haven't been marshaling the eddies of thought recently. I want to dance, sing, write, read, and fuck until I drop.*

Dec. 4. *Don't give up the incredible dream. ... Read Mother's sheaf on marijuana finally. A little frightening but not enough to reverse my conduct.*

Dec. 10. *Kumar thrilled many of us tonight, even the straights. Kathy wrote, and wants me to stay. I am tired and confused. The world is whorling around me.*

In the midst of this, I tried to slow down the maelstrom. In a letter to my friend Mary from the Asian Tour group, now a VISTA volunteer in Tennessee, I wrote: "I have found a basic drone of peace at my source upon which the passionate energies are superimposed and no longer essential. *I have become an eternal youth.*" (There it was, puer aeternus!)

A little episode from December demonstrates the necessity of staying away from Western music during a Hindustani vocal apprenticeship. Leah had a rich friend who was very proud of his new, state-of-the art Akai tape recorder. Ranju thought I would like to hear the majesty of Beethoven's Ninth (which I had sung as a teen with the Birmingham Symphony and been transported) rendered by his magnificent machine, and brought it over to Anoop Nagar to play for us. He turned the volume up and let 'er rip. To my surprise, it actually hurt my ears—not the volume, but the tempering of the western major scale. I tried to listen as long as I could, but finally fled the apartment, hands over my throbbing ears. I had listened so long to Indian scales and microtones—shrutis—that my ear had been re-tempered. Instead of the western system's dividing the octave into twelve discrete tones, Hindustani music cut it into sixteen to twenty, depending on whether or not one actually considered certain shrutis of a distinctly different character than others measurably different as sound waves. As Mother said, the notes occurred "between the cracks" of the piano. Reflecting on this, I realized that a lot was at stake in my plan to become an Indian musician; life would have to be lived essentially within the Indian sound-universe.

But I never completely separated the musical training from other aspects of staying in the Motherland. Though the greatest inspiration was Kumarji's music, I also valued the tremendous freedom I had in this intoxicating fantasy I called "India." The life of an apprentice vocalist would in fact have been fairly austere, more like the *brahmacharin* stage of the celibate student, under the guru's moral guidance—something completely alien to the dissipated life I was leading in the ample, fluid interstices of my few binding responsibilities. So I dreamed of being able to paint, write, and practice my own brand of unlicensed "stoned therapy" on the side.

What I experienced was a powerful rush of "Indian" creativity—afraid that it might last only if I stayed on the subcontinent. It was an upwelling of the Dionysian, a pure subjectivity overflowing my loosened boundaries. The carefully developed container, the Apollonian mold of my "Western" personality had been under concerted attack. But I had no new container, only this rush of raw experience. Reflecting back on the maelstrom of *thousands of thoughts*, I wrote home of the *titanism* of my struggle to decide. Kumarji the singer, Chandu the painter, Maurice the guru: all were models for a new form, one which seemed to require that I stay in India and become her apologist.

But Puer couldn't live with the ambiguity. By late December he was ready to bail. *Set up next year. Roll back the stone from the cave.* However, before resurrection came "redemption," to use Puer's metaphor for the most completely lived fantasy of the year: two weeks in a fisherman's hut on the beach at Goa over Christmas and New Year's, embedded in the tribe of hippy-saddhus.

7 High Noon in Goa

Every Christmas-New Year's during the late sixties and through the seventies, the International Tribe of hippies, freaks, and hangers-on would pick a suitable spot abroad to gather to ring in the New Year. In 1968 the happening place for South Asia was Goa, the former Portuguese colony. I went with Cowboy Don, a friend I had met in Allahabad courtesy of my Fulbright sisters.

We took an overnight ferry, the "Chowgule," out of Bombay, sleeping on a deck crowded with members of the world-tribe intermixed with Indians, mostly Goan. As the human cargo-ship slipped through the night sea off the Malabar coast, speakers piped Billy Vaughn's orchestra playing Christmas Carols. Nearby, a monkey hung about the neck of a hippy-saddhu, attentively fiddling with his beads: *like a funky, loving child.*

I vowed to transcribe my thoughts as a way to work out my mounting confusion. "Retrenchment" became my seasonal watchword for ending what had begun to feel like freefall:

Since Dec. 7, I've been stoned almost every day. Wanted to write, but it fell into God's Black Web. Somehow I have faith that this is all accessible even without grass. But the young can postpone faith, and the hashed writing continued: *The sky is like a vast accordion. The inner pressures say that it's time for my life to be an accordion and retrench.... My mind is shallow today. Even with all the experience around me, it acts like a flour sifter with one big hole. The valve is perpetually open. Close it and you'll get sand in your ears.*

Don was sitting next to me, patiently fielding a Goan Christian. "As a Catholic I am telling you...." Later, "Humanity is *God's* burden, not man's."

Funny, but my chief desire now is a longing for Maurice, as Bombay recedes. [The preacher] *looks past Don at me.*

"I want to convert you too, in Amreeka, your home."

We arrived the next morning, December 23. *Fishing boats like schooners. A land of hope and promise. New, utterly different India.* Don and I took a taxi to Calangute Beach, below Panjim. We quickly negotiated a fisherman's hut, freshly daubed with cow manure and straw. The hut was right on the beach, simple and clean. The straw-manure mix smelled satisfyingly earthy, reminding me of the Shenandoah Valley farm where I worked during one college summer. That had been hard work, but this was going to be an idyll. Subletting was common practice, and the fisherman and his family probably showed up at some relative's house. I felt guilty turning them out for Christmas.

The beach was wide and white, less littered than I expected, lined with coconut palms. The few other huts on Calangute were rented like ours. Less than a half mile south of us was a "Beach Club" which served grilled cheese and canned tomato soup.

We met our neighbors, a motley cosmopolitan crew of hippy kids from France, Quebec, Switzerland, England, and the US, with the majority from Australia. By the second evening, we had discovered our ritual, which I called Redemption. Several of us would go out and stoke a *chillum* under cover of an old beached fishing vessel, its rotting hulk and tattered sail shielding us from the sea breezes. We would stay for sunset, staving off hunger as long as we could. I fantasized that we were pirates, which wasn't hard, based on the sashes, colorful shirts, braided hair, and in the case of the Aussie I named Black Beard, a braided beard, tied with little red ribbons. A few among the crew were paired with women, but most of the Tribe were unattached, and we treated each other like brothers and sisters—though I occasionally had incest on my mind. It took me a few days to realize that the "gulls" the Aussies were raving about weren't birds. *Black palms against starry sky at night. Outlines of ships on the horizon. Every evening Redemption with Michel, Don and the gang.*

We subsisted on a steady diet of ganja and hash and exposure to the hot beach sun. Pigs rooted about everywhere, and would come running eagerly if they saw one of us squatting down in the sand. *One was rooting at Paul's rump the other day and almost knocked the poor guy over.*

On Christmas Eve, I went alone into town to attend Midnight Mass in a dark, somber cathedral. The women wore black and the candles were sparse. Walking there, I saw a freshly painted blue cross over a door, reminding me of Passover. The whole scene seemed contorted, upside down, backwards. I missed having familiar Christmas carols to sing. "Black Mass" I called it. The real energy was down at the far end of the beach, where incessant drumming built towards the climax of New Year's. I went down there a couple of times but recognized that our more sedate end of the beach was more compatible. We were the middle-class hippies, on loan from the Establishment. These folks were hardcore, and the undulating topless women were literally too much to handle, rows of Indian men silently ogling them, hands in their pockets.

Some of the guys went to see "The Cabinet of Dr. Caligari" at the cinema in Panjim. We could have been a bunch of kids in Panama City—until we came upon a rooster's head in the dusty street. Something about the rooster set my mood, so that during the cinema, I was brooding about my impending decision: *you have to re-enter the world and move into the vanguard of those who solve its problems, because places like India and fantasy islands like Goa will arrive at those problems, too.* Returning home, I saw a shrouded body lying next to one of the huts in our fishing village.

On the surface, I was carried along by the fantasy, our little pirate crew bravely toking up several times a day, keeping ourselves fed, fending off any intruders from the sea. We got along pretty well with each other. I enjoyed crooning French folk songs with blonde, classically handsome Michel from Montreal, occasionally joined by sweet, patient Chantelle, a Parisienne. And I delighted in the vicarious pleasure of being around Aussie Fred's ("Twanger") soft, warm Laura. But Twanger began to stiffen in my presence, especially when I'd embark upon one of my stoned, stream-of-consciousness monologues.

One night, as we redeemed our day in Eden, I was rapidly rapping out thoughts, shooting shafts of insight that disturbed Twanger's mind. "Stop running all that shit, man. Don't fuck with my head. If you don't stop fucking with me, I'll bust your ass."

Each time he'd respond like this, it was as if he were throwing ice-water into my placidly babbling face. My revelations were so mind-boggling, such breakthroughs, that I was impelled to share them. I was the group's Coleridge, yet nobody saw me that way. Maybe Laura.

Another night, Fred started bossing her around: "Come on, bitch, let's make our move."

Laura looked at him sullenly. "It's your move, not mine. I'm enjoying the company."

He looked at her archly, frowned, then grabbed her wrist and started for their wattled hut. She hardly resisted, wearing the resigned face of a sex-slave.

Meanwhile, days would go by and Cowboy Don and I wouldn't see each other, except maybe in passing. Most mornings when I awoke he was already gone, out cruising. I guess we were both looking for other connections in India-land, and this was the Tribal Gathering. *Everybody* was here—except native Indians.

We pirates had no weapons. I made up for that with strafing fantasies: the clouds at sunset sometimes turned into fighter bombers. I was a kid again, playing solo war-games in Mobile's Crawford Park. One evening I ran from some Indian girls who I imagined were trying to shoot me down, stagger-stepping through the sand behind Blackbeard as we retreated from our beachhead to the chowline at the Beach Club, our mess hall.

Beneath this sandbox with its shadowplay, the real work went on furiously. In the middle of the pleasure-island there was a sudden plateau:

Don't want to be an Indian vocalist.

Don't want to teach English or philosophy.

Want T-groups and experimental schools. Don't want a PhD.

Want to see Grandaddy before he dies.

Want to see all my old friends again soon. Remember, no matter how much you may get hung up on lieben und arbeiten, *part of life's happiness—a big part—is having and keeping good friends.*

Here we all were in Goa, celebrating our independence, our rejection of roots, clumping together in smoky mellowness like the dried apple the hill people mixed with hash in their hookahs—but how many of us were sharing this with friends? I saw a few folks each day; our meeting was a matter of indolent habit. I felt lonely. I did meet a big friendly freckled guy, Sam, who became a good toking-buddy, visiting Indore a couple of times. Like me, Sam lived in Pittsburgh. But these other characters—friends?

We slid ever more deeply into our escape, our Redemption, this instant tribe that formed a protective hedge against "the real India"—though the protection was imperfect, as that shrouded body attested in the midst of our commandeered huts. Every now and then someone would quietly leave, and the rest of us would close ranks, complicit in denying that this fantasy-play would soon end for us, too.

But for me, there was always a double consciousness, and I was preparing to leave not only this pleasure dome, but Mother India as well. It was as if I had reached High Noon down here, winter solstice the apogee of my India-swing. Like a hoplite in a Greek army, I knew the battle was over because the sun was making that imperceptible move towards setting, and the other army, Mother India with her Black Masses, beguiling Krishnas and stonetranced Shivas had been unable to overcome our assault. It was still midday: only six of my eleven months in South Asia had passed, but I realized with huge regret that India had lost the struggle for my soul.

I knew I had to leave this false place. I said to Chantelle, *"Dans une semaine, il sera une période de retranchement."* Retrenchment in one week.

Life unfolding like a strange paradise with freaks and freakouts on a magical protected island of insanity and sun and water and beautiful people everywhere you turn. When you leave this country, tears in your eyes, not for a lost paradise but for a spent youth, tears of apprehension as the work unfolds before you, tears for too much joy and too-deep friendships, you will be closing the beginning phase of the Work. But I can feel the productive stage, even now, retrenchment surging in my veins.

Though inevitable, this business of retrenchment was not easy. Like an African teen, banished during his rebellion and promiscuity, I would now return to take up the responsibility of life and family. Oh, but the moratorium was so sweet.

Dec. 29. Retrenchment postponed. Will carry this to the finish. . . . Insects bite and crawl all night as I hallucinate. Chantelle left somehow, escaped, fuit le camp.

One can, and some do, trip so much that they forget they be on one. God forbid that happening to me.

Unholy me, untainted yet by wisdom though I've dipped to taste, wants a fuck for New Year's. Could find Carolyn in Madras, or charge someone here like a bull. I still think of dipping as lowering your head like you were bovine and were going to grace and instead got a warm oozy female mouth around a quivering stiff upright prick. Without grass, even. Soft and warm and you spill your seed like a vast sunflower, the sun in your brain smiles in her eyes, and still she flowers, joining navels with orange juice and licking. . . . Find Carolyn with my Wong. I don't want her to lose her mind.

Dec. 30. Exhausted. Flight-sleep like the drone of bees. A scorpion fell on my sleeping bag the other night. Today, another on the wall of the hut, a manta ray on the roof for all you know. Million fleas bite you. Heavy, opium-like stupor. Perhaps a cumulative hash stupor. My throat is bad; it's hard to swallow.

Try to figure out what makes people stay in India or go home. Why run back yourself? To what? A decent answer to that one and you can leave.

On January first, we heard drumming all night long coming from the interior, not the hippy-beach. We'd heard them the night before, and thought it had to do with New Year's. Paul and Don went on reconnaissance and learned the story. Paul said it's because a baby was born who hasn't been able see for six days, but they beat drums to say to the world (and remind themselves): "our baby's still alive."

Island of magic at night. Forms hover, ghosts and witches come. . . . Blankets and lungis become desert dress and night visages dark-Arab under moon radiance. This night, January second, Don, Paul and Blackbeard rushed into the circle.

Paul said, "We just saw a rhinoceros ghost. I swear; we're not shitting you."

Michel and Fred said in chorus, "Sure. Where is he?"

Don stretched his arms up, casting long shadows on the firelit sands, his mournful eyes big, pointing up the beach. "Over there, about a mile. We tracked it as far as we could, then lost it in the brush." I heard his lips crack the way they always did when he got really stoned.

Michel, deadpan, looked along the horizon in the direction Don had pointed, and said simply, "Bizarre. C'est bizarre."

Towards the end of Saturnalia, it became clear that Laura was tired of being yanked around by her egocentric, sadistic boyfriend. Two nights before I left, as we all stood around, a fairly desultory group of sleep-deprived dopeheads, Twanger said to her, "I'm exhausted, let's go to bed."

Laura answered, "I'm not tired," then walked over and stood beside me. I resisted the urge to put my arm around her.

Fred shot me one of his menacing looks. Angry from this put-down in front of the gang, he turned to Laura. "I'm going to bed, and you're going with me, bitch."

Before I could react, Laura answered, "I can't stand it anymore," turned and ran from the circle into the darkness. I wanted to run after her, but didn't. Fred turned and retreated to his hut.

My last night in Goa I wanted "someone," as I put it to the family around the bonfire, to sleep with me on the beach. Actually I meant Laura, but I didn't want to ask her in front of everybody. I looked hopefully around the group, but began to fear none would respond to my appeal. But then Laura answered quietly, "I will." Did she really care about me after all?

We took our straw mats and sleeping bags down to the gently pounding surf. It was quiet, no drums, nobody else around—just the vast, moonless, starry night, the ocean, this gorgeous nymph from Toledo, Ohio, and me. So what did we do? Looking first at her smooth, placid face, perfect in its classically average American features, then at the starry Void, Puer proceeded to present her with the gift of his summary take on the Goan adventure.

All existence is dual, and everyone is naturally schizoid. So insanity is a meaningless category. Everyone's a flipflop of someone else in the chain. Don, Fred, you and me—we're all flipflops of each other. It's like there're two selves: one watches and listens to the other. You may be playing and analyzing at once because there are two of you in one. I'm a Doppelganger—a double—of Don; Fred is my Demian. Fred thinks I am the woman at these times. You were an angel putting on the devil, but you never even knew who the devil was—until I finally showed you."

Laura nodded. This stuff seemed to make sense. Somehow she trusted this guy. He was so sincere, maybe even wise.

Puer continued. *Play and necessity aren't really that different. Did you ever think about that? These fishermen don't know the difference between play and work. Play is work, and being a boy is being a man.*

Laura lay there, eyes open, looking at me some of the time, but with no readable expression. She always smelled so sweet, now with an admixture of salt.

"You know, Laura, you're a witch."

She looked mildly surprised.

"A sweet witch, but a witch."

This new context was exotic, but the monologue was a repeat of my high school defense against romance. Talking was a way of putting off sex. Once my friends fixed me up with the high school "whore," whose name was also Laura. She looked like a Parisian prostitute, hair all froofrooed, bright red lipstick, moles in just the right places, and a wondrously deep décolletage. Actually, I liked her. And she clearly liked me. Looking coquettish, blinking her eyes, she leaned into me as I stiffened with fear. So I launched into yet another Platonic dialogue—the kind that so impressed Mother—and I had more success winning her over to philosophy than she did getting me to cross the fearsome threshold.

So it went with this Laura as well. After a monologue that seemed even to me to go on for hours, I only managed to exchange scarves, gently untying her silk one and replacing it with my coarse cotton one. I couldn't even bring myself to kiss her—which I badly wanted to do—when I left her sleeping by the surf at dawn. "Why are you afraid of sex? It only takes a few minutes," a grad fellow at Winthrop House had said.

Platonic Puer! I remember the afternoon during the Asian Tour when one of the women called me at the Hong Kong Hilton and said, "I want to make love."

"Sure, come on over" I said, but when I put the receiver down, I anxiously wondered what that meant, "make love." As a teen I had seen Marilyn Monroe in the film "Let's Make Love," but the meaning of the title had eluded me and was still not entirely clear here in Hong Kong on the Asian Tour, on the cusp of my twenty-first birthday. We fumbled around a bit, but she realized quickly that she was doomed to frustration, leaving the bitter words of eternal damnation stinging my ears, "I thought you were a man, but you're still just a boy!"

I can still hear the intonation and stress of every syllable in Anthony Quinn's judgment as Zorba: "There is only one thing God will not forgive a man. If a woman calls him to her bed, and he will not come." "Still just a boy"—and an unforgiven one.

The thing is, I didn't love any of these women—Carolyn, Leah, now Laura. Sure I was scared of sex, but I was a romantic: sex only made sense, could only be deeply satisfying with someone you were head over heels in love with. That's how it had been with Kathy. Now I hardly wrote her.

Laura's silence left everything to my imagination. But I had begun to suspect that she didn't have much to say because she wasn't really that bright. It also dawned on me that she had *known* I wouldn't "hassle her," which was undoubtedly how every man had approached her heretofore. Somehow I was different, a safe haven from Fred, the latest in a long line of predatory keepers, or so I imagined. She really didn't want anything more than a quiet, protected night on the beach, one night's reprieve before the distasteful fireworks of leaving him.

So this was the end of Paradise, as Chantelle called it.

8 Indore: Retrenchment

January 1969

Life back in Indore *was* a kind of retrenchment. I submitted my late application to Harvard Ed School for a Master of Arts in Teaching program and started practicing more assiduously, realizing that I had recitals in both Indore and Mussoorie coming up in March and April. I also worked harder at lesson planning and the tutorials I had started giving some brighter students. Chandu and I went to concerts in Bombay where both Kumarji and Vasuthai sang. One was ecstatic, wildly beautiful, student-wife lovingly echoing her master-husband.

Though I finally submitted the Harvard Ed School application, I still gyrated wildly around the decision, wondering how much of the year's experience I could take with me: *Accept the Faustian in you and harness it, or go Eastern? How much can the two be integrated?* Continuing regular trips for lessons to Dewas, I was still reluctant to give up the Plan. But it was the *fantasy* of being a Hindustani vocalist which drew me, for practicing still played only a small part in my daily life. By comparison, Kumarji's most dedicated students, Mukhul and Satish Deshpande, vocalized four hours each day, as much as the voice could comfortably sustain.

At Indian Springs, the glee club director had pulled me aside after rehearsal one day, his wide, Socratic face with buggy eyes serious as he stoked his ever-present pipe. "Are you thinking of a music career?" he asked.

"Maybe, I don't really know," I said. That spring my piano teacher had suggested a stint with a chamber group from the Atlanta Symphony, playing the first movement of Beethoven's First Piano Concerto. The first movement only, no cadenza. I was good but no *wunderkind.*

"Well let me tell you. It's hell making a living as a musician. So you'd better really love it before making that commitment. You have many talents."

I had felt relieved then, having it laid so clearly on the line. Now, with a music career of a sort neither Hugh Thomas nor I ever imagined beckoning, I was balking, yet unable to admit it. I rededicated myself to developing my "talent" for wrestling interpersonal truth from social situations. I would be a labor negotiator, or a leader of self-analytic groups, as I had told Carolyn on the flight to Kashmir. Harvard Ed would have to be flexible enough to help Puer accomplish this, and I penned a long letter to the vague denizens of the admissions office, writing into the night. Puer was straight, ever since the return from Goa's somafest, but his hazy career thoughts were overcast with a romantic haze: *the golden city seems much closer than before.*

Reckoning with Lew

At the end of January, I went to Delhi to visit my dear friend Lew. He was embarked for the year on a world college-cruise, with sojourns in countries representing a broad array of cultures. Lew was my best friend from Harvard, a fellow tenor from the Asian Tour, budding poet and operatic singer. He had an unparalleled zest for life, an infectious sense of humor and an uncanny ability to see through your self-deluding bullshit. As the trip to Delhi approached, I realized how much I missed him.

Lew met me at New Delhi station. As we embraced on the platform, I recognized a pang of longing for the familiar world I had considered abandoning for a superior reality. Lew's hosts' driver, a beaming fellow happy to have such a plush job, chauffeured us to the facility where the touring college convened. En route, we exchanged reports. Puer spoke in superlatives: "India is incredible. The Fulbright has been wonderful. It's true I have to teach English in a university system where everyone learns by rote, but there're lots of vacations, including one that lasted over a month, for Dussehra-Diwali. And the vocal training is the best part. I've been lucky enough to be accepted by the finest and most creative vocalist in the North. Their voice culture is exquisitely intricate, it makes ours seem stodgy by comparison."

Lew, who had been receptively grinning at this little speech, lost his smile over the last remark. He was a serious vocalist, and planned a career as a professional operatic tenor. Now I was looking into his no-nonsense brown eyes: "Hold on, Bob! Slow down! Sure, the two systems are vastly different. But you can't just claim theirs is superior. Besides, you can't really know that much yet. When did you say you started lessons?"

In my excitement, I'd introduced this damned element of competition before we could bask in the warmth of being together again. It wouldn't do to keep up this tack about Kumarji; Lew wouldn't understand. But how badly I *wanted* him to! There were so many other superlatives about Puer's India, the amazing changes he had experienced. I felt sorry for Lew, who was suffering his year abroad in little cultural islands buffered by other Americans, missing Puer's experience of blessed immersion. "It's hard to explain. I just wish you could hear Kumarji sing. How long did you say you'd be in Delhi? I think he has a concert in March."

Lew laughed, eyes dancing, then drew serious, explaining that his group was only in Delhi a few weeks. "Let me tell you about the year I've had." He proceeded to tell me about the carefully designed curriculum focusing on cross-cultural experience. One of the lead faculty was an anthropologist, the other a sociologist. Resident experts lectured the students, who wrote a paper and a journal for each country. He was getting what he'd expected.

But Puer was getting even more. "Sounds great," I said flatly, "I've got so much to tell you about. I wish you could come visit me in Indore while you're here. I want you to meet Kumarji, and my friend Chandu. His mind is so fluid it's like he's on a continuous acid trip...." I was cut short by the driver turning to us, pointing out the building for the morning's lecture.

On Saturday we settled into a long talk. "Lew, I've really changed pretty drastically since coming here. I don't think I could ever be the same person again."

Lew listened with patience and deep interest, but after the exchange the day before, his shit-detector was on. "That's a pretty big claim. I hope you haven't changed so much that we can't still be close. India really has affected you, hasn't it?"

I told him about Maurice Frydman. "The main thing about him is that he is, well, a guru."

"Oh no, not a guru!" Lew said. "Surely there's nobody worth giving up your own independent judgment for, is there? Is he like the Maharishi?" he added, eyes twinkling.

"No, Lew, it's not like that. Maurice is a *jnani*; he wouldn't want me to give up my own judgment. That's the whole point, to learn to discriminate all the shit, the masks, the lies, the fakeries from *Brahman*." I explained what *Brahman* meant, comparing it to the Ground of Being.

"But what about love?" he asked. "And what about our humanness, our wonderful little idiosyncrasies, our endearing follies? Is there room for these in your new philosophy?"

"Brahman *is* love. All the rest, you're just hanging onto sentimental attachments. We've got to learn to drop all that stuff. It's child's play. Now it's time to grow up."

"Sure, I'm hanging onto me, and my mother, and sister, and to you. You're not God, you're Bob. Do you really think you're God, or Brahman if you prefer? I mean *right now*?"

"No. No, I've got a long way to go," I assured him. "But Maurice has given me a glimpse of something so much better, much more real. You know what he said? He invited me to 'join the Brotherhood of the Undeceived.' I'm going to keep working until I become a *jnani*. I want to be part of that brotherhood."

Lew said he was glad I didn't feel like I was on some separate plane. He talked about his visit to Angor Wat the month before. "You see, this is the kind of thing I care about. Taking in as much beauty as I can while I can. From your perspective this is all Maya, just evanescent form. To me it matters; it's beautiful; it awakens me to something grander and more lasting than little me. But it too is ephemeral, like everything that lives."

Puer spoke of the architectural wonders of India—the Taj, the Sun Temple at Konarak, then added, "They only *point* to reality; they are just symbols which raise consciousness to something far beyond their exquisitely crafted stone. It's a matter of emphasis, isn't it? You know Lew, the self I was, the one you knew, was so much smaller, so much more petty and attached to passing things. Like success for instance."

"You've never been overly attached to success. You worked for grades more than I ever have, but that's not so bad is it? What do you mean by success?"

"I mean like getting a good job and making a bunch of money and having little kids running around and worrying about filling a big house up with a bunch of junk that you're too stupid to get rid of. That's success."

"Don't you want a good job, a lovely wife and kids and a nice house?"

"No, I don't. I want to be free to study, to meditate, to work towards enlightenment."

"Sounds pretty heavy, not really fun. But if that's what you want, do it. Do it with all your heart. I just want to stay your friend."

"Sure, Lew."

On the train back to Indore after the showy Republic Day parade the following Monday, I had plenty of time to think over the weekend's encounter. I had been happy to see Lew, but the friendship was strained because Lew didn't buy how "changed" I was. Nor did he accept the efficacy of my "ganja therapy"—Lew, the first person I ever got stoned with. His reality was our relationship back at Cambridge, and he doggedly stuck to that, slowly making me realize that maybe I wasn't really that changed. He pointed out that I still was hung up on sex, and had to work that through until I could get anywhere. This honest observation angered me, and I left him rather coolly at the end of the four-day visit.

Lew had again done the tough job of a mature friend: reorienting me to my own imperfect self, loving me all the while. Back in Indore, I cultivated the seed of doubt Lew had planted. This encounter, combined with ingesting far less *ganja* that month, made for quite a letdown, a reality check. *Funny how Lew's the Hub of the Matter after all. . . . How pompous I was the first day. He made me see I was back where I started when I boarded the plane in New York June 16. Being in a fantasy-land has given the illusion of enormous progress in self-development. Bogus.*

The bogus fantasy was Puer's overlay for the Fulbright year; it was *his* India. Back at the College, I began to realize that the apogee had passed, and that I was going to end the year without having made much headway with my students. This was not really my fault, since the situation required persons trained in teaching English as a second language. So what if I'd been editor of a literary magazine at Harvard. "Sir, you will teach us Poe," the spokesman for the masters students announced. Poe, the subject of my honors thesis—yet they barely understood a word I said. Still, I felt a dawning sense of responsibility, not yet clear for what or to whom. *I am a moralist, always have been. I must have the courage to be one,* [like] *Dr. King and Gandhi.*

One morning in the corridor at the college, the students were all frozen in stances, faces immobile, unmoving, untalking. I was perplexed as I observed the same scene played everywhere. One whole class stood at attention. Afterwards I understood: a commemorative tribute to the Mahatma's martyrdom, January 30. This explained the bell's tolling twenty minutes early.

The bell was tolling, sounding the end of my Passage to India, bringing me back to the reality of these students' lives and struggles, calling me to touch ground before the inevitable return stateside. But then a couple of adventures rekindled all my longing for a more permanent union with India, and ambiguity crept back in. Though I knew in my gut the Great Plan was dead, the India Tarbaby kept exerting it's pull: a wide-eyed Lord Jaganath Puri-doll, Krishna miraculously appearing to the ancient Orissans as an unfinished carving whose arm-stubs forever beckoned.

9 Spinout on the Malwa Plain

February–March 1969

Every twelve years Hindus celebrate the Kumbh Mela, a huge religious fair whose exact date is determined by astrologers, rotating through the four holiest river cities. Nearby Ujjain was one of these, and the imminent site of a "half-mela." A bunch of us accompanied Chandu to Ujjain to experience it, just a short bus journey: Puer, Leah, big cheerful Pittsburgh Sam from Goa, and a perpetually stoned PCV from Bhopal, Doug. After arriving at the bus station, Chandu, who had no interest in the mela, headed to town to meet a client, while we American hippy-saddhus joined the line of pilgrims leading towards the river to immerse ourselves in this confluence of religious currents. Crowd estimates were about 400,000.

The mela was a smorgasbord for the spiritual tourist. There were fakirs on beds of nails, yogis bent in every conceivable position, each with his bowl for *baksheesh* next to little piles of oranges and bananas left by the faithful. I photographed a "transistor saddhu," proudly sitting naked behind his brand-new transistor radio, a reward for his vasectomy. Of course as a celibate renunciate, he should have had no use for the vas cutting. Apparently he did for the radio.

A little way into the milling crowd, we were delighted to find a group of saddhus who might serve as models for Stephen Gaskin's "sacramental" grass-toking inmates at the Farm in middle Tennessee. We arrived just in time to see a short, stocky fellow huffing and puffing like a little locomotive as he stoked a huge chillum to share with the other devotees of cannabis— and Shiva, patron god of the elixir. The chillum was about ten inches in diameter, loaded to the hilt. A man told us that this was the man's sacrificial life, his *tapas*, going from mela to mela lighting the holy chimney-torch. For years afterwards, I would do this in remembrance of Shiva, and it felt right. Leah, one of two women present, bravely walked up to the fiery chimney and gave it a good draught. I was impressed with her *chutzpah*. She turned and looked right at me, smoke appearing to come out of her ears. The time with Leah in Ujjain was the first that her frequent soulful looks finally got through to me, telling me I was special, Sikh boyfriend notwithstanding. It took me awhile, as it always did with romantic currents, to realize what those looks meant. Having ingested these auspices, we were now properly initiated, ready to enter into the polymorphic body, both sacred and profane, of this crowd.

Melas always have a parade, giving its multiple centers a focus, much like a circus. We found good reviewing places in the front row for the gamut of religious personages. Proud, richly bearded swamis in royal mantles of gold, yellow, orange and even scarlet, the color of *rajas*—the fiery, aggressive temperament—marched by. Some were on horseback, with banners or staves. Brass bands followed, one with players attired Sergeant Pepper-style with double-breasted crimson jackets sporting a double row of gold buttons, white felt visored hats. They pranced and swayed like Black bands in the South. The brassy, slightly off-key music rankled and felt out of place. Finally, a long line of naked Nagas from the extreme northeast appeared, ascetics who braved the cold without clothes and very little shelter. The women renunciates in orange robes followed, some with shaved heads. They and the Nagas smeared sacred ash on their faces and bodies. They looked like ghosts.

After the parade, I slipped away from the others. Heading over a little grassy knoll, I found a saddhu standing with his right arm raised heavenwards. There were several such men, some with one leg raised, others with legs crossed, roosting on their hands. But I noticed that many of the others relaxed their poses after each knot of the faithful passed, sitting on little stools, smoking cigarettes. This man was for real. Carefully watching his face, I traced a cycle of pain, lasting about two or three minutes, followed by a look of ecstatic bliss for fifteen or twenty seconds.

I observed the saddhu twice, testing my observations. Then I approached one of his retainers to ask how long he had held this pose. He answered, "ten years." The gentle man told me that the saddhu's arm had atrophied into this position. "Sir, it is too much painful." One testimony to the duration of this *tapas* was that his fingernails had grown through the palms of his hands, curling out the other side in a couple of places. It was as if the arm were an unwithered corpse, crucified by his will, sealed with his own nails. Yes, the Mela is part freak show, and draws crowds for the same reasons circus freaks do. But the look in this man's eyes, both the suffering and the brief ecstasy, lifted him far beyond the merely freakish.

A little after five-thirty, our appointed meeting-time with Chandu at the Ujjain clock-tower, I ran upon the others, glassy-eyed hippy-saddhus shambling along in front of me. Glancing ahead, I saw Chandu, anxiously frowning as he searched the crowd. When I overtook my friends, both Leah and Sam put their arms over my shoulder, each with big stoned grins, and Leah added a smack on the cheek. Nobody wondered at my wandering off. We were pilgrims, not tourists. Or so we told ourselves.

My last adventure was a trip to visit the Bheels, a pre-Neolithic tribal group (*adiwasi*) a few hours from Indore. Chandu knew a PCV there who had lived amongst them for two years, earning their trust. He would put us up in his little house. Leah and a couple of other PCV girls accompanied us.

The Bheels called Russ the White Bull. He was the most dedicated PCV I met in India. He not only worked extremely hard, re-enlisting for a second term, but also became part of the headman's family, so that when his little sister was abducted by a neighboring tribe on horseback, he went with her brothers on the counter-raid to get her back. They were successful, and fortunately nobody was killed. The Peace Corps bureaucrats in Bhopal were mortified. As Russ toured us around the first day, he showed us some poles ringed with doughnuts of dried cowdung, like a primitive game of horseshoes. He told us that early in the century a Catholic missionary happened upon the Bheels during the rite building one of these, and was killed on the spot. No wonder the Peace Corps folks were concerned about the political implications of Russ's family ties.

That evening on a moonlit walk Leah and I came upon a large group of village men dancing a circle dance and joined them. Being in that circle, dancing with the dark, leathery-faced men, their turbans reflecting pastel hues in the moonlight, was ecstatic. The dance wasn't hard, and I had it down so well that I was with them instant by instant as the dance snaked and coiled around itself. The men's faces were impassive, seriously focused on the precision of the steps. In unison our bodies poised, dipped slightly to mark the intervening beats, then uncoiled into a twirl, clasping hands at precisely the same moment at the end of each spin. The drummers held the big taught skins against their bellies, arching their backs, chins up, gazes aimed above the dancers at the horizon. We were a tribe, dancing as one. Leah was behind me, the only woman in the circle, missing the beat at first, but then getting the feel. Her hand was cool, contrasting with the sweaty, warm palm of the guy ahead of me:

Vast dance with clanging drums, writhing bodies, Leah's hand, white moon lighting stoned faces. Hundreds across the wide plain to Russ's hut, twirling, eyes in the stars, feet nimble and limber. My body harmonized finally with my mind. I swirled to Dronatala and swam in the Milky Way.

The intoxicating beat of the drums entered my bloodstream, uniting gut with head. But then a moment came when I couldn't absorb any more. At the point where I was farthest from the village, feeling the pull of the vast arid plain dotted with scrub and the wheeling stars overhead, I made a spin move hurtling me away from the group, and just kept spinning. Farther and farther out into the plain I whirled, until everyone was distant. After a while, I realized that I was alone and cold. When I returned to the dance-ground, everyone had left.

It was as if I kept straining the limit, this time precisely measured by the angular momentum of the dance that night with the Bheels. Unlike Russ, I was not really one of them; I was just tripping. Indeed, my dervish trip across the plain was more like my rag doll dream, the immense vault of stars spinning about me as they had in that dream in rural Bengal. But this time when I landed, it was not the warm comforting hearth of the Master I found, but the cold February plain of Central India. And I was once again alone, needing to be filled.

10 Puer's Endgame

The waning weeks of work at the college were humdrum, but they took on poignancy as I realized this was indeed the end. The long coda from the dance on the plain at Thandla to the final flight from Delhi in late May was bittersweet. I had reached the apogee and simply played out what had clearly become nothing more than a moratorium with as much grace as I could muster.

Encouraged by Kumarji and Chandu, I gave a little vocal concert in Indore in March on a small tented outdoor stage: *Jawa hun desa,* "I am going home." About sixty attended. It served both as a dress rehearsal for Mussoorie and as an opportunity for my Indore friends to hear Kumarji's *shishya*. There were a few other amateur performers, all Indians. My act was last—the curiosity of an Amreekan trying to imitate the master imitator himself.

Mounting the stage, wearing my kurta-pyjama and olive khadi vest, I was nervous, starting to perspire, though the air was cool. The *tanpura* was in good tune, and playing it for a couple of minutes allowed me to compose myself somewhat. My tabla accompanist was Deepak, an accomplished artist and really nice guy who sat watching and listening with a friendly open vibe as I went into my *alap*. The rhythmic section started well, but soon our rhythms parted and I lost the *sum* (the meeting of soloist and drummer at the end/beginning of the rhythmic circle).

When I lose the rhythm, I have an immediate feeling of panic. Some musicians are able to skip a beat or two and jump back in. But I'm lost right away. I usually have to start the whole thing over. This evening, though I started to panic, I decided to appear as professional as possible, and kept singing, trying to meander my way back to the beat. It probably would've been better to ask the tabla-wallah to start over. We remained out of sync for at least three rhythmic cycles. He was looking at me to make sure I knew I was off. I know I looked worried. Eventually I found my way back, and he relaxed into his strokes. But I was tentative, arriving at the *sum* cautiously from then on, rather than playfully enjoying that moment of union. We finished more or less together, exchanged glances, and the audience applauded politely. I was glad it was over.

My lower leg had gone to sleep, so I couldn't get up right away. I reached down to massage the calf and ankle, avoiding the gaze of anyone I might know in the audience. This had been my moment, and I had blown it. I was embarrassed and defeated, and there was no reason to go into the what-ifs the ego wanted to rehearse. I was relieved that Kumarji, in his wisdom, had chosen to stay in Dewas. But the recognition that I was not going to fulfill his hopes for his American *shishya* was devastating. Slowly I unfolded myself, righted the *tanpura*, stood and walked towards the small waiting assembly.

Rahul, *Naia Duniya*'s ("new day") editor, greeted me first. He was friendly and encouraging, placing his hammy hand on my shoulder, cheek bulging with tobacco. Guruji, clad in a splendid tan silk kurta, was his usual reserved self, but smiled warmly. Finally Chandu and I met. He smiled, reached up to my shoulder and said, "You did fine." But what he exuded was sympathy more than pride, certainly not enthusiasm. The performance was polite, but certainly no showcase for an emerging *gharana* at the foot of the Hill of Devi. I was no Jon Higgins.[1]

Vishnu came up and shook my hand vigorously, smiling his Cheshire-cat grin, fixing me with that sincere look he must've learned in grade school., Then, eyelids fluttering, he lowered his gaze, head bowing a little. Looking around, I found I didn't recognize anyone else. Kargonkar, my

---

[1] American South Indian vocalist whose style and voice were indistinguishable from trained classical singers.

tabla teacher who would've accompanied me had he been well, was still bedridden with TB. I was relieved. *Let's get out of here* I thought, and was immensely relieved when Chandu got it. There was no pub, but I wanted a drink.

Not long after my little concert Kumarji gave an afternoon Holi performance in Indore. The atmosphere was festive, the music fittingly ecstatic for Hindu Valentine's, commemorating the love of Krishna and Radha. Tiny old Damukaka—Kumarji's number one fan in Dewas—sang a little bhajan, head rolling so violently I feared it would drop off. Damukaka didn't have much of a voice, but his rhythmic sense was very keen, with several nicely turned syncopations which Kumarji enormously appreciated, grunting responsively, returning the head-rock as he shaved betel nut with the shiny tool that always reminded me of dentists' pliers. *Bhang* candies were passed around, singles for the kids, doubles for the adults, and the whole place was merrily high by the end of the afternoon. As we emerged from the hall, middle schoolers pelted the audience with Holi colors, and the adults soon joined them. I caught Chandu trying to escape around the corner, and plastered him well. In turn, I was covered from head to knee with an assortment of colors: vermillion, yellow, pink, and purple.

South India

Late that same afternoon, I left for South India. Classes were over, and the students had a long break to study for their exams. Forbidden to proctor by Kasliwal, I was free. Feeling auspiciously marked, I wore my white dress shirt drenched with Holi colors to the train station, disdaining a bath. My face and arms remained purple-red. For many years I saved that shirt, rich with colors, one sleeve torn from the hold one fellow gave me as I tried to elude a color-bomb. It was a *samskaric* shirt, drenched with the experience of that mythic afternoon in Indore—a token of the whole Indian adventure. For once, I was clearly one with my Malwan family, and wanted to hold onto that memory as long as possible.

About a hundred and twenty kilometers short of Bhopal, I realized my train was running very late, and risked missing the express I had booked from Bhopal down to Madras. So I slung my pack over my shoulder, hopped off at a small station, and started walking down the narrow highway, hoping to find a lorry to hitch to Bhopal. After about half an hour, a trucker and his sidekick picked me up, perhaps thinking it auspicious to pick up a *foreen* pilgrim who respected their religion enough to wear Holi colors.

I must've looked pretty wild. They sent me aloft in the gaily painted wooden utility carrier atop the cab. On its front a blue-faced, smiling Shiva armed with his trident surveyed a sylvan world. Contentedly I figured it would take us four hours to make the distance. I watched the sunset, counted the stars as they marched overhead and then dropped off to sleep. About twenty-five kilometers outside Bhopal, the driver stopped to sleep for the night. I vainly tried to argue in pigeon-Hindi that we finish the distance so I could catch my train, but he was not to be budged. It was only eight-thirty.

I woke at dawn when the engine started. Birds flew over a misty plain covered with dry wheat stalks, dotted with scrub and trees. It was cold. I kept my sleeping bag wrapped around me and fashioned a turban from a thin hand towel, facing the cutting wind which Shiva plowed with his trident. The cheery driver dropped me at the Bhopal Station, where I learned that another train for Madras would be arriving at ten o'clock. I went over to the water pump at one end of the platform, stripped to my underwear like a native, and proceeded to wash myself, crouching in the foot basin encircling the pump, my Holi markings richly coloring the water as it drained between my toes. It was damn cold. Several curious children gathered around to watch this odd *foreen* perform what was essentially a ritual bath. A couple of turbaned men watched from a nearby wooden bench, hands folded atop their canes. I carefully folded up my Holi-shirt and put on a clean pyjama-kurta. Fully awakened by my brisk bath, I proceeded to the chai-stand to await my train.

The train ride to Madras took twenty-seven hours, for this was not the express I had booked. But I slept well as usual, and enjoyed *masala dosas* for lunch on my arrival. Madras was cleaner than the cities in the North, perhaps with the exception of Delhi. It had some stately buildings built during the Raj, and an interesting museum. The people I met spoke good English and seemed intelligent. But my heart wasn't really in the place, and I longed to see the ocean. So I went to Mahabalipuram, drawn by the beach temples, exquisite miniatures in the South Indian style. A pretty woman in her late twenties selling seashells and necklaces of shell and stone sold me several of her wares. I hung out on the beach, enjoying the sea breezes. But I still didn't feel connected. Perhaps I should've taken a companion along. I was getting lonely. This no longer felt like my India.

I took a train to Madurai, the ancient temple city in the Tamil heartland, staying in a cheap, clean hotel near the huge Meenakshi Temple. The temple featured towering multicolored *gopalams* to the four directions covered with every member of the pantheon, a large tank in the middle where pilgrims could wash before entering the shrines, and two golden shrines, one to Shiva and one to his consort Parvati—called Meenakshi here in the South.

After wandering around the temple grounds, I washed my feet in the tank and paid the fee to climb up into one of the tallest gopalams to look out over the city, covered with pre-monsoon haze. You could almost touch the monstrous bird-billed gargoyles guarding the summit from marauding demons. It was hot midday. After descending, I walked up to the little wire cage funneling pilgrims into the Meenakshi shrine. Approaching the young man at the gate, I asked admittance. Traveling around the north with my Hindu friends, this had not been a problem. He looked at me and asked, "Are you a Hindu?"

Dodging, I answered, "I am a follower of J. Krishnamurthi."

Since he didn't know who this was, he shrugged and let me pass. Once in the inner sanctum, I waited in a modest line to namaste the image of Meenakshi. When I was about eight pilgrims away from the goddess, a burly bare-chested priest, spying me with my camera poised on my belly, bustled over and roughly dragged me out. Puer protested in vain: "What about Love? Isn't that what religion is about?"

The priest smelled of a curious mixture of ghee, sweat, incense, and feminine bath soap. It was his job to remain pure, so he bathed frequently. The rich smell of human sweat seemed to emanate from his armpits, the ghee and incense exuding from his hands, which were clasped about my chest, and his full beard. Remains of the morning soap were still in his facial pores. He was very clean, very priestly, and very angry. The intense palate of smells in the sanctum sanctorum which had saturated me: incense, an admixture of burnt ghee, milk, curds and floral scents of marigold and jasmine, the freshly-oiled woman's hair queued in front of me, was now replaced by this single focus, an unjolly giant dragging me across ancient floors blackened from sacrificial ghee, creased and worn by millions of devotees.

He dumped me with a disgusted look outside the wire cage, and went over to chasten the frightened young guard. I was hurt and embarrassed, but glad that he hadn't demanded my film. (I would never have used the camera in a sanctum sanctorum.) Once deposited on the stone floor outside, the smells of the outer temple area once again assaulted me, incense mixed with the sweat of thousands of devotees and the omnipresent odor of urine and cowdung. I looked up from my position of disgrace to see many pilgrims casually observing me. To one side, the temple elephant attended by his mahout temporarily halted his job of blessing the faithful with his trunk, accepting coins for the temple treasury for his efforts. This was not a moment to be blessed, but rather erased from the records of Meekakshi Temple. But not from my memory. Finally I had been noticed in South India. I *existed*, even if only as an interloping presence.

After the young man was upbraided by the priest, he looked at me sheepishly, then lowered his eyes. He certainly didn't blame me. I have since learned that, unless you're lucky, Westerners must present a certificate of conversion for admission to all Vaishnavite temples but one, and to some Shaivite sanctuaries, including Meenakshi.

And my plea for admittance? It was the closest thing to the truth that I could utter in a pinch. I had read two or three of Krishnamurthi's books, and had been impressed. But a "follower," a disciple? He accepts no followers and debunks organized religion, Hinduism in particular. So the ejection was appropriate, whether or not I was a Hindu. Instant karma.

I longed for Malwa, suddenly remembering sweet old Damukaka's ecstatic little song at the Holi concert, head lolling wildly, skinny shoulders rising as he gulped for breath, neck veins bulging. What a contrast between total acceptance in Indore and being thrown out of this *Shaivite* temple. But I had finally made contact in South India, rudely carried on the prominent belly of that priest, a naughty boy in his father's arms. Father India had noticed me, peeking in on his mother-bride in her private quarters. Better to be punished than ignored.

Now Father India sent me back home to Malwa. I stayed with Chandu and Sulu, where I had more home-cooked meals, Salim having fulfilled his nine-month contract. College duties finished, Stuart was traveling with Lynn. I practiced for the upcoming concert at the Fulbright tutors' final gathering at Mussoorie, a hill station in the North, making the pilgrimage to Dewas a few last times.

Fulbright Farewell

March 1969

The trip to Mussoorie was another long one. Leaving Indore, I took the train as far as Haridwar, then boarded a bus the remainder of the way to Mussoorie via Dehra Dun, about a four-and-a-half-hour ride. I ran into Loren, Jon's roommate from Calcutta at the bus-stand, relieved to have a companion for the final leg. But as the bus ponderously climbed the poor roads, the jostling became quite uncomfortable. I tried to talk to Loren, but was preoccupied with the acute realization that my gonads were extremely tender; each bump made them feel like somebody's punching bag. It was not only painful, but downright scary. My first thought was testicular cancer—this was the end. But a few rude bumps later I remembered Mukhul's face, swollen like a chipmunk absconding with twin walnuts at my lesson the week before. I wasn't dying; I just had the mumps. Towards the end the switchbacks made me carsick as well.

Mussoorie was beautiful, a perfect choice for a final gathering. It was April, so the monsoon clouds were gathering, but you could glimpse snow-covered peaks in the distance in the early mornings. We passed the Woodstock School on our way to our retreat lodge, and I thought of Marilyn, now on vacation. When the taxi unloaded Loren and me, Jon was there to greet us, along with pipe-wielding Holmes, amiable, boy-faced Sharma and a couple of the tutors ambling up behind. Seeing Loren and me together, Jon gave a big smile. But his face turned grey when I told him about my condition. After supper we tried to practice for the next day's concert, since he was my tabla accompanist. Despite my discomfort, I was pleased to hear him tap out a steady *rupak* rhythm. I tuned up a bit, then sang the first phrase. That was it. I was too sick, uncomfortable and exhausted to perform.

The next day tutors presented their papers to Holmes and briefly sketched their results for the rest of us. Then those of us who had studied music and art gave performances and demonstrations. I drank plain tea, shivering with chills, wrapped in a woolen blanket. Those who had avoided mumps kept a safe distance. It was far from cozy, and I felt pretty alone, especially when Jon gave a peremptory little tabla demo in the slot for his concert with me. My Allahabad hostess Jeanie gave a weak sitar performance, blushing at her frequent mistakes. Kathy from Jaipur was far more accomplished; you actually got the flavor of Hindustani classical sitar from her fairly long composition. But she set her angular jaw and never smiled; clearly this was still work for her—as singing would have been for me.

Then Carolyn came on, set to perform two Bharat Natyam dances. She wore a stunning costume, yellow silk bloomers and a multi-hued blouse that left the bellybutton showing, bells on her ankles. Added to these accents on womanly form was a dancer's heavy makeup, producing some unsettling South Asian effects in my blonde friend. She approached center stage, bowed her head, then raised it into that stately serious gaze at the audience so characteristic of the South Indian temple dancer. When she did this, I felt a huge longing for what might have been. This could have been *our* India, not just my little private landscape. That dancer's look is the opening to the world of Bharat Natyam, designed to make the audience understand that they are privileged spectators at the dancer's intercourse with the gods: telling their stories, miming their loves. It was meant to penetrate our dull delusions, to go straight through us to Lord Shiva, quivering *shakti* awakening his inert superconsciouness. I intercepted the ritual glance, took it in, made it mine.

And by god, she could dance. She had the rhythm, her body was supple, and the stamping feet and jingling bells had the authority which always calls me through the Bharat Natyam performance of a grown woman. She was Woman—Mother, Daughter, Sister, Lover—and I was Shiva, pure *lingam*-in-waiting. As Carolyn neared the end of the dance, I saw the beads of sweat gathering on her brow, the look of concern that had crept into her eyes: what if I make a mistake? And sure enough, she did. Her face fell, and she was no longer a temple dancer dancing for Shiva, just a Fulbright tutor doing her bit before her peers, trying to make it through to the end of her performance. The spell broken, I was no longer Shiva, but rather the infantile male figure of the ego, spurned under his heel in the dancing Shiva pose.

Still, she alone among the performers had brought some of the power of Indian music to the brothers and sisters seated before her. Kathy had given us competence, but Carolyn a touch of magic, just by mastering the look and going into her first routine with aplomb. And she was stunning in her costume. And for a brief time, I had been the Shiva I would one day try to be for a wife.

After Carolyn's performance, I felt even more isolated, exhausted once again. I felt like a cocoon was growing thickly around me. It was all I could do to sit politely through the remaining desultory demonstrations. I was unable to make dinner that evening, swilling bouillon in bed. Sharma came to visit me, very sweet as usual. So did Stuart, Demi and Jeanie, Jon, and Kathy. Their attention made me feel better, but the pains still shot through my right testicle, and the fever persisted.

The following morning the tutor group began to disperse. A few were going home immediately, but most were going to stay for one last tour, mostly in the mountains, since it was starting to get really hot in the plains. Increasingly lonely as the year went on, I had finally agreed to the travel fantasy nursed the whole year by Stuart, Lynn, and Carolyn. We had planned to go to Nepal and Sikkim. We had also discussed traveling on to the Middle East together. Carolyn was especially interested in Iran.

Thus in March when I phoned Gyalmo, Hope Cook, the "New York socialite" married to the King of Sikkim to request a royal invitation, I had added Carolyn's name to mine after Gyalmo had recorded my name and visa number. "Carolyn? Carolyn WHO?" shot back on the line, sounding like the Queen of Hearts. I had written for my permission earlier, explaining that I was Harriet's friend, Hope's schizophrenic sister who lived in the other half of our Central Square duplex my senior year. A royal invitation was the only way you could get in, and I had an inside line. But I had not mentioned Carolyn, nor Stuart, nor Lynn in my letter. I was spelling Carolyn's last name when the trunk line went from scratchy to howling to dead. The Queen and I never reconnected.

So our travel plans had to be altered. With my royal invitation in hand, I was not going to miss the trip to Sikkim. Logistics for meeting the others somewhere in the mountains of Hindustan or Nepal got tedious. We had decided that I would go my separate way the initial part of the trip, with tenuous plans for meeting in Iran.

I was feeling better, clearly on my way to recovery. The main lodge had been shut down, but the staff had agreed to feed me and keep an occasional eye on me until I was well enough to leave. I was in a little cabin which had been hastily arranged for my quarantine, propped up in bed after breakfast, finally feeling well enough to read. There was a knock at the door. In walked Stuart, Lynn, and Carolyn, come for farewells. They all looked somber, as if I were on my deathbed. I was sorry for myself and lonely, yet relieved that I was mending. They gathered at the end of the bed, a chorus of long faces. Stuart spoke first.

"Bob, we wanted to tell you good-bye before we took off. We're really sorry things turned out like this for you."

"So am I." I managed a weak laugh. "Where're you headed?" Lynn smiled and answered, "We're still going to Nepal, then over to Dharamsala and Darjeeling. I wish we were all going to Sikkim together."

Carolyn wore an absent grieving look, like a little girl who had lost a relative and couldn't assess yet how she felt, but knew how she was supposed to feel. Out of make-up she was pale, at loose ends, her face rendering ludicrous my previous day's longings. The only thing akin to love pangs I felt now was the dull throb remaining in the groin. The truth was, I had asked Gyalmo for Carolyn's permit out of duty, not affection, and freed now from the obligation to travel with them I was relieved. Stranded loveless and without any sexual outlet in this Victorian sub-continent, full of rules saying "keep out," my loins had sung to Carolyn in Goa. Traveling with Lynn and Stuart would've ended my long isolation, and certainly we would have shared a bed. But I'm not sure how long bedded bliss would have lasted. I've always been more into soulmates than spittoons, and don't pretend well. The ego still clung to the daydream of accompanying this china face, but more as an ornament than any possibility of soul union. Now she was speaking.

"Yeh—yes, we wanted. ... I wanted to travel with you ... with all of us together. It won't be the same without you. Could you meet us in Iran?"

"Thanks, but I want to go to Afghanistan first, and I really don't know when I'll get out of here." I was touched after all, though I felt more sorry for her now than for myself.

I saw Stuart's eyes start to dance a little. "Yeah, we certainly won't get to meet Queenie without you." But he was serious again by sentence's end. "You're still going, I mean after you get better?"

"Yes, I'm still going to Sikkim when I'm well enough. Hopefully it won't be too long." I looked at each of them.

"Well ... we'll miss you," Lynn said, echoed by Stuart and then Carolyn. "Have a good trip."

They filed out, Stuart and Carolyn giving me a last look. It was all too somber, and once the door closed behind them, I wanted to rise up like Lazarus and dance. Good-bye friends. I'll take my chances again with Mother India and her loaded dice.

So my provisional monkhood continued. The chief object of my fantasies that year had just walked out the door, and I was relieved. The year had been filled with chances to prove Maurice Frydman right: a woman to a young man my age was simply a seminal spittoon. Leah, though I had realized it a bit late, teen-aged Marilyn, both of us stoned in a hotel room in New Delhi, her big round red eyes saying, "What next, Big Guy?" (somewhere in the back of my mind the concept of statutory rape dimly loomed), the homely English teacher in Jaipur who had taken me up to her room, Laura on the beach that last night in Goa. But it was Carolyn who had given me a point-blank invitation at bootcamp in Kashmir.

Final Days

After my Fulbright tutor friends left me in lonely splendor in Mussoorie, I journeyed alone to Sikkim, a wonderful Himalayan kingdom graced with record varieties of orchids and friendly, easy-going people. The palace guards were fitted in medieval garb with antiquated weapons, and the roofs in the royal compound were of tin. Unfortunately, Chogyam and Gyalmo were out of town, leaving instructions for my care.

The high point was attending Chogyam's niece's Buddhist wedding, where I wore a traditional Buddhist mountain robe. I joined other guests in drinking *tchung*, a barley beer, from tumblers made from large bamboo sections. Sikkimese from every rank of society were present. I particularly enjoyed the earthy presence of two old village women, each with a cigarette in the corner of her mouth. Repeatedly they would arch their heads back, look me up and down, nodding their heads while speaking into each other's ears. Then they would slap hands and look at me again. Their gestures seemed to say that I would be a good match for their girls back home—or maybe for them, the old bawds.

During the music-making a wild-eyed man in rags emerged from the forest, heading straight towards the musicians. He immediately started performing a sinuous dance, arching his back like a limbo dancer. He looked and acted like a madman. Inquiring, I was told that he lived in the forest and subsisted on roots and fruit, supplemented by wedding food. Apparently he showed up and danced for all the weddings in the area, rewarded by sharing the feast. They viewed him as good luck.

After Gangtok, I bussed to Kathmandu, a pleasant, laid-back provincial city. The people were incredibly friendly, less inquisitive and nosy than Indians. I found a "hotel" in the section of town which was fast becoming a hippy enclave, renting floor-space in a large dorm. The first night I ate right across the street at the Paradise Restaurant. My waiter was a boy of ten or eleven, very friendly and quite competent. He acted like he had been doing this for years.

That night, I got really sick, so ill I could barely move. I struggled for three days just to get to the bathroom, which was across the dorm. I mostly slept, remaining hydrated only because the boy-waiter from the Paradise brought me hot lemon and sugar three times a day. He wore a dirty little cap but always had a brightly scrubbed smiling face, and seemed genuinely concerned. He was my lifeline.

I spent a couple of days in Kathmandu after recovering from my fever. The first day I found myself walking past the American Embassy and decided to go in and check it out. It was a small, low-key, fairly relaxed place. I got a Coke and sat down to read some of the American magazines littering the large coffee table. Glancing at *Time*, I did a double-take as I saw

Harvard Yard on the cover, my old fellow first tenor from the Glee Club, Assistant Dean Archie Epps, escorted from the administration building by troopers through a gauntlet of students. I had missed the whole thing. This was one of those rare moments when I realized what a huge gulf stretched between my experience in South Asia and the home front. Yet I had decided to return to Harvard Ed School, and thus exchange realities. Sitting in this backwater embassy, it all felt unreal.

I walked out the door, adjusting my eyes to the bright sunshine. I looked around and saw that outside the embassy enclave this was still Nepal. It felt incredibly foreign, as strange as the revolution in Harvard Yard felt when I was sitting inside. I didn't really belong anywhere. This was not a good time to be without friends.

The aftermath of my return from Sikkim and Nepal is mostly a blur. I returned one last time to Indore and stayed again with Chandu and Sulu. I had a difficult time leaving. Twice I packed my things and went to the station, only to decide I wasn't ready. Chandu and Sulu were at first bemused, even flattered. But then Chandu said, "Look, Bob, you can stay as long as you'd like but you need to make a decision. You're either going to stay or leave as you had planned." The third time, I was able to cross the threshold, climbing out of this sweet little nest where deep down I knew I was in limbo. At my final departure from the Indore train station, Chandu, Sulu, and Kumarji were all there, Kumarji smiling a huge red-lipped smile, teeth streaked with crimson betel. Sulu garlanded me with a marigold wreath. I wore a green-and-white checked shirt tailored from a lungi, my two-quart boy Scout canteen filled with Sulu's boiled water slung over my shoulder. *Jawa hun desa*—"I am going home."

It was late May in Delhi, very hot. I learned belatedly that I was supposed to write a final Fulbright report, which I struggled to complete.

Sam stones me with a marble Varanasi chillum in the mail. Gulp air, fight to the surface for the report. Steady the wild control needle. I'm coming down now and must fight off the pain of leaving. I am as frightened of my forthcoming journey as anything I can remember. Most people would fear the Unknown—not when they left her for homeplate and cherry pie.... The tests of will the next few days will be massive. Pull all the stops to get on your own bandwagon. Bon voyage, kid.

I was leaving India, which felt more deeply like home than anywhere I had ever been. Having contemplated the exile's existence, I was now exiling myself from an alternative world, the dream of another life, and, let's face it, a fantasy built around the prospect of endless psychosocial moratorium. After staying a few days at a Sikh friend's large, comfortable air-conditioned flat, I stepped once again into Delhi's heat, around 110 degrees. I had one last night before flying to Afghanistan, the first leg of my meandering trip home to Boston. Budgeting for the summer-long trip across the Middle East and Central Europe, I rented a *charpoi* on the lawn of a large compound inhabited by a handful of low-end Western travelers. By midnight, it was almost cool enough to sleep.

The next day I woke early to morning dew and birdsong, feeling surprisingly fresh and rested—a photo taken the previous night shows one exceedingly red-eyed curly-haired Puer in Indian whites. Gathering my gear for the autorickshaw trip to the airport, I found I had been robbed. Though my passport and most of my money had been safely tucked under my body, I had left some Nepalese jewelry, chillum with ganja, and some rupees in my shoulder bag leaning against the *charpoi* frame. The bag was gone.

At the Delhi airport I spied another Western youth in whites. His kurta was dirty and crumpled. He looked half asleep. We hit it off instantly.

"Where you headed?" I asked.

"Kabul. How 'bout you?"

We were both returning to the States via Afghanistan. Jonathan from Antioch was traveling on to Pakistan and Iran.

We compared Indian experiences. Jonathan had come for an Antioch quarter, ostensibly studying Hindustani culture, mostly in Benares. "But I seemed to major in ganja," he added, giving me a knowing grin.

I smiled back. "I got ripped off last night. I was staying at one of those places where you can rent a charpoi for the night. I had a really nice chillum and a little stash for the plane-ride. Somebody decided to take care of it for me."

Jonathan laughed. "I prepared the same way. Actually, I need to get rid of the rest of my shit. Where should we go?"

"Divest shit? How 'bout the men's room?"

So we discreetly retired to the Delhi airport men's room and assumed the four-legs-in-one-stall stance, smoking as much of the weed as we needed for the flight. Jonathan prudently flushed the rest down the toilet.

Sitting together on the plane, we moved inexorably to the subject of the highly touted Afghani hash we soon expected to ingest. But being ganja-beshat did not totally insulate me from the feeling deep in the pit of my stomach that I was leaving the best place and the best time of my life.

Though merry with Jonathan on the surface, the massive Himalayan backbone passing beneath us in wave after wave, the sad back-drone was that India was over, and anything that happened on this return trip would be its pale shadow. I had managed to lay off dope long enough to complete the Fulbright report, "Four Months with a Musical Master ... by a Grateful Toddler." Would I be up for the *massive tests* of these transitional days? Looking over at my red-eyed companion in dirty kurta-pyjamas, I had my doubts.

11 Apprentice Teacher

Cambridge: Avoiding the Brahmins

So I didn't stay. The arc of chaos just swung too widely for me to hang on. My return trip through the Middle East, Eastern Europe, Greece, and Scandinavia, was lonely. I arrived in London broke, so I walked the streets of the jewelers' market trying to sell some of my lapis and jade from Afghanistan to pay for my last two days' lodging at a seedy little hotel. Finally, a motherly Indian woman took pity on me and promised to buy some of the lapis. Upon returning from lunch, her husband was furious, but he upheld the honor of his wife's word.

The highlight of this return journey was a stay on Hydra, where I looked up an old friend of Leah's who invited me into his houseful of Western hippies. I contributed some hashish, buried in my tube of shaving cream, and the island yielded a bounty of women to my delectation. Freed of Victorian India and my instinctive reserve in the face of her goddess-energy, I was starved, and the floodgates were wide open.

At the end of that Woodstock summer of sixty-nine, Fortuna dropped me back where I had spent most of my life—in school. Back in Cambridge, now at Harvard Ed School, I pursued a Masters of Education for General Purposes. Originally accepted with a fellowship into the Master of Arts in

Teaching program, I had followed Kathy Hanson's (the sitarist from Radcliffe) advice in India to switch to this more flexible—and far less rigorous—program. The problem was, the fellowship did not follow my program shift, and the replacement aid package was far lacking. I would need to raise some money, fast.

So, while in Kabul, I hired a man to fill the soles of a pair of new loafers with Number One Afghan Hashish. He and the cobbler worked together. I watched as he repeatedly heated the rich dark brown goo, making it pliable, delighted by the return of the rich smell from the den I frequented with Jonathan the night before. He double-wrapped it in four-mil plastic to evade sniffing dogs at customs. On my way through the Middle East and northern Europe, I wore the shoes as much as I could, wading through muddy streets like a toddler for good measure. When I disembarked in Boston, I wore a summer suit with a Nixon tie and straw hat, my hair shorn with some of my last cash in London. I sailed through customs and the leashed dogs. Once on the other side, I did a little jig, but then turned to see if anyone saw me. I suddenly had misgivings about the paraphernalia, well-worn Indian clothes, and funky jewelry in my suitcase. This re-entry was a lucky blessing.

I lived communally that year on Cambridge Street, my housemates mostly working-class hippies, but also including a Harvard undergrad. My rent was sixty dollars a month. Our negligent but kindly Italian landlord pretended not to see the kitten we weren't supposed to have as it ran between his legs during a house visit. We had good esprit de corps, helped initially by our decision to observe an incest taboo, living as brothers and sisters, though that resolution didn't last through the drafty winter.

Our house mother knew a dope dealer, and I quickly gave him the stash from the shoes to deal for me. After a few months of my promised payments, he was arrested. I refused his lawyer's request to testify as a character witness, but Wade definitely had character. At my birthday celebration the next summer, he sent a runner with a big chunk of the stuff to share at the party. I spent that night listening to Janice Joplin sing "Bobby McGee" directly to me, playing inspired riffs on the drum set the band brought along.

My room off the kitchen overlooked a dreary rubbish-filled backyard, but I made the most of it, furnishing it Indian-style, the entire floor covered with old mattresses covered with white sheets. I plastered the walls with posters: Sita, Ram and Lakshman praying to Shiva, who looked down on them from the clouds; Hanuman enshrining Sita-Ram within his heart, exposed by pulling back the flesh with his two hands. A small flight of steps led down to the room, rendering it easy for people to make the cultural transition, leaving their shoes at the threshold. I brought along my *tanpura* and affected Indian attire. For winterwear I bought some engineer boots and white jeans which went great with the navy-blue serge Sherwani coat—the kind Congress MP's wore then: Nehru collars, split tails down to the knees.

Fortunately, the program at the Ed School was not demanding, for Puer was lost that year. One problem was scale. Even in quaint Cambridge, everything felt the wrong size—way too big. The Sixties cars, huge, voiceless steel beasts, seemed like dinosaurs. Each morning, I awoke to a disharmony which I can best describe as being suddenly dropped in an alien culture. I missed the people everywhere in the streets, talking right in my face, the animals milling about, the pungency of the open-air markets. Everything was so cool, clean, and efficient. Shocked by the inflated prices, I tried haggling. Storekeepers gave blank, uncomprehending looks as I muttered "fixed-price shop," leaving empty-handed.

In October, I hosted an Indian slide show for my brothers and sisters, seated on the mattresses like kindergarten kids wide awake at naptime. The previous week in the Square I ran into Carolyn and invited her to come. Among all the hippies, she looked really uncomfortable in her dark slacks and tweedy sport coat. She sat demurely on the edge of the steps, moving the shoes to give herself room, the mattresses at her feet full of Untouchables. Her flesh seemed to retreat as she looked apprehensively at our presumably lousy bodies, lounging easily on my bed. She didn't say a word. Above us was Krishna, the most beguiling god of all, in long curls playing the flute, framed by a nightscene of the Yamuna River. With those curls and sweet face, he looked a lot like Puer's double, gazing down on the crew gathered in his shrine.

Carolyn was still coolly beautiful, yet I felt distant. After our parallel year studying music in the most remarkable culture I had ever experienced, where she learned enough Bharat Natyam to genuinely convey its energy, she had slipped easily back into American culture. You could read it in her face, her manner, her stylish tweed jacket. In India, Carolyn always wore saris. I'm sure she wondered what happened to the polite middle-class young man she'd initially been attracted to. She left abruptly after I sang a few bhajans and a raga. Our paths never crossed again.

I yearned for India, and felt trapped in self-imposed exile. I met some of the more serious Buddhist practitioners and bought books by Meher Baba, willing to entertain the Parsee's claims to be the Avatar—though I wondered how there could possibly be so many god-men in one century, even overlapping. After all, wasn't Ramana Maharshi the real thing? Baba was showy and witty, an extrovert who only asked his devotees to love him. I was struck by his *numinosity.* At a Baba filmstrip one evening my neck hair stood up as the man scurried around the distant room like a water-strider, moving much faster than the ordinary mortals around him. The film was silent, but I had read his message, a hypnotic mix of wit and easy wisdom. But Maurice had stressed the yoga of healthy doubt: *neti, neti* (not this, not that). Maybe Baba was the Trickster Avatar, the joker who could appear anytime in humanity's sordid history, no matter who else held the stage.

Meanwhile, Ram Das, formerly Richard Alpert of Harvard LSD research fame, had returned from India, and gave a well-attended lecture at the First Church Christ Scientist in Boston. He shared a fascinating, powerful story of his experiences in the mountains with Neemkaroli Baba, a North Indian sage. What struck me most forcefully was Ram Das's claim that this Baba had ingested about sixty tabs of pure acid, to no visible effect. After the lecture, I waited patiently to speak to him. When my turn came, I confessed, "I was in India last year. I experienced many of the same things you did, and I don't know why, but I came back. Hearing you tonight brought back this incredible longing. I feel I've made a terrible mistake. This place is crazy; India makes sense. People don't understand."

Ram Das listened attentively, his face pious. After hearing a bit of my India story, he replied with a big smile, his large liquid eyes, shining and rolling like the Ancient Mariner's, "Don't dwell on what you've left. The East is a state of mind. India is here, right in this room. You just have to keep following your practice." But how could this satisfy or comfort me, who really had no practice, had not been initiated, receiving neither mantra nor jolt of spiritual energy? Sure, both Maurice and Kumarji had given me energy and insight in distinctive ways, and Maurice had challenged me to the *jnana* yogin's path of discrimination, the "fellowship of the undeceived." This tortuous path held no easy answers, and some of my habits reinforced deception, both the easy deception of habitual daily life and the larger deception that somehow I could remain the Hindu I imagined I had become. Did I want Ram Das to be my mentor? Perhaps, but mainly I was embarrassed not to have a practice after all the opportunities I received in India.

I never knew where you were supposed to study at the Ed School. From my Yard-oriented perspective, it was a commuter place. So I did most of my studying at Lamont, the undergrad library, the same place I experienced the tachycardia episode which absolved me of military service. Going back there was familiar and comforting. But one fall night about six weeks into the semester, I suddenly began throwing myself against the wall, over and over again. I was alone, with nobody else around. The culture shock lessened after that, the self-enforced shakeup physically inducing some of the scale adjustment that had been so difficult to achieve otherwise. But the continuing use of drugs was also self-medication against the clash of India and Cambridge, the Hindude self and the liberal western teacher trainee.

Culturally conflicted as I was, I dearly wanted to merge my two worlds, the Ed School with my commune. One afternoon at the Ed School tea, I invited my brothers and sisters to come. Three of them did, but the connections were tenuous. It felt really awkward having these flamboyant provisional friends dressed as children among classmates who, like me, had accepted the conventional life of teaching. But though I was embarrassed that afternoon, I didn't change my costume. I badly needed to hang on to my Hindu persona, to proclaim how changed I was.

I used drugs regularly that year. Our house was typical: cannabis was the mainstay, with mescaline and LSD also prominent. Once when we were asked to babysit Abbie Hoffman's eight-year old son, the boy sat with us in the kitchen after dinner, two joints going around in opposite directions. Brother Denny with his long red ponytail found them both arriving at once, and started crossing his forearms repeatedly, feigning confusion at the sudden wealth. Looking to his left, he found the boy. He hesitated, then smiled his winning smile around the table, placing the acrid weed carefully in front of his small neighbor's face with a gentle, solicitous look. The boy stared at it disdainfully. "No thanks; not tonight."

And I quickly found women. The floodgates that opened on Hydra remained wide, delivering a whole succession of women who shared Puer's comfortable den off the communal kitchen. There was Esther Amaryllis, then Denise, one of the Hydran heads who arrived in Cambridge to exact more tribute, then Alicia, who I literally met at the door at a Liberation News Service orgy, with two Susies in between. Twice, once with Pittsburgh Sam's girlfriend, and once with a woman I met at a party, I wrongly assumed that handholding was a prelude to yes, only to be rebuffed. It certainly would have meant yes in India, sheltered but heavily encoded India where a glance is all a man needs. The fearful, then discriminating youth who had always waited for the "Real Thing" had learned how easy sexual compatibility was, descending willy-nilly to the gourmand. Maurice Frydman's "seminal spittoon" had been only generically correct the previous year in Bombay. Now that Puer was surrounded by willing fruits, my guru proved a prophet.

The General Purposes degree allowed me to dovetail my interests in Hinduism with those in education, so I took an independent study each term at the Divinity School. In the first, I planned a high school course, "The Hindu View of Life," which I would teach the next year back at Indian Springs, the boys' prep school I had attended in Birmingham. In the other, my final paper was a critique of Carl Jung's ambivalent dismissal of Hinduism. Later, I learned that the sage Jung refused to meet for fear of losing his bearings was Ramana Maharshi! I understood Jung's caution, for Puer had indeed lost his bearings in India, though not due to Ramana, who counseled the ordinary householder life within one's birth tradition. Jung had become unmoored, seriously lost during a tribal dance he joined in Africa as a young man, and wanted to be damn sure it didn't happen again, using old alchemical texts as amulets against India's thick web of vibrations. My dance with the arivasis on the Malwa Plain was much the same, threatening a re-descent into chaos, nullifying the "retrenchment" of my degree work.

That winter one of Ram Das's disciples, a Buddhist psychology PhD named Danny Goleman, pulled me aside at a party to elder me. "You don't belong with these people. They're not right for you." I was offended, but by year's end, I began to agree, though I had been put off by my visit to his austere Buddhist commune. More discipline, less drugs, and different company would probably have quickened the transitional process that year back in Cambridge.

The Heart of the Heart of Dixie

Is Shelby County, Alabama, smack dab in the middle of my home state, south of Birmingham. My plan after grad school was to return to Indian Springs and work under the school director, my mentor Doc Armstrong, who had awakened me to a lifelong "search for self" as well as an enduring fascination with interdisciplinary inquiry. Doc obliged, hiring me to teach "Basic Studies" after receiving my Harvard Ed degree. Daddy drove me down to Birmingham from Pittsburgh when I reported for the job, pleading with me the whole way to cut the hair, shave the beard, and "For godsakes put on normal clothes!" In fact, I presented myself to Doc Armstrong unshorn, still affecting the Indian garb of kurta-pyjama and *rudraksha* necklace. Doc greeted me cordially, though the hair became a target later in the year when a students' "appearance policy" became an issue. Daddy left relieved that his son wasn't fired on the spot.

Puer went down to his lakeside trailer and sat on the front stoop, looking over the water, contemplating his new estate. The janitor's wife and son sauntered by, fishing. Seeing the young man in his whites, the child said, "Look, Mommy, an angel." I took this as a sign that the Age of Aquarius had arrived in Dixie.

As a teaching alum at Springs, I taught my own variation of Basic Studies, "The Function of Myth." Myth was my key to reading the world, and Doc had given me a cover by having the faculty read and discuss Ernst Cassirer's "Essay on Man," in which the Yale prof argued that myth and religion was one of four basic symbolic modes of inquiry. Doc and I had a running debate on what I called my teaching subject. Finally he said, "I know what you're trying to do. But you're an English teacher, understand?" I was habitually late to my early morning class, and the classroom was adjacent to Doc's office. I carefully walked around the boxwood hedge, avoiding the windows to his office, then slipped in the door. The boys didn't seem to care.

My office was next to a very conservative older French teacher's classroom and office. When the maintenance head told me his staff would paint it any way I wanted, I opted for alternate walls of white and black, which I offset with a fire-engine red rug. I don't know where that impulse came from, though it looks in retrospect like adolescent counter-dependency. It certainly wasn't some holdover from my interest in Poe. My abrupt appearance in the midst of his turf was unsettling for the older gentleman, who challenged me to a fight before the first month had passed, his cigarette dangling from his lower lip. I demurred, two years before my exposure to Quakerism (thanks to the father of a student, who founded the Birmingham Meeting).

I punctuated ambitious Socratic teaching sessions of ninth graders with guided meditations in an effort to give an experiential dimension to my subject. In my favorite, I led the students through a series of imagined transformations: "You are lying under a huge oak tree … you are an acorn … you are a squirrel eating the acorn. …" After each transformation, I intoned the refrain, "What happens to the Self?" Instinctively, I lay down with them, students arrayed in a loose circle, most in preppy clothes, some long-haired like their teacher. We were seekers together. The point, of course, was that everything *but* the Self is always changing.

After one such session, a fundamentalist freshman went to complain to Doc that I was "teaching false gods." Doc defended me, knowing I would never push any particular theology. As the Vedas say, "God is one; wise men call Him by many names."

In "Aleatoric Epistemology" we read Blake, Nietzsche, Black Elk, and Ramana Maharshi, whose inquiry into the Self was my inconsistent meditation practice. One class convened at the sewage plant, and we ate at a variety of restaurants, each on a five-dollar budget, comparing the trade-off between value and style. The seminar met down at my trailer after school, and was the first co-ed class at Indian Springs.

Yet another elective on "Alternative Communities" included field trips to Koinonia Farms, the racially mixed community near Americus, Georgia which spawned Jubilee Partners and Habitat for Humanity in Jimmy Carter country, a "Black Maoist" cell in Selma, and Stephen Gaskin's infamous The Farm near Nashville.

In Selma, a black man from Detroit with a fancy car, gold necklace, and a flashy ring for each finger got into a discussion with me about Gandhian non-violence. "Okay. If I was to lock you up in that outhouse out back, let's say three - four days, what would you do? How would your pacifism help?" Several months later, I learned their leader had been murdered.

I drove an eager crew in the White Elephant to The Farm in Summertown, Tennessee, where we were met by a "gatekeeper" whose job was to admit only those sympathetic to the community ethos. One freshman, an enthusiast of Ayn Rand, stubbornly argued on as night started to descend, but finally the gates swung open. Immediately, the students were separated from me in the darkness, and I was hustled off to the "rock polisher"—where miscreant wives who questioned their husbands' authority were exiled. Presumably, my students were taken for brainwashing and ritual cannabis ingestion, The Farm's sacramental practice. Thankfully, I was reunited with my students just before Stephen Gaskin's Sunday sermon, cannabis smoke wafting into the poplars from the assembled communards. It was a long, quiet ride home to Birmingham in the White Elephant.

In addition to the core classes on myth and the "Hindu View of Life" elective, I taught an extracurricular lakeside meditation course and made the rounds to public high schools chanting, singing bhajans, and talking up the

Hindu worldview, which I thought could transform the errant West. The high point of these efforts was at Berry High, where I was invited to address assembly. I appeared onstage in my Hindustani whites, *rudraksha* beads and *tanpura*. I warmed up with parroted stories from Ram Das at First Church Christ Scientist in Boston—especially the one about his guru Neemkaroli Baba's ingesting the entire stash of LSD he carried to no effect—interspersed with my own peak experiences. Then I started plucking the *tanpura*, feeling a trance set in as I sang several chants to a rapt audience, eyes closed. When I opened them again and saw the looks on some of those kids' faces, I thought I might take the show on the road. I was a serious Hindu apologist, and tried to evangelize counterculture students, my peers, and family at every opening.

So this was my work, my life at Springs. Romance? Kathy and I had been writing for three years. We had a bittersweet farewell at her base camp for India in Wooster, Ohio in summer 1970, making love for the last time on a floor pallet in a suite with her neurotic psychiatrist father brooding in the next room. Now I was back teaching at my alma mater, and she was entering her second year in India, apprenticed to a flute master in Madras. She wanted me to come to India. Embarked on my first job, I wanted her to come to Alabama. The aerogrammes sailed, but we were stuck in a holding pattern.

I was desperately unhappy. Isolated in the Shelby County woods on weekends, I had a couple of desultory affairs. The wave of euphoria over the new job, the highs from chanting to hushed high school audiences, healthy attendance at meditation classes, and the daily reinforcement that I was *special* —looking in the mirror at Puer's earnest babyface in Hindustani dress, *rudraksha* beads and long wavy Krishna tresses—finally spent itself. One particularly long, lonely weekend, I threw my body into a heap on my disheveled bed with tie-die sheets and sobbed for what seemed like hours. I could think of nothing else to do with my life. This was all I ever imagined.

PART TWO
KRISHNA AND RADHA

12 Trouble at Springs

Another dreaded weekend was approaching. Friday night my friend Sybil the librarian called. At the heart of the school, she counseled many a lost soul. "Ida Martha wants you to meet a young woman med student she met at a medical meeting in Atlanta. Are you free tomorrow?"

Ida Martha was both the assistant librarian at Springs and secretary to the director of the Alabama Regional Medical Program, a Nixon-era federal program supporting rural medicine. Judith Goldman came south from Albert Einstein Medical School in the Bronx to attend a rural medicine conference in Atlanta the spring of 1971, wanting to be a country doctor ever since serving as flower girl at her doctor aunt's wedding at age four. An unseasonal snowstorm canceled her Appalachian Trail hike, but Ida Martha rescued her, suggesting she go to Birmingham to interview for a job in an interracial inner-city clinic. And she had just the man for Judi Goldman as well, the hirsute new teacher in white pyjamas and rudraksha beads who lived in the trailer down by the Lake. Judi hitched a ride with "some Okies," who kindly delivered her to the Regional Medical office in Birmingham.

So on Saturday Ida Martha drove up in her big, spotless dark blue Ford

Fairlane with this attractive, buxom long-haired young woman wearing a long print Granny dress. She looked promising. I proceeded to squire her around campus and the adjacent state park in the White Elephant, my aging white Ford van carpeted in crimson with a black border, posters of Meher Baba, Gandhi, Ramakrishna, and Jesus encircling the interior, fitted with an eight-track tape deck and mattress covered with a yellow floral India-print bedspread. This hippy-van was my first vehicle, bought with a personal loan from Doc.

We were immediately relaxed and easy with one another. Judi was no southern society girl from finishing school. I took her for a walk in the woods at Indian Springs, showing her the Tarzan swing fashioned from a huge grapevine, a place of initiation for my student friends. In the shadow of that vine, she removed her braless blouse, and we took a step towards Eden.

That evening Puer fixed Judi his locally famed mixed veg curry, whose fieriness pleased her. After dinner, he changed into white kurta-pyjama, tuned the tanpura, and performed chants and devotional songs, ending with "Shobe Jata," a composition in Raga Bhairav with a humorous refrain about Shiva's unruly, matted hair—Shiva the *rastaman.* Unruly it was not, but Puer had shoulder-length wavy hair, looking a lot like his two-year old portrait, holding a bunch of keys. After the serenade she sat gazing at "my Krishna," then doubled over with laughter, rolling on the floor. Krishna decided to join the fun, and dove in. He found Radha suitably devotional as they frolicked and nuzzled like puppies on the rug. She finally stopped laughing long enough to blurt, "Ida Martha says I mustn't stay the night." Puer had other things in mind, but this was after all a boys' school with proprieties to be upheld, as the assistant librarian well knew. So we obeyed.

She got the job. The task was to develop a racially integrated community health clinic in an inner-city neighborhood, and market it among poor whites and blacks. Her partner, an imposing black man in his thirties, served both to model with his female Jewish partner the behavior the Alabama Regional Medical Program project tried to encourage, and to protect her. "I didn't know enough to be scared," she later confessed after the clinic became a successful reality.

As for the romantic interest, Puer seemed to be the only guy in Birmingham who was a vegetarian practicing Hindu meditation. She was an inducted yoga teacher with Integral Yoga Institute in New York City, and a disciple of its director, Swami Satchidananda, the Woodstock guru. You can see both teacher and daughter-disciple in the film. As a first-year medical student, she served a useful role as medic at Woodstock, repeated at the Dallas Rock Festival, where she was flat-out decked in the first aid tent by a paranoid tripping man. In Dallas she hung out with the Hog Farm, who successfully redirected her to med school, two large men like bouncers ushering her to her seat on the bus to New York when her resolve faltered. Her graduation fantasy was to drive a van along the California coast distributing free medical care in exchange for life's essentials. The grounding in hatha yoga and meditation, along with her Redbone Hound Quarry, enabled her to survive med school in the Bronx.

Back in Birmingham that fall, she was surprised to find her Krishna still interested. Indeed, she was number one *gopi*. So the relationship began in earnest. During our first week together that fall, after a quick dip one afternoon in the chilly Springs lake, Judi talked about her spiritual aspirations. She got right to the point: "I expect to reach Enlightenment in this lifetime."

Flabbergasted, I looked at her closely. She was perfectly serious. I laughed heartily. "I'd love to be there to witness. I wonder if I'd be able to tell."

"Probably not, unless you get enlightened too."

She proceeded to point two. "You know, I've thought about it a lot, and Swamiji is right. I've had my share of serial relationships, and it's really not conducive to a centered yogic lifestyle. So I've become celibate."

I wondered about the casual ease with which she'd slipped off her blouse that first afternoon in the spring. Something didn't jive here. "How long have you been celibate?"

"Ummm ... since late last winter ... six or seven months."

"But what about that afternoon on the ridge last time you were here?"

"I've thought about that. I had pretty much decided to become a yogi, but I'm not really sure I want to give up the possibility of a householder's life. I've decided that if I ever sleep with a man again, it will be for keeps. So if it happens with you, it won't be like the others. If we sleep together, we're going to get married."

I didn't know what to say. After a long pause I answered, "That's a pretty serious proposition. I'm not so sure I'm into that."

We initially overnighted at the apartment Judi shared with shy, boyish Man Mohan across from West End Baptist Hospital, where I had my earthly origin. Yes, there was a second male vegetarian Hindu wannabe in Vulcan's city—and Judi Goldman found him, too. But I didn't like Man Mohan, who was gamely trying to establish an Ananda Marga presence in Birmingham. In fact, I found him downright creepy. So eventually we broke Ida Martha's injunction, staying more and more at my lakeside trailer at the far end of the campus. Judi left early each morning to avoid crossing paths with faculty entering the dining hall for breakfast. But it was hard to disguise an orange Chevy Nova with a staved-in passenger door and a plastic-bandaged window traveling through the heart of campus.

By mid-October, it was clear I needed to make a choice between my two women, one ever distant, and one who had rapidly totally entwined with my life. I couldn't manage telling Kathy in her Libran birthday letter, but by late November I wrote of this revolution of the heart. In her reply, Kathy wrote that she met a congenial fellow in Nepal shortly after receiving my news. He nursed her through a severe illness, she nursed him, and they married a few weeks later. One pole of the triangle thus resolved itself.

One fall Sunday morning, when she should have been in Sunday School, I looked out the back window of the trailer to see one of the faculty wives snooping about behind my remote trailer among the pines, peering through the windows in her Sunday finery. Puer challenged her. "Ina, what do you want?"

"I was just looking for wildflowers. Have you noticed any back here?"

"No, just pine needles and an occasional weed. Isn't it time for Sunday School?"

She flushed. "Why yes, I do believe it is. I wanted some flowers for the children."

"I really don't think you'll find any here, unless it's the Inner Flower you seek."

Confused, she quickly walked away. At her pace, it would be twenty-five minutes before she reached her house, imperiling not only Sunday School, but the sermon. The Flower she sought was indeed there, but Ina failed to spy her specimen.

Soon the campus was abuzz, and one day in late fall Doc called me into his office. When I entered, he was leaning back, hands comfortably clasped over his ample belly. Leaning forward, he gave me a fatherly look conveying both toughness and concern. Even seated, he towered over me. From behind the big custom mahogany desk, the craggy visage spoke in his thick Oklahoma drawl, "McGahay, I hate like hell to have to say this, but they're all talking about you and that woman. When the first reports came in, I told 'em to mind their own business. Then more and more came to complain. I told 'em the same thing, get back to your work and stop meddlin' and gossipin'. But now I've heard reports from most of the faculty—all the families. I've fought 'em off as long as I could—the petty bast. ... Look, we've got a real problem."

I had dreaded this. It had hung like the proverbial sword over our guilty heads. "Okay, Doc. It's true, there's no way I'm going to deny it. But this is an intrusion on my privacy. We've been very discreet. If I lived in the dorm circle or the faculty circle it would be another thing, but down by the lake. ... Neither the Petersons nor Stegner cares."

"McGahay, you know very well there are certain restrictions that come with teaching at a boaz' school. None of 'em can have girls in their rooms, and you can't tell me they don't know what's goin' on."

I remained defensive. "Nobody but us and God know that—including you, Doc. We don't have an ordinary relationship; it's a spiritual friendship."

"You seem to have a serious relationship, and that's good. But I have to keep the peace in this community, and I'm afraid like any small town, appearances matter, like it or not."

"They don't understand. They don't even examine their own lives. They're sheep. You know that."

He shook his head firmly. "You know they're mostly good people. Like I said, I was disgusted when they filed in here one after the other. But this is a political thing. You may know something about spiritual life, but you've still got a helluva lot to learn, especially how to think politically. The world isn't made for idealists. Like I've always said, you've got to choose your battles. We don't really have any choice—you can't bring that woman to sleep over at your place anymore. If you do, we'll have to let you go."

I was righteously indignant, feeling particularly wronged by Ina, the one person who had shown her cards by snooping around the trailer during all the hushed buzziness. But I knew after a few moments that I wanted to stay as long as Doc was still at Springs, and that I'd have to obey his dictum or find a way around it.

Of course the implied celibacy was untrue, but to plead a "special relationship" was an honest confession. Puer *was* special, and every relationship that meant anything to him was, too. The bottom line was that he was Doc's chosen apprentice, and though the Yankee doc might represent his future, Doc Armstrong was the rock of his past, the person he respected most from his youth.

After that, we obeyed the letter of our agreement with Doc. When not staying in Birmingham, we sneaked across the swamp at the end of the remote trio of trailers and across the highway to a friendly colleague's off-campus residence. Once, Judi slipped and fell in the muck as we attempted the trek by nightfall. "Shit," intruded through her mantra. I succeeded in holding back laughter. It was a long year to continue this subterfuge, and I drove into Birmingham and her West End apartment much more than I would've liked. Fortunately, before Christmas Man Mohan moved on to a more promising mission assignment in Atlanta.

13 Kudzoo Kastle and A Wedding

In August 1972 the lovers moved into a spacious, wonderful old house built in the Twenties in Birmingham's Southside which they shared with six to eight other flower children—including Judi's younger sister Patti—and three dogs. Doc had retired, and I didn't like the Board's replacement, so I left Springs. The loose arrangement worked reasonably well. It was the last house on a dead-end beneath a densely wooded lot, overlooked by the towering statue of Vulcan, though the hillside was so thick with trees you couldn't see him. Since the vacant lot across the street was teeming with the stuff, its quivering tentacles migrating our way, we called the old manse Kudzoo Kastle.

When I brought my grandmother and great aunt to see the place, Gaga insisted she didn't want to go in: "I'll just stay in the car," she said as she lit up, sticking out her chin the way she always did, jaw shifting as if to chew the mouthful of smoke. She knew there would be much to disapprove.

Aunt Dinny was an insatiably curious type, and I had witnessed her tolerance before, so I ushered her in with an eager, even jaunty step. The house was reasonably tidy, but not clean, as usual. Nobody was there, which disappointed us both. But I was free to give her an unimpeded tour of the spacious, rambling old place. "Everyone has their own room, except for Ross and John and their little baby Sonia."

When we reached our room, I showed her the queen bed: "This is Judi's room ... and this is mine." I had led her through the large bedroom with generous floor-to-ceiling triple windows into the "meditation closet" as we called it, a tiny vestibule attached to the large bedroom with a puja table at one end, a pallet, and a tiny window. This was our room for yoga, meditation, my chanting and infrequent vocal practice. She nodded as if she believed me.

As we got back into my grandmother's Ford Falcon, Aunt Dinny wore a spacey look, in full denial of what she'd seen. As Gaga gave us a disinterested glance, I realized her wisdom, resting in the billowy comfort of her cigarette rather than confirming her suspicions about what would have seemed a dive to her. Other suspicions had already surfaced when I brought Judi to her house on Country Club Road on Christmas morning. She had turned to Dinny, commenting: "They act like they're already married."

Judi interned at the University of Alabama Med School teaching hospital, averaging about 105 hours per week. I would make her supper, and she would return too exhausted to join us at dinner, so I would serve her bedside, like bringing in hospital food. She worked many weekend shifts at the ER, and got really good at sewing people up, since she treated a lot of knifings. She also developed a lasting aversion to alcoholics, who celebrated every Friday payday.

My interim job after Springs was counselor-in-residence at the Med School, working mostly with first-year students and faculty on issues involved with "humanizing" the medical curriculum. It was a revealing year and a difficult one, for as an alien humanities person, I was the outsider. When I was introduced to the second-year class, standing at the podium in the lecture hall, one of the students asked my qualifications for the position. I thought a moment, then answered, "Dean Meador hired me primarily because I spent a year in India, giving me a perspective that might enrich your medical education." A stunned silence followed. I had said too much, doomed to irrelevance as far as most of these future docs were concerned.

Judi was committed to marriage, though she briefly ran off with another guy that summer, one final fling. My nuptial movement was steady, but halted shy of the final leap. One afternoon in the fall, I was sitting on the Kastle roof, a favorite spot for looking out through the tops of the trees at the Birmingham skyline, and found myself realizing that I was "ninety-five percent" ready to get married. This seemed worthy of reporting, and I started to go fetch Judi from the hospital to tell her. I quickly realized that this milestone wouldn't be the gift I imagined it would be. I remained on the roof, ascending the final steep resistance curve with a leap of will, feeling a touch of weightlessness in my stomach. Just as I completed the leap, a drop of rain alighted on the tip of my fleshy nose from a virtually cloudless sky. Puer had his sign.

So married we got. When I phoned Gaga the news, she shot back, "You can do better." Realizing how hurtful this was, she quickly added, "Forget I said that"—as if I could. It wasn't that Judi was a Jew, it was a class thing, I realized as I later listened at the supper table as she talked about the "nice" Mountain Brook Jewish families. She was the lone person in my family to verbalize opposition. On the Goldman side, Judi's father Harold expressed concern about my lack of generosity and general obliviousness to the needs of others. Fair enough.

We chose the Indian Springs Library on New Year's Eve 1972. The ceremony was our own: a document which now seems an idealistic eon away from our compromised adult world. Judi first envisioned a rabbi, a minister and her guru Satchidananda as presiding triumvirs. But Mother Culture intervened, and we followed tradition by asking my preacher-uncle to preside. At the last minute, Uncle Billy came down with a severe virus. This was the Lord's work, for he was a conservative Protestant, which worked for my cousins' more conventional ceremonies. *This* wedding would have been extremely difficult for Uncle Billy to officiate. Conveniently, we had invited the UAB chaplain, so I called him and asked "a little favor" on the eve of the ceremony. The result was a middle-class hippy wedding, with a Hindude/Episcopalian ceremony.

We sat on a red Chinese rug from Hyman's, Uncle Stanley Goldman's Rock Island furniture store, before the library fireplace. It was the first time a fire had ever been lit there. We wore white wool, Puer in tailored kurta-pyjama, Judi in a long laced-neck dress. The fire sputtered throughout the ceremony as the groomsmen fed it, slyly passing kindling behind their backs to rescue the ritual moment. Fire and light were the central images of the ceremony, as they are in a Hindu wedding, where the couple walk around the fire *hoven* seven times while repeating their vows, the woman tied to the man by a string. We omitted the walk and the string. This bride would never be strung along by anyone.

As prologue to the ceremony, Puer invoked the solstice symbolism of the world's religions. Capitalizing upon the captive audience, he got in his licks against Nixon's war before dutifully joining the middle class:

> *It is the darkest time of the year. We are in the darkest era of human history, which Hindus call Kali Yuga, the Black Age. Once again darkness covers the face of the earth, an ugly cloud of pollution and bombclouds. The dark underside of the tapestry of American life is exposed daily by THE WAR which continues to rage from the screaming silences of the air amidst belated promises of peace. Despite ample reasons for hopelessness, Judi and I refuse to despair. We choose instead in this dark hour to light a candle in the darkness, to proclaim the hope of a new year, new spring, a new life together, and the dawn of a New Age. ...*
>
> *The fire which burns at the altar before you speaks as the Light and Power of the Lord of the Universe. This is the same fire which smolders in each of our hearts. May tonight's celebration rekindle that Inner Fire and remind us of our common divinity.*

We each wrote a set of vows. My pivotal vow was "I vow to give Judi her own life-space so that she may grow along her own path. I also vow to accept responsibility for my own growth and never to forget to live my own life, though our two lives are intertwined." Judith's key insight was, "I promise that when we come upon a problem, I will try to straightforwardly work it out with you, and not resort to hurtfulness in thought, word, or deed."

The assembled company sang "Longtime Sunshine" as a recessional, and even Puer's stoic, unmusical aunt sang as the impure but glowing white couple led the way through the cold night, a few snowflakes in their hair, candles held high, to the school dining hall and a New Year's Eve reception. At the reception we flew around the room in a torrid polka as the crowd clapped and cheered. The chappals were a nuisance, so I kicked them off, leaving me barefoot in the Springs dining hall, one last rule infringement amidst a night of redemption. I looked over at Judi's dad Harold, who was in his element, popping champagne with a cigarette clenched in the corner of his mouth, sporting the baby-blue kurta our tailor had fashioned for him.

We waited until midnight to honeymoon so we could greet the New Year with guests and friends. By the time we reached the funky little

North Alabama resort where we'd reserved a cabin, it was almost three a.m. The lovebirds drove the last stretch in ten-minute shifts, dead tired. Alas, we arrived to find the cabin locked, nobody around to help. The sheriff's office was closed, and a friendly telephone operator's idea to try a credit card didn't work. So we spent the night, which went down to 17 degrees, in the car, me in the back seat, Judi getting up every hour in front to turn on the heater full blast (the medical training helped here). At least we didn't have to pay the first night, and were treated to breakfast the next morning, a consolation prize for our thrift. And they had remembered to equip the cabin with television, so Krishna could watch his Alabama Crimson Tide play for the national football title on New Year's Day.

14 Inauspicious Honeymoon

July–September 1973

I feel uprooted. Alone in a sea of foreign faces and signs that aren't even romanized. I don't have a clue. My insides chafe and churn at Judi's dominance in our dealings with the world. For the most part, as we walk through the streets of Japan, backpacks on our backs, i walk behind, mainly because she's such an incredibly fast walker. I want to take in the world, not scramble to keep up with this damn tour-guide wife! Of course there's the shame of walking behind the woman.

I vowed at our wedding "to build a community around our marriage which, while meeting squarely the requirement of daily coping among its members, reflects the light of Eternal Truth within us all." As wedding gifts, we received a large commercial-grade double boiler and stainless settings for eighteen, having registered with family and friends that we planned a permanent communal lifestyle once married. We methodically focused on forming an ecumenical intentional community, setting our sights on the mountains, the "Four Corners" of Alabama, Georgia, North Carolina and Tennessee. In preparation for this ambitious move, we met every Wednesday night at Kudzoo Kastle, hosting other potential communards. The cell included Jews, social gospel Christians, Unitarians, agnostics and our Hindu wannabe bride and groom. We began with a breathing and meditation ritual, then went around the circle, each person reporting on their psycho-spiritual progress that week, and ended with chanting. Judi led the first part, but was often so exhausted from her hospital duties it was all she could do to drag herself to the session. Yet it was always rejuvenating. The deep sharing solidified our trust in each other, engendering hope that we could bring the dream to fruition.

But first I had some unfinished business: to take my bride to India. Now we would embark on our real honeymoon—a pilgrimage through Southeast Asia, Japan, and India. I had completed my consulting year at UAB Med School, and Judi decided after a year she could no longer tolerate the pressure as the lone woman in an old-boy ob-gyn residency. Judi's folks provided around-the-world air tickets as long as we agreed to meet them "next year in Jerusalem." It was one thing to give their daughter away to this curious young fellow in pyjamas, quite another to have her disappear into some fakir's cave.

So what did we want from this extended honeymoon, taking us halfway across the world, away from our avowed purpose of founding a community? I wanted Judi, who had already been strongly affected by Swami Satchidananda's package of yoga and Vedanta for westerners, to experience Mother India herself, to awaken as I had to the yearning for *moksha*, deliverance from this sordid dreamworld. After all, hadn't my wife unabashedly declared that she was determined to "achieve enlightenment in this lifetime"? I knew from experience that being in India increased that desire many-fold. Judi knew that I didn't consider Satchidananda to be an authentic master. Didn't my beloved deserve to sit at the feet of the Real Thing?

But before I could realize my fervent wish, I had to run the gauntlet of Judi's own wish-list, heading to Japan and Southeast Asia. After crossing the US by train, supplemented by hitch-hiking in Colorado and Nevada, we spent time with Judi'a mother Miki and sister Patti in Hawaii. I felt like we were spinning our wheels, especially after reading *The Way of the Pilgrim* on the beach at Waikiki, waking from dozing to acres of womanflesh, the scent of their tanning oil filling me with revulsion. And Mother Miki resented every time we off alone, since we would soon be "gone a whole year."

Flying into Tokyo, we were alone together at last. Avoiding the crush of the megapolis, we took the train to Hokkaido immediately, arriving the next morning in Sapporo. At a little teahouse near our hotel, smitten with Japan, Judi started working on me. "Why don't we stay here a month? More, if we can afford it."

"There's nothing spiritual in Japan. The Japanese are materialists, just like Americans. Just wait 'til you get to India." I was taken aback, unprepared to defend my choice to spend as much of the year as possible in India. After all, she had agreed to the plan.

"India will always be there. Don't you just love it here?"

So it went for the next two weeks. Fortunately, Japan was expensive. That first night at the Sanno Hotel, we disbursed a week's housing budget on a closet of a room for $80. We spent the next night on a park bench.

The following day we hitched north, towards Mombetsu, camping in a farmer's field by the Teshio Gawa River, serene and lush with tall reeds and rice paddies bounded by hardwood breaks. After we assembled our barely serviceable army poncho lean-to, the farmer himself arrived. Glancing at the troubled sky, the kind, simple man said we could stay at his farmhouse if it got rainy and wet. We gambled on the small patch of blue and were rewarded with starry sky and a wind brisk enough to shoo the clouds gently along. "Russian roulette," Judi called it.

The Japanese who picked us up were courteous and friendly, offering us "Cocacora" to drink—no refusals accepted. Once in Mombetsu, we went straight to the temple to beg lodging, like traditional pilgrims. The Shinto priest wore dark red silk, smoking a cigarette in an ebony holder. We had the usual difficulty being understood, and our conversation was interrupted by a teenaged boy presenting his shiny new Datsun for a blessing. The priest, after clapping to call the gods, chanting, and waving a paper wand over car, boy, and altar, wrote the license number down. Was this for the feds, or accuracy in reporting to the gods—or both?

"Komban tomette kudasai?" Could we sleep here tonight? We repeated our request. We gathered that we couldn't stay at the temple, our pilgrims' desire. The priest asked repeatedly if we had money. *"Skoshi"*—a little—was Judi's reply. He kept talking to his wife, who would disappear to make phone calls. Then, with elaborate bowing and handshaking, he transferred us to her care, and she drove us to a *ryokhan*—a traditional inn. Before the shy, pretty maid turned down our fluffy comforters, a steward came and asked if we wanted a bottle of scotch, which we refused, being pilgrims. We had a fine big vegetarian meal with chopsticks in our room, and settled into our pile of down for a cozy evening. Suitable honeymoon lodgings at last!

We returned by ferry and train to the main island of Honshu and spent over a week in Kyoto and Nara, the spiritual, aesthetic and cultural center of Japan. We stayed several days in Kyoto with a Yogi Bhajan sect, only slightly less foreign to us than the postulants at a Christian sect we visited called Kiyo Mizu. In the mornings, we rose at five-thirty for exercises, consisting of holding certain yoga poses while breathing vigorously. I was neither very apt nor enthusiastic about this early morning activity, and found it particularly difficult to perch on three limbs while breathing forcefully from alternate nostrils. I felt like a rhino being trained for a perverted circus routine. After breakfast and cleanup, we would gratefully leave for the day's activities. Much to my tour-guide's chagrin, I would soon find myself looking for a park bench for my remaining winks.

On the train from Tokyo to Kobe, my frustration and anger spilled over. "You know, Jude, I'm really tired of this treadmill. Every city we reach, you grab the map and plan out the whole visit before we've even found a place to stash our gear. I feel bulldozed, fucked over. Instead of seeing everything there is to see, why not just sit in one of these magnificent formal gardens and watch a rock?"

"Traveling is hard. There's so much to see and so little time. I'm sorry you're not comfortable with how we're doing it," she said.

"And the forced march bit. I have to run sometimes to catch up with you. It's really embarrassing in Japan to be dragged around by your wife, always bringing up the rear. I take things in slowly and deliberately."

"I'm sorry you feel that way," she said with a look of genuine concern. "Maybe we should do less. But I don't know when I'll get the opportunity again to be in Japan."

So we decided to be more mutual in our planning, and it felt like a brewing crisis was averted. Today the turnabout in murky blackness of soul was clear as the pure sunlight of Hokkaido.

We went to the Taiwanese consulate in Kyoto to get visas for our freighter's shore visit. The official refused to grant me one until I cut my hair. "You look like a girl," he said. When I arrived shorn the next day, he gave me the visa reluctantly, a "favor," since he thought it still too long. I was attached to my wavy locks, but it felt okay.

On her birthday, September 9, I awakened Judi with a kiss. We spent the day hiking around and picnicking at a monastery and park preserve, a soothing spot outside Nara near the Horyuji Temple. The day's pace felt good to both of us. The monastery, like virtually all others in Japan, had dwindled in numbers. Eight aging monks lived in seclusion, frozen in a time that predated Commodore Perry's visit.

We left Japan from Kobe port on September 12. As the Tjiwangi pulled away from the dock, banners of pink, blue and green fluttered gaily, well-wishers waving vigorously. Judi felt sad to leave. It was a good thing Japan was so expensive, or she would have wanted to stay longer.

Once we settled into life on the freighter—all-you-can-eat Scandinavian food, pleasant crew and fellow passengers—I left Judi with her book and went to the railing to survey the Sea of Japan, taking stock.

Several self-destructive fantasies since coming on board ... jumping in the ocean. "She'll be sorry"—and our families will be heartbroken. The ego holds tightly to its self-defeating dance. The sense of urgency to get together tools of self-honesty, non-reactiveness, concentration, meditation alternates with a sense of despair which says, "our marriage is hopeless, when you gonna face that and get out?" Some honeymoon.

Japan was difficult. When we lived at Kudzoo Kastle, Judi worked over a hundred hours a week. We led fairly independent lives, not a bad thing for two introverts. Now we were together twenty-four hours a day, and I was learning what our couple-energy felt like when we were supersaturated with each other. This honeymoon was proving a challenge.

Lion's Head Monastery

Judi's old boyfriend Michael told us we shouldn't miss Lion's Head Monastery, not far from Taipei. The Tjiwangi docked there for three days, giving the pilgrims a perfect opportunity to experience a working Shinto monastery. On the train, a young Chinese man kindly took us in hand, telling us where to get down for the bus which would carry us the rest of the way. Then another man assumed the role of host, insisting on buying our bus tickets. It took us right to the base of a steep path leading up to the monastery.

Magic world up here. Like mounis, since nobody speaks English. Felt those hushed vibes as soon as we were in the shade of the rainforest. ... Very peaceful, blending crickets and Chinese voices. ... We could hear chanting, gongs, drums, bells. Fine, simple meal with the monks, monkinis and lay workmen. Everyone ate together. They worship Shin, the God of Heaven.

It's like being in a dharamsala up in the Himalayas. Tonight before dinner i lay in never-never land and floated into this world. Enveloped by forest sounds, the cool breeze, the amazingly calm vibes. Very cleansing. I can see why folks sometimes don't want to leave remote temple retreats like this. It's like the whole trip to India we're taking is encapsulated by this one day at

Lion's Head. Sure, there's peace here. And i can get quiet and centered. But then you leave, and then what?

Thank thee Lord for leading us here, away from our luxury boat to these simple people, insects, and mountain land. Please show Thy Path for me.

Though he spoke no English, the abbot made it clear to us pilgrims that we were free to stay indefinitely. We were also welcome to sleep together in one room, something I had worried about on the way up. He implicitly accepted the householder-monk lifestyle we were experimenting with. But I had plans, and this was premature. My goal still remained escorting Judi over the threshold into Mother India's lap.

We cruised on to Hong Kong. On the windy deck, I took stock once again: *Yes, it has been a problem letting go of desire for wife, for her inner yoni-fire. Must let go ... and yet not use [it] as the rod of punishment by withholding the seed necessary for our child. You're a fool to think that seed would wither just by the strength of my puny will.*

Stripped of belief, flailing around for want of faith, i stand naked and helpless before the eye of God. May this body, this ego-sheath, burn to dross in the fire of His Truth.

Praise be God for this ocean, a shadow of the mighty sea of His love. The ship sails west, straight into the sun. The East in that west is red with this body's blood, fashioned of dirt on the path and the creator's spittle, gathered each evening by the sun's truth-dealing sickle. ... May these thoughts penetrate my innermost heart, forsaking the dolphin-like forays into and out of consciousness. A mere head-dance. Praise be the Lord of One Sun, One Life, One Blood of Truth. I'm thirsty.

Okay, okay, my sweet, earnest young self, my friend, my twin! What's this about "withholding seed" on your honeymoon? What good fortune to grow middle-aged and take it all more lightly. But lest I grow too lite, I have your voice to return to, sometimes startling me into forgotten truth.

Thailand: Another Monastic Invitation

"Let's not go to India yet. Why don't we go hang out in Bali? We won't have the chance again," she said.

"But there're lots of places we could go. Malaysia, Australia, China. You just don't realize how incredible India is. I can't describe it. That's why I'm taking you."

"Everyone says Bali is fantastic. It's more basic and simple than India. And it's cheap. The people are supposed to be beautiful—and they're Hindu," Judi chimed back.

"Bali's a sidetrip. You're nervous about going to India, like you fear something." I was beginning to see what was going on.

"Oh?" she shrugged. "I don't think so. I just really want to go to Bali."

"But we're already spending a lot of time touring other countries, and Bali wasn't in the plan."

So the discussion would go. We were in Thailand, and loving it. In Bangkok, by government decree, the tallest buildings were the many *wats* whose spires punctuated the skyline. Covering the walls of the main *wat* was an outstanding mural depicting the *Ramayana*. I particularly liked the forest scenes of Rama's little family reclining at a picnic, Hanuman bowing in reverence at Ram's feet. Most people got around on bike and motor scooter; we moved about on the efficient bus system. But our favorite transport was the water taxi, which plied an extensive system of canals. Though a large Asian city, Bangkok was remarkably peaceful and low-key; not the crowded, noisy place with the world's worst traffic jams it is today. We stayed at a reasonably priced hotel full of foreigners, whose most memorable feature was the air-conditioned storage room where patrons checked their cameras when not in use, scores of them, all perfectly secure, tagged with owners' names. Leaving my camera behind for the day, easing the tourist burden, was something I had learned to practice in India.

We were eager to see the old Hindu temple towns, Sukothai and Ayyudhthaya (Ayodhya in Sanskrit), forest abode of Ram and Sita. We also were keen to visit a Buddhist monastery in the north beyond Chiang Mai. Several serious Buddhist seekers recommended the place to us, including an extremely earnest American I met in Bangkok who had been a monk for eight years. During our conversation, he asked me, "Have you ever experienced the space between thoughts?"

I thought it over, and thinking I distinctly remembered doing so at least once, answered, "Yes, I have."

"Impossible! You can't have attended your undisciplined rush of thoughts so carefully! Do you know what you are saying? *I* haven't even achieved this yet." The Buddhist convert was enraged. The query had been his lead-in to an important point about stilling the mind, and this spiritual tourist, this hippy, had the audacity to claim he had reached one of the milestones of meditative practice, cutting short the lesson. Turning from the bewildered Hindude pilgrim with a flourish of his robe, he stalked into the darkened recesses of the *wat*.

After taking a bus to Chiang Mai and wandering about that tranquil place—not yet the tourist trap it has now become—we bussed to the remote forest *wat* the angry American monk had urged us to visit. The bus carried us to a town on the edge of the northern forest. Then we climbed into a second bus, which soon left the paved road for a gravel one, ultimately becoming a mud track. Fortunately, the monsoon had almost ended. After several hours of arduous, lurching diesel propulsion, we disembarked at a jungle crossroads, pointed down a long path by the conductor. We finally arrived just past nightfall after a three-mile trek. We were greeted solemnly and told that it was best to arrive earlier in the day.

Despite our unmannerly arrival, the monks shared leftovers of the day's culinary gifts from the surrounding villagers, which we ate in an anteroom off the kitchen. Buddhist monks take one meal in the middle of the day, and never take food after nightfall. The honeymooners then joined fifteen monks for an evening meditation, which lasted about as long as I could stand. Not only did I have problems taming my mind, but also a congenital stiffness of the legs and back. I was numb. When it was time to greet our hosts, I was unable to stand. While I sat alone, rubbing my legs and feet harder and harder, Judi engaged in conversation with an American monk. They moved over to me, still rubbing my legs. I smiled wanly and made some comment about poor circulation to the extremities.

Joseph nodded his head and smiled briefly. "Difficult prognosis in this business."

We met a few other monks, who quickly went their way, and then briefly spoke with the abbot, a man in his fifties, greying at the temples, lean and fit with keen, searching, intelligent eyes. He said he would meet with us in the morning after tea to answer questions and discuss our reasons for coming to this remote place. We stayed in Joseph's cabin. He explained the daily routine—a series of bells signaling meditation, and two meals, lunch and pre-sundown dinner. After Judi fell asleep, he shared late into the night his ambivalence over whether it was time to leave the monastery.

When the morning mist burnt off, we realized that the wat was perched at the base of magnificent Chung Dao Mountain. The jungle tendrils seemed poised to overtake the little cluster of buildings at any moment. It had been built fairly recently, Joseph's little cabin only the previous winter. The smell of green wood lingered. It was stunningly quiet. All you could hear was crickets and birds amidst acres of banana and papaya trees. We had a very fine meditation in a cave, *but i need[ed] something more solid than temple-hopping and the occasional decent meditation.*

After tea we met with the abbot. His office was paneled in thin bamboo sheathing, with a few pieces of finely crafted furniture of rattan and teak. Trim, alert and athletic-looking, he received us in a dark, polished teakwood chair.

"How did you sleep?" the abbot asked us.

"Fine," Judi said.

I hesitated, since only my ear stopples saved me from the sound of scurrying mice. He leaned forward towards us and got right to the point. "So what brings you here deep in the forest to an austere community of monks?"

The pilgrims looked at each other, hesitating, then Bob answered, "We are on a pilgrimage. Our principal destination is India, where I lived a few years back. We have each practiced meditation and yoga, and I am a follower of the South Indian master Ramana Maharshi...."

Judi added, "And I am a disciple of Swami Satchidananda of Integral Yoga. His teacher was Swami Sivananda in Rishikesh."

The abbot nodded, waiting. These names meant nothing to him.

I resumed. "We would like to start a spiritual community, perhaps. So we are interested in communal spiritual life. We were told by a couple of reputable people in Bangkok that we should be sure to come here."

"One was an American monk, another was a lay teacher we met in the main *wat*," Judi specified.

The abbot looked at each of us frankly and smiled quietly. "We are a practicing monastery since the Second World War, though there was a group practicing here earlier in the century. We have had some Americans join us, including Joseph. Most of the other monks speak little English. Some of the Americans are now in Bangkok; others have returned to the United States. Since you came this far, you must be serious seekers. If you decide you want to join us, you may stay."

The question of Judi's place in a male institution came up the night before, but Joseph assured us that was a secondary concern; the abbot would arrange something so we could stay and partake in the monastic community, like oblates.

Again we looked at one another, each shocked into momentary silence. "We will have to see," I managed to say, "but we still have plans and people to see in India.... I have a teacher there, the one who led me to the Maharshi." I was thinking of Maurice Frydman.

Judi nodded, adding, "And I am led to visit Sivananda Ashram in Rishikesh."

"I see," said the abbot, again looking at each of us, smiling briefly. "If there are any questions Joseph cannot answer, I will be happy to speak with you about them.

I thought back to the long talk the night before with perplexed Joseph while everyone else observed monkish silence. The decision we reached after a brief discussion seemed imminent for him as well.

Later that morning on the monks' circular walking path through the jungle, an experience hastened our decision. Seeing me headed for the path, one of the Thai monks stopped me to explain the method. "You want to walk in our forest?" he asked, breaking silence.

"Yes, I would."

"Let me explain. One must be careful here. ...One simply meditates as usual, observing the breath. Walk slowly and make sure to finish the motion with one foot before engaging the other."

"I understand. Like this," I said as I practiced for him.

The monk held out one hand to stop me, adding, "But before you proceed you must know one other thing: there are cobras in this jungle, smaller but more deadly than the King Cobra. If one were bitten by such, he would die in less than three minutes. There is no antidote. A monk died three years ago after being bitten."

I paled instinctively, freezing through all the sheaths of being, right down to my onion center.

The monk saw my look and continued, "If one remains fixed in meditation and keeps to the path, the cobra will not strike." He turned and walked away.

I surveyed the prospect. The path was less than a meter wide, and tendrils of forest crept out so that in some places it seemed that one could not pass without brushing the vegetation. I looked as far as I could see for any sign of snakes hanging from the adjacent branches. The path soon disappeared into the jungle. Timidly, I took a couple of deliberate baby steps, carefully waiting to lift the toe of my right foot before planting the left. All I could think about were the cobras lurking in wait for each novice, and fear gripped my stomach, rising to my throat. Not only was Puer abandoning his walk, he was leaving this place.

I retreated to Joseph's cabin and started to pack my things. Judi came in. We were to inform the abbot of our plans in an hour. "Judi, I know we're not going to detour here for long, but I was thinking of hanging out long enough to climb the mountain."

"It's beautiful, but the jungle looks impenetrable. I wonder if there's a road or a path," she interrupted.

"There's a path right out back, but we'll never know if it leads to Chung Dao," I replied. I shared my jungle path experience on our way to lunch, ashamed at my cowardice. We agreed to take the next convenient bus back to Chiang Mai. We both felt the remoteness of the jungle, which made me lonely, vulnerable, and oppressed. I marveled at Joseph's ability to stay in this remote place for over five years. Judi was simply matter-of-fact about leaving a place that didn't feel right. But I felt a kernel of desire to follow the *dharma*. *The readings i have recently done, the demeanor of some of the monks, the little bit of the Buddha's teachings, contemplating the body in a detached way, seeing it as one would a piece of hair in one's food, or a toenail, bone, or blob of flesh, have given me a profound disgust with my life as it is, the foolish running in circles, chained to one gross desire after another, the craving for experience, for living instead of Be-ing.*

In Sukothai, the original capital and oldest city in Thailand, we resumed a more typical tourist's journey, though we still saw ourselves as pilgrims. We stayed at a simple lodge reminiscent of a dharamsala. In the ruins of the old city, a young girl stood crocheting with a cool demure expression, a slingshot thrust into her back pocket as she guarded the buffalo. Following Judi's pilgrim impulse, we walked several miles from Sukothai, surprised to stumble upon a remarkable image of the Buddha. In a country full of interesting Buddha poses, especially huge reclining ones, this statue was built into the earth, a stone sculpture seated within walls which sloped to a ceiling with an opening sufficient for the devotee to see the figure from above. A small boy led us through a path in the walls which led to the ceiling vantage point. His hands, arms, feet and knees were encrusted with an intense, rich, green moss. The full effect was of Buddha being received and contained in the earth, an earth-creature, a pupa containing future Buddhas.

Laos

In early October we followed a European traveler's tip that Laos was opening up for Americans. That is, for tourists, since our army had already come uninvited. We booked passage on a *sampan* which sailed from Chiang Rai, crossing the Mekong River and stopping at every large village to discharge and add passengers—self-sufficient peasants who were friendly, healthy, at ease with themselves. The pointy mountains of sculpted rock and pine trees abruptly rising up all around the river reminded me of Chinese paintings. They weren't as stylized as I had imagined. In a country with only twelve miles of paved roads and virtually no industry, everyone appeared well-fed, due to paradisiacal growing seasons. It was a wonderfully languid trip, enabling us to observe the steady, industrious life of the river people from our little love-seat in the rear of the boat. Things were definitely getting better. *Since the incredible evening at the wat of the forest dwelling sect in Ayyudhthaya, where we were surrounded by God's peace, i have felt very close, warm, peaceful, and playful with Judi. Up to then, i was getting the feeling of being trapped, resenting her speedy, prideful trips, even looking for outs from the relationship.*

It felt like a long drought was ending.

At Luang Prabhang, we met a dynamic young Swiss doctor working for Doctors Without Borders who was working at a leper's colony downriver and accompanied him on his rounds. I was impressed with the ease and lack of fear with which the non-lepers lived among the lepers. It was beautiful to see very crippled folks, some with open sores, cohabiting with healthy people who treated them as family, none of the traditional stigmas. The colony was a mixture of health and affliction, the ongoing cycle of Mother Nature: a woman with hand-stubs held a fat, normal baby who nursed at a large healthy breast

The next day, Judi went back to help the Swiss doc minister to the sick, and I decided to stay in town. I joined a little boat-tour at midday to a cave-temple downstream with some of the other Swiss, mostly young women. This was my first day away from her since the trip began, but her image clung to me still. As I described our pilgrimage, *I called her "my mother,"* and blushed.

On the final day of our stay at Luang Prabhang, we set out for a swimming hole the innkeeper told us about. At breakfast, we got into an argument about my camera.

"Are you going to take your camera today?"

"I was planning to."

"Whatever happened to the idea of leaving it behind sometimes? In fact, I'd prefer you never brought it. Because when I'm with you clicking away, I'm an intrusive tourist, too."

"Who says I'm a tourist? I'm a photographer and you know that. This is my art." I was instantly angry.

"You're not a professional," she snapped. "It's an extravagance. And it gets in the way of relating to people."

"But it can work the other way, too," I said. "Look, I don't want to argue. For today, at least, I'll leave it behind. But there's nothing wrong with taking pictures of Southeast Asian peasants."

"Thank you." She got up without finishing her breakfast. Like her father, she was a brooder. Sure, I had planned occasionally to leave the black box behind, and realized right after the argument that today would be a fine occasion not to have the albatross dangling from my neck. But she was always so damned self-righteous and I was still pissed. The camera was just the tip of the iceberg.

On the way to the swimming hole, I worried about leeches. But once there, I headed straight for a small freshet, leaving Judi to stew in her own acid as I sat under its forceful stream.

On a day when Judith felt like the devil personified, the Lord put it to me with the powerful stroke-rush of the waterfall. My heart leapt forth and i laughed as heartily as i can ever remember. Laughing, laughing, the sound merging with the dense rush of packed molecules from the pounding water. Such release, and i thanked the Lord for cleansing me, freeing me, as i floated downstream to the quieter pool. Just let it happen, flow with the water. When i first got under, i held tight, bracing against the powerful stream pummeling my back... Then the mind backtracked, reversing in a split instant, and i relaxed. Instantaneously came the freedom, the release not only of muscle tension and negative nerve potential, but of all the strung-out shit with the wife. Praise the Lord, who waits even now for release, total release, from the fetters of my iron heart.

Burma

Burma was run by a repressive military oligarchy. I could barely wait for our long-awaited journey to democratic India, where spirit was the real currency of the land. Now that India loomed, I could feel the excitement rising. But I felt some anxiety as well, since Judith had resisted Mother India throughout the trip.

We explored several temples, including the central one in downtown Rangoon, distinguished by its height and the density of saffron-clad monks and nuns converging upon it on motorbikes. The tin structure, covered with colorful prayer flags, was a wedding cake, layer upon layer of terraced wats, each with a larger Buddha at its center. It was like ascending into Buddhist heaven. But this was not the heaven I sought, any more than the Taiwanese or Thai monasteries had been, and I quickly tired of religious sightseeing.

Traveling by ferry and unreserved train, we journeyed to Pagan, the ancient capital to the north. The train was very crowded, dirty and smelly. Luckily, it was October and not unbearably hot. The ferry was even worse, for there was even less room for the bulging load of passengers. It felt like the Indian trains all over again. We watched in curious fascination as a woman picked something out of her friend's hair. We didn't know until Judi discovered head lice in Delhi that she was picking nits.

During the night, I slept poorly, as other passengers flopped and rolled against us. As usual, Judi slept soundly. But Pagan was worth the discomfort. Away from the bustle of Rangoon, people were more at ease. We were hosted by two young girls. They were extremely friendly, wrenchingly innocent, so relaxed and natural with us. They seemed too young to be paid by the State, but they clearly didn't expect tips. The nearly abandoned city was chock-full of temples, some with traces of exquisite murals and handsome stone sculptures. From high in one wat, we looked back at all the other sanctuaries studding the landscape. As far as we could see, fields with sparse livestock and occasional herdsmen or gopis interspersed the vista, giving the false impression of an easygoing bucolic theocracy.

The day of our flight to India, we joined a gaggle of Burmese in back of a large canvas-covered truck to visit a wooded retreat spot. Lost in taking photos, I was late for the return departure. I arrived just after the truck finally left, Judi hanging out the back, hand outstretched to help me on. I ran after the lorry, screaming for them to stop. I was terrified that if I overstayed my visa, I'd be incarcerated by the unseen thugs who ran the place. I was wearing a Thai sarong, camera bag bandoliered across my heaving chest. When the lorry finally halted, my lungs were burning for oxygen, and I was apoplectic with terror. Judi reached down to help pull me up as our fellow passengers eyed us impassively.

"Calm down, Bob, everything's going to be all-right."

"But if I missed the plane, they'd have jailed me. Our visas expire today!"

She laughed. "There's no way they'd put you in jail. You'd be sent out on the next available flight. Don't you think I'd wait for you?" She put her arms around me, rocking me like a baby.

Of course the real reason for my panic was the terror of being separated from my bride at the most important moment of the whole pilgrimage, our entrance into India. The novices were crossing the threshold.

15 India: Dragged Across the Threshold

On the flight from Rangoon to Calcutta, we picked up the *Times of India*, where we read that a few nights earlier, on Yom Kippur, the Arabs had pulled a surprise attack on Israel. My Hebrew bride was bound and belted next to me, and we were finally headed for India. But, having resisted my goal, wanting to put it off at every turn, especially as she chanted the Bali refrain, she now found a way out at the last desperate minute.

"I'm going to Israel to support the soldiers," she announced with determination.

"What?"

"When we get to Calcutta, I'm going to call the consul and offer my medical services if they need me."

"You mean, we're finally going to be in India and you're leaving me? This was the whole point of our trip."

"I know, Bob, but things change. The world challenges us and we have to respond. Life is hard. This feels like what I have to do."

"You just want to avoid India, just like you have the whole trip."

"No, I don't think so. If they don't need me, we'll explore India together like we planned." Rational explanation complete, she settled back in her seat.

After a few more efforts at protest, I could see that she was stubbornly set on her mad course. We landed in Calcutta, and, with dread and apprehension, I waited in the airport lobby in limbo, helplessly suspended while the bride whom I'd finally delivered to my place of spiritual awakening summoned our fate. I felt empty, alienated and betrayed.

When Judi returned from the phone, I couldn't tell the verdict; she wore her gambling father's pokerface. The tension was unbearable. She reported that the consul had genuinely thanked her, but they didn't need additional medical services. The war was quickly winding down. I was immensely relieved. But the episode ruined my fantasies of her receiving India like a child arriving under the Christmas Tree.

Calcutta was the scene of great excitement five years before as I sped around the city on the back of Jon Grace's motorcycle during Durga Puja. This time was far more mundane. We did not spend our time in coffee houses getting to know Bengali intellectuals, bumping into Satyajit Rai, as I had imagined. We did get out to Ramakrishna's ashram at the delta of the Hoogly River, where we observed monks and lay volunteers feed the poor from huge vats of dal and mountains of rice. We visited the shrine to the Mother, Sarada Devi, Ramakrishna's chaste wife, at her old dwelling. But Judi did not relish the beggars, the huge mounds of filth, the occasional corpse on the path. For the first time I noticed the death-carts, larger versions of the bike-wheeled garden carts gardeners use. Guardians of public sanitation, Untouchables loaded up the unclaimed dead, sometimes heaped three or four high, and carried them to the nearest mass crematorium. Unlike my arrival in Bombay five years previous, Calcutta really did have corpses in the gutters.

We took a ride on a human pedicab, a cart attached by two poles to a scrawny barefoot fellow clad only in a *dhoti*.

"Jude, don't you feel guilty with this guy pulling us around like this? He must require a mountain of rice as fuel," I worried.

"He's making money to feed his family." But she looked uncomfortable.

So we didn't stay long, quickly leaving for Buddhist territory to the northwest. Though we planned to visit Darjeeling, we ended up staying in Bodh Gaya. At a tent encampment for Tibetans we read political pamphlets and drank buttered tea with gentle refugees robed in traditional maroon. A small group of Americans clad in rainbow attire approached to tell us about a Vipassana Buddhist retreat on the outskirts of town. We decided to check it out.

The retreat was led by a young American Buddhist, prematurely wise, an early Jewish crossover. All our fellow retreatants looked American. Their flat accents offended me, mirroring what a spiritual tourist I was. Since I experienced difficulty sitting cross-legged, I was intrigued by the idea of walking meditation, this time on a dusty beaten-earth track, clear of cobras. I eagerly took up the challenge to focus upon walking to keep the mind clear. But as I and the other spiritual Olympians circled the little track cleared in the sparse jungle, it felt uncomfortably like just that. We were practicing some sort of sport, learning the technique, keeping one foot on the ground at all times like an Olympic walker. Didn't we have a pilgrimage to get on with? Neither of us felt particularly Buddhist, so the idea of a week-long retreat with a bunch of Americans eating bland, *sattwic* food that was supposed to induce peacefulness—unspiced rice, boiled veggies, and yogurt—didn't appeal. This didn't feel like India, so we left early.

Before heading for the Hindu heartland at Benares, we made pilgrimage to the site of the Buddha's enlightenment. The streets of Bodh Gaya felt much like other small North Indian cities, bustling, but not overwhelming. We saw several European and American dharma bums, most dressed in Tibetan costume, or with some badge attesting their sympathy: meditation beads, the brightly colored striped shirts, heavy silver bangles. By now Judi wore a sari, I the traditional pyjama-kurta.

We may have looked Indian, but ancient threshold guardians were alert to our incursion. On the way through the crowded central market to the shrine built alongside the Bodhi tree, out of nowhere somebody threw a couple of cherry bombs which exploded painfully near my ears. They hurt for several hours. Once there, Judi was drawn to the tree, one of many planted in succession at the site of Gautama's enlightenment. She had a long meditation while I balanced like a kid on sections of the low crumbled temple wall. "Now *this* is *India*," I said as we left. Judi smiled back beatifically.

Our spiritual trip had now begun in earnest. On our way to Benares (Varanasi), we spent an evening out under a starry sky curled up in our sleeping bags on the banks of a river. In the middle of the night, I woke and looked around, momentarily concerned about how vulnerable we were. It was totally quiet, not a soul stirring. We were pilgrims hewing the dharma of discovery, protected by the Mother.

The first day in the Hindus' holiest city, I was amazed and delighted to see Jon Grace, my Fulbright tabla-wallah from Calcutta, speeding ahead of the crowd advancing from a downtown intersection on a bike, dhoti and kurta flopping in the wind behind him. "Hey, Jon," I yelled and he pulled up. "What have you done with the Harley?" I asked. He smiled and explained that he was now field director for the University of Wisconsin's India program.

We visited Jon and his wife Joan in their flat for tea. Joan was very worried about the fact that her hair was falling out. Could Judi give her a diagnosis? I shuddered a bit as I saw how old this made his young bride look, thin wispy islands dotting a growing cranial desert. Associating the Buddhist meditation on hair as death, I resisted the temptation to touch my locks and confirm their body.

Once in Benares, Judi met some older Bengali gentlemen in white *dhotis* down by the ghats. We joined them for an informal *satsang*, watching the scene at dusk: water taxis and other craft plying the river, tiny candle-lit boats floating by, along with debris and omnipresent tufts of marigold. "Your timing is most excellent," said one, for their guru, Ananda Mayee Ma, was holding a five-day retreat later that week in Vrindaban, the site of Krishna's fabled youth. "You will attend," a serious man in thick black-rimmed glasses concluded. And so we would.

We proceeded from Benares to join Ma's retreat in Vrindaban. On the train we sat with a handsome monk in his forties who was also attending, Swami Vishwananda of Bangalore, a follower of Ramana Maharishi. We were brothers, *gurubhai*. He had the air of the gentleman about him, very debonair, penny-loafers protruding beneath his immaculate, neatly folded ochre robe. He had classic Tamil brahmin facial lines and unusually broad shoulders for an Indian. The swami read a newspaper, which he carefully folded and tucked between his pleats while we held an urbane, not particularly spiritual conversation—mostly about his handsome hometown and the beautiful countryside we shouldn't miss in his native Tamil Nadu.

Vrindaban

If you loved a stone or a piece of wood with enough intensity, you would learn to love all mankind. For any object of true faith reveals itself as the One God.

Vrindaban was an unexpected delight. A mid-sized town, it had virtually no motorized traffic, and a very relaxed pace of life. We stayed with many other pilgrims at a large *dharamsala* near the Yammuna River, Radha Bhavan. After settling in, we attended *satsang* the next morning in the adjacent hall with about a thousand devotees. Unfortunately, all Ma's talks were in Hindi, so we could only pick up her strong vibe. We wanted her *darshan*, but decided to wait. There was magic in the air, and we wanted to explore.

Swami Vishwananda led us to Nikunjaban and another jungle playground of Lord Krishna's. We also went to the Kaliyuni Temple, where a tremendous force radiated from the image of Mother Kali and the site of *mahasamadhi*, the final absorption, of the founder-Mahatma of the temple. Some South Indian friends of Swami Satchidananda, Judi's guru, were along and felt the same power with hushed wonder. At the main Vaishnavite temple Judi and I as non-Hindus were not allowed inside to see the images of Vishnu and his consort, Lakshmi. But as we shuffled around the entrance waiting for our Hindu friends to re-emerge, a procession formed within, and the images came out to greet us, rocking gently on their palanquins. The priests were thus unable to keep Vishnu chained. Like a liberated Gulliver, he bobbled unbound right into our path. Judi leaned and whispered, "It's the grace of Krishna."

Krishna's birthplace was uncanny. The air was so sweet that I felt like dancing; the faces around me seemed to mirror my mood. While we toured the temple courtyard at Nikunjaban Gardens, bearing busts of great saints and historical figures, I experienced numina. At two distinct moments, the statues nodded or winked at me. One was of an old saddhu who had founded a medieval shrine to Radha. To test this unexpected experience, I turned suddenly a couple of times to see if they were doing it behind my back, maybe catch another numen. But I had been given my share, and the rows of images faced me with stony nonchalance.

Ever since deciding to make the trip to Vrindaban, I had experienced doubt about this place and its god, a mythical character of ancient legend who lacked the force of a divine being who actually walked the earth. The style of worship that appealed to me was *jnana*, the Hindu version of negative theology, where the basic idea was to doubt every apparent divine manifestation. The Sanskrit, from the *Upanishads*, was *neti, neti*: not this, not that. And the deity who pulled me was Shiva (Ramana Maharshi was supposed by many to be his reincarnation), not Krishna. The only Krishna people I knew were the tasteless, rude Hari Krishnas back in the States, whom I pitied. I went once to visit their Boston tribe, chiefly to requite my desire for Indian food, brushing aside their evangelism. Judi, by contrast, was wide open. "The Mother is guiding us," was her refrain.

Now I was in Krishna's hometown, where the avatar supposedly played as a boy by the banks of the little river. Upon examination, I could see the different channels it had taken, creating rills and dunes underneath the neighboring foliage. I had merely intended a side-trip en route to the Main Events. For me, these were visiting Maurice Frydman in Bombay and a long sojourn at Sri Ramana Asramam at Tiruvanamalai; for Judi, sojourning at Sivananda Ashram, our next destination. But the Trickster-god had something else in mind.

"You are so lucky to be here in Vrindaban!" How I struggled to comprehend the old man's comment back in Nikunjaban.

"You're lucky too," I responded, but he vigorously shook his head. Then I realized he was remarking upon our liberation from Amerika: its crass focus on material wealth, its functional atheism, reeling from setbacks at its attempt to establish empire. This westerner had wandered into the place where Lord Krishna Himself played with gopis and flute. *Yes, what wonder this jiva's karma has wrought. Jai Krishna!* I had previously thought of divine *lila*—divine play—as a metaphysical concept. Here in Vrindaban, everything had the trickster-lover's touch. I experienced it daily as hide-and-seek, Krishna lurking at the edge of public places, still haunting the alleys, shrines and gardens,.

One evening, just as we headed out to visit the Krishna shrines for *darshan*, we heard a salutation: "Psst, psst." It was a young boy around twelve calling from the brush at Banki Bihari Gardens, carrying peacock feathers. *"Juldi, juldi!"* (quickly). He motioned us to follow. We looked at each other. Again he urged us, "Come, come, we mustn't waste time." We smiled, shrugging, and raced off under his tow. We called the boy Banki Bihari, an epithet of the wondrous cowherd himself. We raced from shrine to shrine, arriving at each just in time for the noisy, jubilant darshan. *Ringing in the pilgrimage with the soul-piercing arthi of bells, gongs, and kitchen pots clanging so that it set my gross body dancing like Nataraja.*

The various images of Krishna and Radha were hidden in curtained altars, looking like so many four-poster beds, modestly shrouding their amorous activities. But at sundown each day the priest-puppeteer would pull aside the curtains to display the lovers for their expectant devotees. Amidst the general din, pilgrims would crowd round to see the little images swaddled in doll-clothes, cast a prayer, *namaste* deeply to the tops of their foreheads, then move on. The whole business usually lasted not more than thirty seconds, when the curtain would fall once again.

As I said, these displays were supposed to occur at sundown. Somehow

Banki Bihari rushed us to each shrine in the nick of time for the unveiling, sunlight flickering across the images' faces for one ephemeral moment. Ours was a rolling sunset, time suspended as we rode the milliseconds to the sun setting at each little temple. We were not part of the general flow of pilgrims, following a leisurely sundown as the crowd moved from *darshan* to *darshan*. Sometimes, we went with the flow, while at others, Banki Bihari had us darting down back alleys and around corners. "*Juldi, juldi!*" he beamed, his head held high. He was pleased, he was proud, he was sweet as the cane we chewed at a horse fair in Tiruvanamalai. And at the end of it all, he quickly vanished with a smile, disappearing with his bundle of peacock feathers into the sparse jungle. I had been bracing for the inevitable *baksheesh*; he had been simply unparalleled as a guide. But he disappeared as suddenly as he appeared, no thought of *baksheesh*.

The whole episode made me think aloud, "Could this have been Krishna himself, guiding us in the form of this dervish of a boy?"

"Why not?" Judi answered. "If Hari was able to simultaneously entertain ten thousand gopis, each girl thinking she was his sole beloved, why couldn't he have escorted us, and many others at the same time?"

"To a serial view of his Vrindaban sites, arriving at each precisely at sundown?" I interjected. But the grace of Vrindaban prevailed, my doubts suspended.

Radha Dass, a Modern Mira

Vrindaban's grace abounded: shining faces everywhere, sly little sidelong glances, and teen-aged girls dancing and skipping down the narrow alleys at night in complete safety, like so many gopis heading for trysts with the flute-god. And after having a prepubescent Krishna tease us with his presence, a fully mature Radha showed up. That day I had stayed back in our musty cell at the *dharamsala*, enervated and miserable from diarrhea. My misery was broken once, when Judi stopped by to feed me flax seed mixed with some yogurt to stop me up. Coming in and out of feverish sleep, broken by trips to the dank latrine, I could hear the women's ankle bracelets tinkling in the streets aside, their laughter. Like an old wounded king, I was jealous. Why couldn't I be Hari, and all these women mine? Then, I heard musical voices; the laughter was right outside. Judi was at the door with another young woman.

Her face aglow, Judi reported that they had spent the day together, walking around the city under the full moon feeling a presence like nothing she had ever encountered. "Bob, meet Radha." A young woman in her mid-twenties smiled at me shyly, a bit awkward with the abrupt transition from the full moon magic of Vrindaban, dancing with the other gopis. She was dressed like a Boston Hari Krishna—plain sari casually tied around her waist, head wrapped in an Om scarf. But she had a clear, honest look. Now there were two gopis to serve me. Both women smelled lotus-fresh, and I basked in this double attention until Radha quietly left for the night, bestowing one last soft smile. I thought I saw the phosphorescent glow of peacock dust on her collarbone as she turned to leave.

I was now gloriously awake, and after Radha left Judi told me about their day. They had taken *prasad* at a little temple—the same *prasad* they had so sweetly brought me. The priest there told them the following story. He was a saddhu, merrily doing his saddhu thing here in Vrindaban. One day while in the garden of Nikunjaban, idly scratching in the dirt, he came upon something hard. The next day he came back and dug up first an image of Krishna, then another of Radha. He made the rounds trying to find a suitable place to give the images proper attention for puja: bathing, clothing, bedding—the usual amenities. Finally he found a temple, where he asked if they would take the images, since they had none. "Gladly," the *pujari* responded. That night Lord Krishna visited in a dream, saying, "Don't give me away, I came to you only." The saddhu responded, "But how could I care for you?" Krishna replied, "All I require is millet."

So the saddhu reclaimed the images, and procured a small place where he installed them in a corner. Gradually a small shrine evolved to encompass the little house. The images of the divine cowherd and his beloved drew increasing attention from the world of Krishna devotees. In the beginning, the man, now a pujari, was frustrated to leave the roaming life of a saddhu. But gradually he learned to accept and love his dharma, which was to continually care for the images. This love overflowed to all the visitors.

So what might this story have to do with our pilgrims? Married, thus *grhasthanas*, they set out immediately as wanderers. Not just the honeymoon fling, but a full-fledged pilgrimage. The saddhu who had set out to be a wandering ascetic was called by a buried Krishna to be a father, tied to feeding and housing the god. Even here in the home of the Hindu Puer, the god who remained a teen lover, the lessons of the steady householder were in the air, if one noticed. We didn't.

By the following afternoon, I was fully recovered. Feeling cleansed, I joined Judi and Radha Dass for tea at a little shop near the *dharamsala*. Shy the night before, she was more talkative.

"So you have a guru here?"

"He stays here every year during the rainy season. So this is his base, yes."

"And what does he teach?" Judi added, setting down the smudged little glass which served as a teacup.

"He is a devotee of Krishna. I try to watch him as carefully as I can to learn how to love and serve Krishna. There's a holy hill near the town where he took me. Every fifty meters or so you'd see a devotee, prostrating, then getting up. Every step they took they would prostrate."

"Circumambulating the hill? How long would that take?" I asked.

"Oh, it's several kilometers around. Actually the saddhus prostrate one hundred eight times at each step, one for each divine name; this is their *tapas*," she clarified.

Judi and I looked at each other in wonder, then back at Radha. She did not smile.

"And you did the same?" Judi asked.

"Yes, we spent quite some time on the hill. It was a real blessing to be there." The shopkeeper asked if she wanted more tea. Radha started to wave him off, but realized that we probably would. He refilled the small glasses.

We discussed *tapas* for several minutes. Radha felt it had essentially nothing to do with pain, but was simply a natural overflowing of devotion.

"I don't have much appetite for pain," I said. "I think my sickness the last couple of days must be a kind of enforced *tapas*, Krishna's gift of pain for the fainthearted. It will help me remember Vrindaban."

Radha looked me straight in the eye and answered simply, "The true *tapas* is of the heart." I was instantly ashamed to realize how shallow and self-congratulatory my remark had been.

Recalling Radha now brings a shudder of humility, reminding me what piety is all about. Compared to the jockeying of Swami Satchidananda's New York and Miami devotees, with their easy judgments and ranking of gurus, Radha Dass seemed like the real thing. She had a big-boned, square-jawed, wide-eyed kind of beauty. I was immediately drawn to her, appreciating her honest, direct gaze flowing from an unassuming self-acceptance. But Radha also bore the imprint of sadness at the corners of her eyes and mouth. She seemed like someone who had known the world and had enough of it, and now simply wanted to seek and serve God.

Radha owned two saris, the classic complement, washing one and wearing one each day. She also wore cheap little *japa* kerchiefs around her head, the ones you saw the hippy-saddhus wearing everywhere. For them it was ornament, being cool, but for Radha, they were literally her cocoon of prayer. Whatever else Radha was doing, whether it was conversation, walking, or laughing at a pleasantry, you were aware that at a deeper level she was in prayer, saying her Krishna mantra.

Many of us toyed with Indian spirituality. It was an identity thing, making it important for us to *wear* Hindu habits (though I didn't see any naked hippies with ash smeared over their bodies and *tilakas* on their brows). Radha had given herself over to it. Like their Buddhist counterparts, Hindu monks have a ceremony where, after progressively letting go of their possessions, they bundle up the remaining clothes, books, mementos, and send them down the river in a little boat. Radha had given up even more. She had thrown away her passport, and had thus become a vulnerable animal, like an archaic Greek outside the polis walls with no papers. No protection of the Embassy or the Aussie army. No money, no possessions, no citizenship, nothing but her devotion to Krishna.

Radha gave me some verses attributed to the medieval saint Mira, which she had copied from a sickly old saddhu's translation in the room next to us at Radha Bhavan:

> *The world inside and out ... nothing appeals to me.*
> *Without the Beloved everything is insipid.*
> *Where shall I go to light the lamp, friend,*
> *When my Beloved dwells in alien lands?*
> *To me the vacant divan looks like a poisoned bed.*

Radha reminded me a lot of Mira. Mira was the quintessential female saint, a woman who felt as a child she had been promised as a bride to Krishna. When she was married to a warrior instead, she refused after his death in battle to serve his family, choosing instead the life of a wandering *bhajan*-singer, praising Krishna and realizing her girlhood prayer. Her husband had been a Rajput, whose ethos required martial courage from the men and chastity and obedience from the women, the very model of the feudal patriarchy. The famous Rajput custom of *jauhar*, a variant of *suttee* where the women committed mass suicide by fire rather than falling into the hands of the enemy, was the ideal, and Mira flaunted it.

Around Radha, I began to experience myself as Mira's grasping husband, especially chastened that I fantasized both Judi and Radha serving me. Judi may have thought of me as her "Krishna" back in Birmingham, but in the presence of Radha's fiery purity, that fantasy was outrageous. I was immensely pleased when I heard that Radha, like us, was going to Sivananda Ashram after leaving Ma's retreat.

We finally met Ananda Mayee Ma. She was kind and gracious, radiating love and understanding. I kept telling myself, "this woman is a saint, a realized being, there must be something she will teach you just being in her presence." But we were among a group of two dozen waiting to be with her, and since her English was rudimentary, we did not have a "spiritual talk."

As we waited to see Ma, a woman with a strong, proud face, brindled hair tied in a bun, walked back and forth, eyeing us narrowly. Finally, she approached Judi, pulled her aside and asked in Punjabi, "What's a *pukka* brahmin girl like you doing with *him*?" The bride who had mightily resisted India, risking war service to avoid it, now wore a sari as if swaddled from birth. Her gestures were close enough, and her Semitic features smacked of the northwestern plains. It hurt to be judged by the woman. I wished that I, too, could "pass" as Judi now clearly did. But I was also really proud that my bride was finally home, and we had been here less than two weeks. As for sitting at the foot of a realized master, I preferred to have the opportunity to do so with one who spoke English.

16 Sivananda Ashram

So the circle of attempted sadhana continues. My eyes come to rest on doors locked, questionable doors, doors i fear to open. i continue to make pilgrimage like the good, devout folks of Vrindaban, around God, rather than to Him.

Judi learned shortly before we left on our pilgrimage that one of her closest associates within the Integral Yoga movement, a woman she trusted, had accused Swami Satchidananda of sexual abuse, a charge which she later reinforced by representing—now as their lawyer—a whole series of women, all of whom had been his secretaries, each surprised to learn they were not the only ones. "If only it were someone else making these accusations," Judi wished out loud. She carried this burden with her to Sivananda Ashram, and the struggle to resolve it would occupy her initial days.

My own position was that I had yet to meet a guru in the West who I thought was authentic, including my wife's. When we returned from India, I wrote Satchidananda regarding his plan to build an elaborate Lotus Shrine at his new ashram in Buckingham County Virginia, under which would be his *mahasamadhi*. Did the good swami not see the ego aggrandizement involved in such a project? I suppose that his writing me back showed class, but he politely brushed aside my youthful idealist's suspicions. I never trusted any gurus, preferring the response an old swami made to Judi when she broached the mantra topic with him, "Only the mantra of the Satguru can give one God-Realization." So how does one know which earthly beings, if any, represent the Satguru? As for mantras, I suspected they were a vibrational trick, operating at the psychosomatic level.

I was frankly apprehensive about being in Rishikesh. Having dragged Judi to India, it was now her turn; Sivananda Ashram was her thing. She was ready and tremendously eager for a solid grounding in ashram life. Unlike her, I was not a karma-yogi; I could neither envision myself in the bustling general hospital, nor in the leprosy project, nor the large publishing business that specialized in Swami Sivananda's countless homely formulas for spiritual growth. To me, his aphorisms sounded too much like Dale Carnegie. And the prospect of spending several weeks in an institution which I suspected was the model for the simplistic tone of Integral Yoga back in the States disturbed me. Having met Swami Satchidananda at one of his retreats, picture-perfect, new age, but fundamentally flawed by an egotism in which his western disciples bathed unawares, it was hard for me not to associate the mother institution with the same charade.

But we had met Swami Chidananda in Vrindaban, a close associate of Ananda Mayee Ma who felt like an authentic, no-nonsense teacher. He was a brother swami of Satchidananda; they were both initiated by Swami Sivananda, the ashram founder. As president of the Divine Life Society, he had written a letter authorizing a long sojourn at the ashram, which I hoped, despite my misgivings, might bear fruit for both of us. Judi had provisionally accepted the yogi's life before committing to the householder stage. Now was my opportunity to give that path a fair trial.

We arrived by taxi from the Haridwar train station in late afternoon, registered at the office by the main road which ran through the ashram, then climbed dozens of steep concrete steps with our backpacks to the main campus on the opposite side. Our simple cell was next to the forest, full of black-faced gray monkeys who checked us out with more commotion than I would've liked. We deposited our luggage and went to supper in the austere, dingy dining room.

After chanting lengthy prayers in Sanskrit, we ate the simple, unappetizing food seated cross-legged on the floor in rows on long rattan mats running the length of the room, greasy from food droppings. My lower back is like a block of concrete, so it was extremely difficult for me to bring the food to my mouth, cupped in my untrained forefingers, without contributing to those greasy stains and soiling my clothes as well. Men and women ate separately. I felt suddenly isolated and estranged. I missed Judi, who I couldn't even see, since the women sit behind the men. Watching the servers return to the kitchen for more provisions, I glimpsed huge black iron vats operated by heavy levers over roaring wood fires. Except for the bare lightbulbs, we could have been in Medieval India.

We attended *satsang* that evening, sitting on the floor in the cozy main hall among seventy or eighty people. For some reason, men and women sat together, mixed in with some children. Only the swamis sat apart, a phalanx along the wall beside the platform dais where the speaker sat. Judi was clearly energized by the evening's company, saffron-clad monks and cultivated Indian householders prominent among them, and the program: story and commentary by the witty and erudite Swami Krishnananda on the *Mahabharata*, bhajans, finally the sharing of *prasad—laddu* sweets and fruit sections. I still felt weak from my Vrindaban illness, but had no problem eating the bland food.

During the program, Judi looked at me several times, smiling with contentment, her eyes holding the question, *does the ashram suit you?* Krishnananda entertained me, and I smiled back reassuringly. We exchanged nods and *namastes* with the other devotees as we left the hall, but moved quickly to our quarters as dusk fell, eager to get to bed so we could roust ourselves for meditation the next morning. We talked a little, Judi sitting on my twin bed, and she went immediately to sleep right after dark. I lay in the bed, apprehensive about having to wake early and face the contents of my resistant mind before breakfast. In the morning at 5:30, the bells started ringing. It was dark and cold and I was very tired, so I declined group meditation, rolling over for more blessed sleep.

The ashram was a pleasant place, high above the holy city of Rishikesh, on the cliffs of Ganga's western bank. Everything and everybody was neat and scrubbed, a refreshing contrast to the filth of Calcutta and untidiness of Varanasi. Young *brahmacharins* played merrily as they washed, slapped dry and hung ochre robes on the roofs, and painted dancing graffiti Om's on the walls. The evening satsangs, with the promise of *prasad*, were the main events of the day, since the morning meditations were extremely difficult for me. Other sittings were offered during the day, but attendance at the pre-dawn monastery ritual was expected of pilgrims. If I managed to make it through the hour, frequently refolding my aching legs, I'd go back after breakfast to our room and sleep an hour or two more. Otherwise, there wasn't much for me to do except read and write letters. We did make a few hikes around the area, including a memorable trip across the river with a young swami, climbing up to the cave of a famous *mouni* who exuded quiet rapture. To Judi he was the model yogi, sitting in continuous meditative silence. I found him remarkable, but a diversion. This was something I neither wanted nor could ever aspire to. In that cave, she was the aspirant, I the spiritual tourist.

As soon as she was able to see him, Judi spoke with Swami Chidananda about her dilemma with Swami Satchidananda. Her teacher had given her mantra-initiation and carefully trained her to be a yoga teacher. If the mounting stories of sexual abuse were true, then wouldn't this negate him as her guru? Swami Chidananda would not judge his *gurubhai*, but instead counseled Judi to take her worries to Sivananda himself. She went down to the dead Master's *kutir* by the Ganga and followed this advice, meditating there every afternoon on the little cliff overlooking the holy river. This brought her peace and acceptance that the *lineage* was genuine, whatever the behavior of her immediate teacher, with whom she mentally made a tenuous truce.

A trio of swamis ran Sivananda Ashram. Kindly Chidananda, thin and ascetic, was the spiritual head and president. Swami Nirmulananda was the comptroller: a friendly, bright and practical fellow with long tousled brindled hair and beard. Krishnananda was the most entertaining, a great raconteur with a fabulous wit, bald, somewhat plump, often fastidiously adjusting his bright new orange habit, giving him an added measure of dignity. I always looked forward to his tales from the *Mahabharata*, told with great relish. The evenings when he played bard and those when Chidananda gave homilies were by far the best. Thankfully, these talks were in English, chiefly to accommodate the many South Indian devotees who did not speak Hindi. But I knew Hindu spirituality could be a lot more hip than this place, and I longed for more. Sivananda Ashram was full of pious middle-aged, middle class versions of what I imagined the young Integral Yoga Institute folk from the States would grow up to be: boring and carefully good.

During the first week at the ashram, we learned of a rival institution across the Ganga. Intrigued, we boarded a launch the following afternoon to visit the ashram of the Maharishi Mahesh Yogi. It looked oddly like an

American motel, and inquiring about the cost, we learned that it was just as pricey. The Maharishi wasn't there; the chokidar (watchman) told us with some hauteur that he was in the United States, but showed us the bank of videotapes of the Master in the library, saying we could watch any of them we should like for "only a small fee."

Even though Sivananda Ashram was too sedate for my tastes, there was *life* there, connected to a tradition extending straight back to the Vedic era—a huge contrast with the Maharishi's empty, lifeless motel. No library stuffed with videos, moving idols of the guru rather than scriptures, no suspension of authentic ashram life, awaiting the pleasure of a carefully scripted personality. Who was the Maharishi anyway, just a janitor from Benares Hindu University who had hatched a clever scheme—or so Cowboy Don, who was enrolled in philosophy there, had told me five years earlier. As far as I could tell, George Harrison was dead right when he put this guru behind him.

But our struggles would continue: mine to establish some kind of sadhana; as a couple, the struggle over sexual desire. Judi was ready for serious *tapas*; she would subdue her flesh and fast on a once-daily ration of fruit and yogurt. By the end of the week, she undertook *moun*, a vow of silence. Worst of all was the lure of chastity.

By the time we had reached Sivananda Ashram, the transposed marriage bed, the traveling honeymoon bungalow, had become a battleground of frustration. Its setting in Rishikesh was a room about ten by twelve, with twin beds on opposite walls, each with a small bedstand. There was one bare bulb on the ceiling, a couple of candleholders blackened with use from frequent power outages on the bedstands. Cupboards for clothes and personal items were built into the thick cement walls on each side. One small bare desk with a metal chair was in a corner near the window.

The second night, I found *satsang* uninteresting, and was glad to be alone with Judi when we returned to our spartan quarters. She looked good in her orange and red sari. With the bindi (that red dot)on her forehead, restruck by the good swami after satsang, and the streak of red running from the brow through the part in her hair, she looked like a Hindu wife, clutching her *prasad* wrapped in one end of her sari like a gunny sack in her small Ukrainian peasant's hand. The image pleased me. I walked a little faster, catching up with her and putting my arm around her cool white waist, pulling her towards me. I relished the unfamiliar feel of flesh, but immediately realized this was an unsanctioned public display. It was dark, and a few others were scurrying towards their rooms in the gathering chill. Nobody stared at us, and though Judi had given me a glance that acknowledged my indiscretion, she was easy with the hand.

We got back to the room, and she unlocked the big brass padlock. When I turned on the overhead light, she wheeled around. "It's too harsh; turn it off."

She went to her pack, pulled out a small flashlight and rummaged a side pocket for candles. She lit two, placing one on the windowsill, a second by her bedstand. Her face, a canvas stretched over her skull with its strong jaw and high cheekbones, instantly softened in the candleglow. I went over and sat on the bed, putting my arm around her shoulder, pulling her to me. But she pulled away and reached for her hardback tome of Sivananda's teachings.

"What are you doing? Can't you leave Sivananda alone for an evening?"

Laughing, she put it down beside her on the bed, "I was just finding the place for my next reading. It might not be 'til morning. Do you think you'll come to meditation with me?"

"Frankly, I'm not thinking about meditation. I don't plan my day ahead like you do. I'm into the *now*."

She nodded absently. "So what do you think? Did today go any better than yesterday?"

"Not really, I said. "Krishnananda is fine, but the food is unappetizing."

"So things are still tough for you. I'm sorry. But think of it this way: it's an opportunity for you to create your own discipline, your own sadhana. Maybe you need a mantra. I bet you could talk to Swami Chidananda. He could give you one," she said too brightly.

"I'm really not interested in a mantra. That's just not my style. You know that. Right now I'm interested in you."

"I know. You always are. Be patient. I came here to deepen my yogic practice."

"Patient! What the hell do you think I've been for this whole trip? When did we last make love?"

"Recently. ... Uh, not Vrindaban. Yes, at Bodh Gaya at the retreat center. Remember?"

I thought a moment and remembered the furtive act. "Yeah—another dormitory. I don't feel like you care that much whether we do or don't. You put me off as long as you can, then you give in just to pacify me, because it's your wifely duty."

"But I *am* your wife. I chose to be because I love you."

"You make it sound like you're just accepting your *dharma* when we make love. I want to be *desired*."

It was getting late, and the temperature was dropping fast in our unheated room as the cold Himalayan air drained from the foothills. I was tired, and was reaching the point where a warm bed and sleep were the most I could hope for as the day ran steeply down, like the temperature. I kissed her, and we embraced in her narrow steel-framed bed. I was sitting up, poised to cross our little divide and retreat to my side when I felt her pull me back.

"Don't you at least want to get warm first?"

Surprised, I lay down with her and we wrapped ourselves in her down bag and the wool blanket the ashram had supplied. "This is so hard, Judi."

"I know. You've just gotten here. It will get better."

And that night, at least, it did. When I finally returned to my bed, immensely relieved, we were warm again.

Two days after we made love, on the afternoon of a somber gray day, we replayed our continuo refrain, returning to our little cell to get ready for dinner, the high point of my day. The night before, Swami Chidananda had led the evening satsang. Judi had again carried *prasad* knotted in the end of her sari, even more precious because Chidananda himself had blessed it this time. The previous night's cold had penetrated and never left.

"Jesus I'm glad we're not going to be here when winter comes," I said.

"The ashram clears out after Diwali, leaving only the permanent residents. The *dharamsala*'s open again in March. I'm planning on coming back then," she said, "Will you come with me?"

"We'll have to talk about that. I don't think you're going to get me back to this place."

"Maybe that would be a good time for you to stay and work with Kumarji in Dewas."

"Maybe. But here we are already planning time apart and this is supposed to be our honeymoon. I feel so anxious, sometimes hopeless, about our sex-life. Every time I look at you, I'm confronted with the image of a holy woman, not my bride. It's like you're doing what you told me when we met in Birmingham. So why'd we get married, if this is what you wanted?"

"We got married to support each other in our spiritual lives ... to do together what we couldn't accomplish apart."

"You keep throwing at me the problem of desire, the problem of attachment. I mean its *all-right* that I want you, even that I want you a lot of the time. It's normal. I don't care what Hindu orthodoxy says. Sure, I want some balance, some channeling of this energy. But you're threatening to cut it off entirely. How do I know you'll actually come out of all this extreme tapas? Now you're threatening to go *moun* on me. ..."

"It's not a *threat*, Bob. It's what feels right for me to do now. I have Chidananda's blessing."

"And what does Chidananda say about your duty to your husband in all this?"

"He knows you're having difficulty. He'd be happy to talk with you."

"Like I have a lot of choice. You're ganging up on me. I feel like I'm being forced into monkhood. ... I'm just being stoic about my sadhana, doing the work in the grim realization that there's no other choice, rather than out of love for the Divine. It's like taking a vow not to eat meat while you're still attached to it."

"You sound like you're setting a trap for yourself. It is not so serious as you're making it. And it's not a permanent situation."

"What's permanent is the problem of attachment and desire. You can't run away from it, you must either ignore it or deal with it, at every moment when desire arises. Not permanent, hell."

"You're so philosophical. It's too bad it doesn't get you anywhere."

"Judi, you don't have any more desire. I can feel it. I think we should just shelve it—shelve the marriage. What's the point?"

"I still love you. Passion goes in cycles. It'll come back. I've not taken any vows except the ones we said to each other. Maybe you should look at them again."

"Goddamit, Judi! You always sound so cool and rational, even when you're talking about love." I rudely pushed aside some of her papers and the prim Sivananda-tome she carried around all the time. I had an impulse to throw the little pile of *prasad* on the nightstand which she guarded like the contents of a little girl's stocking at Christmas in her face. I stormed out of the room and headed for the hills above the ashram, walking as fast as I could.

After about a kilometer of climbing, some of it steep, I reached a stony little field surrounded by scrub oak where I met a goatherd with his small flock. He was disarmingly friendly, and we had a brief conversation in Hindi. I was still feeling embarrassed and wanted to continue my walk alone. But after this little interlude, I saw there was really nowhere else to go. Turning to his goats, I bemoaned my sexless fate. They merely bleated as I contemplated the irony of it all.

The next day I met with Radha. We wanted to share what we had been reading. She looked pale, drawn and underfed to me, but when she looked up and saw me her face was transfigured by her sweet desireless smile, crinkling the wrinkles around her eyes, making her suddenly look older.

"Are you and Judi happy here at the ashram?"

"Yuh—yes," I stammered, lying. "Judi really likes it here especially. It's almost like home for her."

"So tell me what you've been reading."

"Here. I want you to read this." I handed her the Sufi classic, *The Conference of the Birds*.

"What's it about?"

I found I could summarize the book in academic fashion, but what had impressed me were its literary qualities and the potential for spiritual growth it contained. I realized that it hadn't really changed me;, merely entertained me with the possibility. She had shared the old saddhu's Mira poetry with me at Vrindaban, and I wanted to give her something back. I think what I really wanted was what was feeling more and more inaccessible with my bride.

"I'm leaving the ashram tomorrow. My teacher wants me to go with him to Delhi for a *satsang*."

My heart sank. I wanted to be around this gopi, kinder and more mysterious than my super-serious wife, to ease the difficulties of this place. "You can keep the book."

Radha smiled. "No, I'll read it tonight and leave it by your door with a note in the morning."

So what happened to Radha, this modern Mira who quietly lit up our lives? Is she still wandering the hills of North India, reciting her japa, prostrating at every step? Or did she reclaim her Australian citizenship and raise children who grew up singing Mira-bhajans and reciting the *Bhagavad-Gita* like the four-year-old girl I met in Dewas a few months later? At the rate she burned, it is more likely that she was absorbed into the substance of Krishna, like Mira.

In a letter to my parents, I spoke with awe of the creature unfolding before me, and of the difficulties on the Path: Judith is flowering like a Ganges wildflower, indrawn with devotion and sincerity, seeking God. But her Virgo nature is fulfilled by the variety of sadhana. She went every day to learn to recite portions of the Gita in Sanskrit, followed by meditation alone by Sivananda's kutir. At sundown she went again to the river for arthi, then after dinner to evening satsang. I only joined her for that last piece, and of course the meals, where we sat apart.

The letter complained of a long-standing cold, of the severe diarrhea in Vrindaban, attributing both to the struggle to subdue the ego. *Before, India was one big "trip." So many exciting things to discover, so much good ganja to smoke, holy men to play with like a kid. This time i know what is at the heart of Indian culture, the source of the attraction I've always felt here. But it requires* work, *more work than i have ever done, maybe more than i have the guts and discipline to handle.* While Sivananda Ashram was precisely what Judi wanted, its disciplines felt like an iron vise to me.

Puer's journal recognized his response of *terror, expressed in little-child tantrums. The fear of giving myself to anything. Knowing that this is all that matters, no other fruits to taste. Judi has found herself in an orchard with so many fruits she can't decide which one to pick. I find myself in the world's final orchard with no taste for the fruit. Paralyzed, backing off, realizing I am trapped, nowhere to return, because behind me is unreality. Full of existential dread.*

The next day, November 17, filled with frustration, I had a key talk with Swami Chidananda. His office was on the second floor above the Divine Life main office. The building was light yellow stucco, and the saffron of his robe had the same color value, only a richer hue. The study was not large by western standards, very tidy, with a large gleaming-faced photo of Father Sivananda on the back wall, garlanded with a fresh string of marigolds, another variant of the basic ochre of renunciation. The modest hardwood desk displayed photos and paintings of several saints, most backgrounded by the Ganga, and a photo of Gandhi. Chidananda, a Keralite, was in his mid-fifties, head shaved like all renunciates, thin and wiry, with strong, angular features and a beautiful smile. He greeted me warmly, and I namasted, bowing my head as much as my ego would allow.

After ascertaining that we were comfortable in our spartan quarters, he asked, "So what did you want to speak to me about?"

"Swamiji, I have been drawn almost my whole life to the spiritual life, yet it seems that every time I approach any real progress, I back off. It is as if a wide chasm appears, and I'm afraid to cross it."

The Swami nodded, and I went on.

"I mean, the attraction of the liberated life is so strong—my teacher

Maurice Frydman in Bombay ... he's a close friend of Krishnamurthi—called it the "fellowship of the undeceived." That's a good example. Maurice gave me a photo of Ramana Maharshi after I promised to meditate on it half an hour every day. But I don't think I ever have more than three days in a row. I have seen the possibilities of liberation, but I guess I don't want to give up life's other riches."

"And its pain and heartbreak?" the swami answered.

"I have had some, but not as much as others."

"You are young still," he said.

"Yes, but it's not just that. I fear giving myself totally to anything or anybody. I want to preserve all the possibilities." I was onto the heart of my dilemma.

"Perhaps you have too many possibilities in your life. Do you think you might be happier with fewer?" He would not be the last teacher to say this.

"I have met many in your country who are, which humbles me. Maybe I am simply too habituated by my Western upbringing."

"You are here in India as a pilgrim. But what of your vocation? I know your wife is a medical doctor. She tells me you are a teacher. How do you find it?"

"I like teaching ... in fact I love it. I particularly like it when I can awaken a young person to deeper levels of meaning by getting them to question their experience. At the boys' high school I taught a course called "The Hindu View of Life." I taught the *Vedas*, especially the *Upanishads*. I think the students gain an appreciation of Hindu values, and some of the big ideas. At the same time, I am so aware of the final goal at times that I want to teach *that*. But I lack the authority of immediate experience. You see my problem."

Chidananda nodded, his brow furrowed.

"I want to jump over all the in-between work, all the dirty work, all the little things. I understand the *concept* that *atman* equals *Brahman*, but *realizing* the identity is another thing."

Chidananda laughed. "What you see and experience as separate are in fact already united. You are not alone in making the quest more difficult than it needs to be. Maybe more of a Zen approach is needed. Be Zen-like in spontaneity. Yes, you are right that it is a leap that must be taken. But not necessarily all at once. The leap sometimes takes years." He smiled.

"And I am not becoming a *sannyasin* now," I said, chuckling. "I am a householder and will return to teaching when I get back to the States."

The swami continued. "Being drawn to the infinite does not mean that you must make that the express focus of your teaching. Instead, I advise that you transform the burning desire to teach into the effort to see *Brahman* everywhere, in everything. The desire itself is also *Brahman*, and must be recognized for what it really is. As for your students, you should teach them right living, especially the conservation of sexual energy. This is the hardest thing for youth, and with the permissive atmosphere of your culture, it is something they especially need."

I was not particularly pleased to hear this ethical laundry list, since I was trained in *ideas* and learning them through Socratic inquiry. This felt like a step backwards, playing the Sunday School teacher. I knew he was right, but it was a task for somebody else. I wanted to serve my *daimon*, my own particular gifts, rather than being an ethical soldier, doing my dharma. I felt so unfinished, at Sivananda Ashram a bit like pablum-mush, but my *daimon* had in fact brought me here and was awaiting me upon arrival.

Chidananda went on, recounting a parable he had heard from Swami Sivananda. "It's like this. Even though a guest in your home is really *Brahman*, you give him tea, biscuits and fruit, because as long as you perceive him as a guest—and yourself as host—then he must be treated according to that relative reality. That is, he is *Brahman-as-guest*. You do not use the same language when comforting a lost calf that you would a lost child."

As I listened, I thought of Meher Baba's "provisional ego." You use it as long as you must, but it is not finally real. Chidananda had politely shown that my efforts at teaching shards of wisdom which I had not experienced were foolish. *Now the image of a dog yapping at the moon comes to mind—with a whole pack* [my students] *in attendance. I seem to have a great ability to play the fool unawares. Teach whatever form Brahman takes. Drop all theories, preconceptions, plans. ... So back to the mill of life, abandoning the drawing boards.*

I thanked this kind, patient man and left his study, buoyed by the clarity and energy he had given me. Judi and I slept comfortably apart in our thinly padded twin beds that evening. I was feeling more grounded, more self-sufficient, and eager for *my* turn. We were headed for Bombay and my reunion with Maurice Frydman.

17 Morris and Little Atman

"Your wife is your guru." —Maurice Frydman

This is a honeymoon?—*more a trial by fire!* —Puer

We took the train to Bombay in early December to visit Maurice Frydman. When we arrived at the flat, I learned from his secretary Arvind that Maurice and Miss Petit were in the South, either at Ramana Maharshi's ashram in Tiruvanamalai or at the regional hospital in Vellore. She was battling heart disease, and needed medical attention in a drier climate. Arvind said there was no way to contact them, but that when I came to Katpadi Junction, I would *know* which way to go. So we headed south. On the train down, I prepared myself, quietly focusing on the choice as we neared the junction. When the moment of decision came, I knew they were at Vellore, so we remained on the train.

    Maurice was a little taken aback when we walked in. I had not come to comfort this gentle old mound of flesh that he had taken a vow to care for, and he knew it. It was one thing for him to receive hippy-saddhus at their flat on Nepean Sea Road, but quite another to be tracked down, and he was clearly irritated. I always bothered Maurice, who told me more than once that he was unsure if I was fit to follow the path. Still, he was the closest to a living guru that I knew, and I dearly wanted Judi to meet him.

So we resumed our guru-disciple relationship, Judi listening in. He reminded me that my mantra was "charity and clarity. Love and truth." He hit hard at my self-centeredness. Eager to change the tone of the conversation, I sang him one of the *bhajans* I learned at Kumarji's and Vasuthai's feet.

"That's nice; you pronounce the Hindi well. But what is the purpose of this song? Is singing it part of your *sadhana*? What does it mean to you?"

I didn't know what to say. Why should I have to defend the joy of competent Hindustani singing? I looked at Judi, as if to say, "see what I mean about this curmudgeonly little Polish Jew?"

Maurice continued, "As I listen to you sing, I still get the sense that something is missing. You are uncooked, incomplete in some way. And you are not going to change that by simply hopping from ashram to ashram like spiritual tourists." As he glanced at Judi, who listened with great sympathy for her Puer, his demeanor softened.

Maurice went on. "Try to make this missing ingredient the focus of your meditation. Perhaps you don't have the heart-quality for *japa*. Try discursive meditation."

"What's that?"

"In discursive meditation you penetrate, try to work through a thought or a problem. You must bring this before the Maharshi when you go to the ashram."

I nodded attentively.

"If you do persist with some form of *japa*, the importance is not the mantra so much as the *gap* between mantras. Focus there, where nothing happens. The goal is to expand this gap until it is continuous."

Sitting here in the Vellore Hospital, challenged yet again by this wiry little hunchback, I recalled the intense young American monk in Bangkok who had asked me if I had ever observed the space between thoughts and his disgust at my affirmative answer. Well, if I once had, I certainly wasn't finding much success in catching it again.

But meeting Judi perked Maurice up. At least this wayward seeker had chosen a wife who would firmly tread the path, setting him an example. She was not only a sincere, strong-willed seeker, but also someone I could *serve*, perhaps unraveling my cocoon of self-absorption.

"Your wife is your guru."

I was startled.

"Don't you know the story from the Vedas? In an auspicious house the man always prostrates to the women as goddess: servant, wife, daughter, grandmother." He saw my doubtful look. "I'm not joking. Now that you have been smart enough to marry this woman, your job is to look out for her needs. And the little one's," he added in his reedy voice, smiling his thin-lipped smile.

Judi, who was always regular as clockwork, had missed her period and was convinced she was pregnant. When he heard this, Maurice chuckled, telling us he had recently dreamed of people singing, "We're gonna have a baby" over and over. Since we were at a regional hospital, she took the pregnancy test. It was positive. Modern medicine and the Guru agreed. Judi's immediate concern was to remain as healthy as possible during our remaining time in India, which we expected to be at least four more months. And Puer?

I am deposed from the throne as of now. Dig it.

I've always loved nicknames, playing with, inventing, re-inventing new variations. In Japan, I started calling Judi "Takuji." I learned from a swami in Vrindaban this was one of Krishna's names, meaning "Lord of my heart." So I had been preparing. It was now a matter of becoming fully conscious of it, living a continuous prayer, rather than indulging in romantic play. I called the new life in her womb "Little Atman," little soul-breath.

Maurice continued. "When you go to see a saint, just *love* them. Don't have any expectations. They all say the same thing about awareness, the Buddha, Ananda Mayee Ma, Krishnamurthi. You need to practice awareness all day long, from the time you wake in the morning until the last flicker of waking consciousness at night. Buddha said that being steadily aware for two weeks produces Realization. He also said that with no obstacles to normal spiritual development one should attain Realization by twenty-eight to thirty-five years. The rishis say that with devoted effort, it can be attained in six years. So there you are. The choice is yours."

"I still haven't really made a choice, Maurice. I want to be free, unencumbered by commitments. Yeah, I know, this defeats the purpose of spiritual work." I recalled Maurice's offer to join the "fellowship of the undeceived" five years earlier, uncomfortably aware that I remained outside the fellowship. Now he was matter-of-factly inviting me again.

"We don't make the decisions which lead to events in our lives. Life leads us where it will, directed by the universal computer. We feed in new data by our acts, and it processes the data. We must learn to accept this destiny, churned out moment by moment by the computer, in fact to *love* it. Karma is love."

"I thought karma was the cycle of divine rewards and retribution, based precisely on our actions."

"You're confusing karma and the computer. They are two different concepts. Everything in the stream of life is for our ultimate liberation." Maurice studied my face, then forged on.

"The mind, heart, and will must be integrated. It's not enough to think good thoughts. The mind cannot train the heart. And if thoughts do not become deeds, then what's the use? The mind must know, the heart must love, and the organism act through a will in perfect synchronism with that knowing and loving."

Puer struggled to assimilate his prickly teacher with the reedy voice. "Let's see if I have this. So, given the day's numerous choices, each a crossroads of karma, there is only one right way at each crossroad? The form of action may differ somewhat, but the motive decision is only one: the truthful and loving way. Right?"

Maurice barely nodded. He was on a roll. "Take my relationship with Miss Petit. It is my job to take care of her. I decided that when I moved into her apartment in Bombay. I've surrendered myself to this. So I am not bothered by all kinds of decisions about what to do with my life, which would deflect my energy. I am free always to live the inner life. Having an orderly, simple lifestyle likewise gives one freedom. Every day is perfect monotony... and perfect freedom."

We did not get to meet her during our short visit and her busy rounds, but another manifestation of Maurice's devotion was his adopted daughter, now an internist at this same Vellore hospital. He had told me about her arrival in his life, abandoned on the landing beneath the "Tibetan Refugee Center" sign. Tiny, emaciated, and shriveled she "looked like a skinny rat who had been flushed from the river, barely alive." Nursed to health, she became a beloved daughter.

The next morning, we left Maurice and the quietly resting Hilla Petit to journey to the temple town of Tiruvanamalai. Puer summed up the day's lesson: *Maurice made me see quite clearly that my searching after perfect fulfillment, perfect happiness, the perfect place, was a lie to myself. As he put it, I was 'cheating.' The question is not can this job or this community satisfy me, but what can I offer? He pointed instead to choosing a place which would be appropriate for raising Little Atman, get a teaching job, and give. Nothing else needed, no trapesing about searching for a more perfect place.*

As the Episcopal prayer-book reads, "Service is perfect freedom."

18 Tiruvanamalai and Ramana Maharshi

The pilgrims left Vellore with Maurice's blessing to visit the ashram in Tiruvannamalai which had grown up around Ramana Maharshi. The South Indian countryside was lush and green: neat cottages, coconut palms, farmers plowing rich reddish-brown earth with sturdy wooden plows behind magnificent creamy white bullocks. Though many of the cottages had thatched roofs and waddled dung walls, the people looked more prosperous than rural folk in the North. As we neared the ashram, the rolling hills gave way to ancient, gently cragged mountains. Looking over at Judi, I met her smile, happy that she was accompanying me to *this* ashram. Once among those mountains, I dropped into a state of wonder that continued through our arrival. We later learned that the Eastern Ghats were among the oldest mountains on Earth.

Tiruvannamalai in 1973 had a population of thirty thousand, a typical South Indian temple town with a large, magnificently sculpted temple, Arunachaleshwar, defining the main square. Its precincts were huge, comprising eighteen acres, laid out in the classic style, with a towering central *mandir*, smaller outlying ones at each wall. Puer's misty dawn photo renders an organic quality—something like a human body, with head, arms, feet, dominated by a central heart-place. That is the idea of a South Indian temple, representing the body of the Creator, Purusha, as he materialized into the cosmos.

But most striking of all was the mountain overlooking the town, which ashram inmates simply call "the hill." Though only half a mile high, Arunachala dominates the countryside. It has an ancient, primordial feel to it, a Grandfather with huge boulders strewn all about, like the aftermath of war between Olympians and Titans. It is predominately laterite, the red mineral characteristic to the whole range, accented by the yellows and browns of winter grasses. The colors in the early mornings (*arun*, dawn) and evenings are particularly beautiful, subtly changing minute by minute.

We came here because this was the place Maurice's beloved Master Ramana, born Venkataraman, came after his realization. Devotees call him *Bhagavan*, an incarnation of the Lord. Maurice had given me his photo five years before to anchor my meditation; now I would have the added reinforcement of basking in the Maharshi's earthly place for several weeks. The usual length of stay for westerners was three days, but we carried a letter from Swami Chidananda recommending that the ashram accept us for a longer sojourn, since we were serious pilgrims. It felt eminently right, as I wrote home:

December 1973

It is extremely peaceful at Sri Ramanaji's simple and humble abode beneath the sacred mountain Arunachala. There is a powerful presence here, personified in the bodily form of the sage Ramana, and continuing to manifest in the laterite of the huge red (fire) mountain, really not material at all. Legend has it that Siva once manifested himself as a lingam of light, later transmuting into the present-day mountain. When queried on whether things were different around here since Sri Ramana died (1950), one of his old devotees said, "I never considered Maharshi to be a person." The Grace which i need so much to undergird my puny efforts at so-called "spiritual life" has begun to flow here more and more evenly. ... Believe me, being Phi Beta Kappa is absolutely no help on this path.

How Ramana came to Tiruvanamalai is classic in its simplicity, like everything about the sage. At age sixteen, this South Indian brahmin went into his room, lay down, held his breath, and experienced death. As he felt his body grow cold, he realized that the Self lived on. After an indeterminate period, he rose, but never left this realization, living out of its unassailable certainty from then on. Having heard the sacred mountain Arunachala mentioned by a visiting uncle, he realized it was his "Father." A few months later, after stealing a few rupees from his brother, he journeyed here by train and foot, ending at the great temple Arunachaleshwar at the mountain's base. He entered *samadhi*, living on virtually nothing in a cave-like room underneath the thousand-pillared hall, oblivious to the insect-bites covering his skeletal body.

After this, the adolescent sage moved to the mountain, and at each of his cave-dwellings, devotees followed, establishing shrines. His mother tried in vain for years to convince her son to return home, but finally joined him. It was only then that he agreed to let devotees build a dwelling for her comfort at the base of the sacred hill. An ashram grew up around her grave after she died, which Ramana accepted, though unsought. The sage lived there, ministering to the animals and souls of the faithful who flocked to him, until his painful death from a sarcoma in the arm. At the moment of his death, a large meteor appeared in the sky over Arunachala that was seen widely. In faraway Bombay, Hilla Petit reported seeing it from her porch on Nepean Sea Road.

We arrived at an auspicious time. Deepam, which the northerners call Diwali, was the day after our arrival. In fact, several festivals intersected our stay. For Hindus, life is a series of auspicious moments just waiting to happen, and you pass your time waiting for the next one by celebrating as many festivals as you can. We joined a group of mostly European devotees to climb the sacred hill. That night on its crest a flame flickered visibly. December 9, 1973. *Last night the Fire of the Universe was incarnate on Arunachala. As we walked round the mountain, i thought how appropriate a time it was. The sun is now in Sagittarius, a fire sign. Judith is carrying a baby who will be born under a fire sign, Leo. Our marriage, which we are about to re-consecrate, was symbolized by fire—fire in the hearth, fire on our wedding bands, fire in our hearts.*

This awareness of the fire-child framed our entire time at Ramanasramam, which extended, with a couple of breaks, until January 20. It began as a missed period, was confirmed as a pregnancy by a woman ob-gyn in Vellore, finally blossoming into a whole mythic panoply texturing our thoughts, dreams, and fantasies.

Life at the ashram was much quieter and slower than it had been at Sivananda Ashram in Rishikesh. During Ramana's lifetime, there were scripture readings twice daily and regular sessions where devotees would sit silently in his presence or pose questions, spoken and unspoken, which he invariably answered. Now, other than the continuing ritual of scripture readings, nothing much happened. This meant Sanskrit or Tamil, vibes for us, not conceptual understanding. Without language, it was like *satsang* with Ananda Mayee Ma. Only this time I felt at home and deeply connected to the teacher. As the devotees insisted, he had never left.

Before breakfast the second day, I dragged myself through darkness for morning meditation along with Judi. You could still sit in the "Old Hall" where Ramana received visitors, which retained tremendous power for me. The room was kept just as it was the moment he died. There was the divan where he would prop himself with bolsters, the plastered walls a chalky baby blue. Directly behind the divan was a stand that supported two clocks, which he always set meticulously. Next to the stand was a reading light, its scalloped plastic shade the color of mother-of-pearl. The divan was covered with print spreads of unmatched colors and patterns. From photos I knew that underneath should have been the tigerskin rug upon which he sat, traditional seat of the rishi who had mastered desire and felt no fear. I oddly missed those glassy vacant tiger eyes I had often seen in photos, so incongruous beneath the Master's penetrating, yet loving gaze.

This morning perhaps fifteen people sat in the hall, mostly Indians. I sat down creakily and stiffly, adjusting myself into a modified half-lotus on the cool floor. As usual, I needed to change positions often, though I probably lasted almost twenty minutes in my first postural set. We grouped ourselves around the large photo of Ramana propped on the divan, smiling out at us, long legs stretching out from a loincloth that looked like big diapers. The atmosphere was very peaceful, and I appreciated the relaxed style, contrasting with the formality of Sivananda Ashram.

After breakfast I was overtaken by my usual wave of tiredness and returned to our room for a little nap. When I got up, the Old Hall drew me back. Nobody else was there, so I could have a personal audience with the Master, just the two of us. I also knew that he didn't care how I sat, and so I was able to relax even more, freely letting one knee pop up in the same posture I used for playing *tanpura*—much more comfortable than half-lotus. It didn't take long for my question to take form. "Bhagavan, why can't I take my sadhana more seriously, actually treading the Path which I so clearly see before me? Why do I continue to hold back?"

The Master seemed to look at me. It was eerie. I felt like he was on the verge of a response and held very still. Nothing at first. Then, it felt like he was saying, "Okay. We have our question, something to work on while you are here. Keep it before you as much as you can."

We met some of the older Indian devotees, even more Westerners, including an intelligent, well-scrubbed, *sattwic* group of Europeans who shared a loose community in Paris, alternating with extended periods at Sri Ramanasramam. Their leader was a German homeopath, Hugo Maier, a longtime ashram resident. Hugo was friendly in a fatherly kind of way, easily accepting the deference the other Europeans showed him, as well as some of the Indians. Our favorite "old-timer" was Raja Iyer, who introduced himself our second day: "Good morrow and welcome to Bhagavan Sri Ramanaji's asramam. You are new here, I think?"

We smiled agreement, bowing in *namaste*.

Rajaji smiled broadly, then grew little-boy serious, bowing deeply in profound *namaste*. "And from which country you are coming?"

"We are Americans."

"Ah, Americans. We have had so many Americans come here. And Europeans. People from all over the world. Just last week there was a Japanese man.... But you must know all this."

We smiled and nodded.

"Myself, I am Raja Iyer, ex-postmaster of the asramam. I am retired you see."

He then took us to the post office, which he showed us with obvious pride. It had its own "Sri Ramanana Asramam" origin stamp. Raja reported the many famous persons who had written letters to Ramana that he had personally delivered. The young queen of Denmark wrote for many years, finally visiting a few years back. "The queen and her new husband sponsored a huge feast. It was like something out of the *Mahabharata*, a wedding feast. The poor lined up on one side, the saddhus on the other. The lines stretched far beyond the gates." Rajaji looked up at Grandfather Arunachala, adding wistfully, "It was like old times again for just a few days."

We took meals in the ashram refectory. At the entrance was a hand pump for washing hands. Inside, you sat on the floor, filling in the rows set with stitched banana-leaves. Serving boys stood by the walls, quickly placing more leaf-settings when a rush of hungry devotees arrived. Breakfasts were either *iddly* or *uppama*, both served with delicious coconut-based chutneys, crushed coriander seed and fresh green peppers, sometimes garlic. I especially loved the *iddlies*, a dumpling made from fermented dal and rice, served with hot ghee. At Sivananda Ashram I never got quite enough to eat, being unable to sufficiently gorge myself during the brief meal-sittings, but here the servers, both boys and older men, would smile as they indulged me. Dinners were simple, standard South Indian meals with a lot of rice and usually *sambhar*, a savory spiced broth of tomatoes and dal, with seasonal vegetables thrown in. Sometimes there was a side vegetable, always plenty of yogurt. Though simple, the food was perfectly prepared, everything fresh. It was like home cooking.

In the North, we learned to eat with our hands. But it was customary to use *chapathi* to scoop or enfold the food. Here in the South, diners would actually knead their food thoroughly before swilling it into their mouths. North Indians, after deftly sweeping the immediate area, piling and mixing, would cuff the food in clawlike fashion to the mouth. Some appeared quite dainty in the act, especially marriageable young women. But down South eating was more like finger-painting. Instead of pressing outward just enough to include some of every substance to be mixed for the mouthful, the fingers deeply splayed, pushing across the banana leaf, then sweeping back.

Communal eating brings people together in celebration daily. But eating like this was more like a lovefest. The sensual delight, the re-entry into the touch-world of the very young child, was liberating. With little conversation, undertaken in low murmurs, the dominant sound was swilling, a little slurping, and smacking. We were a pack of happy monkeys. At the end of the meal my fingers would be wrinkled and shriveled as if I had been swimming. Mutually smiling, inmates would operate the hand pump for each other in turn as we left the refectory with pasty hands.

We made *pradakshina* (circumperegrination) of all the key sites, the Stations of Ramana, including visits to Skandashram on the lower slopes of the mountain, and to the dank cell under the main temple where the teen boy had spent the first several months in deep absorption. But Arunachala was the main attraction, either to walk along its slopes on our own, or to mount with the crowds on feast days.

At the Deepam festival, crowds climbed the mountain-god to contribute little pots of ghee to the vat which burned through the night's festival of light. Devotees experienced that light as *jyothi*, the feminine inner light burning at the heart of creation. I remember especially one ample old woman trudging upslope all the way to the top, breathing heavily. But the look on her face when she arrived was more *jyothi* than pain. At the top was a young Dravidian man, his skin almost as dark as the oft-used black cauldron, receiving the buttery gifts, which he deftly poured into the smoking pot. I chafed at the waste of all that *ghee* in this poor country.

Yesterday afternoon, the awe of that long line of people snaking up Arunachala. The flashes of sunlight glinting from little pots of ghee. A human thread interspersed with occasional jewels of light. Light going to light, brilliant sparkles from the body of this long devout Python headed for its cauldron.

After descent from the sacred cauldron, we discussed our blessings.

"It's like being in Jerusalem for Passover," I said.

"I was thinking the same thing," Judi said. "We'll be there next summer with the folks."

"The crowds, setting up tents in the field, bringing horses and bullocks for trading, the *bhava* of a religious festival—it's like the Jews of old. ... But no *pesach* lamb." Suddenly I thought of Little Atman, and then of the Easter Sunday in Kinston at Gran Howard's church when Judi and I had been so moved by the sermon that she was crying openly and I had tears in my eyes. We almost answered the Eastern Carolina pastor's altar call.

Judi broke my reverie. "The people here are so humble and simple—not at all like the madness in Benares for Diwali, with all those firecrackers and cars honking."

I thought of the air of expectancy as sundown arrived, the hands going together instinctively at the chest or the forehead, touching the third eye marked with ash, all eyes fixed on the mountain top fire which superseded the sun.

Then I remembered my behavior on the way up.

As usual Judi climbed ahead of me, and I struggled to catch up. As I pushed past one man, he reached out his hand to slow me down. "Good sir, do you realize why we are here?"

A few days later, returning from a visit to the main temple and market, we witnessed a chilling accident. Careening widely around a curve in typical fashion, a bus driver smashed into a horse-tonga. The horse took the brunt of the collision, but the tonga-driver appeared also to have a concussion. The panicked bus driver immediately ran from the scene, heading for the scrub forest at the town's edge, leaving the bus diagonally blocking the road. Several of the male passengers lit out after him, an instant vigilante posse.

At this point Hugo Maier arrived, his handsome Germanic face framed by closely cropped curly brindled blonde hair, wearing his usual colored lungi sans shirt, barrel-chested like a *mridangam* (South Indian drum) player. Judi had already spoken to the driver, who was being attended by paramedics and female relatives, quickly on the scene (his male relatives had presumably joined the vigilante mob). Hugo and Judi knelt on the pavement to look after the horse, who was still alive but had multiple fractures and was bleeding profusely. Hugo ran back to his bungalow to get a syringe and sufficient poison to put the dear beast out of his misery. I approached to comfort the tonga driver, who had plunged into a deep depression. He could only look at me dully.

After administering the injection, Hugo explained to us that Tamil Nadu had no clear laws governing fault in such instances, so the police tolerated a certain amount of vigilante action. As for the tonga driver, the horse and rig were everything he had. He faced certain ruin.

When we arrived at the hospital the following day, the man was in a large open ward, lying with his head bandaged in red and white checked scarves. We commiserated with him through facial and hand gestures. He tried very hard to smile. We handed him a hundred rupees, much less then he would need to purchase a new horse, and he broke into tears. Perhaps they represented gratitude, but I think the insufficient gift chiefly reminded him of the impossibility of ever recovering from this blow. The whole scene was deadeningly somber.

The crowds of people came and went, but the regulars kept a low profile. There were many animals around, especially peacocks, monkeys, and cattle. Bhagavan loved animals. He fed them often and was a keen observer of their behavior, often pointing to them as a kind of living Aesop's exemplar. One of his closest devotees told of his first visit to Ramana at Skandashram. He had told himself that whatever Ramana told him when he arrived, the first utterance, would give him direction for the rest of his life. Ramana was fixing a thin porridge, shallow bowls awaiting their humble contents. The Master quickly finished, and asked the man, a highly educated brahmin, to give the plates to the dogs, waiting in the shadows. Dogs in India are usually treated simply as scavengers, more like jackals than our pampered pooches. And a brahmin is not supposed to touch lower caste folk, let alone a dog.

I found living at the ashram immensely soothing, and the peace and depth steadily began to sink in. Judi was in her "floating" mode as she later called it. Though she was not drawn to this teacher, she drank in the atmosphere and continued japa meditation with her own mantra.

The night before we were to leave for a Christmas trip to the cape, we went for a short walk through the sparsely peopled ochre dirt lanes opposite the ashram, strolling through flower gardens maintained at ashram expense, patrolled by peacocks. We crossed the lightly trafficked road, a warm breeze bearing a hint of jasmine commingled with the smell of cow manure. Judi wore the blue-printed sari with purple and white border she had purchased in Varanasi. I wore my usual white kurta, but now that we were in the South, had switched from pyjama pants to a magenta *lungi*. We shared the road with a bullock-cart driven by a leathery cocoa-skinned farmer swaddled in white dhoti, turbaned against the winter sun by white cotton, and a brightly colored horse tonga carrying an ample woman in a rich silk sari. The thin driver clucked at the spare-ribbed horse as a few bicyclists passed, dhotis or saris wrapped tightly to avoid the spokes. It was late December, and the sun set rapidly.

When we reached our room it was growing dark. I unlocked the padlock, and we went in. The quarters were somewhat roomier than at Sivananda Ashram, and we had some luxuries: a small sink in the corner of the room and mosquito netting. Tonight Judi lit candles, putting one on either side of the wash basin. She unwrapped her sari, removed her sari blouse and washed her face and underarms. I moved the little desk from the corner over near the basin and wrote a brief entry in my journal, sharing the candlelight while she washed her hair. When she was done, she wrapped her head in a thin towel, and I quickly took a half-bath, gripping the basin as I washed each of my dusty feet in turn.

Judi doused one candle, placing the other on the table between the two beds, and we ducked under the mosquito netting into one of them. We sat facing each other in half-lotus, the candle flickering on her face, framed by wet tendrils of dark hair.

"So where will we live?" she asked. The baby was due in August, and we were meeting her folks in Jerusalem in May. It didn't leave much time to get prepared.

"Well, we have our community in Birmingham. We need to get land as soon as possible." But I knew this wouldn't be soon enough.

"We're going to have to support ourselves right away. Who knows when we'll get land—housing is even more important. I can't expect much maternity leave."

"I hadn't really thought about that. Jyothi Mary really changes things," I said, the reality of our situation starting to sink in.

"What do you think about going to Kinston and staying with Gran while I have the baby? Rudi's there and I trust him," she went on.

"I don't know about Kinston. I'm afraid I'd feel enmeshed. It's so amazing to think that we could almost live *here*. I mean a two-bedroom bungalow with meals for eighteen hundred rupees a month...."

"We could live on that with interest on our savings, if you figured it at ten percent. Of course, there'd be travel and clothes and school for Jyothi Mary. ... We probably don't have quite enough," she replied.

"But you could work in the local hospital. And maybe I could teach English. We could do it—I'm just not sure I want to."

"My main concern is prenatal care and a competent ob-gyn for the delivery." She was practical, as usual.

"Think of it. Living here the rest of our lives after working another couple of years. But what would we *do*?" I asked.

"Hugo seems to manage all-right."

I thought a minute and shook my head. "It would be too perfect."

But Judi was not finished. "We'd have to learn Tamil. And we'd have to figure what to do about Little Atman's education. But if this is what we want, we could make it work. Whatever we decide, we've got to make a plan. This baby's on its way."

I looked at her thin serene face, the dark curly strands of hair starting to soften as they dried, and reached my hands around her stomach, trying to imagine this new life which didn't register yet as a thickening. It was good to be playing house, finally. Ramana always counseled devotees that the life of a *sannyasin* was rarely appropriate, and that most of us should be householders, living as ordinary a life as possible. Now that she was pregnant, Judi had become a householder and wife, embodying a different field, no longer playing the holy woman.

We curled up in each other's arms, Judi in sari slip and fresh blouse, me in fresh lungi. A few mosquitoes came prospecting at our curtain, and I looked up at the dark ceiling, listening intently for their whine, thankful to hear but little. She was soon sleeping heavily on my shoulder.

19 Mary and Joseph in the Deep South

As Puer had done with Goa in 1968, we sought a Christian setting for Christmas and New Year's, this time at Kanya Kumari, the subcontinent's cape. En route, we spent a couple of days near Coimbatore in Chettipalayam with Swami Satchidananda's brothers' families. They were prosperous but simple brahmin farmers, extremely warm, hospitable and generous, proud to show us their fields and healthy animals. It surprised me that the women cooked on an earthen charcoal hearth with inadequate ventilation, as in the poorest of homes. The kitchen was black with soot, the women hunched from leaning over the stove. Leaving, I wrote home:

We are both—apparently all three—quite well. Heading tomorrow for Christian Kerala, seeking a Christmas home. I keep feeling like Mary and Joseph—who also didn't know where they would spend Christmas. Particularly last night as we rode by ox-cart beneath a huge starry sky which harbored a large comet, as yet unseen. Om Shanti.

We made our way by bus and train from Judi's New York Swami's village to the cape via Coimbatore, Madurai and Trivandrum, where we spent a tough morning trying to catch a bus for the cape. Now there's a train from Bombay which follows the coastline all the way, but in 1974 the journey was more arduous. The large depot lot was jammed with people, and each time a bus arrived, the crowd jostled for position. All seats were unreserved. Twice our bus for the cape appeared, but we were pushed aside by more experienced travelers. The second time, Judi got lost in the crowd surging in front of me. When I saw her again, she was gasping for breath, sandwiched between two corpulent men. I was furious, screaming at the top of my lungs, "Hey, that's my wife. She's pregnant; let her pass! Can't you stupid people show any manners?"

People looked at me with a mixture of concern, bemusement and pure neutrality. Hoarse with useless shouting, I reached Judi just after she had dropped back with several others who failed to squeeze onto the vehicle. More shaken than she, I embraced her: "Are you all-right? You don't think you had a miscarriage?"

Her face drawn and jaw still set, she answered, "I'm okay.... It's too soon to worry about physical pressure on the baby."

I was relieved, but still angry and very frustrated about the bus. Then I realized how absurd I must've seemed. How many of the women around us in this over-fertile country were in various stages of pregnancy, yet throwing themselves into the fray with abandon? What an overprotective wimp I was. When the third bus came, most people who wanted to go in our direction had already left, and the crowd was manageable. We made the bus, even got seats.

Kanya Kumari, the cape of India washed by three oceans, is a Hindu pilgrimage site, a fine place for a tropical Christmas, with magnificent beaches and the requisite Catholic churches. The leathery fishermen plied skiffs with aerodynamic sails resembling a school of sharks darting about. The fisherfolk were very friendly as we hung out with them on shore where the boats brought in the catch and they spread their nets to dry.

The Lord shone upon this piece of flesh and rags today. Beautiful sea, sand, rock, sun, palms, brownie kids, white smiles. Simple, elemental. Scant speech. A tinge of Christmas in the air. Running by the sea, feeling young, boyish. WHO AM I?

We stayed at a clean and comfortable dharamsala, Meenakshi Bhavan. The South Indian meals were solid, and I enjoyed the beach while Judi read scriptures. But on Christmas eve, I caught the India Sickness again and was bedridden. I had planned to take Judi to re-experience the incredible, sudden view of the cape mountains rising above palm-fringed waters beyond the rocks and eloquently angled fishing boats with white skin like old, vulture-picked bones bleached by the sun. To bathe in quiet pools. To go to Suchindrum Siva Temple. To attend Midnight Mass at the large cathedral downtown on Christmas morn. Plans, plans. But the Lord disposed the day as usual, exposing these plans with severe clarity.

Christmas morning, we waited for a four-thirty AM bus to ferry us to a junction to meet the Trivandrum-Madras express. We were going to stay in Kathy's old flat where her sister now lived in Madras. I felt better, though tired. We passed at least a dozen little gaily-lit Catholic churches through whose doors we could observe pre-dawn services—my glimpse of their Christmas. As we waited in the darkness by the road for the bus, along came a truckload of cheering carolers, replete with Santa Claus, who waved.

We shared Kathy's old flat with sister Debby and her Keralite Christian boyfriend. It was your standard suburban high-rise flat, replete with security features. Madras was hosting a superb line-up of Indian music and dance, and on the third night we attended a concert by Subalakshmi—India's most renowned female classical vocalist—seated on the stage with pools of water dripping from our rain-soaked clothes. Suddenly I was seized with severe chills and the runs. Moments before, at dazzlingly close range, I was delighting at the interplay of sound with the glinting reflection of spotlights from her nose-jewels, and now I was wrenched in the gut with acute pain and a desperate fear that I wouldn't be able to make it to the john. I hung on until the end of a mercifully short composition, tumbled off the stage and ran for the toilet.

After two days of severe nausea, diarrhea and vomiting, Debby became alarmed by my illness, imagining she saw a yellow cast to my skin, though my physician wife did not. She was nervous, almost panicky to get her jaundiced guest out of the flat. Disease in India surrounds you, and you do everything you can to guard the woefully porous boundaries of the flesh. I didn't blame her for banishing me.

December 28, 1973. *i am struck down with queasiness. The winds howl beneath gray skies and hints of rain. This is a lonely place where Kathy lived. Look in the mirror at the familiar boyish face: the cruel full mouth, the weak chin, the warm eyes looking for the ever-flowing breast, knowing at the same time that they will never find it. What's missing in this unbaked cake?*

Suddenly this day has become very much like one in Indore almost five years ago—early-mid January, the annual nadir of despair. Grey sky, a feeling of absence, and the upwelling of desire from my soul to be whole once and for all. The desire rested on several significant women, from Leah, the closest manifestation of shakti, to Mother Virginia. Nowhere did i find peace, consolation. i was desolate. No woman, *i realized, could fulfill this incompleteness, this yawning absence.*

Now i have the same desire, the same despair, welling from the core, yet i am married to a woman i adore as goddess-Devi. Still the sense of being left alone and incomplete.

In the examples of these two days, five years apart. . . . i begin to see more clearly what Maurice has been talking about. For in both cases i first perceive myself as nothing, worthless, incomplete, and then try to see how to fill that self up. But the perceived self and the filling are both unreal. The expression of this is always in the realm of kama, desire. What can i get, how can i be whole and happy and blissful like a babe at the World Breast, willfully ignoring I AM THAT I AM. *The whole question is wrongly put, the whole game self-defeating and intrinsically painful, binding to Maya.*

The realization that my problem right now is one of dharma, not moksha, points the way out of this deepening mess, compounded by age and habit, samskaras piled upon samskaras cutting a rut as deep as an iron phonograph needle in soap. For the false view of moksha is just the quintessence of this maddening disease "I-want," missing the point that moksha is from start to finish a selfless operation. . . . The more i look at it, the more it's clear that this reassessment from the treetop where i was flung by the storm at Sivananda Ashram was the first step in the dawning realization. . . . It is dharma i have neglected more than anything else. It is dharma Mother was calling me to in her own way over five years ago as i embarked on my sojourn in the land of moksha (and i severely bit her back for this piece of untimely advice). It is dharma that Doc Armstrong has been calling me to for several years: "You may call yourself what you want, but you will teach English." It is dharma my father has called me to, so concerned that I have a job.

And so it was of dharma that Maurice not so gently reminded me at Vellore. He pointed clearly to the dharma of my situation: i have a pregnant wife and no home to take her to. Equally clearly, he pointed to the element of ashram-hopping in our proposed travels South. . . .

So i am blessed by the situation. i know exactly what i must do; whereas five years ago i could not respond to the call of dharma because my whole existence was by definition without it. And i am fairly sure this is why so many young converts to the "spiritual life" lose their enthusiasm after several years. i must become perfect in dharma before i even attempt moksha. As the sage responded when asked to sum up the Hindu aims of life, "Dharma."

The place Debby arranged for me was an excellent choice, the nearby Nature Cure Hospital, definitely part of a real neighborhood, with little shops, street-life, motley smells (oh, the queasiness, that attraction/repulsion response to the Hindu palate of smells when you're gut-sick and wasted). I was treated with all kinds of naturopathic therapies, including enemas, steam baths for the hip, green mud packs imported from France plastered upon my stomach, and fasting. When I emerged a week later, I felt my best in years. It was a real cleansing.

We Lose Little Atman

We arrived back at Ramanasramam January 7, in time for Ramana's *Jayanthi* celebration, reckoned by the lunar calendar as January 9 (he was born December 30, 1879). Pongal, the South's New Year's harvest celebration, followed shortly after. This time we stayed at Rhoda McIver's garden guesthouse. Rhoda was the wealthy widow of one of Ramanaji's longtime disciples, who built her a beautiful bungalow. She augmented that beauty by her love of flowers and shrubs. She was an extremely kind, generous hostess who gave us afternoon tea, inquiring keenly about our ashram activities.

But our private celebrations were premature. Arriving back at Tiruvanamalai, Judi had noticed a spot and worried it was a miscarriage. The first pregnancy test had rendered a false positive. The diagnosis for her first-ever missed period was malnutrition and the stress of excessive travel. Thus our Christmas fantasies turned out to be doubly dashed, first by my illness, then by the results of this second pregnancy test. The "unseen comet" of the Advent oxcart trip never materialized.

Judi was disappointed. Nevertheless, she appeared stoically to accept the false pregnancy. But she clearly did not like the professional embarrassment of being duped by poor science. And Puer? The whole episode had shaken him, shocked him into recognition of incipient fatherhood—if not now, then soon:

I see that my notion of freedom was false ... what i want most of all is to fulfill my dharma in this life and be a father and family man. ... To make room for another being to share Judi's mother-love, which would be a good kick in the ass for young Scrooge.

So we proceeded without delay in efforts to *purposefully* conceive a child, right there in Rhoda McIver's guesthouse. According to Vedanta, sex within the marriage union is not only proper for the purposes of conception; it is even celebrated. But I find it hard to believe all those erotic temple carvings are purely in service of childbearing.

We joined a group of quietly enthusiastic ashramites led by Hugo for a *pradakshina* eight miles around the mountain Bhagavan called Father to honor his *jayanthi*. We set out jauntily at midnight, heartily singing the "Arunachala Shiva" hymn (in boringly basic raga Bilawal, India's C-major). It was chilly, and I was glad the pace was crisp, since I was not quite dressed warmly enough in my dhoti, kurta, and light wool shawl. Judi was ecstatic in her white sari with gold-trimmed aquamarine border, going barefoot, as did Hugo and most of the Indians. She was once again "floating." I worried about all those worms embedded in the dusty road, waiting to cross her sole's membrane, but hell, I once bathed in the Ganga at Benares, heedless of worse threats. I was tired when we go back. Judi glowed.

Near the end of our stay at Ramanasramam, which had begun to feel like home, I went for one last vigil in the Old Hall. I frequently felt a sense of peace, but this time a deeper current steadily surged through me, washing away all my cares, especially the concerns about how to meditate. Though I had sometimes forced myself to lie prostrate at the foot of his divan, today it happened spontaneously. I felt myself emptying like a spilled vessel; no fear, only deep joy and relief that I finally had sufficient devotion to receive this overflowing grace. I cried with gratitude, body shaking, lying there for a long time. Rising from the floor, I looked at his face which just smiled at me, totally accepting. "Yes, this is it." I did not want to leave, but my karmic life insinuated itself again, and I found myself walking out into the clear sunny day of the ashram courtyard, among the stately prancing peacocks.

20 Bombay: Death and A Blast from Morris

At Maurice's urging, we returned to Bombay in late January to attend two public lectures by J. Krishnamurthi, making one last pilgrimage to the holy town of Kanchipuram with its panoply of splendid temples before leaving the South. We also went to see the aged heir to the spiritual position of the great reformer-teacher Shankaracharya. At a modest little cement block cottage on the outskirts of town, we sat in quiet meditation with a few other devotees, looking in the barred window at the peaceful old man resting in his bed.

That afternoon Judi sat rapt in one of the large temples while I scurried about taking photographs. Catching the bus to the train station to board the Madras-Bombay express, I was late as usual, preoccupied with finding the perfect photo. As I sprinted after the moving bus, Judi held out her hand. I just managed to jump onto the running board after losing my lungi, which I gathered in one hand as the camera bounced on my belly.

On our way north, Judi got down at the Lonavala Institute for yoga and ayurvedic medicine. She would stay a couple of days before joining me in Bombay. Once in Bombay, I went straight to Maurice's by the Nepean Sea. Maurice was out, but Arvind came by, breathlessly running around like the White Rabbit, making arrangements for the Krishnamurthi events. We had talked about accommodations the last time I was in town, when he said, "Don't worry, all will be arranged," which I understood to mean that he would work something out. Many foreign and Indian visitors were in town for the occasion, including some of Maurice's close friends who were staying with him at Mrs. Petit's. Seeing my gear on the living room floor, Arvind assumed all was taken care of. I was anxious to talk to him about our accommodations. Caught in his White Rabbit mode, he put me off, promising to return in the afternoon to talk further. Arvind did not return that day, so I spent the night on the couch at the Indo-Tibetan Refugee Center while the invited guests occupied upstairs bedrooms.

The next day Maurice spoke to me after breakfast. "So, have you made your arrangements yet?"

Comfortable in my set-up at the hearth of the guru, I was taken aback. "I thought Arvind had taken care of that. He said yesterday that he would tell me the arrangements, but he—"

Maurice interrupted, confronting me with more cold fury than I had ever known. "You have no right to expect Arvind—or me—to take care of you. He has a lot to worry about right now, and you are not his responsibility. You are tourists, and like other tourists you are quite able to make your own accommodations. I find your presence here exceedingly unmannerly. You were not invited, we have limited accommodations, and you've just settled in like you were an old family friend. You are impolite, unconcerned about others, an encroacher and a grazer-goat. I must ask you to leave."

I had never felt such rejection in my life. I immediately choked with tears of self-pity from a sense of betrayal. I tried a few times to speak, but it was impossible, a huge knotted ganglion of rejection in my throat. Arvind, who had slipped in the door in time to witness the Teacher's rage, was horrified. He was incredibly gentle, and tried to calm Maurice down enough to let me speak. But every time I was given the space, words failed me. Finally I was able to blurt out my sense of betrayal, "Because Arvind said ..." Damn Arvind, preoccupied with everything but his promise to me.

Maurice was unimpressed. "Don't bring Arvind into this. You are not his responsibility, and even if you heard promises from him, you should simply have taken them as a gesture of good-will and proceeded to make your own arrangements. The fact remains that you maneuvered yourself here as an uninvited guest and made yourself at home. That has nothing to do with Arvind."

I was devastated, completely destroyed. Not only had the Guru, who had become mother and father to me, totally rejected me, he wouldn't even hear my case. My expectations were reasonable, based on Arvind's promise. My sense of justice—my deepest ballast—was violated. As I got my things together, a huge stone of emotion lodging from my throat to the bottom of my gut, Arvind came over and said quietly, "I'm so sorry. They say he's a realized man, but at such times as these he shows a side that is terribly human—even brutal." This was really no consolation, though his kindness was a sweet gift. I simply could not undo the huge projection of all-knowing Spirit with which I had mantled Maurice. Maurice, the *mythic teacher ... the father-of-fathers.*

Later Maurice softened, clarifying that he was teaching me *manners*, not rejecting me personally (though the "tourist" remark cut particularly deeply, and could not be undone). He repeated the earlier understanding that we were always welcome at his and Mrs. Petit's flat, but that a stayover would require a proper invitation. He reaffirmed his hospitality by inviting us to dinner the evening following Judi's arrival.

Judi and I ended up staying at Peacock Palace in nearby Breach Candy with the family of two young Muslims I had met during the Asian Tour visit. They were very gracious to us, and Judi really hit it off with Mrs. Mecklai's mother, Mrs. Carmully, a Sufi delighted by our deep interest in spiritual matters.

But the wounds suffered from the Guru's razor tongue were deep. Desperate as I was for the father-of-fathers, I took to heart as best I could Maurice's points about my self-complacency and infantile trust in others caring for and loving me. I wrote my parents of the Guru's *telling me I wasn't wanted ... who ever says that to me, who expects unquestioning acceptance everywhere i roam upon the World-Breast. ... I always assume I am the favored child.*

Death at Sagar Darshan

When I took Judi to see the Patels in nearby Sagar Darshan, we walked into a flat crammed with grieving women dressed in white saris. The men were all at Padmaben's cremation service. Udayan had told me just days before that his mother was very ill with a kidney infection. Now she was dead of a heart attack.

We returned the next day to offer condolences. When I entered, I received a privileged glimpse through the master bedroom door of a sight which brought wonder to my WASP eyes. Ramanlal was sitting on his huge marriage bed surrounded by women in white, enfolded in the arms of one, leaning against another. I was shocked to see this strong man, one of the leading psychoanalysts of India, soaking up mother-love like a young boy. Shocked too by the revelation of such overflowing love. For an instant, I imagined myself being surrounded by all the black nannies and maids of my childhood, soaking me with whole-hearted tender comfort. From my familial experience it was doled out much more carefully, for it might run out.

A somber Udayan greeted us, explaining the circumstances of his mother's death. While Judi talked with Anuradha, he spoke to me of what this experience meant for him. Surprisingly, he said that though he was incredibly grieved, a huge hole where his mother had been at the center of his being, it also gave him a tremendous input of creative energy. Her death put him in touch with the inner "mother" that he knew would give something back to the world.

Ramanlal came in a few moments later and greeted us, face still smudged around the perimeter of the teary flood, though he'd made an effort to wash up. Learning that Judith was headed to Rishikesh from Bombay, he got a gleam in his eye. "Would you be willing to take some of my wife's ashes with you to dispose of properly in the Ganges?" Moved, we readily agreed. He said our being present at the time of Padmaben's death was an indication of our having had some "past association," and he found it particularly significant that Judi was going there as a pilgrim. We felt bonded more closely than ever to this family, and I was once again impressed by the depth of Hinduism's power. Here was a modern Freudian, an atheist, and yet he wanted Padmaben's ashes not only to be joined with Mother Ganga, but the proper rituals observed. Perhaps this was her wish, and he was simply honoring it.

Krishnamurthi's talk was on the evening of January 26, outdoors in a banyan grove. The crowd must have been around 1,500. Before K appeared, some representatives of the Organization came out to make an appeal for its educational and publishing work. Having prepared for a session with a spiritual anarchist and debunker of tradition, I feared I smelled the leavings of the Order of the Star, which he had disbanded as a youth, refusing the mantle of Avatar that Annie Besant wanted him to carry. We were after all in India and he was speaking before a row of swastikas struck on the columns, probably during the Hindu renaissance at the end of the nineteenth century. Could one really escape the all-pervasive Hindu tradition? Certainly the Muslims and the British had not.

Once K stood before us, I set aside my reservations. Clearly *he* was not here to talk about any organization, moving quickly to remind us not to follow anyone or any group, but to pursue one's own unavoidable truth. He was slight and trim, with large liquid eyes and a beautifully angular face with thin lips. I had seen his youthful photos, and heard the stories of women falling for him. I could see why.

He sat on a dais before a large terraced structure. It was a very pleasant evening, with crows wheeling through the dusk above us. K was a gripping, piercing speaker, refusing to truck with any ritual, any conceptualization of the Real, any organized religion, any sanctified scripture. Listening to him describe with shattering eloquence the lonely path to the unembellished truth of human existence felt like a dip in the clear cold Ganges at Rishikesh on a winter's morning. His command of English was impeccable as he carefully explained etymologies, freeing words from habitual usage. Each word was always new and fresh, for he abhorred established, lazily accepted meanings.

Focusing intently on his words, sitting in the hushed crowd under the gnarled banyans, crows occasionally swirling by, I achieved a profound meditative state where everything was clear, each moment sharp and charged with the life beyond the reach of sense or conceptual thought.

Not so for Judi. She leaned over and whispered, "I'm not really into this." From then on, whenever I looked over at her, she was fingering her rudraksha beads, muttering her mantra, tuning K out.

At the end of the talk, he entertained questions. The most penetrating response was in answer to a question about the difference between life before and after liberation. I set down his words: "One single mark identifies every manifestation of pure, universal, life: it acts but does not react."

21 DEWAS:
A TRIAL APPRENTICESHIP

The archetypal scene is one of adoring, intensely dedicated disciples ranged around the master-artist seated on deerskin, straining to reproduce his Godgiven sound, still the most captivating music i have ever heard.

We returned from Bombay via the Ajanta caves to Indore and Dewas. I weighed 123 pounds (my college graduation weight was 160) after emerging from the purges of the Nature Cure Hospital in Madras. I needed fattening on the excellent Malwan cooking of Vasuthai and Sulu. The train brought us to Khandwa, where we boarded a bus for the final leg to Indore.

The ride here from Khandwa went through the Malwa country i love. Parts of it felt like the North Alabama hills, and the huge falling leaves of an unknown—but characteristic—tree reminded me of the Alabama catalpa (it was teak). It looked like something out of an ancient Irish fairytale.

The countryside was dotted with lovely yellow stucco farmhouses, intersected by streams, patched with fields of cotton, grain, bananas and grapes. Many of them were fenced by rows of thistles and cacti. Egrets gracefully alighted in huge expanses of green grain fields. Finally we were in Indore country, passing Daly College, Leah's tiny house, and then Government Arts and Commerce College, the road leading into more and more familiar territory.

Now we are ensconced for five days at the House of Music at the foot of Devi's Hill, where the most stressful moment is when you occasionally overeat the superb food. Kumarji really loves to eat and delights in watching his guests' reactions to the daily delicacies as much as he does in sharing his effortless, breathtaking taanas (complicated fast musical patterns).

Judi was more at home here than at Chandu's. Though he hung out with the hip Maharashtrian artist crowd, Kumarji was a devoted Shaivite, and householder life at Banukhul had a traditional basis. Vasuthai welcomed her into the kitchen, and their cook became a wreath of smiles whenever Judi joined her. More importantly, both Kumarji and Vasuthai really loved her, treating her almost like a daughter.

Nirguni Capital

When I last wrote of Dewas, I spoke of the singular tradition of the *nirguni bhajan*, the devotional song directed to the *nirgun*, the formless. Someone told me that Dewas was the "world capital" of the tradition. For a person drawn to the *jnana* path, where you continually work at discriminating the real from the unreal (like catching the space between thoughts), the idea of *singing* about it was a delightful variant of the discipline. And it obviated, for the duration of these musical interludes, the occupational hazard of becoming a mere philosopher. Since I had expressed a strong interest in the *nirgun* tradition, Kumarji started right off teaching me a couple of nirguni bhajans, both by Kabir, the fifteenth century Muslim weaver-saint from Varanasi.

The "world capital" claim turned out to be authentic. The last in a long line of *nirguni* yogi-singers, reaching back to the fifteenth century, had been a teacher named Sheelnath. He died sometime after the First World War, but his ashram still stood on the other side of Dewas, Dewas Senior. Kumarji and Vasuthai were devotees of this being who spent the last decades of his life in Dewas. Kumarji recorded the most famous of Sheelnath's compositions, and it had been a hit *bhajan*, like a hit gospel song.

To whet our interest, Kumarji ordered us a horse tonga for an afternoon visit. The tonga took us through the mildly decrepit streets of Dewas Junior, then, from the Maharajah's statue eastwards, Dewas Senior: past all the dry goods and heavy equipment dealers, open barber shops and children playing hoops, finally into fields of leaf vegetables, potatoes, onions, dal, and wheat. On the outskirts of town, we came to a ramshackle wooden tower, with a double row of plane trees bordering a dusty ochre road leading towards a shaded site.

This watchtower dated from the latter days of the Maharajah of Dewas's reign. Now the *chokidar* and his family lived there, and when the gateman let us in, three of his children with smudged faces in clean rags stopped to smile and wave, then ran merrily on. The tonga parked outside the inner gate which led to a courtyard and an unpainted ramshackle Victorian bungalow opposite a rankly overgrown garden. This had been a country retreat house for the Maharajah, who then donated it to Sheelnath and his disciples late in life.

We were received by the middle-aged, slightly crumpled *chokidar*-guide, a devout Sheelnath man, the soul of the living energy you could still feel in the place. Our tour began with the *hoven*, the firepit in the central courtyard at one end of a raised swept-earth floor, surrounded in all directions by wire fencing—probably to discourage monkeys. The fire had burned continually since Sheelnath's *mahasamadhi*, a semicircle of fresh marigolds with little cairns of devotional *lingams* around it. Then we entered the musty house.

Our guide was clearly delighted to host us. All the rooms were preserved just as they were when the master died. The furniture was in terrible repair, and mosquito-netted double beds looked like something out of the middle ages, they were so small. One of the rooms had suffered water-damage due to the leaky roof and was roped off, but you could see the profuse mildew stains and ripped fabric, the occasional rodent. They couldn't afford electric lights, so our guide led us with a candle through the dark shrine.

Judi turned to me, speaking quietly: "Do you feel it, the *bhavana*?"

"Yeah," I said, grabbing her hand and leaning closer to her ghostly face. There is a holy aura here—stale, but definite."

The highlight of the tour was our visit to Sheelnath's top-floor bedroom. In one corner the *chokidar* indicated a trap door, tapping it with his cane asking, "Are you knowing what purpose this door is having?"

I answered, "It's a dumb-waiter for serving and removing food from the kitchen."

He laughed with glee, shaking his head: "No, guess again, sahib." He turned to Judi, "You are perhaps knowing memsa'ab?"

"Some kind of closet?" she ventured.

Our guide shook his head, assuming a look of calm satisfaction. "This is passageway where Master would be traveling to visit his friends and attend very sick people in distress. There are so many reports of Master's appearance at such distant places while we were seeing him in this room only. But we were also knowing about this little door, of course." He smiled broadly.

At that time, I had not studied shamanic bilocation, yet somehow was grabbed by the possibility that someone could train themselves to do this with the subtle body. Judi agreed. "In *this* country, virtually anything is possible."

Pleased, the *chokidar* went on. "Most famous time of Master's power came when he had need of being at Kumbh Mela at Haridwar, and was being seen there by several persons, fleeing through this door during nighttime. In morningtime, he was here doing puja and taking breakfast with us. No train could go and come that quickly."

Towards the end of the five days we spent at Banukhul before Judi took the train north to Rishikesh, Kumarji reminded us that he was serious about his offer for me to be his live-in disciple. Chandu had come for lunch, and was our interpreter. Kumarji led us out to the front yard.

"Kumarji says he will build you a bungalow on the back part of the property … over there." Our eyes followed the two Maharashtrians' hands, and we exchanged glances as we took in the cozy spot amongst the bougainvilleas. Kumarji then led us a little farther towards the shops of Dewas Junior. At the edge of a four-foot stone wall, we stopped. Kumarji spread his right arm over the top of the wall, a bit like one of his sweeping concert gestures, as Chandu added, "And this is where he would build Judi an office and dispensary. If Bob decides to stay and apprentice at Bhanukul, Kumarji will set you up in practice. As you can see, he has the land," pointing to the fair-sized adjacent lot.

"Hunh!" Kumarji nodded, showing his betel-stained smile in confirmation. I was humbled and embarrassed, shrinking from his generosity, my words dying in my throat like stuffed cotton. Judi responded, "You have made a very generous offer to us, Kumarji. We will give it serious thought."

I nodded. "Thank-you, Kumarji. I'm not sure I can be a *shishya* worthy of such a gift."

Back in our room, we sat down on the big teak bed designed by Chandu. It was late afternoon, quiet except for the voices of a few kids playing down the street and the cry of a nearby mynah.

"What do you think?" Judi asked.

"I'm overwhelmed. These people are so good to me, and yet I'm afraid they have the wrong guy. The trouble is, I *am* musical, and this is the most incredible music I've ever been exposed to. I mean working with Leonard Bernstein was great, such an energy charge, such musical intelligence. And Ozawa and Leinsdorf. And Charles Munch, who used his face and hands to show us how to sing when he didn't have the English. My piano teacher in Birmingham was in the line from Beethoven, via Robert Cassadessus. I've been blessed with so many great musicians in my life. But Kumarji puts them all in the shade—he's India's Mozart and Bartok in one. And yet I'm not sure this is it."

"Why not give it a try? You'll never know unless you try." She was always so upbeat.

"I've done that once. I didn't have the desire or the discipline—just awe, the inspiration of being in the workshop of the music-gods. Besides, to really become an Indian musician I'd—*we'd*—have to live here."

"But you heard Kumarji's offer. He's repeated it twice. He's serious."

"I know. Would *you* really want that? Would you give up a medical career in the States?"

"The only thing which would be difficult would be getting set up with the office and equipment, and Kumarji's willing to do that. I love it here, and if this turns out to be the life that fulfills you, then we could both give it a real try. Look at all the incredible things which have happened in India that we didn't expect," she replied.

For the first time, I felt more attraction than fear. My head danced slightly, and I felt a little adrenalin surge. "So it looks like once again it's really up to me. You know I don't get very much out of Sivananda Ashram. That's your thing, your teacher's place. Kumarji is taking my dream of studying with him again and laying it on the line. Maybe being here will motivate me."

"Good. You know I believe in you, Bob. Try being Kumarji's shishya for a month, then we can meet up North and talk about where we go from here."

"But what about our promise to meet your folks in Israel?"

"Don't worry about that. We'll do what we have to when the time comes. Trust the Goddess."

"Okay." Trusting Mother India had meant wondrous turns, little fate-gifts accompanying our pilgrimage. But this was not an adventure or a pilgrimage; this was life, and I feared other doors closing if I chose this one.

Our last afternoon in Dewas we decided to circumambulate the Hill of Devi, the local home of the goddess, known throughout central India for her auspiciousness. Bearing masabi oranges and water, we climbed the path into the afternoon sun. It took much longer and was more arduous than I expected, the sun beating down on us, a silent, implacable witness to our hatless condition. The vegetation was sparse and the earth dark brown, almost black moon rock. As we treaded higher, the atmosphere grew more unworldly, and I experienced a different force-field than in the town. Judi concurred. We finally reached the little cave-temple, catching a glimpse of this little lacquered doll-figure in the rear of the cave. Nobody else was on the mountain, no priests, no children begging for *baksheesh*, only implacable stillness and the steadily setting sun. We dipped our heads as we entered the cave, which would have been quite dark if not for the fact that Surya beamed his light into the shaft just at that moment, the glow lighting Devi's dark red face. Devi (Tulja Bawani) was less than a foot high, bright open eyes rimmed with kohl, a fresh ochre cloth wrapped around her tiny frame. The painted plaster icon was folk-naïve and felt cool and distant, yet oddly welcoming. Strange yet familiar, she seemed to say, "I've been expecting you."

We remained with Devi around fifteen or twenty minutes, sitting quietly before her, I on my knees, Judi with legs neatly crossed under her sari. I sat with my eyes alternately closed and open, trying to fathom this enigma staring back at me. Then we honored her, bowing in *namaste*, and left. I felt reluctant to leave, but the sun was moving past the little cave, hastening to end another day.

Our descent was calm and smooth, and I picked up a moon rock as a memento. We had time for a cold bucket-bath before joining the Komkali family for dinner. That evening as we lay in bed I tried to hold on to Devi's image, that unfathomable look in her eyes, for as long as I could.

As promised, we spent a few days in Indore, eating under Sulu's appreciative gaze, who remarked on how thin we had become. Now that I was safely enlisted once again as Kumarji's student, the feeling of tension I felt during our fall visit had dissipated. Chandu could live with Judi going off to Rishikesh now that he heard her talking about doctoring in the region, doing real work in the real world. I was fortunate to be an artist with a loyal spouse who could support me. So when Judi's train pulled away from the station headed north, feelings were good all around.

Back in Dewas the next day, Kumarji escorted me back to the large comfortable room upstairs, overlooking massive bougainvilleas which partially screened the street below. Outside was a large patio from which I would have a commanding view of the Hill of Devi just behind us. My first night, Mukhul came up to see if everything was satisfactory, asking if I wanted water. I did, and he brought me a steel tumbler. This became a nightly routine until I realized I could get my own water.

In the morning, I took *chai* early, performed yogasanas, tried meditation, and read before breakfast. I attempted yoga outside on the patio, but the morning proved to be too cold. Breakfast was parathas, which I ate with Mukhul, Satish and Pinu. Extraordinary parathas, with finely chopped cabbage and onion mixed in the dough, they were served with creamy yogurt, sweet lemon and tart mango chutneys, both made by Vasuthai. Kumarji rose late and passed frowzily by, his sleeveless undershirt tightly stretched to contain his little belly, sleep clinging to him. He gave me a big smile on his way to the bathroom. I spent my days reading, writing deliciously long letters to Judith—*it's actually romantic being separated like this*—walking into town to mail the letters, and occasionally practicing music. Mukhul and Satish both practiced about as much as their voices could sustain, around four hours a day. I peaked at about an hour and twenty minutes (once). The best times were those at table with the family, and the lessons. This time, instead of Vasuthai, my teacher was Mukhul, now twenty years old and a serious young musician. Kumarji frequently sat in, grunting, nodding, occasionally instructing Mukhul, pointing with the caliper-like tool with which he carefully shaved betel nut.

In my town walks it did not take long for me to run into lay practitioners of the *nirguni bhajan*. After dinner the end of my first full day at Bhanukul, Mukhul turned to me with his super-serious look and said, "Do you take *paan*?"

I hesitated briefly and answered, "Yes, occasionally." So we went out among the shops of Dewas Junior, brightly lit and moderately busy. Mukhul, who had been sizing me up ever since that first year, faced me abruptly, looked me in the eye from point-blank range and said, "Bob, you must seize the moment you have been given. You realize what a precious opportunity you have, being given the chance to be a *shishya* in the home of Kumar Gandharva?" He spoke with challenge in his voice, clearly hoping to awaken me from the torpor he sensed already.

"Yes, Mukhul, I am quite aware of it. And I'm glad you're being so straight about telling me. I'm going to do my best to make the most of my time." Yes, I would try to allow myself to be transported by the Master's voice until I couldn't help but sing unceasingly myself.

Shortly later we ran into a group of older men who invited us to join them in the back room of a shop. I think Mukhul actually arranged this, for the man out front ran to the back of the shop as if he expected us. The men in the back room welcomed Mukhul, greeting me with warm leathery handshakes, some holding my hand between theirs. Chai appeared, and one by one they started singing. Mukhul turned to me: "You recognize?"

"Bhajans?" I responded tentatively

"Bhajans? Bob, these are *nirguni bhajans.*

After a third man sang, the leader of the group turned to Mukhul. "Mukhul, do you have an offering?" Mukhul returned the evening's currency, singing fluidly, almost effortlessly, with an occasional Kumar Gandharva gesture, arm out, face turned to the side, looking up with closed eyes, then bringing the hand down at the same instant in which he turned to greet his listeners on the *sum.*

The leader turned to me after all the old guys bobbed their heads like lanterns and exchanged gentle hand-slaps, saying, "And one day you will also sing one of our songs for us." I demurred, feeling blessed to be with these sweet souls, already fearing I was inadequate to the discipline.

Afterwards we found the *paan-wallah,* who smilingly started assembling our orders, piling the leaves, sprinkling the betel nuts, spices, lime paste, and in my case, sugar. He deftly folded each together, handing them to us in the same motion. Mukhul was disdainful of the fact that I declined the tobacco portion: "You take *meetha paan.* That is for children and women. Don't you like tobacco?"

"No, Mukhul, I've never been interested in it," I said.

He replied, "Smoking is of course bad for the throat—though I do occasionally. But with *paan,* it enhances the betel nut. A man needs that."

Shivratri

The second week of my sojourn at Banukhul coincided with Shivratri. I wrote Judith, *the moon is now at the penultimate Shivratri stage. The air is electric with expectation. Kumarji returned a few hours ago and has been telling beautiful stories about Shivratri.*

On that day, February 19, 1974, Kumarji spent the afternoon making *bhang*. He also oversaw the preparations for the feast which would follow the concert. How he loved his fresh vegetables—scraping with obvious glee. He was the master-priest. He was everywhere.

Hanging out with Satish, I felt mutual appreciation in being *shishyas* in this household on such an auspicious occasion. I sensed, as well, the budding music critic, like his father in Bombay. Satish was part of the inner circle. And I wasn't the only non-blood relation in the household. His was an independent perspective, and I needed that.

And Mukhul. Was he Kumarji's heir-apparent? Did he feel pressure to step into shoes that he could never fill? This evening, he was simply in awe of his father; we all were. After the singing commenced, Mukhul and I exchanged glances. In that glance was a recognition that we both saw his father as an incredible musician and human being, *a genius of the heart*.

Before Kumarji's cozy family concert began in the music-den, he passed around glassfuls of the carefully concocted *bhang* to all the guests, abstaining himself. These guests included a handful of good friends, including Chandu, Guruji and myself, and a few fortunate townspeople. I was particularly drawn to a simple, warm, beaming mill worker named Onkar. Unlike the Fulbright year, during this pilgrimage I had abstained from cannabis, dating back to my time teaching at Indian Springs. As the singing commenced, I realized that I was enfolded by Kumarji's impish devotion to Shiva, sober Master of the stoned saddhus, and, for good measure, saturated and entranced by the hallucinogenic beverage. All of us in the blessed music den were strung like beads on the endless river of sound coming from Kumarji's throat, which emitted *taana* like *musical rivets ejaculated from the flashing stream of sound*.

Kumarji sang a medley of *bhajans* by three great singer-saints: Mira, Surdash, and Kabir ("Treeveni"), by the afternoon/evening raga Gaud-Malhar and followed by the night raga Chandra-Kauns. The sarangi player, whom I had never heard play more sweetly and hauntingly, accompanied the opening raga. Though a solo instrument in its own right, Hindustani music often employs the sarangi as a figured drone, playing a continuo pattern overlaying the tanpura framework of open octaves and fifths. But tonight the sarangi-wallah went further, performing Gaud-Malhar in concerto fashion with Kumarji. Onkar the factory worker and I exchanged appreciative glances. Before the first composition Kumarji gave him *prasad* of fresh leaves of black pepper, which the unassuming man accepted as if from a saint, bowing low, crushing the sweetly pungent leaves to his nose, eyes full of love and humility. I looked over at Thai, seeing in her eyes what it meant to be married to a genius and truly appreciate it. Later, as Kumarji began the third in the "Treeveni" series, a composition based on a *bhajan* by the blind saddhu Surdash, he turned to me and said by way of introduction, "a God-musician." Puer's journal continues:

Kumarji suddenly a small, princely Napoleon. The triumphal return of the emperor after the successful tour. His finger into everything: the apple juice, whiskeywine. And the nadi *just flows on.*[2] *Me the devotee with Kumarji at the temple of Banukhul. But the bhakta of bhaktas is the freedom to leave puja at any time—and any price.*

I had attended many rehearsal sessions with Kumarji, and at least one private concert, the informal concerto-session with Bhimsen Joshi in September 1968. But that had been a "men's" session, lubricated by Indian whiskey. Tonight was a family affair, a domestic celebration of the key moment in the Shaivite calendar, with disciples and a few invited guests from the community. Banukhul *was* a temple this evening. Just about everyone there had imbibed Kumarji's sweet lassi milkshake, laced with cannabis and spices, but the evening's madness had been dedicated to Shiva himself, so any egos which appeared to go astray were all within the god's ample sheepfold.

Thinking back on this evening, I see not Napoleon so much as Dionysos, pictured on a *cylix* at the center of a whirling bunch of orgiastic devotees, his hand in the Buddha's mudra of peace, the still point in the dance. We were all flying, but centrifugally, Kumarji directing the rite from the center in complete control, mixing our bhang-shakes, seeing that everyone had just what they wanted, finally sitting down with his sarangi-wallah to spin his masterly web of song. It was his day entirely. We were delighted children at his father's feast, and he was the "God-musician," Shiva's servant.

One Less Shishya at Banukhul

With respect to the Hindustani vocal career these were not auspicious beginnings, as I knew deep down. I was a privileged *shishya*, but I was

---

[2] The sound-essence of the material world. As OM is the sound of creation, so the *nadi* are the coeval sound of its ongoing dance, a preserving chorus.

not ready to be devoted to my teacher. I still wanted to be free. Besides, my heart just wasn't in it, which I realized in a flash when Mukhul asked me towards the end of the first week, "Why do you spend so much time writing Judi? You have the rest of your life to be with her." This was my chance of a lifetime here at Bhanukul, and I tried in dutiful bursts to avail myself of it.

Judi and I were working on a rather complicated plan to meet Radha in Vrindaban for Holi, the Hindu Valentines, commemorating the youthful dalliance of Krishna and Radha. Our Australian friend's artless, Christ-like guru lived there, and she planned to be with him for Krishna's Day. I was feeling acutely the pangs of love, preoccupied with the fantasy of being with my bride in Vrindaban for Holi/Valentines to mirror Krishna and Radha's devotion—not to mention being with the earthly Radha again. Kumarji, on the other hand, very much wanted me to be with *him* for Holi, when he was giving a home concert.

Thai spoke to me after breakfast, her tone serious, "Bob, Kumarji wants to talk to you about your plans." He was going on a tour for ten days, and would be returning just before the concert. "He wants you here for Holi when he gives a special homecoming concert." Kumarji was sitting close to us, pudgy in his white underwear, and I could feel this father-yearning from him. I smelled his aftershave.

Feeling cornered, I looked at my guru and blurted, "Impossible," feeling as surprised as they did to hear it.

Kumarji looked sad and a little hurt, but would not argue with me further after such clarity. Thai mirrored a complex feeling. On the one hand, I was a fool, even a traitor. But on the other, she admired and respected Judi tremendously, and there was a half-grudging, half-pleased recognition of the love and respect I had for my bride.

So who was the guru here, Kumarji, or Judith—as Maurice had insisted? It was more a matter of love than authority, and ultimately I would do what I felt was right. This guru business had never really persuaded me. Love and respect, yes, but total devotion and obedience, no. The letters are full of this plan, that plan about Holi and Vrindaban, Rishikesh and Bhopal (where Kumarji would give the last concert of his upcoming tour).

The night before, Mukhul came up to my room for a lesson. Smiling confidently, he said, "We're going to have a good lesson tonight. Now that you've learned some nirguni bhajans, let's get into the real business of learning some ragas."

"Mukhul, I want to learn *both*. Kumarji has been showing me some ragas portraying the change from day to night, night to day. He promised me I could learn them. Let's rehearse the introduction to Shri rag (pre-dawn) that we went over last night."

Mukhul was angry. "You haven't properly learned the other compositions—how do you expect to learn so much at once? "

I responded, very frustrated, "But it's *boring* to practice all those little details over and over until they are perfect. I don't have enough time to reach that level of perfection. I want to learn as much as I can while I'm here."

Mukhul looked at me, and I realized that I had just acknowledged what I had implicitly admitted in the music den with Kumar and Thai two days before: my days were numbered at Bhanukul. He tried again.

"Bob, I want you to do something *real* and *Indian* while you are here. Let me hear the Kabir composition one more time."

So we were finally trapped into doing what neither of us had wanted to do that evening. The attention to detail he demanded (like his father) would be what yielded real results. I had been thinking in terms of *quantity*—x number of bhajans—rather than producing something "real and Indian."

Like anyone in the guru(kela) system, i am the low man on the totem pole and by rights stand last in terms of practice space—and lessons. Yet like any infant, i am demanding and feel very dependent. Because i am a guest and a favored person in Kumarji's eyes, concessions are made, and i have realized that i therefore disrupt a fairly stable system. Though there are inherent jealousies in its normal functioning, i make it worse. Since i do not plan to devote my life to this music (which everyone realizes now), it's an energy-drain on the others for me to get the attention i feel i deserve. This has been particularly hard on Mukhul.

The musical movement was in fact virtually dead. Indeed, as I wrote Judi, I had vented my frustration on him, and he found subtle little means of retaliation, which I recognized as *normal and righteous*. Still, Mukhul tried his best to provide inspiration *and* discipline in his father's absence. But my "impossible" had been answered on more levels than I realized, like an ejaculatory prayer in answer to the deva's "I will grant you a wish." I got what I wanted, not what I thought I wanted.

The plans for Holi at Vrindaban never materialized; Judi never got in touch with Radha Dass. So I was with Kumarji for a sweet little Holi concert after all. If he failed to gain a musical disciple who would do him honor, he did teach me how to *listen* to Hindustani classical vocal music, giving me a lifelong appreciation. He also initiated an American Hindu wannabe into the wonder of Hindu festivals from inside a modern brahmin vocal artist's family—a great gift, graciously bestowed.

The final gift was the family's invitation for me to return with Judith for Kumar Gandharva's fiftieth Jayanthi (birthday) celebration April 7-8. I carried this offer with me when I went to join her for the Kumbh Mela at Haridwar in late March.

22 Crisscrossing North India in Hot Season

I took the train to Delhi, then changed trains for Haridwar. Detraining there, I looked over at the Ganga and her bridges, vainly searching for the hordes of pilgrims come for the Kumbh Mela. But the traffic appeared only a little heavier than normal. Something was wrong. Somehow, I had missed it—missed the Big One. I made my way to the *dharamsala* where Judi had instructed me to meet her—an island of propriety, a privileged bed amongst the thronged millions, thanks to Swami Chidananda. I was immediately struck by how clean, sweet-smelling and middle-class the priests were who greeted me at the office. A young ochre-clad priest escorted me through the neat flowered courtyard and past a marble fountain to Judi's room. She was seated on the floor next to a little writing table about eight inches high—the kind the swamis used at Sivananda Ashram, studying scripture. She looked up with a quiet smile, the young swami bowed, backing out the door, and we were together again.

"So where is everybody?" I asked after we hugged, a little too demurely for my taste. She was still enfolded in renunciate energy.

"You missed it. The main day was two days ago—it was crazy. It's much better now. "

"I don't know how this could've happened." I was hugely disappointed, but this was a really nice *dharamsala*, and we were together again. "At least *you* got to experience it."

"I think one Kumbh Mela is plenty for anyone. Now we've both been through it. Isn't this place wonderful?" She switched the subject. "You must be disappointed things didn't work out in Dewas."

I hesitated, then shrugged a little. "Sure I am, but at least now I know I'm not cut out to be an Indian vocalist." There was definitely more to report, but I didn't want to get into it right then.

It was a relief seeing and touching Judi again after our long, romantic time apart—five weeks. I was happy to hear that all my mail had arrived. After all, those letters were my chief accomplishment at the House of Music. Judi had written me briefly about Padmaben's final ritual, but now told me in detail how the swami had taken her and the urn of ashes out in a little skiff to the middle of the Ganga and intoned a long Sanskrit prayer for the dead. Then he dumped the urn in the river, and Judi strewed marigolds. She had written Udayan and Ramanlal about the whole thing.

Once I was oriented, I went outside in the garden to absorb any remaining sights, smells, and sounds accompanying a mela. No crowds, no dope-smoking nude Rastafarian Shaivite saddhus. I was late to the party! But we still heard drumming in the distance.

In the morning we went down to the Ganga for ritual baths. Only a hundred or so pilgrims remained, playing in the water like serious children, all intent on modestly changing clothes while remaining in holy water. I was amazed at the suppleness with which Judi did just this, removing her underclothes in the water with ease, calmly and efficiently rewrapping the sari as she emerged onto the ghats. We took this as yet another sign that she probably lived here in a previous lifetime—maybe several.

That afternoon, we went early to get a good spot for viewing the mela parade. Again there were far fewer in attendance than I had expected. We were able to get a front-row view because the Punjabi Mataji from Sivananda Ashram who had once challenged Judi about why she, a "brahmin," had hooked up with this Amreekan, had saved us a spot. Now she accepted me, broadly beaming her slat-toothed smile at both of us as we sat down beside her, hugging Judi like a daughter. The parade reminded me of the one at the Ujjain artha mela in 1969: lots of color, with fat bare-stomached priests royally bedecked in jasmine and marigold astride fancy white horses in regalia, naked rasta saddhus smeared with ash in a long thin line, either unshorn with matted hair or bald, and women renunciates in ochre, arms, faces, and hair streaked with ash. Midway came Kali, patron goddess of our era, her dark snarling ferocity oddly softened by the freshly painted white filigreed wood frame behind her and the crisp colorful new clothes on the clean-cut smiling retainers walking alongside her float. The float was pulled by a spanking new red tractor, gleaming in the sunlight.

But this mela felt like a movie rehearsal of the real thing, not the ambiguous underworld carnival I had experienced in Ujjain five years earlier. I still can't figure out the calendar. Supposedly the melas occur every twelve years in each of four holy cities—Varanasi, Haridwar, Ujjain, and Allahabad. But apparently the astrologers disagree on which years are auspicious.

After our little retreat, we took a cab to Rishikesh, riding through scrub forest, casually eyed by many monkey families. At the ashram office in Sivananda Nagar, we confirmed our spartan room once again, and I tried to be positive about re-entering ashram routine.

We stayed at Sivananda Ashram for one final week. Before we left, we went to speak one last time with Swami Chidananda. He was quite clear that a more extended stay in India was *adharma*—disordered and not timely. He was particularly stern with Judi, knowing how drawn she was to ashram life: "Go home, serve your parents, raise children. Follow the householder *dharma* and your profession." Then, turning to me: "You, Bob, should teach. Teach what you know best and don't worry about trying to teach Hindu religious ideas. Teach *values*—that's what young westerners need so desperately now."

"Yes, Swamiji," we both answered, like children before their father.

Tehri-Garhwal and Sunderlal Bahuguna

Swami Chidananda still had one more darshan for us before we left India, instructing us to visit a Gandhian activist in the nearby Garhwal Himalayas, Sunderlal Bahuguna: "This man is doing the most important work I know in India to help the poor. He is a disciple of Vinoba Bhave, Vinobhai. Here, take this letter of introduction. He is a good friend." So we took the bus to Tehri, the Garhwali capital. It was twenty-odd kilometers from Silyara, the village where Sunderlal had his little ashram. Tehri was a four-and-a-half-hour bus ride through beautiful forested mountains, sparsely populated with funky little shacks and occasional slate-roofed farmhouses. The traditional homes were of stone, wood only utilized for the joists and headers. At Tehri the bus parked by a large greensward, the high school on one side, a tented bazaar on another. We were greeted by friendly mountain people in colorful hats and scarves. Since we were cold at the six thousand-plus altitude, we bought a woolen Scotch-plaid shawl to supplement the one Judi was carrying. When folks learned the reason for our visit, they smiled warmly. Our man was well known here, and greatly loved.

The townspeople told us to take another bus to Gyansali, then get down and walk to the ashram. At Gyansali, a small market town, we disembarked and were instructed to follow a path through the mountain passes to Silyara. We strapped on our packs and hiked six kilometers, traversing the last three valleys on three-point rope bridges, the sisal dipping deeply beneath our weight. The ashram perched high on a bluff overlooking the town. We arrived in late afternoon, and were greeted by a couple of friendly, handsome girls, about fourteen years old, who were rhythmically pounding rice with large wooden bats in a hole pressed into a cement pad. They took us to Sunderlal's wife Vimla, who quickly instructed one of the other women to put on more rice for the guests. Sunderlal, she said, was out helping some farmers nearby, and would be back later in the evening.

Dusk had fallen and we were already well into our simple meal when Sunderlal arrived, laden with a huge backpack. He was a vigorous, ascetic man in his late forties, close-cropped greying beard and hair, kind but intense eyes. He walked huge distances talking with villagers about self-reliance (*swadeshi*) and claiming their rights (*gram swaraj*), nourishing himself on pre-cooked barley which he made into gruel and wild berries—the mountain folk call them "gooseberries"—from the Uttarakhand area. He claimed these berries held more vitamin C than any other fruit. Sunderlal's children, two boys and a girl, aged roughly eight to twelve, slept in the bed with Vimla, while he slept on the floor, which seemed to me a tremendous act of self-denial. The ashram at Silyara was home for Vimla Bahuguna and her three children. For Sunderlal, it was a base of operations.

The ashram consisted of a little grammar school, where Vimla was the chief instructor, and a small subsistence farm. They had planted guava trees, grew a meager vegetable garden, some paddy, and some wheat in a rocky field on the ridge above the school. Beneath the ridge was a copious spring which emitted freezing water, a tiny concrete bathhouse and a couple of privies. There was a cow, her calf, and couple of yearlings. Like other Garhwali farmers, the women walked fairly long distances to gather fodder, returning with huge sheaths on their heads. Once I saw the cow with her front legs braced against one of the shir pines, straining her neck to reach a branch. The girls who had greeted us husked the grain daily, rhythmically pounding with their stout wooden poles.

Sunderlal had amassed a rather impressive library, specializing in environmental, botanical, spiritual, and social action texts. My chief job while on site was to re-organize one of its sections. I found a lot to divert me, which may have been part of his plan. We also worked in the wheat field, stopping each day precisely at noon to pray in solidarity with Sarvodaya workers all over the subcontinent. Sunderlal explained, "I have done this ever since living with Vinobhai. All Sarvodaya workers, wherever they live, stop daily at noon to pray silently for the poor. We pray for justice, we pray for the crops, we pray for all who work to build up village life." Vinobhai had been Gandhi's chief lieutenant and Sunderlal's teacher. He was now in his eighties, living at the big Gandhi ashram near Wardha, in Maharashtra near the Madhya Pradesh border.

Vimla sent out word that an American woman doctor was visiting. On the third and final day of our visit, a line of about sixty women from neighboring villages waited to present their ailments to Judi, who received them in the library, assisted by Vimla, another woman teacher, and one of the older girls. Since Judi had virtually no medicines, it was mostly a laying on of hands—which made the women very happy. Judi was practically overwhelmed when she saw all these women, no medical infrastructure to back her up. She dispensed a few pain meds and diagnosed two cases of TB, sending the women to the nearest hospital in distant Srinagar.

The time came for Sunderlal to walk the villages again. "Come with me," he said with a smile and an outstretched hand. But we declined, wanting to visit a Gandhian retreat in neighboring Kumaon, next projected stop in this final whirlwind tour of our adopted Motherland. But he convinced us to go see Vinobhai. Since we were going to Kumarji's fiftieth jayanthi celebration on April 8 in Dewas, we added the historic ashram to our stuffed agenda, for it was within striking distance.

Kumaon Wedding

In Kumaon we spent a comfortable few days at Annapurna Ashram in Kausani, where Gandhi had written his *Gita* commentary. The mountain bus rides were alternately exhilarating and harrowing. The drivers were more careful than those in Central India, rarely "playing chicken" except on the occasional straightaway. But the roads often dangerously perched over high passes, no guardrails, and like roads everywhere in India, were only one and a half lanes wide. The papers routinely report bus crashes in the mountains. Usually everybody perishes.

Hiking the hills the day we left, we encountered a village wedding party just as it turned to mount the steep path to the bride's parental home. The bride's parents, the smiling groom translating in his dark suit, tie and hair blowing in the wind, asked us to join the wedding party. They explained that it was auspicious for us *foreens* to encounter the party at this precise moment, and the couple would garner good luck from our presence. We gladly agreed.

So we mounted the trail with them. I watched the shrouded palanquin containing the bride with some concern, for at each switchback it looked like they were going to dump her—definitely not auspicious. Halfway up in the mid-afternoon heat, the party stopped and brightly clad sword dancers performed their stately dance, accompanied by cymbals. I think this was for us, for they performed a more elaborate dance during the festivities. It also gave the palanquin bearers an opportunity to rest.

At the little farmhouse, we were seated as guests of honor, and given the best food at the wedding feast. Before the ceremony, Judi joined the women accompanying the young bride (she was fifteen or sixteen) to a ritual purification at a spring downridge. She told me she was shocked at how frightened the girl looked when she removed her veil for this little rite, kum-kum smudged by tears streaking down her cheeks. This was perhaps the last time she would see her parents, since her husband lived far away, and her life henceforth would be serving her mother-in-law.

The groom, who wore a mask of confidence, told us that he was on leave from his MS studies in chemistry, and that he had to return the next day to the university for exams. Perhaps that was the cause for the anxiety I sensed.

The wedding ceremony was less elaborate than I expected. When the bride removed her veil afterwards to reveal a clumpy moonface augmented by a huge nose-ring, she managed a brave smile. The food was modest, and I was greedily thankful that we got to sample some of everything. I was oblivious, but Judi noticed that most of the guests, poor farmers, got only the basics: rice, thin dal, chapathi. But we all got sweets—greasy fried *jellabees* so sweet they hurt your teeth.

We spent that night under my army poncho along the main path beneath a large deodar tree. The next day, we had a full day's hike, reaching our destination at dusk. We knew from a few glimpses on the way up that it would be a beautiful Himalayan panorama. We had run out of water, and I clambered down the mountainside in the direction of the spring. I was so thirsty when I reached it that I drank copiously before filling my Boy Scout canteen and Judi's army one.

There was a Forest Guest House on the ridge, but it was locked, so we pitched the poncho nearby and quickly went to sleep. I was dead tired. At about one a.m., a *chokidar* appeared, shining his big flashlight in our faces. He told us that we must leave at once, since this was a spot to be enjoyed by reservation only. I told him that we had not known that, and were just staying this one night. He reluctantly agreed for us to stay, but only until daybreak.

So Judi woke me at daybreak and we decamped. I didn't feel well, wanting desperately to go back to sleep. We didn't take time to make tea, and had virtually nothing left to eat, though I didn't feel like eating. Even before I put my pack on, I knew I was too sick for hiking. But we had no choice. I stumbled down the path as best I could, stopping to vomit every few minutes. I was soon totally exhausted and beginning to dehydrate once again. Halfway down, somehow Judi secured my pack as well as her own, trudging on like a pack-mare while I stumbled the rest of the way. We found a bus stop a half a kilometer or so from the bottom, and once we ascertained that a bus would be coming to take us back towards Kausani by late morning, Judi walked into town to see if she could find help. I felt awful, simply grateful to find a bench where I could once again sleep. Her medical opinion on my illness was that I had induced water-intoxication the night before when I gorged at the spring.

While Judi was in town, a brahmin entered the street to see if there were any travelers needing to be fed, a traditional Vedic hospitality ritual. He encountered Judi, so she received her meal. Afterwards, he helped her find some medicine for me. I felt queasy on our bus ride back to Annapurna Ashram, but after the long, heavy nap I was able to stomach a little plain rice and curds, along with some clear tea.

Kumarji's Fiftieth Jayanthi.

Leaving Kausani and the mountains, we made our way back down to Malwa. I felt extraordinarily refreshed after my inadvertent cleansing. As we entered the familiar landscape, I felt like I *belonged*. I experience a sweetness in Malwa that eclipses the contentedness at Warden Road by the sea in Bombay, the allure of the girls in the South with fresh jasmine in their hair, and the exhilaration of Himalayan vistas. But when we arrived at Banukhul, I was disappointed, for we were taken to quarters above the house at the Shivomtirth Ashram. I wanted to be *family*, and family should stay in the Komkali compound. Prince Puer wanted special treatment. But I recovered, reasoning that there were many guests, many of them lifelong friends.

It had always appeared to me that Banukhul was the last house, right at the base of Devi's hill. But beyond the ample bungalow was this tiny ashram, mostly hidden from view by a large peepul tree. Mukhul walked us over there, very friendly. This was the first time I had seen him since he had sternly confronted me with the truth that Hindustani *khyal* was not my path. That was behind us now, no regrets on either part. He was our host and still my brother.

The ashram was very clean and orderly, with a *hoven* at the center of a neatly swept dirt courtyard. Our room was swept the same way, with a cool concrete floor and a gentle breeze coming through the barred rear window. It was quite warm outside, around ninety, yet we were comfortable. We met the gentle *chokidar*, who told us we would meet the priest later. He turned out to be a shopkeeper from Dewas Senior, a good friend of Kumarji's.

As we settled in, I realized what a blessing this was. At the main house, there would constantly be people to meet, the expectant vibrations before the next day's events rising to disturb the peace I felt. We took *chai* with the presiding brahmin as he told us about its history and its inspiration, Sivomtirth—another *nirguni* teacher. We were on familiar ground, and Kumarji's friend was quite comfortable with casteless guests of the Nameless God.

So we decided to make this stay into a mini-retreat. We wanted to take advantage of the peacefulness of the site on the flanks of Devi's Hill. Before dinner with a small group of friends and family at Banukhul, which wasn't until ten, we alternated resting, doing yogasanas and meditating. When we went down for dinner at dusk, I was a little taken aback. The atmosphere was like a cocktail party. "So I hear you are Kumarji's student. . . ."

"Well, not exactly. You flatter me. I am just a baby. ..."

The next morning Judi happily joined the festive meal preparations. The birthday meal was served at midday in the large living area as well as the adjoining front porch and patio. It was a veritable feast, regally served from brass buckets and platters. Though virtually everyone there was a brahmin, Thai gave Judi the honor of serving, functioning like an elder daughter or daughter-in-law. Orthodox or not, as guests of the master they dared not show any sign of complaint. Clearly we *were* family, and I proudly watched as my wife gracefully leaned past distinguished brahmin women in their elegant silk saris, serving them with her own dear small hands wreathed in a rainbow of bangles—just like the ones Mother had admired so long ago on her Aunt Londa. She wore a silk sari Thai had given her, saffron bordered with a gold-threaded motif in a deep fire-orange background.

After lunch we heard tributes to the master by friends, music critics, and other musicians. These were in Hindi and Marahti, so we only understood an occasional word or phrase. I sought Chandu's help with translation, but it all went by too fast. So I tried my best to look interested, but mainly noticed that I had overeaten and that most of the women on the patio wore too much perfume. Kumarji sat in front, beaming, nodding and namaste-ing graciously as the praises flowed over his dear head. I was briefly introduced and stood bashfully, joined by Judi, the American *shishya*'s wife.

After this rather long and sticky ordeal while the sun rose to its apogee, it was time for music. Several singers offered short compositions. Some really interested me, others were merely competent, or sang in a style that didn't particularly move me. Finally Kumarji himself sang, a familiar treat, and though I was tired, he lifted me into that sweet ease islanded with moments of amazement that his gandharvan vocal play invariably aroused. Chandu was near enough that I could catch his eye appreciatively, and occasionally we gasped in chorus, "Wah, wah, chia wah"—eyes locking. Judi was at my side, for here in the intimate circumstances of home, the sexes could mix freely.

Visit with Vinoba

We took the train from Indore to Wardha, then got down and proceeded by horse-tonga to Kasturbagram, the ashram at Paunar near the Maharashtra-MP border where Gandhi's wife Kasturba had presided. It was now Vinoba's headquarters, the Mahatma's right-hand man, whose remarkable contribution to the movement had been to persuade wealthy landholders to give away *bhoodan* parcels to the landless poor in the early fifties in south-central India. Acreage the size of France was voluntarily distributed in this way, damping the progress of the Communists in the fledgling Indian democracy, who wanted to accomplish by force what Vinoba achieved by awakening the heart. Much of this was later taken back, but a sizable portion still remains in the hands of descendants of those newly empowered farmers. We were here because Sunderlal had spent almost a year under Vinoba's tutelage in his youth. Swami Chidananda had sent us to Sunderlal; now Sunderlal sent us to Vinoba.

It was mid-April. When we arrived, dusty and tired, it was mid-afternoon, and the heat was unbearable, peaking at 108 degrees. Everything was in various shades of brown, the earth a parched hardpan. Things would not green until after the monsoon. It was a brick compound, standing within the outer perimeter of the larger Kasturbagram, whose historical significance—holding over a thousand Gandhian workers during the Independence struggle—was duly noted on a plaque at the gate.

We were ushered to a tiny cell opening on the courtyard with a door and one tiny window. I do not remember a fan. We had tea with our hosts, after which I tried to rest on the thin floor mat in our cell, but Judi went outside to read on the slightly cooler veranda. We were dripping with sweat, and continually thirsty.

In the evening we joined thirty or so inmates for a simple meal in the ashram refectory. Everyone but us was clothed in white *khadi*. We had thin yogurt with kitchari. I could have drunk a quart of it with ease, but there wasn't enough. We were tired, but stayed up talking to the soft-spoken Gandhians as long as we could, because it was still too warm for sleep. When the time finally came for bed, we found our little cell much too hot, removing our bedding to the barely cooled earth of the Central Indian Plain, draping dhoti and sari over our respective heads to ward off mosquitoes. The stars were magnificent as usual, and the mosquitoes only moderately pesky, their periodic humming more bothersome than the occasional nibble. It was well past midnight before it cooled down just enough to sleep.

Judi especially suffered from the extreme heat at Paunar, as she did throughout the last few weeks on the northern and central plains. Too uncomfortable to eat at noon, she ate only sparingly at the evening meal, though it was still in the nineties. I missed the Malwa Plateau and its merciful cooling evening breezes. It was hard to believe that we had been at Kumarji's Jayanthi only ten days before this oven. There it had been summery, somewhat muggy, but tolerable, especially when *Shabe* Malwa arrived—the "nights of Malwa."

In the morning we visited some of the cottage industries, focused on empowering women, though most were inactive. Paunar seemed more like a desultory museum, harkening to the full-blown Gandhian days. The one thing which did impress me was the biogas dome, the only alternative energy installation we saw during six and a half months on the subcontinent.

After lunch we went into the long rectangular hall for *darshan* of Vinoba. We had been instructed to write down our question. Thirty people sat in the hall; we sat up front near the master. He was a striking and original figure, skin tan and leathery, thin, dressed only in the Mahatma-style white *khadi* half-dhoti swaddled around his loins, a blue New York Mets baseball cap on his head. I looked at his wiry legs with appreciative awe, knowing that they had carried him over south and central India many times. He nodded and smiled at us as we were seated, then put on thick glasses to read the queries.

When our time came, his young black-haired assistant read my question aloud: *"What is your advice for a couple who are spiritual aspirants going to build a rural ecumenical community in the belly of the Beast, in Alabama, the Heart of Dixie in the USA?"* Since the old man had been observing silence during his last years, the assistant also read Vinoba's response: "Love the Lord thy God with all thy heart, all thy soul, and all thy mind. Love thy neighbor. Love thy enemies." He smiled at us again, and proceeded to the next question.

I was disappointed. I had expected more practical and strategic advice, something more political, reading Vinoba through my expectations of Gandhi. But here was a Vedic scholar who had spent his many years in jail studying, writing commentaries, and following Gandhi's lead in learning Christianity, which offered more social gospel than the Hindu texts. Great teachers always throw you back upon yourself. Vinoba had thrown me back upon my religious heritage as well.

Last Days

Chandu and Sulu feted us royally during our last precious days on the Malwa Plateau, and we went to Dewas for one last meal at the House of Music. Sulu presented me with a colorful tie-dyed red-white-and-blue beach shirt, Hindi scrawled all over it. Thai gave Judi another sari, for which she had a couple of blouses tailored—the Nafdes insisted on paying—and Sulu presented her with a *salwar chemise*. These last days in Indore were bittersweet, and I found my gaze often lingering in Chandu's crinkly, expressive eyes. This was really it. The background melancholy was my refusal of the call to be a disciple of Kumar Gandharva, Chandu's inspiration. We both knew it, but managed to celebrate nevertheless.

We boarded the train for Delhi after breakfast, heading back into the heat of the North Indian plain. The first night we stayed in a flophouse, where Judi got lice. The final night in India we stayed in the guest quarters at the Gandhi Peace Centre. It was so hot, I just felt like staying in our room, lying under the ceiling fan. The room was small and musty, but very cheap; we were running very low on cash. We were leaving Delhi and India on April 25, which had not seemed a summery date when we booked it. But it was 112 degrees. Even with the fan running full speed, the mosquitoes feasted. They had figured out via countless mosquito generations that they could go into a glide pattern and gradually home in on their victims, tacking with all their strength across the whirling crosscurrents of the fan.

By our last morning in the capital we were reduced to the tourists Maurice had insisted we were. We had some rupees left to burn, so we went to a nice little cafe off Connaught Circus and ordered lassi and snacks. A small trim older Sikh at the adjacent table struck up a conversation with us, graciously accepting Judi's offer of chai. Like every Indian, he wanted to know what our "purpose" had been in his country. When we told him about our spiritual aspirations and the ashram-hopping, he smiled, then gently shook his head. He told us that while our intentions were laudable, we were going about things in the wrong order. "Go home, serve your parents, have children and teach them properly until they leave your home. Then come back to India and you will be ready for these teachings."

We gave each other a look of recognition, so simple and direct his words, so understated his manner. Swami Chidananda had given us the same advice a month earlier, but we still had an agenda. During these last weeks, we had swung up and down India, saying our goodbyes, duly meeting each guru recommended by trusted teachers. But our *dharma* had been laid out at Tiruvanamalai during the false pregnancy. Judi's thoughts especially turned towards our yet-unknown home and the householder life that lay ahead of us. We were householders without a household. We didn't belong in India anymore.

PART THREE
RETURN TO INDIA

23 The Siren's Call

Who is Shiva, Lord?

September 9, 1976
(Judi's thirtieth birthday)

Doing Jacob's diapers tonight, the smell gave me a flash of Indian latrines and I missed them. ... I was transported and for a moment didn't want to come back.

September 1976

Retreat to Rock Creek: After passing two rattlers, one dead, one erect and rattling at me, (read ValleyoftheShadow from Psalms), then braving a jungle of rhododendrons and briars, I reached a little knoll and pitched camp. Bed at seven. The heaviness and misery and confusion welled up, and I cried almost til nightfall. Slept with a hundred dreams 'til 10:30 a.m. Bright open day, and I found my way with ease. After a jungly stretch, I reached a small quiet, beautiful tributary of the Rock. Hopped down it to the Rock itself, a wild gorge of the river. Bathed in waterfall-pool. Lay on rock and a Shiva chant found me. The sun came and went behind the clouds. Some kind, very poor folks picked me up in their old car, looking for their heart attack-prone uncle (who was safe at his place up the holler).

Winter Solstice, 1976
In the quiet, amidst the whiteness and whirling wind outside, I feel hope of Christmas, of Light in the darkness—a New Year's dawning out of the void. Old issues of a dying year remain, but when the heart is at peace, these things come much more easily. Can I remain so calm, still, watchful even as I argue? Who is the antagonist/protagonist? All is Shiva. The world is divided and enshrouded for divine play. Play with Shiva, cut loose from bondage of national pride, I am man, I am woman, I am child, I am father, I am brother. See that I AM. And from that vantage point watch the play. . . . It all leads to Deepam, to Christmas, to rekindling the hearth. Power of Alama Prabhu's Shiva poem:

> O Lord of Caves
> if you are light,
> there can be no metaphor.

Yesterday, I teased Judi about her solemn statement in the early days of our courtship: "I plan to reach enlightenment in this lifetime." Today, I read from Echu: "It is a rare privilege to be born as a human being, as we happen to be. If we do not achieve enlightenment in this life, when do we expect to achieve it?"

Inspired by folks I met at a Quaker gathering near Asheville, Judi and I began to visit the Quakers in Celo Community, a land trust in the mountains to the east. Several of our commune-mates and both dogs from Kudzoo Kastle accompanied us in the White Elephant. Eventually, work opened up for us and we moved there after returning from India, Judi pregnant with our first child. Judi took a position as a family doctor at the Celo Health Center, while I became a core teacher at Arthur Morgan School, a Gandhian boarding junior high, where we also served as houseparents. My personal dynamic at AMS was quite different from Indian Springs, where I had been on the radical fringe. Here we were the conservatives, tying to encourage the sexual abstinence Swami Chidananda felt American teens so desperately needed.

My chosen method to pursue enlightenment, courtesy of Maurice Frydman, was to meditate on the photo of Ramana Maharshi he gave me. Sometimes, this would lead to the self-inquiry that the Master taught, following thoughts and experiences back to their source: "Who am I?" Progress was slow; I practiced less and less. But my connection to Shiva's supposed incarnation remained a powerful undercurrent. During those first months in our mountain home I dreamt: I am observing the reddish banks of a great river, and see the ankles and toes of a huge embedded figure. As I look closely, I realize it is Ramana Maharshi. The Master gave form to the river of my life, bestriding it like a colossus. But this remained hidden from awareness.

"The only death from which we do not recover is when a parent loses a child." I was sitting in the parlor at his Nepean Sea house, declaring my undying affection for Maurice, declaring how much I would mourn him when he died. He scoffed at me.

While Judi was hanging diapers one afternoon, a car drove up and a middle-aged fellow with a backpack got out. Hans was a Swiss hitchhiker who tracked us down after his visit to India in 1976. His mission was to tell us that my beloved teacher had died of congestive heart failure. That night I dreamt that Maurice morphed into a praying mantis which folded itself carefully, prayerfully sliding into a matchbox lowering into the darkness of Hades. Waking from the dream, I knew the guru was right again. The news had been difficult to hear, but I did not grieve deeply, merely filing him in my personal Underworld, on reserve should I need him again.

In India, practicing the alap—the slow development of a raga's character—was also a method for centering consciousness. I seldom found time for that, with two toddlers and three or four junior-high age youth in the house. "Won't you play your sitar for me?" I heard this often. These mountain transplants didn't get that I had studied vocal music, and the instrument was simply a tanpura. Not every gourd-and teak stringed instrument from South Asia is a Beatlesque sitar.

My life as a teacher at a rural Gandhian junior high in a Southern Appalachian land trust was not working. The setting was idyllic, the people wonderful, and I was learning mechanical skills that I had neglected along the way. But as the Rock Creek passage above reflects, I was often out of sorts, bordering on depression.

I was thirty-four, and had just finished building a house in the community for Judi and our two young sons. As we neared completion, the crew talked behind my back. "What's he gonna do now?" I had terraced the southeast side of the house for a garden, and was working on a plan to lease the adjacent hillside from the school. I would plant an orchard there, and had ordered blueberries for the slope beneath the garden. My friend Joe up at Mountain Gardens had raspberry cuttings. I would be self-sufficient, at least in vegetables, fruit, berries and firewood. The house was passive solar, featured in *Fine Homebuilding* in my illustrated article, "Mountain Passive." Liberated from the functional sheds of typical solar houses of the seventies, it was not only functional but beautiful: post-and-beam, with dormered tin roof and board-and-batten hemlock siding. Born in the Deep South, growing up a city kid, I was now a Southern Appalachian yeoman. Or so I thought.

After my talk about myth to interested community folks one evening, a friend gave me some advice. "Next time, try to explain it with a fifteen-year old in mind." Responding to his advice, I began teaching adult education classes for a local Baptist college. In "Myth and the Modern Condition" I led the students in dream work and guided meditation as well as studying anthropological material, scripture, and literature. One or two of them got what I was trying to do, though most were merely fulfilling their aesthetics requirement with this curious teacher. But the graduate dean was worried what the Board would make of a course whose premise was that myth was more fundamental than religion, so he pulled the class. In its stead, I volunteered to teach a class on "Critical Thinking," one of my chief goals as a teacher. After teacher and students alike endured a nightmarish semester of what was actually a class on informal logic, "Myth and the Modern Condition" was restored, but I began to mull options past the EdM degree, so that I might move beyond adjunct status. I was tired of operating at the Dean's whim.

Something was still missing. When Judi showed me a flyer advertising a men's retreat with Robert Bly at Lama Foundation, New Mexico, it didn't take long for me to decide to go. I had read his poetry and his article on the men's movement and was intrigued. Maybe I even hungered for this.

Once we gathered at Lama, our hosts told us there might be a problem with Mr. Bly. Here we were, forty men from all over the country, and they were still dickering over his fee! Suspended by these negotiations, we went around the circle, sharing what had brought us to this gathering. When my turn came, I heard a strong voice: "I am a teacher and scholar who has turned his back on his gifts. I need to serve them." So it had finally crystallized. I was a Householder in Paradise, wired as a teacher-scholar. It didn't matter whether Robert Bly showed up or not. I had gotten what I came for.

There was a lot more, much of it bearing on the energy balance in my marriage, but working with my parents' wounds brought out something huge. One morning Bly had us perform a mystery-rite which unlocked a repressed memory which says it all. While we were living in Mobile I experienced an early onset of puberty, age eleven. Daddy was traveling for US Steel, four or five nights a week, plus sales conventions. Fearful, Mother put me in the marriage bed with her, a golf club underneath to arm the Little Man should an intruder breach the house membrane. We were both light sleepers, and she forbade me to move. I would carefully, secretly lift my head from the pillow, turning it imperceptibly by excruciatingly slow degrees to the other side, then inch my legs into a new position, as slowly as possible. It was at this age that I started noticing the bloody sponges in the bathroom. Why did I have to sleep with that? This was all so clumsy and scary that I totally repressed it until Bly's rite revealed it again.

January 1984

A letter arrives from India, Bhanukul, Mataji ke Rasta, Dewas, MP. It's from Vasuthai. "Bob and Judi, Kumarji and I would very much like you to come to his sixtieth jayanthi on April 8. You were at the fiftieth. It would be auspicious for you to be there as well. You must come." Judi flies into motion, securing flights and arranging child-care for our two sons, aged eight and six. "I wonder what sari I should wear."

"Why the one Thai gave you, remember?"

After the initial excitement, I feel the dread hands of panic reaching up, chest tightening, mind a whirling tornado. I am waiting to hear back from the doctoral program at Emory I applied to– late, just like my application to Harvard Ed School from India, fourteen years before. The India Siren has resurfaced, and I am not about to be robbed of my new career by her untimely return. "I'm sorry, Judi, I can't go. The ILA application is in limbo. I may get sidetracked by India again. I've got to be here to answer any questions."

Indeed, when I phone on the appointed day from a campground booth at the beach in May, they ask if I will accept a full tuition scholarship to Emory's Graduate Institute of the Liberal Arts PhD program. Somebody else has just surrendered hers. The next day, she called to ask for it back. Too late, for I am launched on my true career.

24 Reconnected with Sunderlal

When we left India in 1974, Swami Chidananda banished Judi from Sivananda Ashram, telling us to return to the States, raise our children, and serve our parents. This was our dharma as householders. After the children grew up and our parents passed, we might come back and pursue ashram life. By the mid-Nineties, I was teaching a tenure-track job at Moorhead State University in Minnesota, and Judi was working as a family practice doc in a huge multi-specialty practice. She had lost both parents and the boys had left the nest, living together in Asheville during Jesse Ananda's senior year at Carolina Day back in Asheville, while Jacob Ramana worked at a bike shop, training and racing relentlessly. We were content together, and our love-life was the best it had ever been. Moorhead State was a "comprehensive regional university," not a liberal arts college, but I carved out a niche in which my gifts prospered. Dharma rolled on.

At a conference on "Inner and Outer Ecology" which we attended in D.C., I met Satish Kumar, editor of *Resurgence*. Satish and our old friend Sunderlal Bahuguna were brother Jain novitiates as young men, later disciples of Vinoba at the ashram near Wardha, where we had sweltered. I remembered the last time I saw Sunderlal, a few weeks before we ended our Indian honeymoon, jauntily setting out with his huge backpack to teach remote Himalayan villagers about *gram swaraj*, village power. His face clouded with concern, Satish told me about Sunderlal's most recent fast in protest of the mammoth Tehri hydro dam, lasting forty-five days and sending him to the Dehra Dun hospital. I was stunned and remorseful; I hadn't thought about Sunderlal in years. Maybe I should try for my sabbatical.

So I wrote Sunderlal asking if I could follow him around and write about his work. I submitted an application for sabbatical from Moorhead State for the following fall, year seven, and a grant application proposing to explore the cultural impact of my Big Three: Kumar Gandharva, Maurice Frydman, and Sunderlal Bahuguna. Both the sabbatical and the grant were refused, but I decided to return, sabbatical or no, requesting an unpaid semester's leave. Sunderlal was almost seventy, his protest fasts lengthening. It was 1996.

Sunderlal remembered us, noting that our son "Hanuman" (Jacob) must now be almost grown. He accepted my proposal, but was uncertain about conditions in Tehri in the fall. The Tehri Hydro Development Commission timetable called for flooding the town after June 30, so I shouldn't expect him to be around in September. I knew of his vow never to leave unless dam construction was halted, so I imagined that he'd go down with the town, or else fast until death. I was worried, especially when I learned that he had begun another fast.

Predictably, Judi wanted to join me. Back in North Carolina, we had considered returning to the Motherland with our sons, but her concern about tropical diseases led to a decision to wait until they were older. She and Sunderlal exchanged letters. He wanted her to give clinics for the Garhwali women, but she was unable to find a Rotary connection (my Stanford activist was now a Rotarian) to facilitate an ongoing health project in the Tehri-Garhwal area. She remembered the waves of women who came in 1974, when her supply of medicines was insufficient. She learned then that practicing her art in Tehri-Garhwal was futile unless the villagers could be connected with a medical infrastructure. Perhaps she would need to find a project elsewhere in India.

SLB's fast mercifully ended after an unimaginable seventy-four days, when he accepted juice from the new prime minister, Deve Gowda, at Gandhi's Rajghat shrine in Delhi. The PM agreed to order a comprehensive review by two commissions, one scientific, the other environmental, but he did not halt construction. Sunderlal was again admitted to the

Dehra Dun hospital, but was recovering as I left for India. He was not going to die on me.

Sunderlal was the only one left from my Big Three. Maurice Frydman was dead, and declining Thai's invitation to attend Kumarji's jayanthi meant I would never see my dear, brilliant classical vocal teacher again. But I still wanted to know what became of his music and his family. Meanwhile, Judi found a Rotary volunteer medical slot at the Kodai International School in Kodaikanal for five weeks beginning in mid-October. Kodaikanal is a lovely hill station in South India.

I planned my arrival in Tehri for the end of monsoon, late September. My instigation to return was not to retire to an ashram, but to apprentice as an environmental journalist, maybe even an activist. *No sentimental return*, I told myself, but a new passage to India. I would go on pilgrimage, write it up for the *Sun*, then join Judi in Kodai before visiting old friends. We would see Udayan and Anuradha in Bombay, then Chandu And Sulu in Indore, just down the road from Dewas and the House of Music. After my work, I would collect my reward. They would feed me, listen to my stories, and bathe me in the warm ghee of friendship.

Delhi Again

In 1968, Puer arrived at the Delhi airport and transferred to a plane taking him and his Fulbright siblings to Kashmir, crossing many a high snow-peaked mountain and lush green valley en route, the beautiful Carolyn at his side. This time I was alone heading north, not to embattled Kashmir, where only the brave or foolhardy would now venture, but to find Sunderlal in the Garhwal Himalayas. I arrived late in the evening at a Delhi airport cleaner and more orderly than I remembered, though the air was stale. Once again my clothes stuck to my body. I was lonely and wished I had booked a hotel.

All that was available at the booking desk was the pricey Ambassador. Only later did I remember the thrifty Delhi YMCA, right off Connaught Circus. The hotel lay on one of the outer rings of the city, and it took the cabbie an unbelievably long time to reach it. He must've asked directions four times as we meandered the large loops. He had no idea how to read my map, didn't seem to understand what a map was. Driving around past midnight haphazardly tracing those rings was disorienting. I certainly didn't feel like I had *come home,* Puer's sentiment in 1968.

Waking that first morning, I peeked through the curtain for my first daylight view of India in a quarter century. What once must have been a lawn was now littered with rubble from a previous version of the Ambassador—broken glass, some frayed couches, several dilapidated trucks and cars. At the breakfast bar I picked up the *Hindustani Times*, where I learned of an epidemic of dengue fever sweeping the capital—ten thousand reported cases. Would I be exposed?

After a jetlag nap, I went for a walk, searching for signs of the Delhi I remembered, some familiar ground. The filth was piled high, and I encountered makeshift cardboard houses and tents across sidewalks. The people, though, seemed absorbed and content. No beggars, for the authorities no longer tolerated them. The little streetside markets were busy, but I worried who was going to buy all that fish and mutton littering the steamy roadfront. On my return loop, I walked along the filthy Yamuna River, a virtual cesspool where kids played amidst little cairns of animal and human feces.

Returning for dinner at the hotel's pleasant South Indian restaurant, I thought back wistfully to the old Fulbright days and the comfortable headquarters at 12 Hailey Road. Ena Nader, secretary extraordinaire, had presided over the place with competence, dignity and grace. She always asked if we wanted tea and biscuits. With her ample figure and wide, dark-red lipstick smile, Ena was mother for us lost Americans. I missed the sparse traffic on the wide boulevards, clear skies, wheeling birds, and far more ruminants casually redirecting traffic. In 1968, Delhi had displayed herself as a capital of India should, with spacious dignity.

After dinner I went to hear a concert of classical music at Max Mueller Bhavan. The flutist was superb and the young Sikh on tabla showy but talented. I remembered my first live performance, sitting with the men at the concert hall in Dewas, women with children in their laps across the divide, the electricity of the music, my sense of belonging as the new *shishya* of Kumar Gandharva. But now the emcee, a society matron trying to become a sarod artiste, was playing. She was awful, and many walked out.

On the short journey back to the hotel, I hassled with rickshawallahs demanding inordinate fares. The trip over, a metered rate established with the help of the doorman had been fifteen rupees. The best offer I could get from these sharks was forty. A friendly middle-aged fellow with a pleasant face and brindled hair saw my plight and escorted me to the correct bus. The fare was one and a half rupees. Relieved and thankful, I paid for both of us. The bus was full, so we stood in the aisle, dangling from the ceiling bar amidst the crush of sweaty bodies. He leaned into my ear: "Surruh, you understand that the unemployment is getting more and more. In my neighborhood alone we are having forty percent with no jobs, or only little-little. I myself have no job since last six months. I have many peoples in my family, and my wife is sick in the bed. ..."

The bus approached my stop. He became desperate when he realized I was not going to pay him fifty rupees for saving me forty. Lowering his voice to a whisper, he blurted, "Sir, you want girl?"

This was a such a shift in conversational direction that I asked him to say that again.

"You want girl, sir? I can get you nice young girl very cheap." It was now time for me to get down. I gave him a firm no and handed him ten rupees. He hung onto the bus with one arm as it departed, his face a gray flag of disappointment. As I walked past the tall doorman with a handlebar moustache in Bollywood costume, I thought about how comforting it had felt to be cared for and how betrayed I felt when deceived. Was the sweetness and humility of the Indians I regularly encountered in the Sixties now something one bought, a commodity like any other?

The next morning, I negotiated a reasonable fare with a Sikh autorickshaw driver to ferry me on my Delhi errands. We hit an impenetrable traffic jam while still far from our destination, halfway across town. Three-wheeled autorickshaws are humble conveyances, two-stroke motorcycles with a rear seat and roofed cab, open on the sides, low-slung. As the hydrocarbons drifted downwards, my lungs seemed to thoroughly filter them all; the exhaust gases almost made me gag. I wished I had a handkerchief, like so many others I saw, clutching it to their nose and mouth, or a mask like the men puttering in and out of traffic on scooters (they also wore helmets, though not their wives and children seated behind them, apparently being more expendable). I warded off the momentary panic induced by fear of suffocation.

Errands accomplished, I was anxious to quit Delhi. Judi had told me something about the train, but the rickshawallah knew this travel agent, a guy in a pink cap who could get me a deluxe overnight bus. Thus began my bus adventure. To begin with, the shopkeeper where I was sent to wait was thoroughly absorbed in a cricket match. I anxiously watched a steady stream of busses pass during my forty-five-minute wait, befuddled by the darkness and my inability to read the Hindi destination placards. Observing my nervousness, my keeper reassured me, pressing his palms down in a quieting gesture between drags on his Wills cigarette, then returning his rapt gaze to the tv set suspended from the ceiling at the rear of the shop. I tried to relax. A few minutes later he realized we had missed the bus and sprang into action, calling two boys to help me lug all my gear to another site, only to find the bus had also left that place. So he arranged a rickshaw to take me to the last possible pickup in Delhi—two and a half hours after the time stated on my receipt.

It was around midnight, yet everywhere the night bustled with workers: road construction, warehousing, metalwork, engine work. Often the road was blocked by lorries or oxcarts unloading, the bearers, glistening with sweat, heading into narrow unlit lanes and dimly lit warehouses. Many intersections were torn up and marked with detours. Once we had to go the wrong way down a huge busy street. And I thought New Delhi Station was busy! Many tent communities spread into the streets, covering the sidewalks, almost everyone still awake, including young children lined up in rows on *charpois* like baby birds in their nests, waiting for mother to arrive with scraps of food. Some of the older kids were quietly playing board games by lamplight, recalling the neatly scrubbed children playing caroms back in Breach Candy with the Glee Club in '67, framed by fresh laundry fluttering in the sea breeze. It was the middle of the night, everyone was busy, and the day-long traffic jams continued unabated. It was like an unending Underworld carnival.

When we finally reached the bus, I thought for a moment there was some mistake, because this heap was hardly "deluxe." Settling into my seat, I inquired of my Nepalese seatmate, traveling with his wife and mother-in-law, and learned he paid less than half my fare. Cheated again.

The bus featured the narrow seats which became the bane of my travels in the mountains, beset with hip bursitis. I was never able to sleep for more than fifteen minutes at a time due to the road condition, which was abominable. This was a main road, but the monsoon had been particularly heavy, leaving gaping potholes everywhere. So every several minutes we would hit a crater and everyone on the bus would go flying towards the ceiling in a perceptible sinus wave. I had placed my laptop in the overhead luggage rack, and watched nervously as it mirrored our motion.

The Nepalese man next to me was so tiny, it felt like sitting with a young child. He and his family slept through most of the bounces, though with the biggest their eyes would momentarily half-open, closing again upon landing. A couple of times, I launched into the aisle. At the rest-stop, the bus headlights eerily lit a field of towering sugar cane which must have been eight feet tall. I flashed to the fields next to Ramanasramam, seeking the comfort of familiarity.

Tehri Besieged

The green-and-yellow state bus was old and dilapidated, and appeared to have been running continuously since our 1974 visit. It wound slowly out of the valley, through the goats and chickens and drifting trash. The road was wider than most, leaving plenty of room for oncoming traffic, so the shoulder was free for scores of black-faced monkeys who emerged from the forest to watch the traffic and scavenge for food. It was a grey, monsoony day.

When we entered the Bhagirathi Valley from the west I saw evidence of extensive earth moving. It was a nice wide valley here, chocked with huge storage sheds, trucks, and bulldozers. Everything was in motion, and the vehicles raised clouds of dust. I could see the vast potential for hydropower. There was a sign detailing the dam's sterling points. All I had time to read was "Afforestation of 1,100 hectares," a line I would see everywhere the next fortnight, testimony to the excellent job the Tehri Hydro Development Corporation did at greenwashing.

The engineer seated next to me shared his lunch. We did not share opinions on the Tehri Dam. "I work for the THDC, you see. Actually, the dam is critically necessary to the development of this region." We stopped at a large dusty bus-stand several miles out of town and my companion got down to change for New Tehri, the "model Asian city" built countless switchbacks above the valley floor which will one day sell real estate overlooking the giant lake formed by the dam flooding old Tehri town. Up to this point virtually all Indians I met were for the dam, because it represents progress. And if it collapses, inundating downstream Haridwar and Rishikesh, then, as the wealthy Brahmin farmer PK Agarwal told me en route in Kotah, that is the "will of God."

Returning to Tehri was disorienting. I thought I recognized the suspension bridge over the Bhagirathi, its one lane of macadam deeply creased, folded, and pocked. But I strained vainly to find the grassy bucolic town square where the bus disgorged us in 1974. I suddenly missed Judi and the time we spent together here. We pulled into a busy docking area near the commercial heart of the city: grimy, noisy, and muddy. Tehri was now a dirty, bustling town, not a pleasant backwater. I asked for the River View Hotel as instructed, which was right above the docking area. It was dusty and smelly, lots of flies, cowshit littering my path.

The big news is that the town was not flooded on June 30 as originally planned. Sunderlal and friends were able to get a stay from the Supreme Court, ruling that the Government had no right to evict the townspeople with only the coffer dam completed. But the stay was only a partial victory, for the court also refused to halt construction to await completion of the review. And that construction bustled along, sometimes extending into the night, a constant backdrop to life in Tehri, vast clouds of dust punctuated by frequent blasting. My nostrils were black.

My Moorhead State colleague VJ's relatives, comfortable Uttar Pradesh farmers I visited in Kotah en route, were right. Tehri is a dumpy town. Below me a constant stream of buses alternates blaring horns with birdlike whistles from conductors shepherding them into their docking places. With evening's descent, the din lessens. The hotel itself is primitive, drenched in the constant smell of urine, the filthiest place I have stayed since the dive in Kathmandu in 1968.

In the morning, lieutenants at Sunderlal's *kutir* confirm what the Riverview desk clerk told me the night before: SLB is on a speaking tour, returning Oct 1. The *kutir is* staffed in his absence by an impressive young disciple of the Dalai Lama, Tenzin. His Hindu colleagues simply call him *bhiksu*, monk; but he is anything but generic—the only *Punjabi* Buddhist monk in the world as far as I can tell. Tall, with close-cropped hair and intense dark eyes, Tenzin is passionate about ecology and the simple life. The solar cooker, his points about always using as little as possible, thinking of the animals, not just human well-being, are clear Buddhist responses to modernity.

"You see, Robert, I actually prefer feeding the monkeys to humans, because with the monkeys the cycle is complete; their feces go back to earth, rather than polluting the rivers." But he seems pleased to feed me, a gentle, welcoming host. Tenzin is not impressed with the West. "You in the West haven't changed your lifestyle." Perhaps George Bush Sr. was simply stating a fact in his defiant remark at the Rio Earth Summit, "The American way of life is unnegotiable." A defining moment, like Harry Truman's triumphant glee when the Hiroshima bomb went off.

The Ashram at Silyara

Since Sunderlal is not going to arrive for a few days, I decide to make a quick visit to the ashram at Silyara where Judi and I first met him, about twenty-five kilometers up the Bhilganga Valley from Tehri (the Bhagirathi and Bhilganga meet at Tehri, joining the Alaknanda downstream at Devprayag, where they all become the Ganga). The little towns along the route are busting at the seams. Gyansali, the end of the road when we visited Silyara, is crowded, now a developed market center.

No more rope bridges. Today the bus stopped right below the ashram at a chai-stand. The roads now reach higher and higher into the Himalayan valleys, as do the terraced slopes. Climbing the steep path, I have trouble remembering the place until I reached the old grain mill by the entrance, a cement pad with a hole in the middle which the girls pound in rhythmic succession with long wooden bats, just as they did in 1974. Finally, after being back in India a full week, a familiar place! But I was without my familiar life-companion. I recognize a few of the buildings, some with huge fissures in their walls. The library and school are completely rebuilt, all the result of a quake whose epicenter was at nearby Uttar Kashi in 1992.

Roughly eight people live here full-time, including a young couple and their baby, a few teachers, and two orphaned young teen girls who help with chores. Devendra and Surita run the ashram in SLB's absence, now almost ten years since he began his Tehri action. Though SLB does not have many active supporters on a daily basis, Devendra makes an impressive lieutenant. He and Surita seemed at first to be like the youthful Bahugunas. With Devendra's burning desire to take the work to remote villages, Surita is often left to hold the fort, as Vimla did for decades. Ironically, in both cases the Gandhians are repeating the Garhwali pattern: the women stay and do the homestead work, while the men go away to seek a livelihood. Devendra is passionately restless, extremely idealistic, yet worried that the farm is not run properly because he has to go off and work for the Movement like his predecessor. But unlike Vimla, a social worker who chose this life knowing that SLB would be a Gandhian activist, Surita is a city girl, with a masters in Sanskrit, and her distaste for this enforced country life comes out in a shrewishness, mornings punctuated by vituperative machine-gun harangues of her cohorts in the world's fastest Hindi. Still I like her, and by the time I left Silyara, sympathize with her situation as a misplaced scholar-teacher. She is Puer before he left Edenic Celo to pursue his PhD at Emory.

The school has grown, reconstructed at the top of the property beyond the cowshed. I remember climbing up to this spot among the wheat stubble with Judi and Sunderlal our last visit to pray at noon, joining disciples of Vinoba's Sarva Seva Sangha movement for peace and right livelihood for the poor throughout India. Devendra's view of education surprises me: "Our teachers not well trained. These children need to work. Beyond eight grades—what use?"

After a morning tour of forest and field, I go for *chai* at "tea master's" shop in Silyara village. He is friendly and verbal, but his eyes are bloodshot, with that dull alcoholic look, seeming to bear out Devendra's claim the night before that he ran the town pub after-hours. At the chai-shop I meet Oman Singh, a man in his mid-thirties, a self-described "Chipko soldier." Singhs are *kshattriyas*, the warrior caste dominant in the Garhwali hills.

"We need Sunderlalji here in the forests. He is making big mistake fighting the Tehri dam. Timber companies are plundering us and falsely accusing our women of thievery and harlotry. I would ask you to tell him to come back, but he will not listen."

I had heard stories of the women being verbally abused, called whores, and in a few cases actually roughed up by forest company men. Sunderlal set up a fund from the Right Livelihood Award purse he received on behalf of the Chipko Movement that pays one woman from each village to guard the trees. She can dispense it as she sees fit, but the number of forest guards remains insufficient for the task.

That night, I go to bed hungry. This is the only place in India that as the Guest I haven't been given "the best." The women eat with the men, something I have only experienced with my rich educated friends in Mumbai. Yes, they are poor, and the rice and dal is wearing on me. But they have a self-reliant spirit, and gritty dedication to their work.

25 Old Man of the River

I return to Tehri early the morning of October 1 and head straight to the *kutir*. It's still rainy. Sunderlal arrives shortly, returning from a talk in Varanasi. He is a tiny, wiry man of seventy with long wavy white hair and beard, a twinkle to his eye and a piercing sense of humor. He wears white khadi, khadi scarf wrapped around his hair. I think back to the earnest, disciplined iron-willed Gandhian, sleeping on the concrete floor, his wife and children in the double bed above him, surviving his long treks to the villages on *sattu* (powdered roasted grain, traditional food of trekkers) and "gooseberries" very high in vitamin c, like sailors on the old Greek ships. The iron will is still there, but he's mellowed.

Though he must be tired from the all-night train and subsequent bus from Rishikesh, Sunderlal is quite cordial. "So you want to learn about the Tehri Dam first-hand? Stay awhile and you will learn much. And how are Doctor Mrs. Judi and Hanuman? He must be a grown man now."

The *kutir* is a tin shack with one leaky good-sized main room cluttered with journals, mail, baskets of guavas from Silyara, old typewriters, and a second little room off to the side with two beds. Over his bed, a large photo of Swami Chidananda of Rishikesh, with images of Krishna around the base, and one of Ganesh. He has an old rucksack and a vintage North Face sleeping bag. In the main room are two paintings, one of SLB with the Dalai Lama, slapping each other's hands with glee, and one of his youthful teacher Dev Suman, looking like Nehru in his white khadi cap and blue vest. Dev Suman died in the Tehri jail after an 85-day fast protesting the lack of civil liberties under the Maharajah in the 1930's.

Over the next four days, I hang out at the *kutir* as much as I can, asking Sunderlal more and more questions as I digest the pile of material he has given me. Several images stand out: squatting in the morning sun, sifting his daily millet while setting up the solar cooker; chasing away the monkeys; laughing his toothy grin and slapping my hand as he told story upon story of the corrupt pols. Best of all is a scramble down the steep, boulder-strewn embankment of the rushing Bhagirathi to join him for a bath. Despite his age, Sunderlal is nimble as a monkey, and I must hustle to keep up. Once we reach the bottom, he puts his arm around my shoulder, turning me to direct my gaze at the Bhagirathi. Speaking above the roar of the diversion tunnels, he says, "See what they do, diverting the river from the farmers who need it to feed our people. You understand that none of the power they plan to produce will go to the Garhwali people."

"None?" I echo. I wonder about the "regional development" the engineer had applauded.

"None. It is highway robbery. My idea is to have many small dams that will help the local people, especially the women who must walk far to bring water."

"I've read about these dams. Run-of-the-river," I eagerly chime in.

"Correct. And do you know what we could do? We could have a small dam at each major village and pump water up to the villages, so the women could get drinking water without having to build more roads or walk many hours each day. And we could erect cables for small gondola cars to carry people and materials."

"What a great idea." SLB not only has a will of steel, he is brilliant. Later, with Judi in a Bangalore fabric shop, I meet an Indian seismologist who confirms that Sunderlal has anticipated some of his findings on Himalayan drainage, adding this is not the only instance of SLB's scientific acumen.

So we bathe in the frigid water. Sunderlal laughs as my flesh recoils from the shock, sharing the Himalayan bark he uses as soap and shampoo. It is difficult to believe that he made this daily trek unaided right up to the end of his 74-day fast just a few months before.

Apparently Sunderlal eats millet out of solidarity with the poor, though the villagers I ate with always shared their rice with me. He laughingly explains that he doesn't eat Tenzin's *kitchari* because vegetables and rice are "rich man's food." Living in his tin shack, refusing gift-money, he's proud to still earn as a journalist. Sunderlal is critical of the NGO's—the World Bank is anathema amongst the Gandhians and social workers of India—because they "rob the people of the will and ingenuity to solve their own problems." He claims that most NGO's are fronts for Western governments, and compares them to missionaries of old.

In the evenings I join the little group on the *kutir*'s small terrace for chants and prayers by the tiny shrine to Shiva/Ganga, a red railway warning flag fluttering in the wind. SLB ends the ritual by leading a prayer to Mother Ganga, which he follows by inviting introductions and open questions from visitors. I remember one man in particular, the Deputy Director of the Special Protection Group of the IPS (Internal Protection Service), assigned to protect the Prime Minister during an upcoming visit. Ramchandran is from Kerala, tall, a soldier's bearing, extremely intelligent and well-read. He tells me he has admired SLB all his life, now meeting him for the first time. Sunderlal smiles at him as he nimbly scrambles forward and bends low to touch the Gandhian's feet. After some pleasantries, he brings up his moral dilemma. "Bahugunaji, how can I discipline my men when the government officials over me continue to break the law with impunity?"

Sunderlal laughs "This is India's problem, isn't it? We must achieve a true and lawful democracy. Everyone must work for it, in each town and village, as well as in Delhi and Lucknow." Several meters behind her husband, his wife in a lovely sari and pretty pig-tailed daughter about seven move shyly forward for *darshan*. Ramchandran has a comfortable life in return for the ironies of his position. So do I.

The issues we discuss during the next four days range widely, including SLB's personal history, Indian politics and global economics, and the relationship between science and Vedanta. "The blueprint for survival should be based on the scientific facts of the West, but have the mystic vision of the East. Isn't it?" Sunderlal is in unassailable territory.

This certainly makes a lot of sense to me, but my biggest question concerns the transition to a sustainable lifestyle in India. Sunderlal claims that converting farming from annual monocultures to fruit and nut orchards is the way to feed humanity and restore the ecosphere. I am skeptical.

"How can everyone live off the land? What happens to the huge number of city dwellers here and elsewhere if we quit the industrial model?" I asked.

"The present rate of growth of the world economy cannot be sustained. Those only will survive who adopt traditional subsistent lifestyles. All others are lost," he said.

"But I don't understand how this jives with the Hindu belief that the aim of creation is to recognize, once it reaches human form, that it is God, merging back into the godhead. After the great die-off, maybe even extinction of the species, what happens to all those souls and the desire of creation to join the Creator once more?"

Sunderlal smiles. One man says, "It takes a very long time. Kali Yuga is the end of an era, not the end of time."

Tenzin adds, "Hungry ghosts. The Buddhists speak of this. There will be huge numbers of hungry ghosts desperately seeking bodies to incarnate in. They will circle the globe, endlessly."

Sunderlal nods his head in agreement. "Don't worry about Hindu cosmology. Go back to America and tell your political and industrial leaders to get off the backs of the poor. Encourage the farmers you know to plant nut trees. It will take time. And we have no time to waste."

Gangotri: A Midlife Yatra

Finding translators for my pilgrimage to other villages proves to be a virtual impossibility, since my visit coincides with the Uttar Pradesh elections, and all suitable translators are swamped with election activities. As we draw near the end of the last day's interview, Sunderlal suggests that since I am unable to go to the villages, maybe I would like to make a more traditional *yatra* after all. He points me not to Badrinath and Kedarnath, the principal pilgrimage centers, but up the Bhagirathi Valley to the Ganga's traditional source, rushing out of the mountains at Gangotri. As a devotee of the River, he often makes this pilgrimage, and in retrospect I think he wanted me to see something more inspiring than dumpy old Tehri. Besides, he has run out of pure water for ceremonial purposes collected from Gaumukh, glacial source of the Bhagirathi, and wants me to bring him back a liter.

I am disappointed not to walk the villages with Sunderlal, but the idea of a trip to the headwaters of the Ganga appeals to me. Many Hindu men make a yatra at age fifty, and I just turned fifty. And I'm curious to see how far upriver modernity reaches. I have read a back issue of *Bhagirathi Pukar* which discussed a Gangotri yatra made by some of the younger members of the Tehri Andolan. They observed disturbing patterns of development: the proliferation of chai, soda and potato chip stands along the final 22-kilometer pilgrimage route from Gangotri to Gaumukh. They also wrote with dismay and horror of finding two westerners fornicating in a saddhu's tent in the very shadows of the holy glacier. SLB wrote of his great sadness at the removal of a large *deodar* (Himalayan cedar) to provide space for a luxury hotel in Gangotri, a traditional pilgrims' center.

The morning bus labors the last several kilometers of steep switchbacks to Gangotri. We traverse thick forests, including some patches of native oak, cherry, mandel, and deodar, then break out into magnificent open views of the Himalayas. Once there, I mount the main street. Inquiring in the market, I find a suitable little hotel with a large room and a thick cotton mattress. This is where I will crash after my two-day trek.

Feeling energetic, I fairly bound up the steep cement steps rising from the river floor at Gangotri to meet the contoured trail cut into the ridge above. This is a mistake, compounding my failure to spend at least one night in Gangotri conditioning my lungs to the altitude (about nine thousand feet). Besides, I'm already out of shape. Very soon I start feeling like I don't have enough oxygen, and slowing down doesn't alter the feeling. I succeed in calming the mind, decoupling the feeling of oxygen-starvation from the panic impulse. This is more difficult than I have imagined.

I hike virtually alone the first several kilometers, but later join a steady stream of trekkers, mostly Indian. Some of the Europeans have snowshoes and ski-poles. I learn from one young man with a German accent that Tapovan, the alpine meadow another four kilometers above Gaumukh, has received twenty inches of snow the night before. I am impressed at the number of Indian women in their sixties steadily pulling the trail. This is probably their trip of a lifetime, a holy *yatra.*

But I don't sense much spirituality. As a young Indian college student emphasizes, they are "sportsmen." Though the route is punctuated with chai and chips stands, some with soft drinks in large coolers, I don't experience the sacrilegious atmosphere which SLB and his camp do. Of course, I have not seen the trail before the commercialization process began, so don't have their virginal image. It has only been in recent years that the bus even reaches Gangotri. The best place is the relaxed camp at Cheelbassa, with its little earthen terrace by a spring, accessed by pump with handle, with tables and chairs to take chai. Too bad I overlooked the camp on the way up, when I needed it most.

As darkness encroaches, I find a sufficiently level spot below the trail protected from the wind. I pass a cold, near-sleepless night, in good part because SLB's sleeping bag does not zip. But it is too cold for snakes, and there are too many humans around for bear or cat. Only a mouse bothers me, taking fright each time I roar at it in Hindi. In the middle of the night, suddenly the half moon beams across the valley at the snow-peaks, lighting them up as if by spotlights. Above, thick clouds, with deep holes into the firmament through which I see stars. Pre-dawn brings an even more magnificent scene, an absolutely clear, starry sky, with sparkling light from the unseen moon and sun across the whole rim, including a spectacular glow on Sivling.

Increasingly tired, I stash my pack at the "11 km" marker in a cave above the trail and proceed to Gaumukh with daypack, camera and lenses. As I begin my final approach to Gaumukh, a handsome young naked saddhu beckons with a drinking gesture while I wash my face in the Bhagirathi. He's going to give me some blessed Bhagirathi water as a kind of *prasad*. I go up.

The saddhu has a clean neat little tent. He's picture-perfect, his skin unblemished, hair in long Rasta-style Shiva locks, well-oiled. He is *moun*. He waves me towards the clean spread of blankets forming a terrace between his tent and the river. all this is very pleasant; it's nice to slow down. Mounisiv worships Ganga Ma and Shiva, a good combination in this place, and the sunny moment seems auspicious. No holy water, but he serves me warmed milk and some parathas, gritty from the glacial water.

Then comes the charade. He pulls out one of his primitive drawings of Ganga Ma and begin his silent pitch, dark eyes glinting expressively as his hands weave their own magic. It will bear my name plastered on the side, which he indicates by showing me a sample from some other foreign pilgrim. "10,000" is scrawled haphazardly on the border. I demur, feeling trapped and cheated. When I finally give him something, I ask for change, ten rupees back from my twenty: payment for breakfast, no longer a free offering.

Mounisiv is pretty cool about our little transaction, though he first asked for ten dollars, showing me a bill from his enormous plastic bag stuffed with a global array of currency. He reaches into the jungle of notes to pull out the ten-rupee note with a long set of tongs with great delicacy and deftness. He won't deign to touch money; it is unclean. He remains pleasant, backing off his hard sell once he realizes I won't play his game, now more bankclerk than saddhu. Later, I wonder how he manages to be the only saddhu in the shadows of the sacred glacier. Then I realize this could be the guy who provided the horny pilgrims his tent.

The glacier itself, reached through an increasingly boulder-strewn path the last few tenths of a kilometer, is gray and somber, dirty from the grit it carries, chafing the mountains as it moves. It feels alive and very vulnerable, and I worry that it will start melting before my eyes in the mid-day sun. It reminds me of Moby Dick rising up in the old Gregory Peck movie, and the sudden empathy I felt for that magnificent hounded creature. The water issues from underneath a cave, icicles lifting like stalagmites in its maw, the river source bubbling up as in "Kubla Khan." Some "sportsmen" are roaming around back under there. A young European man tells me about a great camping place about one hundred fifty meters above the cave. All I can imagine is camping on the glacier's back. I worry they're disturbing this living creature, more gentle dragon than "cow's mouth" (*gaumukh*), snout easing out of its hoary Himalayan lair like a huge exposed gray slug.

Near the Source is a group of about fifteen Indian soldiers in great spirits, undressing to bathe in the icy water. They ask me to take their picture. Oh dear! I know from past experience that they will want me to send them all copies, and I have either obliged or born the weight of guilt when I failed to follow through. So I refuse. Their faces fall with disappointment, and I feel guilty. I take in the scene for a few minutes, and scoop up two liters of Gaumukh water—one for me, one for Sunderlal.

A kind American woman—thirtyish with pigtails and decent Hindi—helps me negotiate with a porter a 100-rupee descent fee, since it has become clear I won't make it down alone with my entire load. The 18-kilometer descent the last day on virtually no sleep in this rarefied mountain air proves tough enough without it. I barely make it back down, even with the assist from the friendly young porter. When he tells me at the top of the steep steps down to Gangotri that his license does not allow him to descend into the valley, I am disconsolate. Newly burdened, I redescend the steep steps in utter exhaustion. I am asleep in my huge bed under scratchy wool blankets by dusk.

The next morning at the river, a priest gently asks if I want him to do a proper Ganga puja for me, and I politely decline, preferring to sit on a rock in the sun and quietly meditate after my chilling bath. The water is clear and cold, with a surprisingly high grit content, attesting to the Tehri Andolan's claim that modeling siltation from this river on the slow-moving Danube has produced inflated expectations for the length of the dam's service.

After the shock of being in Delhi again after almost twenty-five years, remote Gangotri feels like my India of the Sixties and early Seventies. Some people seem genuinely pious, and there is an atmosphere verging on innocence, brought into relief by Mounisiv's charade. I pay my respects to Ganga Ma at the funky temple with its tin roof, passing the open Tahitian-looking hut where King Bhagirathi supposedly performed his *tapas*, then enjoy an open-air shave from a grizzled old barber between the Ganga Temple and the River as I listen to its roar, huge boulders rising on every side, the breeze crisp.

Back at Tehri, Sunderlal debriefs me. Yes, I had a good *yatra*. No, it was not overly filthy, only moderately overrun. Yes, many European young people, as well as young Indians who identified themselves as "trekkers" and "sportsmen," and finally a good number of middle-aged and older Indians, making their *yatra*. I tell him about my difficulties finding accommodations, both at Harsil and at the Gujarati Ashram in Gangotri, and of my night spent by the trail in his sleeping bag. He feels like an insufficient host with the breakdown in bungalow accommodations, but he chuckles when I tell him about the broken zipper, which he has lived with for some time.

As I leave Tehri later that morning, I manage to get off a letter to Judi. I am pleased to receive phone confirmation for my visit with Udayan, looking forward to being at ease with the Patels. And in just two weeks, Judi will arrive in the South. But I have some grueling over-mountain travel before such urban comfort. This yatra is not yet over.

26 End of the Road

My plan upon leaving Tehri was to stay in a Himalayan hill station with a fine view of the snowy peaks as I wrote about Sunderlal and the Tehri Dam struggle—a reward for my hard work. Sunderlal has another idea, which is for me to go to the Gandhi Ashram at Dharomgar, deep in the Kumaon hills. He knows Sobha Behn, the Indian woman who had inherited the mission from Mira Behn and Sarla Behn, two Englishwomen who were dedicated Gandhians, giving the measure of their lives to decentralized hill development. He writes her a letter introducing me.

It takes two days to reach Kotmanya, a short jeep ride from Dharomgar. Alas, the jeep driver says that Sobha Behn had just left for Tehri Garhwal; we have crossed paths. Meanwhile, I have gotten to know a young biology teacher, Ashok, en route home to his parents' farm. A grimy little priest from the town had assured us that nobody was home at the ashram, inviting me to stay with him at the local temple. Mercifully, Ashok has given me a counter-invitation, and a battle for the prize foreen guest ensues. I thank the jealous priest, whose manner I find offensive, gladly accepting Ashok's offer. So we take yet another bus, forging on at dusk towards Paunkir, the end of the line. The road soon turns to rough, pitted gravel, and we proceed for seventeen kilometers, an hour and twenty minutes. This really is the interior of the Kumaon Hills, as I realize the following morning when I find the bus parked where the road withered against the forested mountain, marked by a lone chai stand. The end of the road.

When the driver drops us off that night, it's pitch dark, and I struggle up the steep path with my huge load of baggage. Then Ashok's mother, armed with a flashlight, ambles down to greet us. When she reaches us, Ashok bows low to the rocky earth to kiss her feet. He introduces us, and we follow her bobbling torchlight up the steep hill. The farmhouse is old, framed with rough wood, more solidly built than the stuff they throw up nowadays, a small square dwelling over a half basement created by the steep slope upon which it is built—probably a stable for the water-buffalo. The furnishings are spare, two old wooden chairs and a loveseat with stuffed, fraying red cushions, and a divan with a wood bottom and cloth cover on which Ashok regally seats me.

He introduces his wife, a small daughter and infant girl, clinging to her mother. His wife is pretty, though she bears the flat nose and wide, low cheekbones of the hill people, as opposed to her husband's more Aryan look. The family—everyone except Ashok—speaks Kumaoni, not Hindi. Ashok tells me that only fifty percent of the people in the region speak Hindi; virtually nobody speaks English. I ask if he's raising his daughters to speak Hindi.

"No, Doctor Robert, what is the point?"

His mother returns, watching me with delight, hovering with a bemused smile on her lips. She seemed fairly old in the dark, and once inside I have confirmation. She looks maybe mid-sixties, her face deeply lined, yet her hair is just beginning to grey. Ashok tells me she is "48 or 50." It feels odd for someone looking that venerable to be younger than I. When I show surprise at her age, Ashok acknowledges women's tough life.

The meal is not good: too salty, rancid ghee. Ashok recognizes this, and is embarrassed that he can't provide something better. I eat more of the chapathi and lassi, but can't handle anything else. After dinner, I inquire about the privy, and they send me to the edge of a little stream. It is obviously also the water-source, but one needs water for hygienic ablutions as well.

On this tiny farm, they grow rice, bread-grain, a little dal. Veggies are a luxury. The buffalo provides milk. Ashok has one sister, virtually exiled due to the distance of her married household—Ahmedabad, capital of Gujarat on the far West Coast, half a continent distant.

Ashok had told me on the bus that he was a high school biology teacher in nearby Kumdevi, but at dinner he confesses he was actually temporary, and that someone had been sent to take his job. He was returning, in fact, from fifteen days' unsuccessful effort at the UP high court in Allahabad to get a stay so he could go back to work. The judge had dismissed the case for lack of evidence and sent Ashok home to fetch a copy of the position ad for the post he felt he was being robbed of. He is returning to Allahabad in four days to wait his turn before the judge once more. In the midst of this burdensome ordeal—upon whose outcome the whole family depended—he receives me as royally as he can, excusing the simplicity and inadequacy, always calling me "Sir." He is incredibly kind to me, to his girls, very tender with his wife. His kindness overwhelms me, and I break into tears.

He wants me to stay, to visit his little apartment in town and have a proper bath, then go to the temple with him. He will play harmonium for me. When he sees that I am determined to move on to Kausani, he says we'll discuss these plans tomorrow. Tonight is for relaxing, and he'll treasure his fantasy until morning. He's interested in my work, the articles on Sunderlal, photos of Judi and myself, material on Kerala. He makes it clear how vital it is to have contact with these other worlds. But no Hindi for his daughters.

When I ask Ashok who is his *ishta devata*, his personal deity, he smiles. "Hanuman," turning his gaze in the direction of the nearby altar. But he adds most of the local people don't know these Hindu gods, worshiping the sun, moon and earth. He says he would, too, if he hadn't learned of the monkey-god Hanuman. They call the sun *Din*. When I affirm this is the name for "day" in Hindi, he says it's the word for god to the Kumaoni tribes. The day is god, and the sun rules the day.

So I spend one night at Ashok's farmstead, a poor Kumaoni family with a few steep, rock-strewn acres, in difficult straits after a light monsoon, their outside income jeopardized by his misfortune. Though I have been unable to visit the poorest villages of Tehri-Garhwal and hear their plight in the wake of the Tehri Dam project, I have been thrust willy-nilly into a "rural northern hill experience."

The bedding is thin and uncomfortable, yet as I drift off to sleep, smelling the rich buffalo dung from the paddock below, I contemplate how real this place feels. What would cloistered, antiseptic suburbanites back in the States make of this? I am a committed Hinduphile, and following Sunderlal's advice, an adventurer. What good fortune.

In the middle of the night I wake up disoriented, almost choking with severe claustrophobia. I feel like I can't get enough oxygen. I try to meditate it all away, but it starts to spiral towards full-blown panic. I get up, looked beseechingly at Hanuman on the altar, then out the tiny window into the thick darkness, and realize the dull despair of this place, barely held at bay. The reality which seemed so attractive at bedtime is now overwhelming. Ashok's hut is indeed the End of the Line.

I can't stop the spiral of panic on my own, so I take two sleeping pills and start the anti-depressants I have used periodically since a breakdown in grad school. I get past the near-panic, but wake in the morning exhausted for the predawn trek down the hill at 4:30 with Ashok to catch the bus. As we make our descent, he points out the farmers toiling by lanterns in their fields to finish the harvest so they can plough.

My dream of a writing retreat at the ashram in Dharomgar dashed, I proceed to Kausani, arriving October 10. It is still beautiful, but much more developed—lots of tourist hotels. Fondly remembering our honeymoon time at Gandhi's Anasakti Ashram, I request a room there. The ashram still stands in its strategic place overlooking the distant Himalayas, but the tourists and pilgrims now stay in a large multistory *dharamsala* behind and below it, no views to the Himalayan north. Standing at the door of the former ashram waiting for the manager to appear, I turn towards the mountains. The oak in the middle of the courtyard is now huge, so I squat down low to see the mountains under the branches. As I glimpse them in this prayerful posture, I feel the momentary intense presence of the two young lovers, Puer and Judi, Krishna/Radha, and ache for the sweetness of our youth. Yes, we were at our most content during our stay here.

I sense immediately upon meeting the new manager that things are very wrong. The old ashram where sweet old Guruji had lived and Gandhi had sojourned has been usurped as his personal dwelling. He is a comfortable burgher rich with European cologne and expensive clothes who greets me with slick deference. In the recesses of the house, I see numerous servants scurry to their tasks. My heart sinks. Another dream, another precious image, smashed. After meeting this new boss, I take a crude meal in the refectory behind his bungalow, buoyed only by the humble cheerfulness of the kitchen workers.

So instead of historic Anasakti Ashram, I stay at a congenial little hotel, where I recover from a violent illness that assaults me during check-in. I realize that it is the "tinned lassi" which Ashok's wife had given me, though the past two and a half weeks' stress had probably softened my gut. The two servings I drank had in fact been "tinned" with water from their spring/latrine. I take some of the powerful, broad-spectrum antibiotics which Judi has supplied as a precaution and spend a couple of enervated days in bed.

In 1973, Judi and I joined the wedding party of a Kumaon couple, the bundled bride lurching her way up the steep path in a palanquin. Though the bride's family had sponsored what for them was a lavish function, replete with costumed sword-dancers, it was the most meager wedding I ever attended. But the simple hospitality overflowed, and I felt it again at Ashok's hut at the End of the Road, right up against the impenetrable Himalaya. So much has changed in India. So little has changed in Kumaon.

27 Urban Adventures

letter to Judi, October 1996
Hating Delhi (aka hell), and all the stinking cities of the Gangetic Plain. Incredibly filthy, polluted, crowded ... people at you all the time.

After my recovery in Kausani, I leave the Kumaon hills, taking a "deluxe" overnight bus from Almora to Delhi. From Delhi I will fly to Dubai for a lightning visit with my sister Barry, then return to Bombay before joining Judi in South India. During the steep descent through the mountains, many of the Indians, unused to mountainous travel, vomit out the windows. The window right in front of me is streaked the rest of the journey. When we stop for snacks, chai, and urinal shrubs outside a small city, a sturdy cheerful young chai-wallah tells me that he's a disciple of Neemkaroli Baba, guru of Ram Das and Danny Goleman, the social psych grad student who tried to convince me to leave my Cambridge commune. Judi and I had felt strong vibes at his mahasamadhi site during our honeymoon, but I was so taken aback by the filth in the overburdened Ganga that I have no stomach for guru-talk.

The "Hilton Paradise" turns out to be a moderately seedy, overpriced businessman's getaway in an out-of-the-way neighborhood. The air conditioner is noisy, dripping copiously. Because of the location, you have to eat their food, like prison fare. I abandon Paradise after one night, finally going home to the YMCA just off Connaught Circus. But my feelings about Delhi and the urban North have permanently soured.

I write Judi a few times, but hear nothing back. She's due in the South soon—is it today? It has been an intense and difficult three and a half weeks. "Pilgrimage" is wearing on me. *Yatra* ended, my purpose now is to be with her in the South, and I'm just treading water. I miss being tended, having a simpatico friend with whom to share my sense of betrayal over the loss of a more innocent India. Maybe I have changed, too, dropping my rosy glasses, but it seems like the spirituality that suffused everything in the Sixties has vanished, replaced by a nation on the take. Joining her at a resort destination in the more civilized South seems like something I deserve.

The Bootblack's Box

My last evening in the capital, I attempt to chase my loneliness by dining at one of my favorite restaurants in Connaught Circus. As I head towards my goal, hungry but cheerfully expectant with a pocketful of rupees, a bootblack emerges from behind a pillar.

"You want shine suh?"

I inquired at the Y earlier in the day if this service was available nearby, and got a negative reply. I am delightfully startled. Since he doesn't have a bootblack's box, we walk over to a nearby car bumper, where I prop one foot at a time for the job. While he shines my shoes, this Rajasthani teen tells me his story. His father, a farmer, had died and he, his mother and two younger siblings moved to Delhi to seek a livelihood. They live under a tarp on the street, and he makes just enough each day to purchase their food. Then comes the inevitable request.

"Suh, could you purchase me a box? If I have box, police no more will be chasing me from the streets, and I am making enough money for my family to live better. It should not cost more than four hundred rupees."

Here we go again, I think. Like the good Scotch Presbyterian I was raised to be, I explain that he needs to save a little bit each day until he has enough to purchase the box. Perhaps I can give him a little to help get him started. But he needs to develop middle-class saving habits, not depend on the largesse of tourists.

He looks at me with this disarmingly earnest look. "But suh, to you it is nothing." This pierces my defenses like an arrow. I think of all the beggars I've encountered over the years and ask all the requisite questions needed to make this a bona fide deal. Yes, he would be happy for me to accompany him to make the purchase. He has located the box he wants, a used one that will work fine.

We wait on a dark corner as several buses pass by, sweaty citizens pushing and swinging on as best they can after their day's struggles, the tail-ends of the buses dragging perilously close to the pavement from overweight. This is not the kind of corner where I would normally hang out, and I'm happy that my young friend is along. As I reach for my money he warns, "Be careful!"

The area where our bus disgorges us is a large, highly organized shantytown several blocks square, with tiny thoroughfares leading among the huts, mostly of cloth and plastic. I later learn that this order is a product of mafia control. The government would never dare tear down these people's homes, as they regularly do in unprotected communities.

When we get to our target neighborhood, a wedding party is underway, accompanied by cacophonous music. The family engulfs me in their wave, giving me a choice between the separate celebrations, male and female, progressing in adjacent tents. Advised in a whisper by an older woman that the women's rite is "more interesting for you, sir," I enter a tent with a friendly multigenerational bunch of women, a supple teen dancing suggestively to a sinuous reedy *shenai* in honor of the bride's upcoming sexual initiation. I immediately realize this would not have been appropriate at a village wedding, or any higher caste one. This is a new experience, and I am a bit uncomfortable, feeling the voyeur. But the women are simply pleased that a Westerner has graced their ceremony in a place where few of us ever come. It is auspicious. The men don't seem to care.

After the dance, I compliment the young dancer, acknowledge the bride, and rejoin my patiently waiting bootblack. He takes me into a nearby wooden house with two rooms, palatial by local standards. The dealer greets us; it's clear that this transaction has a previous history. A young girl watches television on the divan while we haggle over the price. We finally close the deal at four hundred fifty rupees, which my friend tells me immediately after we step outside was too high. I misread his head nods. *To you it is nothing.*

But the deal is done, and I want to celebrate. Now I'm really hungry. My friend shows me a simple but adequate shop where I get a complete *tali* for twenty-five rupees, the most ample meal I have ever gotten in Delhi for that price. But Prakash refuses to join me, saying that his mother will have supper waiting for him when he returns. I keep shoving bits of my fare towards him, but he won't even eat a *pappadum*. I have befriended this boy and become his benefactor, but I am not *family*. I feel greedy eating in front of him. My own sons would devour these talis, Jacob two.

On the bus back to Connaught Circus, I look over at my companion as he gazes fondly at the box between his feet. Though the merchant got a modest steal out of our exchange, this is still the best ten dollars I've ever spent. My stomach is full, and I have seen a side of Delhi I would never have experienced otherwise.

Bombay: Return to an Island of Privilege and Comfort

The great crawling sea: breakers crashing in patches of gray-green amidst the sullen brown.

"We will pick you up, anytime in the night," my host said over the phone. "We" means Jayanthi, the Patels' driver who I remember from the Seventies. It is indeed night, and Jayanthi's route takes me through acres of slums built of tarp and tin, but now very few sleepers lining the streets. I am back in Bombay with my old friend Udayan and his wife Anuradha before heading south to join Judi in Kodaikanal. Shaibya, their fifteen-year-old adopted daughter, stays on a pallet in her parents' bedroom while I sleep in her bedroom plastered with movie posters, most prominently Leonardo Di Caprio, who looks down beatifically. I always feel welcome at their flat.

From the ninth-floor balcony, my fortress, I can look out and see it all. The seafront would now be a dunghill if not for the tides. Where before genteel ladies stood on coal-black rocks lifting their saris above the swirling waves, poor men defecate on the same rocks, their products masked by the brown tides each afternoon. For days I watch as street-people go down the pathway burrowed between three-foot mounds of weathered refuse to perform their ablutions at low tide. Women do their business here too, though for modesty's sake they clamber much farther out, hopping ebony rocks to distant outcrops. This morning ritual is a good example of the encroachment upon the commons of fecal garbage and environmental despoliation in wealthy enclaves in the developing world. The Patels ignore it.

I watch more upscale folk across the road briskly walking in white shorts and cotton sweaters on the path around the grassy flower-bordered walled compound next to the US Consulate. Dead-serious, they remind me of the Norwegian power walkers back in northern Minnesota. And in this tight little seaside enclave, I also observe for the first time a heterosexual couple in India in a mildly erotic public display, arms draped around each other's waists and buttocks. Weekend pony rides are still available down by the beach on old Warden Road. One little girl's head bounces like it is going to fall off, rolling dramatically forward, then snapping back to the pony's trot.

Women and children brush their teeth with actual toothbrushes, more prosperous descendants of the Sleeping Dead I encountered motoring through the night in 1967. They've tossed their neem-stick brushes, and their clothes are cleaner, less tattered. Others will come and bathe in the ocean at the same spots where the morning crew did their ablutions. Unsanitary! Yet we constantly flush our waste into waterways, cleansed by chemicals and settling ponds, to be sure. At least here in India you see the shit right before your eyes. The street people have no illusion that we are some kind of superior being. *The great crawling sea, breakers crashing in, flushing out the shit and industrial waste.*

Bombay, tarnished jewel, Breach Candy fortress island of privilege, buttressing my hosts and their friends against the reality of the urban poor. I observe the different reactions to the squalor from a liberal raised in a "classless" society and brahmins who, though educated in Western institutions, do not question the caste mindset. Of course I mustn't forget that I met Udayan courtesy of the Harvard Glee Club and the international Harvard network of Old Boys to which his wealthy industrialist neighbor belonged.

My favorite Indian city seems much the same, new skyscrapers and many more people, but the same essential character, preserving many of the old Victorian landmarks. Unlike Bangkok or Tokyo, one can see how the city has grown around them. The waterfront is familiar, because the coastline holds its shape. I had hungered for this comforting familiarity the entire journey.

Part of what I like about Bombay I suspect is that I move in a privileged world. It is very different from the trapped world of Ashok in Paunkir or that of the Garhwali peasant whose land is threatened by the Tehri Dam. This urban world is the one which is hungry for the Dam's energy. Sunderlal speaks of the swimming pools of the rich supported by water and energy robbed from the Garhwali people. The electricity from the dammed Bhagirathi flows to Delhi. My wealthy friends will thrive upon energy from a similar dam planned for the Narmada River, near Indore. Someday, as I party with these friends, far to the northeast brave Sunderlal's cremated ash will flow down the choked Ganga to join the sea of lies, corruption, and filth.

The last time I was here, Anuradha was a polite ghost clad in a white sari mourning Padmaben's death. Now she's a person: intelligent, handsome olive face framed in short hair, western dress, a chain smoker. With gregarious Shaibya, she is firmly holding the line, highly concerned over her daughter's poor performance in school, a constant focus of family life.

Memories of this flat flood back. Ramanlal, Bombay's first Freudian—looking at and through me, yet kindly. Padmaben treating me as if I were a nephew, Udayan's cousin-brother. She didn't speak English, just looked at me and smiled that wide gap-toothed smile, big round eyes crinkling in her broad, deep brown face, especially when watching me eat. She nodded firmly when Udayan and Ramanlal told tales of her arrests and jailings during the independence struggle.

Both parents join in Udayan, who has his analyst father's hunger for the truth and his mother's fierce love and joy at feeding you. Last night's dinner gathering brings back old scenes. I remember Udayan as the accepted elder of his peer group, analyzing their words and actions, while they paid careful heed to his comments. Last night guests still huddled attentively around him, and dinner was delayed until eleven.

Ramanlal was close to Maurice Frydman, and Udayan grew up watching my mentor's unrelenting pull towards self-realization, buttressing and occasionally challenging his father's secular Freudianism. They knew J. Krishnamurthi, too, so the family intellectual and spiritual influences combined to nurture a fiercely independent and broadly liberal stance. In common to all of these was a firm adherence to Socrates' dictum about the unexamined life.

Udayan teaches as well as seeing patients. He has eight to ten students in a self-selecting class. It is unclear after meeting them if any of these students plan to practice. The key is that he is continuing the tradition of the Breach Candy flat under his father—imparting tools of the consciously examined life.

A sannyasin looks at me from the cover of a book. I Feel like I am in the presence of an old friend who knows me. My god, it's that fellow Maurice introduced me to! The cover reads "*I Am That*, Sri Nisargadatta Maharaj, translated by Maurice Frydman, published by Udayan Patel." Not only did I not know how to respond to the Master when Maurice took me to see him in 1968, I have totally forgotten the incident.

I recall some of the details, but the gist of it all was descending the ladder and going back out into the twilight air, relieved to escape the dingy confines, yet wishing I could do it all over again. If I had, I might have evoked his fundamental insight: "Love says, 'I am everything.' Wisdom says, 'I am nothing.' Between the two my life flows."

The usual crowd gathers at Sagar Darshan for salon, drinks, and eventually dinner. It is October 27, the date I fly to Madurai to join Judi in Kodaikanal. My bags are packed, and I cram samosas while grabbing a drink. Jayanthi arrives, right on time. As we enter traffic on B. Desai Road, I recheck the ticket. I have misremembered the time, giving Jayanthi another opportunity for racing brilliantly through the streets of Bombay. I arrive, ticket in hand, twenty minutes before take-off, only to find the gate closed. The gate officials are firm. "Airline policy, sir. We're very sorry."

Judi has arranged a trekker to meet me at the airport. My negligence means that I am standing them both up, which weighs on me the whole drive back to Udayan's. But missing the flight also brings fortune. When I re-enter, Roshan, my romantic gateway to India, is across the room, her head turned, giving me a moment to regain my composure. How we change in thirty years. The image of her young face is perfectly preserved in Puer's immaculate memory. But despite time's erosion, she still has those dark smokey eyes that so captivated me. She has matured, her romantic flitting grounded in a more thorough knowledge of the arts. Like Udayan and Anu Radha, she moved away from Sagar Darshan and then back, after her parents died and she divorced. A music critic, she has interviewed both Satish and Mukhul, my *gurubhais*. I ask her to update me on Mukhul's career, sharing my judgment that he had the most potential of any of Kumarji's *shishyas* to carry forward his legacy. I have heard nothing about him all these intervening years. Roshan answers the mystery.

"Yes. He is still the most talented inheritor of Kumarji's musical gifts, but he's squandered them in playing the *mast*. You know, wandering around in a lungi like a saddhu from place to place. It's a pose, you see."

Roshan goes on to recount an interview where he wore a monkey hat, a lungi with shorts underneath, and a wild shirt in a huge flower-pattern. She says he uses *ganja* and *charas* and is frequently drunk. And he throws fits, shouting, even physically abusing people

"Does he still give concerts?"

"Occasionally. But he's usually drunk. I attended a concert in Bombay where he was so drunk—or stoned—that he couldn't go on. It was terrible, I tell you. He has worn all patience among the musical community. Now he is ostracized everywhere."

"And what about Satish? They were really close in Dewas."

"Oh, that is really sad. He desperately needs Satish's friendship and support, but when he's drinking, he abuses him terribly. It's a love-hate relationship. He ridicules Satish's lesser voice and weaker breath-control. But Satish tolerates far more than I would stand for. He's a rock of sanity and stability."

"I would love to see Mukhul. You know he was my teacher during my second stint in Dewas."

Roshan nods, coolly taking this in. "He is giving a concert in Bombay in December. I can get you the date and hall."

"That would be great." I hesitate, adding, "That is, if he can go on."

Roshan smiles grimly. "One never knows with Mukhul."

I leave the party to phone Judi about missing the plane, feeling guilty over having such a good time that I neglected her. "So you missed the plane. I've already sent a jeep to pick you up. Why have you been so out of touch? I've been worried about you."

"Believe me, I'm the one who needs touch. I've tried several times to reach you. Haven't you gotten my letters?" A postal strike has coincided perfectly with my Indian sojourn, and she hasn't received a single one. This extra day's delay makes me keen to see her, to end a distance I now realize is greater than I've allowed myself to feel.

28 Kodaikanal

Judi is at the Kodaikanal bus-stand to greet me, dressed in a light blue everyday sari. Kodai is beautiful, as was the ride from Madurai, both the robust healthy agriculture of the plains and the dense, dripping forest of the long, laborious ascent. I drink in the fragrance of mountain air. My heart jumps as she smiles brightly, heading to the bus to greet me. We will be together here for almost three weeks, then tour South India and make a quick trip to Indore and Dewas before heading back to Minnesota in early December.

She apologizes for not sending another trekker to meet me. I brush it off, since the bus wasn't too crowded and had decent tires. After all, I stood up the jeep she sent the previous day. "It's great to be here—what a beautiful place. But the taxi-wallah at the Madurai airport ripped me off. I thought they only treated you that way in the North."

"Madurai has become a big city. They're all like that now."

How easily she says that; how quickly she has adjusted to Indian modernity. The changes that devastate me don't seem to bother her. But after all our missed communications, exacerbated by the lengthy postal strike and missing yesterday's flight, it is a delight to be together again.

The marketplace is busy, yet nobody pressures us to buy anything. They seem to know her, and once again, as in the Seventies when she passed as a Punjabi, being with her protects me.

Within three blocks lined with vines trumpeting seven-inch white blossoms and huge flowering shrubs lies our bungalow, a three-room stone building, its functional entrance at the rear through a bathroom, the largest room in the house. It's the largest bathroom I've seen in India. You walk through the shower and past the toilet to reach the "receiving" room, our bedroom. On the front adjoining the porch is a long vestibule where I will create an office-space, replete with a propane burner on the counter for tea. We have no kitchen. The bungalow is adjacent to the compound of Bruce and Tamar's sprawling two-story house, where they live with five kids, assorted pets and a trusty *ayya*. Judi is substituting for Bruce while he stumps for money in "a hundred" Lutheran churches back in the States to support his doctor's salary.

As the sun goes down behind the tamarinds and live oaks behind our bungalow, it's suddenly cold. We are at seven thousand feet, it is almost November, and like all Indian houses, ours has no insulation. I hug Judi, as much for warmth as for touch, but she quickly disengages and heads for the pile of sticks by the tiny fireplace in the corner. She lights a smoky fire, and after waiting ten minutes for the draw to improve, asks me to open the windows. Now the smoke is thinly suspended in the room. I watch carefully to see if it will set off her coughing, but it doesn't. We each grab a book and head for the lumpy bed—our first double-bed in India. I can tell immediately that the quilts are musty. "Jude, doesn't the smoke and the mustiness here set off your allergies?"

"No, I'm fine most of the time."

I am relieved. The fire, which nets no appreciable heat, gutters out and the smoke clears. Thankfully, plenty of quilts, and my wife's familiar body.

On our first morning we rise early for a sweet little hike on the "Coolie Road," the old ghat road which links the plains of Tamil Nadu below and the mountainous interior along the Kerala border. The ghat is a terrace across the Southern Ghats built and serviced by coolie labor in the nineteenth century. Our guide is Hans, middle son of Tamar and Bruce, who at eleven is already seasoned, pleased to have hiking guests. As we set out, I recall the morning at Celo when Jacob and two close friends—all elevenish—set out with their fathers, waving goodbye as I stayed behind to write, a sharp pang of regret staying with me throughout the morning.

The road passes neat whitewashed farmhouses, a large field of blue-green cabbages behind a row of apple trees, flowers on every side, through a stretch of jungle, opening upon a massive brown cliff to the northeast. Further down the *ghat*, we reach a vista revealing multiple layers of velvet green misted mountains. Behind us, Hans shows us a foggy ledge under which hang more angel trumpet vines, huge flowers, white with red rims on their throats. On our return, we take another route, passing through a poor but well-kept village, huts of mud and stone with thatched roofs. Hans knows many of the children, who run to greet him. As we return to the bungalow, he says sweetly, "I can take you to a different place every morning before school if you'd like."

The people here are more polite and civil than in the Hindi Belt, but I expected Kodaikanal to be more quiet, clean, and British colonial, untouched by the blight of modernity. When I hear "hill station" I imagine a secluded mountain resort. Kodai is jammed with tourists, most of them Indian, and everyone leans on his horn. It's as if drivers don't trust others to watch the road; they have to *hear* you coming as well. "Air horns prohibited" read signs at each end of town. But the truckers ignore them. Being blasted by one of these at close range is worse than a night at a rock concert. As the horns gradually lessen, folks go out for evening walks.

In the Sixties, the tinkling bicycle bells during mornings cycling to Government Arts and Commerce College buoyed me. What a miserable contrast these air horns make! I look forward to my return to Indore, the dense trees of Palasia, the mango commons along MG Road in spring. But these pleasant thoughts are shadowed by the knowledge that my old colleague Chandel, who once told me the solution to the "Untouchable Problem" was to line them all up and machine-gun them, is now vice-chancellor of the university.

I awaken this Monday morning to the incongruous notes of Christian hymns descending from the church on the corner. I can't tell what language they are singing, but the notes themselves are tired and predictable. What a cultural waste, ignoring the rich tradition of Carnatic music. It's cold until late morning, and I have to bundle up at my writing desk and prepare another cup of tea, just like back home in the North Carolina mountains during winter. Judi's off at her routine, morning rounds at the private hospital, then hanging out at the school, followed by regular hours at the school clinic in the afternoons. She's clearly bored, so she's taking on two projects: one doing "well physicals" for the poor children at a church-supported creche to identify serious problems of malnutrition, development and chronic disease. The second is screening the entire Kodai School staff for TB.

In the bustling morning market, I buy Judi a string of jasmine. But when I present it to her outside the dining hall at lunch, she seems conflicted.

"Bob, that's really nice, but I can't wear jasmine; I'm allergic to the scent."

"Oh, I didn't know."

She smiles, her eyes tinged with regret. I'm disappointed, feeling romantic. As usual, I'm more hurt and angry than sympathetic, but I try to put myself in her shoes. God, I couldn't manage to continue so cheerfully with so many allergies.

In the evening, I go for a run around the large lake that is the central feature of Kodaikanal. The houses are quite upscale. Looking back across the lake, I get a beautiful view of the Kodai School campus. The big hotel rents colorful rowboats, and I see a couple idling in a bright red one, the male a poor oarsman. Like cars signaling each other on the road, we answer farts tonight; a long one from her, then my short answering toot. Boisterous sounds assault us from the corner church, a shouting match, rendering sleep a challenge. Tamar tells me the next morning that both the hymns and the drunken cacophony were from a South Indian college group on vacation.

Our *ayya* Bina is quite decent and competent. She keeps us in kindling and cleans six days a week, but she doesn't cook, so we must seek food every breakfast and dinner. Lunches at the school are satisfying. What a luxury having a cook, like the Bombay-wallahs. It provides employment and, as Judi points out, another set of relations, as well as comfort.

One day at lunch Judi introduces me to Imon Ghosh, a Bengali economics teacher. She has gotten to know Imon well, sponsoring him for the Kodai Rotary Club. I think I'll never get used to her being a Rotarian. We shake hands. He's handsome and friendly, a huge winning smile.

"So you teach economics to these high school kids? That's unusual isn't it?"

"Well, I try my best. It's just an introductory course, you see. But some of them seem to be interested."

We move into a discussion of Indian development, and Imon talks about the model of the Grameen Bank in Bangla Desh.

"And what do you think of Gandhi's approach?" I ask him.

"Gandhi of course had good ideas, but he lacked an understanding of the need for capital to get village economics on a firm footing."

Judi has a meeting, but as she is leaving, she spots a British woman in her fifties heading towards us. She puts her tray down, reaching for her. Pippi teaches biology, has written a book on Indian birds and is working on another on butterflies. She tells me about her family planning lesson for juniors.

"I have them pair up, boys and girls. They are of course uncomfortable with this, even more so when I present each couple with a fresh egg which they must manage to protect throughout the week without breaking it. The egg is their child. They quickly learn the weight of responsibility caring for this egg-child. My hope is that they will remember this during moments when they are tempted by unprotected sex."

I am impressed by Pippi's devotion to teaching and her lively intelligence. Before the end of the meal she asks me to talk to one of her classes about Sunderlal and the Tehri Dam. "But don't expect them to know anything about Gandhi. I'm afraid most of them come from families where he is not discussed."

Nevertheless, the blank looks when I recount Gandhi's civil disobedience campaigns surprise me. The idea of *gram swaraj* (village power) is new to them, as well as the notion that the national government might work so methodically against local interests. They have some questions, but only one student, a tall Kenyan, wants to do follow-up research. Poor farmers in the Himalayas are not an issue for these well-heeled kids, most of whom are bound for college in the US.

Kodai School is very un-Indian, a mild Lutheran bastion paying lip-service to the Hindu world in which it is embedded. (It is one of two American prep schools in India; the other is at Mussoorie, which hosted our Fulbright final gathering back in 1969.) The campus is well-kept, the graystone buildings with orange tile roofs soothing. The realisation tree, covered with red blossoms, is blooming everywhere.

Judi delivered her first baby in India this morning, after hurriedly grabbing a spare set of gloves from the maternity nurse. The glove supply with her special cache of extra-smalls was locked for the night by the careful administrator. She's had some interesting cases, including an attempted suicide by a woman who was married off and came here to honeymoon with the arranged husband. Unfortunately, her family ignored the minor detail that she had a lover. She hung herself by her sari, but the designated husband found her and cut her down in time. Judi thinks the Indian marriage system is at least as good as ours. Perhaps, if you can manage to avoid falling in love.

Over several days I notice the remains of curious little fires in the thick grass in a deep bank along Hospital Road, where I walk daily to and from the school. One afternoon I find a droll little old man in the act of setting one, and ask him what he's doing. He is delighted to explain. He's from a nearby village and had come to the hospital for an operation on a fractured wrist one month previous. The fires are an attempt to get relief for his wrist, which hurts from the cold. After paying the doctor's bill, he is unable to reach home because he can't afford busfare. "If Doctor Bruce were here, my good Christian sir, he would take care of me." He used to be a chef, accompanying treks with the Kodai School. He convinces me to give him twenty rupees for the busfare home.

A couple of days later, I see him again. "I thought you had to go home," I said sternly. "Oh sir," he replies, "if you see me again out and about, I am the world's greatest liar."

About a week later, I again see him, approaching with a big jar of preserves. I am righteous and indignant: "You are the world's greatest liar, and I don't like liars."

"No sir, no sir, I am a good Christian Lutheran. Won't you take this pineapple jam? Here, taste it."

At first I imagine he's making amends, but the idea this time is I could pay him the cost of the busfare and actually get something back. "My thatched roof blew off in a big wind and I must go to the neighboring village to see the carpenter. Please sir."

"I'm not your sugardaddy," I answer gruffly, walking away. Begging by the destitute was one thing, and I always struggled with it. But I absolutely hated lying and manipulation.

One night we listen to Kumarji tapes I bought in Bombay with Lakshmi, whose father brought the violin to pre-eminence in Carnatic music. The violin is so central to the tradition as we know it that it's hard to realize it's a Western import. As we talk quietly, listening deeply in a room lit only with oil-lamps, I re-enter the world of that music, and am almost overcome.

"It's like we are being strung like beads on the flowing line of Kumarji's music." I echo Puer's youthful journal.

Lakshmi nods, a deep smile of appreciation on her face.

"Yes, it's the cosmic thread that holds it all together," Judi adds. "Music and spirituality join so naturally in India."

Listening to the music together, the three of us are strung together for some long moments, silently glancing at each other in the softly lit room, Lakshmi's kind face almost as black as Kali-Ma, the destroyer. And I realize that it is the soul of India, the deep well of spirituality, that I really miss this visit.

The "Unknown Rotarian"

Judi joined Rotary while we lived in Moorhead, which was how she found the volunteer position at Kodai. It fit our yuppy lifestyle, and she resonated with their internationalist values. Two years before, we had attended the Rotary International Convention in Nice with my parents, since my father was also a Rotarian, and we were all Francophiles. Rotary is popular in India, so it is no surprise that Kodaikanal has a club. Geeta has met a couple of the local members, and wants to sponsor Imon.

The District Governor from Madurai, a short, tough-looking fellow with a pocked face, presides at the monthly meeting. After introductory pleasantries, an oatmeal-faced man from Anaheim gives an embarrassingly poor, rambling talk. Then the District Governor introduces Judi, with a dignified, honest display of admiration. Dressed in a splendid magenta sari with gold border, Judi speaks about her work and her gratitude for being able to serve the community. She is low-key, impeccable and eloquently brief, putting in relief the false show of the guy from Anaheim. I have always admired what an effective public speaker she is.

At the board meeting before dinner, the District Governor gives the local club hell for not informing him in advance of Judi's presence as a Rotary Volunteer. Now he gives a folksy speech, ending with an appreciation of my beloved. "Rotarians are nameless, doing all kinds of tasks and giving plenty of money to the foundation, but don't receive the personal credit of the Fords and Rockefellers. Each is a brick in the great Pyramid of Humanity. And lo, here in our midst, the Nameless Lady Doc from USA, doing good works. She, my friends and colleagues, is the Unknown Rotarian."

I am proud of Judi, but the evening's Rotary company reminds me of too many medical society functions over the years. I am the "doctor's wife" no matter what else I might say or do. The context is always so thickly layered with expectations, and usually I am the polite southern boy, loathe to disturb them, though I did practice mild guerrilla forays into the world of intellectual discourse, which often involved ignoring the wives. When Judi became President of the Yancey-Mitchell Medical Society in North Carolina, a position whose baggage included the doctor's spouse hosting the Christmas Party, I made it clear that if she were president, this precedent would be broken. I knew my limits

As we mill about the serving tables I find myself next to the District Governor, my glance shifting from the chafing dishes to the big diamond on his dark, stubby finger. The District Governor does not smile when I tell him that my main work in India is chronicling SLB's struggle against the Tehri Dam.

"You realize, of course that we desperately need the power the dam will provide." he said pointedly. He goes on to tell me he is a Tamil movie producer, India's biggest.

Looking down at this powerful man in his tailored suit, I light into him about what I judge globalization is doing to traditional Indian society and its timeless values. The producer is taken aback to hear this from the Unknown Rotarian's spouse. His careful answer is that the atmosphere in India is one of "ambiguity" in the wake of Rao's opening the economy to the capitalist West.

I am in a fighting mood after an evening of boosterism, ending our conversation with a lament. "What is being lost by damming the farm valleys and trivializing traditional culture in the film and advertising industry is the wellspring of religious depth that India has developed over millennia as a resource for humankind."

The District Governor shakes my hand, bowing with more grace than I deserve, and moves on. He is intelligent and alert, but a businessman. I am a misbehaved Rotary spouse, an uppity romantic intellectual.

As for the "ambiguity" he speaks of, I feel it in the adolescence of that new phenomenon, the Indian Tourist, who blights this genteel southern hill station with his whistles, hoots, and general rowdiness as surely as he does the Himalayan resorts of the North. I long for the beauty, the quiet of bicycles, and the deep religiosity of *my* India. The Indian middle class, now legion, has betrayed me, and their heritage as well.

Back in our bungalow, I heartily endorse Rotary's belated recognition of Judi's contribution. "But my talents are really being wasted here," she demurs. "They just need someone for emergencies at the school, and the hospital schedule is inefficient. And it really bothers me that everyone, including the poor, has to pay."

I think of the old man and his brushfires. "But you have the creche project—and now the TB project."

"Oh, I didn't tell you. ... I talked to Bruce last night and he made it clear there would be no follow-up on the TB tests."

"What! Is this just his sinecure or something?"

"It's not that. Bruce is a good guy. It's just that docs in the West are trained to fit into our richly resourced system. Here, the best of intentions sometimes only makes things worse in a system where only the rich can pay for services we have come to expect routinely."

Though feeling underutilized here at Kodai, Judi is upbeat about India's future. I find it hard to see why. It turned out that more than sixty percent tested positive in those TB tests. But she is really excited about joining the nationwide Abolish Polio vaccination campaign that Rotary is sponsoring next month in Indore. The timetable is to abolish the disease worldwide by 2000, and they are getting close in India. She wants to come back.

I am less sure I want to return, except to see Udayan, perhaps go trekking with my sons. At this point there are no ashrams that pull me. The shock of all those city lights in Tiruvanamalai on the cover of a commemorative book makes me fear visiting Sri Ramana Asramam. I don't want my hallowed images of that sacred place ruined. What I saw in Tehri and the urban North shook me to the core, and though the South is more civil, modernity has arrived here, too. The most important thing that might bring me back would be Sunderlal's Final Fast.

As our time in Kodaikanal draws to a close, *The Sun*'s "man in India" mails off his piece on Sunderlal and the Tehri Dam. We finalize arrangements for a little tour of the South before heading home, much of it planned by Imon, who we meet at Ernakulum Junction, across the bay from Cochin. I have wanted to visit Cochin ever since Stuart's glowing reports during our Fulbright year. Imon and his friend J. Prakash are on the platform to greet us. Ernakulum Station, covered with anti-AIDS government health banners, is nothing special. But once we head across Cochin Harbor to the Seagull Hotel, smelling the salt air as seabirds wheel among the various craft, I feel like we might get what I came for.

J. Prakash is an environmental lawyer who Imon calls a "giant-killer" for his role in bringing some of the industrial polluters to heel. Lean and lanky, sallow-cheeked, with one glass eye, he dresses in grey chino pants and workshirt. Our taxi-boat trip to Cochin Island is peppered with descriptions of exploits, the most famous being the case where they (Imon helped J. Prakash with the research) forced the shutdown of an anhydrous ammonia plant that was right at the end of the Cochin Airport runway. One plane narrowly averted a toxic conflagration when it skidded past the runway in the late Eighties. This Kerala backwater lawyer took his case all the way to the Supreme Court in Delhi and won. As the boat approaches Cochin, J. Prakash points out a waterfront building. He speaks English as if it were Sanskrit, with no word breaks.

"Weshallhavethemteereetdown. They have beelteetintheemarshlands. This is strictly againstheecode." What a waste I think, admiring the architecture.

We meet several other friends in Cochin: KP Joseph, a poet and journalist with a strong sense of social justice, and an elegant Mr. Menon, first cousin of the former Defence Minister. We sit in his marble-floored living room overlooking a verdant garden and the ocean, sipping supersweet South Indian coffee. When Judi tells him I was Kumarji's student, he gives me a long look that acknowledges my remarkable good fortune. He tells me that his brother in Delhi is just finishing Kumarji's biography.

The most poignant meeting is with John Mumpalli, aging editor of the *Malabar Express*, longest continuously running independent newspaper in India. The tottering old man shows us his manuscript collection of impassioned editorials from the Quit India movement, our knees all ganglioned together as we pore over them—Judi surrounded by a bunch of Indian men. She is comfortable in both men's and women's worlds, perfectly fine with our hosts. KP Joseph, whose daughter is married to Mumpalli's son, asks me for help in publishing the collection in the US. "We owe it to him," I say to others in the crowded car as we drive off. I will never forget the lingering look from Mumpalli, who has followed us to the curb with great difficulty, leaning precariously on his cane. My brief subsequent efforts to find a publisher prove unsuccessful.

The highlight of our trip is an Alleppey-Quilon boat-ride, which we take after J. Prakash's family royally host us at their compound. He has arranged for a boatman to motor us across the waterway to the ferry station in Alleppey. We stand on the dock in the morning mist, straining to find the boat. It's late. Finally, the craft appears along the high marsh grass by the shore, the boatman alternately poling the tiny fishing craft, then trying to start the minuscule gasoline motor. I look from the narrow boat to the four of us and our extensive luggage, whispering to Judi, "No way." Fortunately, he is unable to start the motor, or we would've surely capsized. With some embarrassment, J. Prakash is able to procure a car to drive us to the slip in time for departure.

It is a lazy day on the waterways, island homesteads dotting our prospect, coconut trees on every spit of land, uplifted Chinese fishing nets like mantises awaiting their prey. In the middle of the ferry ride, seated in deck chairs, faces slathered with sunscreen, the palmed islands drifting by, the salt air rich and pure, Imon and I resume our earlier debate on economic development. I hold the Gandhian position, where the local community is primary. Imon, though initially sympathetic to this way of thinking, defends global trade and the recent treaties further empowering it. "A rising tide raises all boats."

"Perhaps, but the smallest craft can't always withstand the wakes of the big boys. Besides, there's only so much water in the global pond."

Then Imon makes a statement that is a touchstone for this entire journey to the subcontinent. "Economics is the most important subject of all." When I demur, he adds, "I don't understand why everyone doesn't see this; it's obvious." In postmodern India, *artha*, piling up material goods, *is* everything. But Imon's point remains a corrective to Puer's youthful economic oblivion.

I tell Imon that we need businesses where value-added profits stay in the community, rather than local people everywhere being robbed by the global fat cats. Our lunch stop gives a small example. The tour operators have arranged with the village to prepare a typical Kerala meal, which we eat from banana leaves. All the vegetables, the coconut dishes and the little fried curried fish are local. I relish everything about this stop, from the mud oozing between my toes as I walk across the mudflats to the red-orange fishgrease on my fingers. I walk a little way into the forest to find an old woman with her grandchildren weaving coir under a simple little roofed shelter. Looking closely at the ground, I see that it teems with insect life. Nearby, a neatly tilled field of vegetables. Eco-tourism seems to work here, though I'm sure the boat company takes their cut.

In Quilon, we meet George Oomen, the writer-activist Arundhati Roy's first cousin. Though a lawyer at the Supreme Court in Delhi, as eldest son George returned to the family house after both parents and his aunts died to look after an elderly female servant who essentially watches tv all day. As a southerner from another continent with its own tradition of caring for "the help," I honor this remarkable gesture mandated by a culture whose family structures remain so different from ours. Caste has its privileges, but it has responsibilities too.

George has booked us at Lord Curzon's palatial residence, now a government tourist guest house. It costs sixty-one rupees, a tremendous bargain. The residence is huge, stately, its partially ruined condition invoking the heyday of the Raj. The wood railings on the long stairs and capacious mezzanine hall are glorious, though needing restoration. The door to our room is twelve feet high, the ceilings twenty-two. The nice mattress and large bed present a welcome contrast to the thin straw mats covered in worn cotton of the rural North, and we plop down to sample the loft as I teasingly grab Judi around her bare waist—the sari's holiday. We also have a dressing room and huge bath adjacent. It's a corner room with a wide wrap-around porch like the one at the Dutch colonial hotel in Cochin harbor. The cavernous bedroom requires two AC units to cool it. Looking around like a little girl, Judi remarks, "I feel like at any moment a giant is going to come to repossess his lair and throw us out." But in our story, Goldilocks' boyfriend stays for some bedroom frolic. After we clean up, a skeleton crew serves George, Imon, and us a full meal clustered at one end of Lady Curzon's huge long table in the capacious dining room. It's on George.

The next morning, we walk through the remains of a formal garden, descending to a brightly painted dock, which Lord Curzon must have used when approaching his palace by water. On the way, we see two eagles come to roost in the huge live oak tree opposite the main rotunda. They remind me of us, a royal pair.

This stay at Lord Curzon's summer palace was most like the tourist guest houses of the Sixties: the same courteous service by starched-uniformed servants, the same cheap ancient yellow paper with multiple carbons, the accountant with his huge pile of handwritten ledgers, which still prevail in most post offices and banks. Kipling and Dickens would still be at home in such places. I certainly was. For a day, I was again Puer, colonial prince.

But what were we after all? Now that Judi had left her medical duties and I had completed my journalistic activity, our purpose in India was less clear. Dour old Maurice Frydman may have disagreed, calling us "tourists," but in the Seventies we were pilgrims. Now we *were* tourists, latter-day colonials, though more knowledgeable than most. Still, we were headed to Indore, and Judi was joining Rotary's campaign to rid the subcontinent of the scourge of polio. Maybe this was sufficient justification for her, but what about me?

29 Return to Malwa

Avantika Express, December 1996

Approaching Indore at long last, I watch people on their roofs in the holy city of Ujjain, performing yogasanas, reading newspapers, taking early morning sun. The Madhya Pradesh countryside looks the same. The cities have grown tremendously, increasing industrialization and legions of apartment houses. Next stop, Dewas, where I get down at the station to catch a glimpse of something familiar, a gestalt of buildings, foolishly hoping to see a member of Kumarji's family to wave us on. Nothing but disorientation, anomie. Judi smiles sympathetically as I report my news.

Reading the paper, I continue to follow Anna Hazare's fast to pressure the Maharashtra Lok Sabha, demanding that the Agriculture and Irrigation ministers both be sacked, due to allegations of corruption. Hazare is the man who inspired his townspeople to rebuild the town of Radagon Siri in Maharashtra after it had become a barren ghost town. He's a Gandhian, Sunderlal's buddy. Judi sits next to me in her sari, reading the Vedas.

I observe a single woman bobbing on the wide plain, her sari billowing in the wind. Looking more closely, I see she's on a bike, not floating on the horizon. Areas of overgrazing, turning barren. Fairly sparse fields, though many are under cultivation. Reminds me of a forester's comment in Uttarnanchal about the progressive fate of land in India: forest, cleared for agriculture, then pasture, finally barren after persistent erosion and soil depletion, hastening to desert.

Indore must be soon: the huge orange-blossomed tree in the bazaar next to the film billboard, the funky movie theater adjacent to the Shabe Malwa restaurant, the wide road to the college filled with morning bicycles and their pastoral tinkling, the open spaces and big trees, the "mango commons" in the park where we used to harvest those heavenly fruits, fleshy orange breasts dripping with unbearably sticky-sweet nectar, the cool nights, the smell of wood, dung, and charcoal burning. Indore, jewel of the Malwa Plateau. And nobody beats the cooking of Sulu and Vasuthai. I am excited.

The station sign says INDORE, but I'm still looking for my city, my Indian home. There used to be a hole in the fence where you could take a shortcut into the station if you were running late. I remember Sulu's father closing the eyes on a corpse in the wide parking area out front. The fence is gone, as is the spacious parking area, just the labyrinthine crush of honking streets, tall buildings everywhere.

A woman in a dusty brown *salwar chemise* walks rapidly towards me. She's stunningly beautiful. "Bob? Are you Bob and Judi McGahey?" Then, about fifteen yards behind her Chandu shuffles after, thick, wrapped in a plain grey shawl, bespectacled face old with care. We've both aged—he must be in his sixties. He sees me, and both our faces brighten.

We're off to 40 New Palasia. Neeram's one of his star painting students, and she has a car. Chandu smiles back at me, his eyes crinkling familiarly, our friendship affirmed after all these years. Judi is responsive, exiting her reflective traveling cocoon, and Neeram looks at me in the rear-view mirror, her almond eyes incredibly warm and direct, studying this friend Chandu has told her so much about.

But I am lost, looking for my Indore, searching every possible vista, stomach sick from the fumes and the vertigo of loss. I recognize nothing; everywhere wall-to-wall shops and businesses and especially apartments, all about eight to ten stories, the limits of reinforced concrete construction. Somebody in the South laughed and called Indore "Little Bombay ... but the people are nice." The people are all I have left.

Finally we wheel into Chandu's neighborhood. As we crossed the arched concrete bridge downtown I made out a building here and there. But all the *space* in between which held and grounded them, the trees and lawns and little parks, creating an off-elegant pattern, relaxed and comfortable, is gone. It is just like Delhi, a haphazard pattern of development, barely resisted in Bangalore. Now that we're in Palasia, I start to see more trees—not as many as before, but in some places big ones where saplings were planted before. Then, at last, Chandu and Sulu's house, with higher, thicker shrubbery, and the old lime Vespa which whisked me around Malwa, now under mildewy canvas wraps, retired from duty. "Temporarily," Chandu says.

"Since how long?" I ask.

"Maybe seven or eight years," my friend answers.

A woman is standing in the door of the house. It must be Sulu, she who fed me, then blessed me to run off with Chandu on our madcap adventures. I remember her stunning steel-grey eyes and beautifully boned face. But the lines of her face are lost to sagging flesh, and the eyes do not sparkle, even in anticipation, until the smile actually comes. When she smiles, I recognize her. I can still coax that smile from her, and find myself trying again and again so I can see the person I remember so tenderly. She is old and thick with care, more motherly than before, concerned for our every want, cocking her head to one side, steely eyes under thick lids watching intently for our response. She and Judi greet warmly, two women in saris enfolding one another. Setting aside the helter-skelter of this household, she listens patiently to our stories. That evening they give us their bedroom, as they retire to the living room's large L-shaped sofa.

Chandu still has a furniture design business, the same classy man as shop foreman—now with the snowiest, best-groomed wavy white hair I've ever seen. But the shop sits idle. These days both Chandu and Sulu take art students, who are always around, both for instruction and for the tolerant, wise mentoring. There is one sweet, doting young couple who conduct their relationship under their teachers' liberal gazes, unbeknownst to their stuffy parents (mismatched sub-castes). They are around for most of the morning, part of the household. Their romance, protected by my friends the old libertines, comforts me, reinforcing my western preference for "love-marriage."

Chandu also teaches interior design, and has worked on a couple of projects with their son Milind, including a plush home in Delhi in the trade magazine he shows us. They have a maidservant who comes in for a few hours most days, whom they can afford because rent control has kept their payments at the same incredibly low level since the Sixties. She's bossy and quarrelsome, but they keep her because she's family.

The next morning, brushing my teeth, the power goes off. I emerge from the dingy bathroom to inquire of Sulu, standing in the dim morning light. "Yes, it goes off every morning for four hours. We fill the tank before it shuts down." Shaving the following afternoon, I notice screw-shaped critters in the tank, gyrating up, then down in otherwise clear water. I show them to my biologically trained wife, who is less fascinated and repelled than I. "Tell Chandu and Sulu they might want to disinfect it," she says matter-of-factly.

After settling in we make plans for Judi's upcoming day working for Rotary International's assault on polio. This is a big deal for her, a chance to actually help the needy, rather than the pampered students at Kodai School. Chandu is now thoroughly at home with Judi, whose efforts at development and service have replaced her earlier focus on *sadhana*.

But I am not at home in Indore, my pleasant provincial backwater now infected by the cancer of modernity. On the way to the polio camp the next day, I ask the local Rotary president to take us by Anoop Nagar, where Stuart and I were outlaws in our new apartment on the edge of town, surrounded by pastoral scenes. We are near where it should be, he has heard the name, but he can't find it. Speaking quietly in the back seat, I lament my lost city. "It's so depressing, Judi. It's hard to even get your bearings with all these apartments everywhere. Do you realize how deeply this disappoints me?"

"Enough! I don't want to hear it anymore," she says under her breath. We are honored guests and visiting dignitaries, with concomitant roles to play. She wears her best sari, gold-bordered magenta, neatly pleated, face lightly made up with Sulu's toilette. It's the sari Vasuthai gave her during our honeymoon in Dewas.

The Rotary International President, an Australian, and his wife are guests at the function. Judi, looking professional despite her red "Rotary All-India Halt Polio" baseball cap, gives oral drops to infants and toddlers as I take photos, relieved not to have to sit among the stiff guests. Each dignitary gives a speech; a new set of latrines is dedicated for the poor. I sample one, the only *clean* latrine I have ever experienced in Hindustan outside upscale hotels. We end our long day visiting a school for the retarded on the outskirts of town, where art displays and performances by beaming Downs children trump still more civic speeches.

Banukhul: the Succession

"Kumar Gandharva is dead. He died early in the morning after a brief illness, complications from obstructed lung disease. He was sixty-seven years old. He was cremated late in the afternoon after a procession of the body through the streets of his beloved adopted home in Dewas. His eldest son Mukhul lit the pyre. Rites were attended by four thousand." —*Times of India*, January 12, 1992

"What ten singers are needed to perform in a 100 years, Kumar Gandharva did in a short span of his life." —Asok Rani

The road to Dewas is no longer a pastoral excursion, but a sprawl of businesses and factories from both directions. Few farms remain. Traveling to Dewas with Chandu used to be a refreshing retreat from the bustle of Indore, but now scores of trucks, buses and minivans clog the road. Traffic jams are frequent, and though the road has been widened, a jaunt that used to take forty-five minutes now takes twice as long. The bus stops often to pick up and discharge passengers. About seven miles out, there's an odd trailer park, vast as a Civil War cemetery, with hookups all the way to the horizon. I've no idea who would stay there, other than the steady stream of truckers. The scale of the operation is eerily apocalyptic.

The minibus deposits the three of us in downtown Dewas, which I faintly recognize. We walk the few blocks to Banukhul. It used to be on the edge of town, with only a few houses strewn amongst fields. Just beyond it was the promontory of Devi Hill, with open access to its two temples to Devi, a simple dirt track circling amiably to the moon-rock summit. Now the houses are dense to the very edge of the walled Komkali compound, and beyond, a much-altered Hill of Devi.

Chandu and Sulu have warned us how much things have changed at the House of Music. Since Kumarji died, things have never been the same—how could they? Praful Bidwai, senior editor of the *Times of India* and native of Dewas, speaks of "a sense of vast cosmic emptiness pervad[ing] [Kumarji's] Nirguni Bhajans." Standing on the front veranda of Banukhul in December 1996, almost five years after his death, being welcomed by his wife and daughter, Vasuthai and Pinu, this vast emptiness is palpable.

We have tea and biscuits on the wide, comfortable front porch, Judi and I sitting in the swing, Chandu sitting with his back to the flowers, somber and glum. He has insisted on accompanying us to Banukhul, even though I can tell he didn't really want to come. He remains in a black mood the whole time, uncommunicative, moody, unsmiling. He leaves for Indore after lunch.

Vasuthai, though greying, seems to have changed surprisingly little in twenty-three years. In 1974, Pinu was a skinny, quiet, impish girl of twelve. It was not clear then that she would be a musician, though occasionally she would imitate what she heard. Towards the end of Kumarji's life, after a series of dreadful setbacks involving Mukhul and the death of his tabla-wallah and emotional mainstay Atchrekar, Pinu decided to accompany her father everywhere he concertized, singing the backup vocals, becoming indispensable to him. It was in this period, in her mid-twenties, that she made the decision to become a Hindustani vocalist—right about the age when I finally dropped the idea. Now she is plump, talkative, socially skilled, a singer in her own right, concertizing with Vasuthai and planning her first recording. At thirty-four, she is unmarried, committed to the musician's life, centered here in provincial Dewas as her father had been.

After dinner, we listen to mother and daughter practice, mother taking the lead, daughter following. They are working on a particularly difficult turn of *taan*, and Pinu is clearly competent. She also performs a couple of compositions for us, which are generally pleasing, except for the high notes, which are forced and not very musical—though I doubt my ears at first, she's so confident. Indian vocal technique does not produce much warmth of sound, because vibrato is kept to a minimum. So vocal control becomes all the more important at the limits of one's register. Kumarji, a supple tenor, was able to reach for the highest notes and touch them lightly, sustain them, or sing loudly if he wanted. Pinu, with an alto's range, telegraphs every high fortissimo. I find my gut tightening in anticipation.

When we retire to our bedroom, I ask Judi if she feels the same way I do about Pinu's little recital, especially those high belts. "No, I didn't notice anything uncomfortable. She is a competent singer, and clearly very disciplined. But she's no Kumarji, if that's what you mean."

We listened that night in the same room where I had taken my lessons and spent precious evenings listening to Kumarji give concerts, joust with Bhimsen Joshi, patiently but firmly teach members of his flock, and endlessly shave betel nuts for paan, uttering little grunts of pleasure, intently listening to others' vocalizations. The man lived through the ear, and never listened casually.

Now he is a memorial presence, huge photos dominating the walls, one with right arm raised high in a characteristic gesture. In his last years, he apparently moved his bed into this room. Beside the bed are his house-chappals, the worn imprints of his toes forever empty. Marigolds sit on a small table with some music books and his betel-shaving tool; the presence of an incense burner tokens its use for ritual purposes. The *tanpuras* lining the wall are wreathed in marigolds, a mute line of tributes to the Master. The whole effect is of a small, well-tended shrine. Vasuthai and Pinu have made it clear that their main life-mission is to keep Kumar Gandharva's legacy alive, maintaining the memorial for the occasional connoisseur/pilgrim, making archive recordings, and giving concerts.

Banukhul is certainly peaceful, an atmosphere of reverence for the dead master. But the main feeling is one of loss and sadness, especially from Vasuthai. These women live in a shrine, and those who visit, including Judi and me, come primarily to pay their respects to the vast ghost who haunted it. The music that Vasuthai and Pinu bravely struggle to keep afloat is an echo, evanescent no matter how confidently and loudly Pinu sings. What I heard in this house in 1996 was not the birth of a new *gharana* inspired by Kumar Gandharva, but a grimly determined, careful aping of the master by loyal disciples.

Rebel Son of a Rebel Father

And what of my third teacher, Kumarji's son by his beloved first wife Banu? Mukhul had shown the most promise of becoming a true successor to Kumarji. He was extremely musical, had a good voice, was intelligent and inventive, and dedicated to singing. He had married Nitu, the daughter of Kumarji's harmonium player, who I remembered for his quiet, impeccable dignity and kindness. The marriage did not work very well, and Mukhul began showing signs of instability, abusing alcohol, pot, and worse.

"One night he arrived quite late with another woman, very drunk. Nobody knows exactly what happened, but before the night was over Nitu, apparently while heating milk for their baby on a propane burner, caught her sari in the stove and was burned extremely badly over 80 per cent of her body. She spent two days in the Indore Hospital before she died. She was in agony. Sulu was at her side the whole time," Chandu tells us back in New Palasia.

"Sulu? Were you close to her?" I ask.

Sulu hesitates, then purses her lips to speak. Chandu barges on. "Somebody had to take care of her." Sulu nods, her eyes intense with the memory. "The only one from the family who came was Kumarji himself. He was totally distraught. It was a terrible tragedy. Terrible."

This whole time Judi and I are looking at each other. We know this scene, reported in the press. By the government's conservative figures, twenty thousand young brides a year die in these mishaps, usually after persistent dowry disputes.

"Was there an investigation?" Judi asks.

"Yes, the police made a routine investigation. But no charges were brought. Mukhul disappeared for a while, then showed up at a temple in Indore and has since lived the life of a mendicant holy man. We have seen him a few times—emaciated, unshaved and unwashed, often in a stupor."

"*Mast.* He plays the part of a *mast,* doesn't he?" I add, echoing my conversation with Roshan in Bombay.

"*Masti,* yes. The God-intoxicated wanderer," Chandu says gravely.

Remembering Mukhul's fondness for the *nirguni* afficionados of Dewas, I picture him with *ektara* on his shoulder, singing his way through the streets. After a few years he started giving some concerts again, but he hid behind this persona, often too drunk or stoned to go on, as Roshan had said. It was his "holy" excuse.

"So do you think Mukhul was performing a kind of penance?" Judi asks.

"Yes, definitely," Sulu replies.

Chandu and Sulu continue to fill the gaps in Roshan's account. Mukhul was abusive of his father, who was heartsick and severely depressed over the whole business. This was not only his sole son, the living memory of the saintly Banu, but the person most gifted to continue his legacy. Then Chandu launches into Vasuthai's jealousy, mistrust and over-possessiveness.

The other side of this last complaint is the challenge of living with a creative genius. Thai spoke to us of this in Dewas the previous day. "You know, Bob, Kumarji worked very hard. He was always focused on his music. So I took care of the kids, night and day. It just didn't occur to him—at least not very often. And now we have Bhuwan," she said, looking at Pinu.

Mukhul's little son Bhubeshwar was raised in Dewas by Vasuthai and Pinu after his mother's death and Mukhul's penitential retreat. We meet him after he returns for dinner from classes at Puer's old post, the Government Arts and Commerce College of Indore. Bhuwan is now twenty, a handsome and poised young man with a quiet dignity that reminds me of his grandfather. He ably accompanies Pinu on the tabla when she performs for us later that evening.

I remember Kumarji chuckling over a composition featuring Mukhul as a toddler, repeatedly crawling onto his lap while he was trying to work. The Master brushed him off like an ant. *What a great theme*, I had thought. But I missed the underside of the motif, which was where Thai dwelt, patiently raising the child of a reputedly saintly woman, living in her shadow. Now she is doing it again with Bhuwan.

Chandu explains that Vasuthai has legally blocked Mukhul's inheritance. He is no longer welcome at Banukhul. She and Pinu control all of Kumarji's recording rights and the collection of his taped concerts. They want custody of Bhuwan.

Bhuwan is an adolescent who wants to know his father, a man of some mystery, power and considerable musical gifts, despite his mad antics. Mukhul wants to get a house in Indore and have Bhuwan live with him, but with no inheritance and a spotty career, he really doesn't have the means to do this. It is a frightful mess.

But what of my own career as a Hindustani vocalist? Kumarji had given me a royal opportunity to be trained by the best in the business, accepting me into the bosom of his family in the *gurukela* tradition. But lacked the necessary discipline and the confidence that I could achieve the required transformation of vocal technique. Deepest of all, I couldn't manage to turn my back on my own musical tradition, and my embeddedness in my blood family. Mukhul had tried to understand this, and was sympathetic; the musical systems of West and East were totally incompatible, and I bore the inalterable imprint of the classical West. Yet I was captivated by his father's unearthly music, and now I want *someone* to carry on that exquisite gift.

Devi Hill Revisited

"Would you like to go with me on Devi Hill?" Pinu asks the second evening of our stay in Dewas, slipping on her white Bata tennies. "I walk there every day. It is my exercise."

Judi and I exchange eager glances. "Sure," we say in chorus.

I had noticed the monstrous plaster gates beyond the bungalow, remembering a simple dusty pathway. Now the road leads straight to these oversized gates, painted grey and red, an imitation of the seventeenth century Moghul style. I comment to Pinu, who smiles. "Yes, it is in the Punjabi style." She delights in correcting me, recalling her impish tone towards the American *shishya* as a girl. In the afternoon, she offhandedly compliments my "Muslim lungi" (a colorful blue and green checkered print, rather than the more subdued South Indian white with colored borders). It is a class thing; brahmins wear white, like tennis players at Wimbledon. Other castes wear what they please.

On the other side of the gates, large paving stones create a wide avenue up the side of the mountain. Many people amble over the hill, mostly families with children in a holiday mood. Large speakers blare incongruous Haydnesque music as hawkers sell carnival food, especially pink cotton candy. We rest on a bench under a roofed structure in the same odd style as the front gate. It feels like Disneyland. I look out at the town below, seeing how large it has grown. "Yes, they say we have a population of 250,000 now" Pinu observes with civic pride. In the distance, I spot a windmill farm, which she verifies, "one of the largest in India." This pleases me.

Now we can see the entrance to the Chawmunda Temple. I guess that we missed it during our previous ascent in the Seventies, for then we only entered a cave-like structure of the older, doll-like Devi near the top. But Pinu agrees that this is a new temple. The image has been moved from a more obscure spot so that people can enjoy her more readily.

"Where's Devi, I wonder?" I ask Judi.

"Why don't you ask Pinu?" she replies.

But after what I've seen, I can't bear it; our little doll-goddess has undoubtedly been upstaged by a nouveau temple. Pinu tells us that Madhya Pradesh has transformed a series of religious sites into these park-like places, both to make them more accessible and to swell the state coffers, among India's more impoverished. Standing once again before the temple entrance, the Haydn has receded, replaced by Bollywood film music. No quiet, no religiosity; our pilgrimage spot is now Hindu Disney. I would hate to see what the MP government has done to the exquisite Buddhist shrine at Sanchi I visited in 1968, where I shared the lonely hill with a student, his clothes neatly hung on a *neem* tree branch as he paid respect in his underwear.

A Surprise Appearance

That afternoon, Chandu and Sulu take us shopping nearby in the greatly expanded shops of Palasia. On the way there, Sulu points out a vacant lot on which boys once played soccer, recently closed by the merchant association. She says some citizens brought it before the municipal government on the boys' behalf, but the plea was brushed aside. "Now there is nowhere in Indore they can play," she mourns. This was the last of the commons in Indore as far as I could tell, now facing the same oblivion as those lovely mango trees.

Just before the evening's music session that Chandu has arranged, he invites me outside to present me Kumarji's custom stainless steel betel-nut case, a book-like hinged box with a shelf for the shaving tool and little cubbies for the nuts. "I wanted you to have something of his. Please take it." Tears spring to both our eyes as we hug.

After supper, the musicians start to appear. Vishnu, my original vocal teacher, arrives with guitar and briefcase. He looks exactly the same: huge grin, head rolling like a doll's mounted on a spring, bug-eyes sparkling. Then Deepak arrives, the tabla-wallah from my desultory Indore concert, now a banker. Vishnu begins the program, playing two compositions on electric guitar, one in raga Todi. As Deepak, his thick black hair streaked with white, tunes the tablas for his performance, Chandu, who has been nervously glancing out front, pronounces in a serious but satisfied tone, "Here's Mukhul."

I look out the window to see a frail, slightly bent Mukhul, wearing a long tan kurta, thick mop of black hair greying at the temples. I am unexpectedly moved. When Mukhul enters the Nafde living room, I rise to greet him, giving him a heartfelt hug. He grimaces a little with pain, returning it awkwardly, managing a wan but sincere smile. I can feel all his ribs, and he look sallow.

We share a round of chai and try to reconnect.

"So, Mukhul, are you giving any concerts?" Judi asks gently.

He looks at her very frankly, then at me, answering, "I am trying," producing an awkward silence around the room. "But my voice is not good these days and I feel too much weak." I exchange glances with Sulu.

He asks about my singing, and I tell him of my satisfaction with the Fargo-Moorhead Chamber Chorale. "I am glad you are performing—you love music." Then he shakes his head, like so many times before, saying that Indian and Western music are "so different." This seems to explain for him my failure to progress with Hindustani *khyal.*

Deepak proceeds with his tabla performance. Flashy and accomplished, he shakes his gleaming oiled hair triumphantly after each showy riff. Looking over at Mukhul, I notice he only feigns interest. Now it's his turn, and after apologizing about his voice condition, he sings a very sweet composition, unaccompanied, with graces of *taan* and syncopated riffs characteristic of his father. It is wonderful, but all too short, lasting only a few minutes. I expect him to sing something else, but this is his little gift for the evening. He seems weak, his voice lacking the projective power a performer would need—what his half-sister Pinu has in abundance. As we compliment him, he again demurs over the condition of his voice. He explains that he sings many styles, not wanting to be restricted to any tradition, "Tonight I have chosen to sing in the style of Kumar Gandharva—in your honor," looking directly at me. I bow to him in *namaste*, while Judi looks at me appreciatively. After another ten minutes of pleasantries Mukhul excuses himself, saying he's tired. He shuffles away into the evening, bent over like an old man.

The whole party breaks up shortly afterwards. Mukhul's troubles and early departure have dampened everyone's spirits, even irrepressible Vishnu's, who shakes his head mournfully as we discuss Mukhul's life difficulties. Sulu tells us he complained that his back ached. She wants to take care of him, if only she could. Judi thinks his symptoms point to tuberculosis. Both my tabla teacher Khargonkar and Kumarji died of TB-induced illness, and it appears that Mukhul is headed for the same fate. Seeing Mukhul walking up to the house has been the climax of this whole visit, sending a pang of longing for the time with his family at Banukhul and the musician's life I rejected. I am deeply saddened, leaden with apprehension that this marks the end of the line for Kumarji's genius.

The next morning, Neeram drives us to the Indore airport for our flight to Bombay. The route takes us by Indore Christian College, largely the same as before, a surprising degree of forested land remaining around the whitewashed buildings with orange tile roofs. It is a green oasis in Little Bombay, giving me a feeling of relief, but also renewed longing for the hometown that fostered me during the Fulbright year.

Our airport wait is uncomfortable. So many feelings, such an awkward place to voice them. Finally the time comes to go through security and board the plane. Chandu walks with us as far as the security doors. As we hug one last time, I wonder if I will ever see my friend again.

Except for Bombay, whose character remains intact despite tremendous growth, I feel devastated by the India I discover after a quarter-century. Chandu and Sulu still provide an emotional anchor, but Indore and Dewas had been home to me, the heart of the Dream, and I hardly recognize them.

Judi is upbeat about the Rotary campaign, always looking on the bright side. She has already said she didn't want to hear any more of my disappointment at the fate of Indore, so I am left to digest the knot in my throat on my own. On the plane the speakers blare a juvenile American ditty from the Fifties. I want to ask the attendant to turn it off, but lack the resolve.

30 Bombay Farewell

The great crawling sea ...

Crawls again outside our window in the fastness of Sagar Darshan. It is mid-December. This has been a difficult trip in many ways, great chunks of landscape lost, memory-places supplanted by commercialized ones twice as big, catapulted hundreds of years into the disenchanted present. But here by the sea I experience a comforting sameness, down to the cracked tile in the familiar bathroom off Shaibya's bedroom, crisscrossed by clotheslines, its low toothpaste-splattered mirror set for short Gujaratis.

Having got his address and phone from Vasuthai, we look up Satish Deshpande. He has permanently returned to his native Bombay after spending chunks of his youth as Kumarji's *shishya* at the House of Music in Dewas. Satish is the last disciple, my last chance to see if there is someone worthy of the unlikely possibility of carrying on Kumarji's music. He has a generous grant from the Ford Foundation to master all the old recordings of the great Hindustani classical artists since the beginning of the recording era and document them. So his flat includes a recording studio as well as a large comfortable room for performing. Judi and I sit on the floor, sipping masala chai as we reminisce. "I miss Kumarji," he agrees, "but life has been good to me."

Satish invites me to join him in some of the old compositions he remembered me singing, but I'm too embarrassed. He sings a few excerpts of old Kumarji ragas. They are competent, but now Satish is a musicologist, not a performer. After twenty-odd years, he looks like his bulldog-faced father, but he is anything but tough. His kindness makes me wince as I recall what Roshan had said about Mukhul's abusive behavior towards him. At Banukhul, they were like brothers. None of us mentions Mukhul.

"We would love for you to talk to us about your work," Udayan's psychotherapy class is giving us a party the following night, right before we leave India. Judi agrees to talk about her work with eating disorders, something these folks have not yet seen. They are fascinated, and her talk goes well. I want to demonstrate the method of archetypal psychology I learned at the Dallas Institute, focusing on the dream as image rather than symbol. I have requested dreams from Udayan's class and receive three. Only one of them is interesting, but since it is from an overweight woman and concerns body-image, it feels too charged. Stuck, I decide to present one of my own.

I am learning to play cello with Hank [one of my former Indian Springs students, now a wily businessman]. *It is a beautiful, expensive instrument, with a double set of strings as well as a double set of mutes. Hank shows me how to remove the first mute. Then a Nazi woman jailer is making rounds. In my cell, I am in the midst of masturbation, and have a sticky hanky which I'm looking to stow. She demands to see my fingers, and says they look sickly. Since I know they are removing "sick" parts, I am immediately concerned, and go into the next gathering of inmates to give an impromptu concert of the first movement of Beethoven's Pathetique sonata. I bluff my way through it. She isn't there, but I tell the others to make a point of it to her, proving my fingers are quite strong.*

I feel exposed before these people and their Freudian teacher, and do not succeed in my goal of "sticking to the image"; the symbols are just too powerful—"overdetermined" Freud would say. Afterwards Udayan pulls me aside. "I would *love* to interpret your dream." Freud insisted that living a satisfied life was essentially a matter of "love and work"—both muted. Showing up at Lama, waiting for Bly to finish his negotiations with the organizers, and hearing that strong emergent voice saying, "I am a teacher-scholar" was the moment the first mute started to be removed from my instrument: cello/lyre/tanpura: heartstrings connected to who I really was. Bly called that mute "economic dependency." But a second mute remains.

At my parents' nuptials, the wedding march was the second movement of that same Pathetique sonata. My own marriage, heading into its fourth decade, is a challenge, and must be the setting of this dream-jail, the second mute strongly clamped. I do not have the full range of the *piano-forte* (quiet-loud), and I still keep my eroticism—and energy—to myself, hidden in my cell, cowering from my Woman Keeper. Learning to play "Celo" and removing the second set of mutes begins to look like a lifelong task.

This raw exposure before so many strangers leering at my inner life unsettles me, and I am hugely relieved when the ordeal ends. Presentations complete, we return to the groaning table, where we are rewarded with a mighty repast of Parsee wedding fare. Udayan's class has catered it in our honor. We are in the penthouse of the tallest building on top of Malabar Hill and the place glitters like the city beneath us as Judi and I gaze down from the deck. The air smells fresh, washed by the breezes of the Arabian Sea. Being up here reminds me of the sordid world of Rushdie's *Moor*. This could be the place whence the Moor's mother threw herself into the sea, dressed as the goddess Lakshmi. But all that is beneath us, unseen as the ubiquitous mafia. Returning to the party, our host is solicitous, and the people glitter. But these are good people.

We leave hastily after a series of quick good-byes for one last midnight ride through Bombay's streets. Jayanthi has been waiting patiently for us in the Suzuki, Udayan insisting we have plenty of time—which we don't. Jayanthi does his racing best to get us there, just in the nick of time, and I hand him a hundred rupee note as we rush to check-in.

Returning to Moorhead and Middle America, everything feels just the same—as if we have never left. As she always does, Judi goes to work the next day, having no particular use for transitions. Thankfully, I have Christmas vacation ahead of me before classes resume. A cold I contracted in Bombay has taken a nasty turn, requiring a month to mend. And the queasiness I suffered periodically ever since quaffing the "tinned lassi" at Ashok's Kumaon farm has followed me home. It turned out to be giardia, finally banished by a huge pill. Though I feel nothing like the culture shock I experienced upon returning to the States from my first India sojourn, I am wrapped in a dull depression over the loss of the India I remembered and treasured. At this juncture in my life, America is normal, India the perverted culture.

Judi and I have different readings of India. I see endgame; she sees folks working to make things better. On a visit to my parents in Pittsburgh that Christmas, I enter a dinner discussion with the new daughter-in-law of my mother's best friends. Her honeymoon experience of Bhutan—the freshness, the humility, the simplicity of peasant life—sounds just like mine in India in the Sixties and Seventies. We agree about the paradoxical reversal of Westerners wanting to leave our baggage behind, while the rest of the world grasps to emulate the source of our own unhappiness: the cycle of desire, more and more stuff, never fulfilled. Now India is the regional kingpin, the necessary capitalist supplying Bhutan with much of its foreign trade needs. That kingdom's avoidance of the contagion of world trade suggests another developmental path, their celebrated Happiness Index: preserving beauty, local culture, the richness of many languages, not to mention the integral complexity of the biosphere. The flipside is romanticizing the simple, pious peasant's life as imagined by the privileged observer. Ashok's struggles at his end-of-the-line farm in the Kumaon hills certainly corrected Puer's adolescent fantasy: *One must imagine the Indian farmer happy.*

The Balance-Taking

Being here finally feels like the fifty-year-old balance-taking. So I experienced my *yatra* to the Ganga's glacial watershed. A balance-taking indeed. Puer's deep love and yearning for India was gone. Initially encountering something ineffable, an energy, a quality of being that he had never experienced before during the circumstantial visit to India in 1967, he returned to explore it thoroughly, once on his own, a second time with his bride Judith Goldman in tow. Puer wanted to merge with it, whatever it was.

This is how I see it now. The ineffable appeared in two forms. One was the equation atman=Brahman: "Thou art That," embodied in Maurice Frydman's teaching. The Self was God, and that Self was all that existed. The ego was the agent of illusion, ruled by the goddess Maya. Maurice encouraged Puer to "join the fellowship of the undeceived" and sever the illusion, getting to know the Self as the one Reality by following Ramana Maharshi's disciplined method of self-inquiry, *achara*.

The other form was Puer's merger of separate male self with the Goddess: Devi-Durga-Kali. Being unseen, this unconscious absorption gripped him harder than the first, a fellowship which inspired but continually eluded him. Puer's goddess-union was unwitting, like that of the fly with the carnivorous flower, submerging his Western-identified self in Mother India. The evening's ride carrying the image of Durga to her annual rest in the local creek in a Bengali village embodied this process and its complex energies.

When Puer took Judi Goldman to India with him the first time, he wanted her to experience this deep yearning for union, too. At first she resisted, wanting to flee—better to join the Israelis in the Yom Kippur War than subject herself to this unsettling country. But very quickly, she too had been caught in the Mother's embrace. "Devi is guiding us," she would say as they were led from experience to experience, saint to saint. But in the end Swami Chidananda banished her, knowing it was not yet time.

Puer didn't realize it then, but India's siren call was already moribund when the couple left the gentle old Sikh in the Delhi café, bemused by their ashram-hopping in 1974. The goddess-immersion that pulled so strongly in 1968 was transposed into Puer's choice of a wife. She carried the spiritual values he sought and provided the physical enfolding—just enough—that in tandem drove his initial quest on the subcontinent. And she was big enough to accept Puer's Kali-projections, the role of the Devouring Mother who got into bed with him each night. At Bly's Lama Camp, another recovering Mama's Boy echoed a statement from the Midrash: "A man needs to cut his teeth on something bigger than him—either a woman or God." In the midst of those men's rites, the proverb resonated deeply. Pulled toward spirituality from a very early age, Puer nevertheless managed to avoid Jacob's angel-wrestling and Job's righteous questions. With Judith, he had no choice; she challenged him daily to be tough, clear, and authentic.

Many years of struggle later, Puer gradually receded, and I appeared to achieve a mature ego's liberation from the wife-goddess. If not exactly liberation, at least a beachhead in Goddess Land. Let's say we're less enmeshed than most. As I write now, the goddess still provides my ground. But she is no longer India or an earthly woman. On my best days, she is the Earth.

And I found a spiritual home with Quakers. When I first went to India I had yet to experience genuine spiritual depth within organized religion, certainly not a group mystical event, the "gathered" or "covered" experience that happens with gracious frequency at Celo Meeting. So my hunger during the first two sojourns in India was doubly fed by the time I returned. Returning to disillusionment in 1996 punctured Puer's India-complex. When it loosened its hold, the old India magic no longer worked.

And what about Judi? Why did she opt to tour the South during her remaining time after the Kodai stint, rather than pilgrimage to her beloved swamis in Rishikesh? What happened to her "floating" mode this time? She had come to serve, even to enjoy a tourist's holiday, not to seek. But this would all change.

31 Another Sabbath, Another Passage

"I felt no break in my path." Judi was recounting for me her reconnection with Sivananda Ashram in Rishikesh in January 1999. She quickly fell into the same ashram routine from 1973. Not much had changed, though she missed the huge boulders between Swami Sivananda's *kutir* and the Ganga, now terraced with concrete *ghats* stretching down to the river. But *she* had changed.

I felt this incredible love for everyone. Before, what I felt most was spiritual pride." Tell me about it.

The first day, the now aged Swami Krishnananda gruffly asked her, "What have you lost? You've lost something."

She had no idea what he was talking about, feeling this was a test. So it was, for he proceeded to produce her passport.

"Not ready for renunciation," he said, sternly shaking his large shaven head. She was no Radha-Dass, who had shown the guts to destroy her passport back in the Seventies, becoming a wandering renunciate. Judi was just distracted.

"Learn how to take care of your things!" the Swami said, dismissing her. At each subsequent meeting, Krishnananda remained gruff. Later, observing his politeness with a neophyte young western woman, Judi realized his gruffness was a measure of acceptance of Judi McGahey as a genuine disciple.

In 1973, Judi had studied Sanskrit with roly-poly little Swami Devananda, reading the first chapter of the *Gita* with him. But now Devananda was on tour. Someone sent her to Swami Hamsananda, a disciple of Krishnananda, also the ashram postmaster. She went to his tiny *kutir* next to the post office every afternoon, waiting for a slot to study with him. A young South African woman had secured a regular time, and my wife would quietly slip into the room, listening carefully to her lesson, reading *Gita* over her shoulder. She knew the protocol without asking. Come regularly and on time, don't be greedy, learn from every occasion, be alert for opportunities for service, be patient. Soon she was a regular. The routine was *chai* and cookies, which she helped the swami serve, then read *Gita* with him, following the traditional oral transmission of *jnana yoga*. She read directly from the Sanskrit original, while the Swami corrected her pronunciation, then gave a translation. She offered to clean the dishes, but here Swami Hamsananda drew the line. After three weeks in the ashram she had read four *Gita* chapters with him. The old routine was seamlessly restored.

I finally got the long-awaited sabbatical from Moorhead State that year, the tenth. We spent most of the year back home in Celo, where I worked on this manuscript, laid up firewood and gardened. Judi volunteered for site visits in late winter to South India for Right Sharing of World Resources, a small Quaker NGO on whose board she served. After initially agreeing to tag along as official photographer, I began to pull back, fearing the culture-shock I had suffered so heavily two years before. Then our younger son Jesse thought he might like to go along. I realized I wanted to see India through his eyes, co-experience his shock wave upon arrival on the subcontinent. Jesse's decision became my dominant factor. When he waffled, I waffled. When he finally decided, I booked my flight. Jesse was exactly the age I was my Fulbright year in India, twenty-two.

Our site visits were to begin mid-February, but Judi preceded us, leaving in early January to work on a proposal for a Rotary development project north of Delhi in polluted Moradabad. Afterwards, she moved northeast until reaching Sivananda Ashram in Rishikesh, completing a twenty-five-year circle. In 1974, Swami Chidananda sent her back to the US to accept the dharma of doctor and mother, banishing her from the bliss of multiple hours of daily meditation. Now her parents had died, and her sons were grown. Dharma accomplished, he would now welcome her.

At the end of her homecoming to Sivananda Ashram, Judi sojourned at Sunderlal's ashram in Silyara until meeting Jesse and me in Bombay for our trip south to the Right Sharing projects. She had been invited for the dedication of a small Devi temple to Ganga on the ashram grounds. She reported that it was the most powerful Hindu ceremony she had ever attended. Judi was riveted by the *hoven*, the sacrificial firepit. Seated before it, she "Felt like I was being wedded to Silyara." I listened to her account with both wonder and concern.

So when we meet at genial Udayan's in Bombay in February 1999, my wife is fast transitioning to the third phase of the Hindu life cycle, the forest stage (*vanaprastha*). We don't talk about her shift, but I feel a reticence from her, breaking only when we talk about Jesse's arrival. She retired from medical practice the previous fall and is now finally ready for the next step in the Hindu *dharma*. Both of our sons have left home, and only my mother remains among our parents. So she has fulfilled Swami Chidananda's charge a quarter century before, and though neither of us knows it yet, Sivananda Ashram would now provide an annual sanctuary to ground and protect her spiritual development. On the path more firmly than ever, Judi is resuming the discipleship that was premature in 1973.

Jesse arrives one February morning at 2 a.m., having finally secured his visa in Paris, looking dazed and tired as he emerges from the throng at the airport, surrounded by drivers' greeting placards for other passengers. His is a decidedly different adventure than Puer's, greeted by seasoned parents rather than floating as a casteless, clueless hippy-saddhu in implacable Mother India.

On our train trip South my high extrovert son for once has little to say. He observes everything. Growing up in our household, he already has developed a taste for spicy Indian food, though the manner of its being served—on peepul leaves, old newspapers, and unfired pots—is novel. Jesse majored in anthropology, so immersion in a strange culture is something for which he has tools. Watching him with feigned casualness, I try to restrain my desire to ask for his reaction to it all. Finally, he speaks. "Dad, look at that seam. See how clean the rock is? There's no rubble or flakes underneath. That's good rock. I wish there was more."

Jesse is a rock-climber. When I let go of my desire to see myself in him and start actually looking through his eyes, what I mainly see is rock formations. As our journey progresses, his usual social aplomb starts asserting itself, and cultural differences or not, he can rely on universal underlying motives. Unlike Puer, he will not be blindsided by India. There will be no complex, no conversion.

Having learned that Swami Chidananda would be at a Divine Life Society gathering at the great Vaishnavite temple complex in Tirupathi (where Carolyn lived during Puer's Fulbright year), his mother wants to stop on our way to the Right Sharing sites. The good man was absent while she was at the ashram in January, on tour with her old Sanskrit teacher, Swami Devananda. But she misses him again in Tirupathi, including one final Marx Brothers ride, the swami in the front seat urgently calling the turns to the driver as we anxiously track the ashram president to his cottage. We arrive less than five minutes after he he's left for the airport. I would never see Swami Sivananda's true heir again.

We are now in an enclosed temple town, and Jesse is fascinated. We stay in a huge *dharamsala*, hundreds of rooms surrounding a large grassy central courtyard where picnickers lounge amid drying saris. Jesse decides to have his hair shorn by a temple barber, the pilgrim's traditional sacrifice. We accompany him through the labyrinthine maze of meshed wire chutes leading to an underground chamber where several barbers sit around the perimeter sluiceway which carries the hair to a hidden collection point, where it will arrive washed and ready to be transformed into wigs, source of the temple's considerable wealth. It is an eerie feeling watching our son being deftly shorn by the skilled brahmin barber, like watching a little boy's first haircut. For Jesse it is a casual decision that nevertheless bestows ritual kinship with members of the culture he stood outside a few days before.

The three of us spend the next two and a half weeks on location visiting Right Sharing sites, mostly in Tamil Nadu. Our first site is in Pondicherry, where we visit a remarkable project at the ambitious international community in Auroville, restoring the nigh-extinct dry rainforest which once covered a large portion of coastal southeast India. Pitchandikulam Forest is the highlight of these site visits, and its visionary leader, Joss Brooks, an Australian Quaker our age, one of the most impressive community leaders we meet. Joss and his team, mostly local tribals, have restored more than two hundred acres of native forest over the last twenty-five years, and he has developed an extensive network all over South India for teaching their methods.

At supper in the spacious open-sided lodge, we meet members of the

Pitchandikulam community as Joss tells us his story. "I came to India in 1967 and loved it. I lived among the saddhus in caves for over a year, wearing a lungi and smoking endless chillums. But you know after a while I began to think about it. If I really loved these people, wasn't there something I could do to better their lot? I became involved with Auroville in the early days and have essentially grown up with the community here."

The next morning Jesse and I accompany a jeep loaded with seedlings to a distant plot where a family has tried to guard the young trees from the ravages of goats. Judi accompanies a midwife to nearby villages. The rocky, scrubby site gives us some idea of what it was originally like at Auroville, now an oasis for silviculture, agriculture, and appropriate tech in a multi-ethnic community of four thousand. It would require dedication to persevere in such a godforsaken place. Later we tour some of the adjacent villages involved with the Right Sharing project, talking to elders intimate with medicinals and midwives. A forest preserve which has harbored some of the species for almost a thousand years surrounds one temple. Back at Pitchandikulam, the women make fresh flower arrangements, floating in water, every morning before meditation, and Judi is pleased to take her turn.

I am frankly awed by Joss's energy and accomplishments, especially by the fact that he seized his destiny at such a young age. I was in the subcontinent at the same time, and really didn't have a clue. Unlike Puer, Joss Brooks had a "conversion" which lasted. He gave the saddhu life a serious look, but found a way to integrate his Western sensibilities with life on the subcontinent. Puer *thought* he loved India, but it was an infatuation with the Other that drew him. For him, India's lasting influence was affirmation of the primacy of the inner life and the validity of mystical experience as something a whole people could value, not just eccentrics. And Joss Brooks' Quaker values were a birthright, not a future happy discovery.

Our travels in Tamil Nadu are mostly to organic farms and women's credit-sharing organizations. Right Sharing emulates the success of the Grameen Bank in Bangladesh, giving women's groups seed capital which they loan each other. We are encouraged by their success, and by the spread of organic farming, successfully modeling a way of farming without suffocating debt. At each stop, we give little speeches, listen to reports, are garlanded, given treats, and take photos. Jesse likes the South Indian villagers, and they are intrigued by his bald head and goatee—the part he reserved from his sacrifice.

We encounter one energetic farmer, Tangaswami, who enthusiastically presses everyone he meets to plant timber trees, teak and rosewood. Each of us plants two trees for the farmer's grandchildren, one teak and one rosewood. It feels good putting my hands into Indian dirt, the soil that I revered at a distance as a young man. On either side of me, my wife and son do the same. Solidarity with the Indian farmer at last! Tangaswami even gives trees to our driver to take home and plant. This Hindu Johnny Appleseed shows us his shrine room, which bears no images, only a full-length mirror under which reads, "Know thyself" and "Serve Mother Earth today in every way possible, that is your realization." On the outer wall of the compound, another sign: "Trees can live without man, but man cannot live without trees" (Richard Barbe-Baker). This is the kind of religion Jesse and I can appreciate.

32 Return to Arunachala

Many of these visits are encouraging, leading me to see that in the rural South, at least, India is greening. But I suffer more losses as well. I expressly avoided returning to Tiruvanamalai and Ramanasramam in 1996 after being alerted to the huge growth of the town by way of an album cover photo commemorating Ramana Maharshi's one hundred years. But Right Sharing wants us to visit a women's project in some nearby villages, so here I am back in Bhagavan's temple town.

Our host Murugesan lives near the ashram, the narrow road to his flat just opposite its entrance. I shudder trying to absorb the urbanization around what had been a pristine compound adjacent the old tank on the outskirts of town, the countryside dotted by a few mud-and-wattle farmhouses, sleek milk-white oxen plowing the fields. I recognize the dorm buildings across from the entrance, now densely flanked by taller buildings. Everywhere I look, white faces. En route to Murugesan's, I notice row after row of two-story buildings with brass plaques out front, many in French and German, one in Italian, another in Japanese. Inquiring, I learn that they are residences of foreign devotees who have concocted charitable organizations as fronts to enable them to purchase real estate in India, prohibited by law for foreign nationals.

A plump fiftyish Murugesan greets us, flanked by several young male social workers, some of whom run their own NGOs. His wife, a son, daughter and father-in-law round out the household. Mrs. Murugesan brings us snacks, which we eat in our room while the well-scrubbed young NGO-wallahs seated on the beds pepper us with questions.

Because of the proximity of his house, Murugesan says he frequently hosts paying guests visiting the ashram. We speak fondly of our *pradakshina* around sacred Arunachala. "Oh, yes, they still do it. Biggest time a big movie star came. Over a million peoples in one day. They made huge mess. It took one week's time to clean up."

The next morning, we rise at five-thirty for meditation in the Old Hall, after which we plan to meet Subramanium, one of the social workers, to climb the Hill. Once inside the ashram gates, the place seems much more familiar. Very little has changed within the complex itself, though everything feels closer together. We find the Old Hall readily, marked by a little line of shoes outside the door. This morning's group is mostly western, though some older Indian couples are present, all draped in shawls against the morning chill. Despite having to frequently change positions in my somewhat cramped corner, I feel the vibes of long prayerful association stirring again ever so slightly. I try to envision the Master on the couch, and his image flickers briefly.

Outside, I listen for birds, and peek around the corners for the peacocks I had briefly glimpsed through the gates the previous afternoon. I hear the sounds of a solitary kitchen worker as he readies the day's breakfast. Night is lifting as our cheerful new friend arrives with Jesse, who slept as long as he could before the morning's ascent.

Though the noisy, crowded town has developed willy-nilly, the Hill remains its implacable, peaceful, energy-filled Self. Trees now grow along the lower slopes, protected by fences from the freely browsing goats. Subramanium says he oversaw the planting himself. We soon come upon village women in worn, faded saris gathering fodder, who gravely nod at us. We stop to meditate at Skandashram, joining a few Europeans, then proceeded to climb Shiva's earthly body. Unlike our youthful days, we have promises to keep and people to meet, and now Jesse is leading us, a young mountain goat scrambling up the flanks. I weigh far more than in the Seventies, and I'm in much worse shape, so am soon winded and fall behind. This is not like leapfrogging past the line of old women going to honor the Deepam flame licking forth from its black kettle. Subramanium patiently waits for me to catch up, and we summit with plenty of time to hang out before returning for our day's appointments.

From the peak, you can see the rural character on the other side of the mountain. The summit is smeared with blackened ghee over a surprisingly large area. Over to one side we spy a tiny hut of sticks and burlap where a swami holds miniature court with about five devotees, one a young Californian. The American approaches us twice, first to tell us to observe silence in Swami's vicinity, then to invite us to join a little ceremony.

We are to take some cold chai mixed with herbs and drink it, and then appear before the swami—who remains behind a burlap curtain—to ask for help with a life problem. Judi drinks hers immediately. Jesse shrugs his shoulders as we look at each other, sharing a lukewarm little communion sip. When my turn comes to slide down the bank for my audience, I can only focus on my yearning for the Tiruvanamalai I had once known, and pray for the Spirit to rekindle Ramana's ashram. The swami mumbles something, and I feel some electricity from this shrouded being, a fraction of the magnetic power emitted by the Hill itself.

The path down from Skandashram leads past Virupaksha Cave, where Ramana lived during the early years. Judi and I enter for meditation while Jesse stays outside to study rock formations and chase a wary monkey. It is the most powerful place I experience this time. More than twenty-five years after our first visit, the bustling ashram at the base of Arunachala feels like an impertinence to the mountain, but the Hill and its shrines, the Master's early cave dwellings, are still packed with power.

After dinner that night back at Murugesan's we have a major discussion, where it quickly becomes clear that our host is not a devotee, but rather a principled Communist, only seeing religion as mollifying the poor and dispossessed. Social revolution is what India needs, and this is something the Party could regularize as policy. His skepticism for the doings of the ashram borders upon open contempt. How do we know that this personality was Shiva incarnate, or even a saint for that matter, since we never saw him in the flesh?

I reply, "When we were here in 1973, there was an atmosphere of respect, love, and dignity. The animals were treated well, the place was immaculate, the little boys in school shone in their attitude of service. It's true the leadership had no particularly religious aura, but there were several evolved souls here."

"That may have been. But you still don't really *know* that the man they worshiped was anything but ordinary human being, perhaps even charlatan. People are all too ready to prostrate themselves, to give away their power—even having little. But when you speak of the order of the place, you were experiencing the power of the brahmins who ran it."

"It was Ramana's family, the Venkateramans. His brother's son, I think was the president."

"You are correct. But that is finished. The brahmins have lost control of the place, and now it is chaos."

"Lost control to whom?" Judi chimes in.

"Lost control in general. But especially to Westerners. Did you see all those fine houses along road from the front gates of the ashram?" When we assent, he continues. "They are dwellings of foreigners. Now there are three–four thousand of them. Perhaps more. They are having money, so they think they should be able to run things as well."

I am shocked. This did not seem possible in hierarchical Hindu culture. But I remember the self-satisfied expressions on some of the Europeans in their Indian garb, the looks of false piety, recognizable even in photos of myself and Judi. As Murugesan continues, I realize he has contempt for both sides of this power struggle, for neither is doing much to help the poor and lower castes. And he is lower caste himself, as he pointedly reminds us.

Then comes an even bigger shock. "There is even one fellow named Hugo Maier who has built huge ashram in countryside near here who set himself up as a god."

"Hugo Maier?" I gasp. Judith looks puzzled, and I remind her of the German homeopath who had been at the ashram during our previous stay. "Remember, you helped him put the horse down who had been in the bus-tonga accident."

"So you know him? He has big air-conditioned ashram with high walls having jagged glass—some say electric fence as well. ... And he only allows German speaking peoples to stay there. "

Again I register disbelief, as Judi listens attentively.

"The village peoples call him mother and father, and bow down to kiss his feet. It is true he gives them many things, which is why they bow. But he does not give them power. And he once had big open fight with another swami, a man named Sai Das. They both want to be Bhagavan with Maharshi gone."

I think back to the Hugo Maier I knew. He was self-possessed, intelligent, seemingly pious. But I had sensed a streak of spiritual pride. Murugesan was laying out what could happen if this went unchecked, and unlike some spiritual leaders, Ramana had not chosen a successor. So there was no one to prune outsized egos.

We talk into the night, and Judi and I shift the conversation away from Ramana's *Advaita Vedanta* to Gandhi's example, expecting we might find more common ground. But our host snorts at the weakness of the latter-day Gandhians, claiming that though Gandhi led a great movement to which all Indians are indebted, he had not been able to reform the Hindu religion, thus the old habits undermining social equality remained entrenched. India is a corrupt society, propped up by an outmoded religion which foolishly holds to its hierarchical view of predestined caste.

Murugesan is a forceful advocate, a sober counterbalance to the cult of "floating" where we nestled during our previous visit. I don't leave Ramanasramam doubting the genuineness of the man around whom it grew, who was clearly Self-realized. But now I see more than enough of the transitoriness of cult once the master and evolved disciples leave the scene.

And Jesse? He will return, and not just to climb rock.

33 Sunderlal's Challenge

We return to Rishikesh in late March after finishing our Right Sharing site visits in the South. Though most prospered, some villages were rather stark. One village with extremely poor soil, rank poverty and a communist village council regaled us with gifts, then wanted handouts. We spent another afternoon hearing complaints from those who had been denied Right Sharing grants, demanding to know why. I particularly squirmed as one angry woman rose to say, "The state government awarded our proposal a prize. Why wasn't it good enough for you?" As usual, Judi handled such difficult questions with dignity and aplomb.

On the overnight train from Delhi to Haridwar, we defend our reserved bunks, casually invaded by young men with frequent regularity. I'm glad to have Jesse as a comrade-in-arms, though Judi's Kali-persona once banished a young assailant in the Bronx. The conductors in starched uniforms no longer rule. When one appears in the middle of the night, it is to provide accommodations for a small throng who boarded our car, refusing to leave. I look around nervously trying to see whence these leveraged bunks might materialize.

Our early morning vikram trip from the station at Haridwar to the ashram in Rishikesh through scrub forest is brisk: I barely have sufficient layers to keep out the foggy cold. The ashram is largely the same, as Judi promised, though more dwellings have been built, including a large new temple behind the old satsang hall. But an adjacent transportation center for vikrams, oversized three-wheeled motorcycles which hold six to eight passengers, has appeared and traffic is more frequent, noisily leading right through the ashram.

Judi fits right in here, as she always did, weaving her personal routine of *japa*, clotheswashing and late afternoon *arthi* at the river with the many options for devotees. The key to her day, though, is taking *chai* and cookies and reading *Gita* with Swami Hamsananda. Now nearing sixty, he is short and almost toothless due to his fondness for sweets. Still, his smile is beautiful. Hamsananda has been a monk since twenty-one, like many at the ashram, a South Indian Brahmin by birth. His role at the ashram includes delivering the mail, presiding over *arthi* at the Ganga, teaching foreigners who request his direction, and silently policing the area along the river—a public market area in front of his little cubbyhole. Unlike Satchidananda, Judi's first guru, who had a gargantuan ego to match his Olympian prowess in *hatha yoga*, Swami Hamsananda is exceedingly humble. He treads the exacting *jnana* path upon which I have long struggled, and is a very firm, disciplined, insightful teacher for Judi. Meeting her "post office swami," I feel clearly that she is being led aright this time.

But once again I am here without a teacher, even less comfortable with the routine than I had been during our previous pilgrimage. Jesse and I marvel at how effortlessly his mother fits in, but I still prefer to make my own choices each day rather than have my way prescribed. I do enjoy the afternoon *arthi* honoring the goddess Ganga by the swiftly flowing river in front of Sivananda's kutir. Hamsananda presides beamingly over this ritual, visually nudging Judi to lead some of the chants despite her uncertain pitch. I try to help, but don't know the syllables.

We still eat in long rows on the floor. The burlap mats are so dirty and stained they appear to be the same ones from our previous stay. I have even more trouble eating in cross-legged posture than before, stiffer, now suffering from hip bursitis. Unable to lean over sufficiently, I keep dropping my food, quickly looking around to see if any of the inmates have seen. Seated next to me, Jesse shakes his head in sympathy. The refectory food is still unappetizing, though we have a good feast day meal, as Judi promised. Jesse and I start eating at least one meal a day at the Madras Café, which caters to westerners down by the river, splurging on sweet *lassi*, dosas and scrambled eggs. He is a polite visitor, but the ashram isn't quite his thing.

Judi takes both her men to join the little group for meditation at the evening gathering at Swami Krishnananda's *kutir*. Krishnananda, always a storehouse of knowledge, a great storyteller and expounder of the faith, has grown into a very powerful teacher, regarded by his many disciples as a realized being (*jivanmukta*). He still has a great wit, as he demonstrates by gently prodding me as we are re-introduced, a discernible twinkle in his eye. With Jesse he is respectful and straightforward. When it is time to begin meditation, his attendants fold his ample eighty-four-year-old flesh into full lotus, pivoting him onto the mat. He holds the position for the rest of the hour. As usual, I am unable to remain cross-legged, and opt for a chair. The gathering is right next to the main road, and vikrams roar incessantly like a band of Harleys, repeatedly breaking my concentration. Judi later claimed not to notice, and said that just being around a powerful meditator anchored her meditation more deeply.

One day I wake in time for morning *arthi* at the new temple. I noticed the drumbeats other mornings, but stuffed my ears with stopples and tried to go back to sleep, as Jesse is doing now, turning to face the wall on the other side of the bedroom. Judi is already at the temple, always one of the first. As I approach, I hear the intoxicating bass beat grow louder, and over it, voices chanting, somewhat off-key as usual. But when I sleepily enter the hall, devotees clanging bells line in front of the central chamber dedicated to all the major gods in the pantheon, thick wreathes of incense curling about their upturned faces, I am dumbfounded to find the central beat emanating from a mechanical drum. The chamber of gods with their multiple arms is the focal point for the other devotees, but I can't divert my attention from this eerie drum, mechanical driver of the whole play.

I really want to see Sunderlal again before we leave, and especially for Jesse to meet him. He had survived his "final fast" in October 1997, which lasted more than sixty days. During the Kumbh Mela at Haridwar the following year, he was joined by "storming saddhus"—ten thousand of them swarming upriver on motorized rafts claiming they would occupy the dam site along with Brother Sunderlal. As one rasta-haired saddhu said, the government and THDC were trying to "enchain the holy goddess" who had been "catching impious things" during monsoon when she was "having her period." No saddhu could worship such polluted water. But it was all a publicity stunt, and the saddhus left as suddenly as they had stormed in, leaving SLB chuckling alone. When Judi saw him in

February, he had negotiated a truce with Delhi, agreeing to quit his fasts if Delhi promised not to build any of the twelve additional dams planned for the Himalayas. Tehri's fate is now sealed.

Sunderlal is not at the *kutir* in Tehri. His son tells us that he has been hospitalized at Dehra Dun with pneumonia. But shortly before our final departure, he left the hospital for his daughter's house, where we manage to see him. When we enter the bungalow, SLB is sitting on the living room couch, looking surprisingly strong. His hair is down, lustrous and beautiful. Well-scrubbed, he looks more relaxed than weak. The hospital has been a good enforced rest. He speaks passionately about saving the Himalayas and stopping globalization in its tracks. Jesse later says he has never heard an environmentalist so convincing—someone who obviously lived the principles he promoted.

Judi guides the conversation towards her own wish to serve the Garhwali people, fast becoming her adopted clan.

"If you want to serve the hill people, you need to move to one of the villages and build a little house there. You need to become one of them. ..."

"You understand, Sunderlal, that I would probably not spend more than half the year there."

"Or even less" I interject.

He looks at me, continuing, "...Living amongst them as much as possible, just as Mira Behn and Soba Behn did (British Gandhian ladies). Have you read their biographies? You must, both of you. This is the only real way you can be effective. You must join the village and learn what their needs are as a villager yourself."

"But she also has a marriage. And I am not sure this is the *seva* I would choose."

Sunderlal looks slowly from me to Judi, while Jesse watches it all with intense interest. "I understand. If you could join her as much as possible, that would be my desire. But married people must work together. That is the first thing."

I feel on the knife's edge. We are approaching a choice-point, and I am not ready for the required leap. What will we do?

It is now early April, and we are packing to leave. In the middle of the night, our dormitory starts shaking, and we all scamper downstairs into the darkness below, assuming an earthquake. Our guess is confirmed at breakfast. It turned out to be a 6.9 quake at Chamoli, a hundred kilometers away. Devendra immediately contacts us and asks Judi to come do relief work. We sit down as a family to talk about it.

"I'm really pulled to go join them," Judi says.

I am dismayed. I hate changes in plans. "Deb and Gary are expecting us. We can't let them down." We are planning to visit good friends from Moorhead living in Germany en route home. I shoot a look at Jesse, who maintains careful neutrality.

Judi looks at both of us. "I'm conflicted. Here's a situation where I could help. You're right, it would be awkward to shift plans with Deb and Gary—but I think they would understand. What do you think, Jesse?" Jesse had introduced her to Deb, a story she repeats often. "Mom, I found you a friend," recognizing a potential friendship in bleak Moorhead. Judi always trusted his opinion.

"I'm out of this," horizontally leveling his arms. He has plans to explore Kumaon with a good friend from North Carolina as soon as we leave. The rest is up to us.

"Judi, you know the relief work will take time. Look how long it's taken to rebuild after the Uttar Kashi quake. The work will still be going on when you return next time."

"I guess you're right. But if our plans weren't so intertwined with others, I'd stay."

I am relieved, but this portends more conflict.

Jesse has patiently waited for the chance to explore India on his own terms. Now we tell him good-bye.

We take the train to Gaziabad for one last stop before our flight to Germany. Gaziabad is a suburb of one million due north of Delhi, the road between thickly lined with petrochemical refineries and other heavy industry, hardly a tree or shrub to hide the blight. Our host PK Agarwal meets us at the station. PK was my chief opponent in a late-night debate on the Tehri Dam three years before ("if the cities are inundated because the dam breaks, that is the will of God"). There are no residual hard feelings. He works for the UP state electric company, a broker for the power which he hopes will soon flow from the Tehri reservoir.

In the middle of the afternoon, as we join PK for *chai* in the Victorian drawing room while his wife, daughter and mother-in-law watch a Hindi film on tv in the breakfast room, the electricity fails. Embarrassed, PK goes out back and turns on the generator, which creates more noise and diesel fumes than power. The women resume watching the film, now without benefit of dialogue. We sit around with them, gesturing ineffectively. Nobody can hear anything but the generator.

Later, after the public power flow resumes, PK speaks fervently, seated in a Victorian wing chair in his drawing room, "The people, my customers, *deserve* to have power they can count on. It is their right, and we must do everything in our power to provide them that right." I don't not need to tell him that India's power delivery is the world's least efficient, therefore challenging the need for the Tehri Dam and scores of others the Indian government hopes to build. Why not invest in upgrading power lines and stopping graft, rather than displacing millions of poor farmers and tribals while flooding hundreds of thousands of acres of wetlands? We have been through this before. His passion is unexpected, and reminds me how firmly the battle lines remain drawn in this latest version of the quarrel between Gandhi and Nehru.

PART FOUR

THE TABLES TURN

Awakening in the chilly pre-dawn, women huddling in the dark hall opposite the living area are biting me. They bite again and again, dark forms like snakes dripping down from their hair. I cross my hands over my heart, trying to protect it, and they bite my hands. They swarm at me from the dark hall, maenads, lamias, priestesses of Kali, Kali who gorges on her harvest of blood.

I would be Shiva, who quickens with excitement as Kali dances furiously on his prostrate form. But this feels like Orpheus, assaulted by maenads, his lyre falling uselessly at his side as he reaches to protect the heart-center from their furious assault.

waking image, April 1999

Dance of the Gods

On Saturday night, Memorial Day Weekend 1999, Judi and I join the annual "Dance of the Gods" at the Friends Conference on Religion and Psychology at Lehigh Valley in eastern Pennsylvania, ending our fifteen-year absence. Each person goes in costume, playing the role of one of the gods. As Jungians, we tend to play Greeks; as Quakers, we rejoice in denying that the days of the week are mere integers. Seventh Day? No way, baby, this is Saturn's Day, and we're gonna banish melancholia. Judi has planned to go as the prostitute Pingala whom Shiva accepted because of her devotion to him despite her lowly, filthy status. To Pingala every man was simply a manifestation of Shiva, so her acts did not accrue karma. While I watch, she dresses in her red-and-saffron sari, smearing herself with sacred ash, puts on thick eyeshadow, and giving me one wanton glance, slips out the door of our spartan college dorm room. This is going to be fun.

So my choice is obvious. I go as blind Shiva, seeking not Pingala but Jyothi, the inner feminine light of the Universe. Jyothi, who is dancing around in her sari disguised as Pingala. I don my black sleep mask, tie on my green-blue checkered lungi, smear three streaks of ash on my brow, one across my throat, and hang a brass trident around my neck, dangling down my bare chest. Sneaking looks at the ground, I meander from our dorm over to the ritual hall.

When I enter, people think I am Oedipus. I hesitate. "I am also Oedipus." What man isn't? "No, the one you see is not Oedipus." I keep being lost, then heartened by women coming up to me, clutching my hand, leading me to meet other gods whom I cannot see. Of course, I don't know my own nature, either. Oedipus? Damn, maybe they are right. I am starting to feel helpless. Then a goddess says, "Someone wants to see you." Jyothi! It has to be Jyothi. Blind and disoriented, I am excited. A familiar hand gently touches me: "Do you want *prasad*?"

"No prasad," I hear myself saying, "I want my Jyothi."

"You can't have her now, but she has sent you *prasad*." I push the blessed food away, and she's gone. I ask again for Jyothi, but there is no answer from the cavernous room. I feel alienated from the clutch of divine voices, ranging far over the floor as the other gods lose interest in this Oedipus who won't admit it, every few minutes bellowing "Jyothi! Where's my Jyothi?"

I, Shiva, want Jyothi, my own inner nature, distributed throughout creation. The Jews call her *shekinah*. She's right here in this room, just offered me *prasad*. But I am blind to her, the cow hiding from the bull in the Hindu creation story. I grow tired of being blind Shiva. I want to take off my blinders, and I'm hungry behind the mask.

So I eat, and hang out with the other gods and goddesses. The lawyer from DC who leads a men's group—he always seemed so young before—is playing DJ, all the old favorites, but not many people are dancing. Where is everybody? I sneak out of my blinders and search the room for my Jyothi. She's not there. I ask a friend. She has stepped out. ... Oh. Jyothi stepped out. Where would Jyothi go? Jyothi is everywhere. Shiva is everywhere.

A woman comes up, bumps me with her hip, and we start dancing. I have put my mask back on, rejoined the play. If she is a goddess, she is Earth, Gaia. Instantly I recognize her, the feel of her body, her scent, the way she bumped me with her hip. The risk of being wrong, of merely guessing, shadows my reflexive response like a momentary passing cloud, but yes, I recognize my old dancing-partner after fifteen years. She laughs and we bump and grind.

Hardly anyone else is dancing. I don't feel that close heat and motion of many bodies on the floor together, no trace of a sinus wave in the floor beams. This place is dead, dancing gods an anomaly.

There she is.

I aim my trajectory as close as possible to my quarry, then slip on the blinders again, groping like blind Oedipus for the sari wrapping the familiar form. "Jyothi?" I ask, touching a goddess on the waist, missing. "No," the mortal says, "but she's right here." So we're together. I sneak a look at the kohl-painted eyes I have sought all evening, and ask her to dance.

"I'm tired. I need to get up and meditate early tomorrow. Okay. One dance." I know I look deflated. "Okay, two, then I'm going to bed. You can stay." Jyothi/Pingala dances with me. Neither tune is quite the right beat—too slow, as usual. The tiresome Rolling Stones again. When the beat is right, we can really move on the dancefloor; people stop and look. We briefly discuss waiting for our beat, an uptempo swing rhythm, my hand waiting expectantly on her hip. But Judi-Jyothi is really tired, spent. She leaves with a smile and a little chaste kiss.

I dance with Kali, petite, raven-haired, dressed as a butterfly in her white tutu—so incongruous as the bloodthirsty goddess of destruction—but I can only think of Jyothi, back in our dorm room, and how I wish she were here, now that I am no longer wearing blinders and the beat's back. But of course that's just it, with blinders off, she's unavailable, not a partywoman anymore. And me? *Who is Shiva, Lord?*

34 "Shiva Has Stolen My Heart"

This last winter of the millennium is difficult. Judi retired from family medicine last August, then accompanied me on my sabbatical to Celo. Now it's University payback time for me, but her prospects for spending a year back in Lake Wobegon simply out of loyalty were too bleak. So in the fall she made a long train trip to the West Coast to visit family, then helped crew her sister Layne's and brother-in-law Michael's catamaran in the annual regatta from Santa Barbara to Capo del Gato, returning via the Copper Canyon Railway and interminable buses from the Texas border. Jacob and Jesse surprised me in Moorhead for a family Thanksgiving. What a joy it was to see them in the Fargo airport! Jacob especially, since he had reckoned he was done with Minnesota when he left two years before. All four of us enjoyed Thanksgiving Dinner at our house by the Red River. We're all together again in North Carolina for Christmas before Judi leaves once again for India in January, returning to Sivananda Ashram for the winter. I fly back to teach my final semester, the soul following, trudging on foot through the vast snowfields of the upper plains.

While she's gone, I develop a mean case of bronchitis, missing well over a week of classes, a record. In all, it takes a month to recover. It's no help that I am at the center of Dante's hell, winter in Fargo-Moorhead, and really only have my good friend Dieter to count upon for support during the illness and depression. Discouraged, I call our North Carolina friend Nancy, who grew up in Minneapolis and once visited us in Moorhead. I ask her to come take care of me. She laughs, repeating catty comments from her high school days about Moorhead. "Visit you in *Moorhead*? You gotta be kidding." I am exiled at the end of the earth, indeed woebegone. I must patiently wait for the woman who once took a vow to take care of me, though not too much.

Our friend Eleanor from Mobile. another southerner in economic exile in the frozen north, picks her up at the Amtrak Station in Madison and brings her back to the Twin Cities. We meet at the Saint Paul Hotel, our favorite in the Cities. They've given me an improbably good rate. Judi's worried. "They never give rates like that." Sure enough, she's right. My reservation proves to be irretrievable, given by some sweet young phantom, and I've lost the reservation number. It costs a lot more. Judi disapproves, says we're splurging. Exactly. I am reuniting with my bride, now a transplanted Garhwali matron. *Mataji* has taken a new name: Geeta Jyothi, Song of the Inner Light.

Judith, I mean Geeta, shines with quiet radiance, almost ethereal. At the Saint Paul Grill, she has a very difficult time finding something to eat that will suit her vegetarian regime. And she has forsworn alcohol, so instead of a romantic bottle, I have a little rationed glass of Italian red. But Geeta Jyothi does not need alcohol to be enthusiastic about her time in Himalaya.

"I told you I met an absolutely delightful sannyasin, Swami Premanand. He runs the Sivananda branch ashram outside Uttar Kashi [the last urban outpost before Gangotri]. Swamiji is devoted to the villagers, like a father. And he cooks for them, like a mother. He serves them with unflagging goodwill and total humility. He delights in his flowers, which surround the ashram, and his built a bower for the delight of Krishna and Radha. With his encouragement, I've started seeing local devotees in the villages—mostly laying on of hands, but some more serious cases."

That winter, Geeta gave some health camps, primarily working to assess needs and ways to better deliver services. Premanand works tirelessly, eighteen hours daily, taking care of orphaned boys and cows, and plays some mean badminton. He even plays banker to village people, stashing their rupees in envelopes on which he scrawls his impeccable transactions, circulating their little caches among them. He gives away the ashram's cash donations so generously that he sometimes must borrow from this pool to pay for food, fodder, and books for the schoolchildren. "Somehow there is always enough."

Swami Premanand quickly becomes Judi's touchstone Swami, and her annual visits will be divided between swamis, Hamsananda in Rishikesh and Premanand in Ganeshpur. It's a bit of a dance for her. He will also become our "family teacher" when our sons meet him during a subsequent trip. Their introduction to him is unforgettable. After our arrival for a few days at his ashram, he seats them and gives a serious look, studying their faces.

"I must tell you the rules at this ashram."

Jacob and Jesse exchange glances, and he continues. "There are no rules. Just treat everyone here the way you would like them to treat you, and all will be fine."

Several years later, during a sojourn at an ashram in Tiruvanamalai founded by an American advaitist who taught Bhagavan Ramana's method of self-inquiry, I accompanied Swami Premanand to a tea there, where he was to meet the inmates and spend some time with Stan, the director. A circle of chairs was set up in the beautiful courtyard, a table covered in a spotless white cloth laid with chai and sweet biscuits. As we approached the reception, Swamiji grabbed my hand, picked up his step, barely acknowledging Stan as we walked through the chair circle to the floral bower in the center of the ashram grounds. He seated me on a bench, his arm around my shoulder, looked around with his huge, infective smile, saying, "Isn't this beautiful?" After a couple of minutes, he said, "Come, let's go." We then returned to the tea reception and the usual social graces. Vintage Swami Premanand.

Back in St. Paul, after dinner we retire to the conjugal bed on the ninth floor, overlooking our beloved Ordway Theater, where we would hear Hugh Wolf and the SPCO the next day for one last time. We are old pros, but inert Geeta is elsewhere, albeit smiling benevolently. I feel like Rilke's Orpheus, forcing Eurydice back from her comforting Underworld. I've never had sex with a thirteen-year-old, or a virgin for that matter, but this is what it feels like. She's trying to be present, but her body just isn't there. This is premature.

Reunited, we return to dreary Moorhead and her late winter landscape, snows sullied by dirt blown from the plains. We walk into the bedroom, standing by the second marriage bed I built for us, faced with some nice oak boards from the roadswath I cut to access our house in North Carolina. Geeta, still trim but less buxom than she had been as a bride, her long brown hair just beginning to salt with gray, as if she had lightly brushed against silver roof paint, reaches for my hand, gently turning me to meet her brown-eyed gaze. "Shiva has stolen my heart."

So grave, so compassionate, so sensitive, but very firm. My mind races back to the first time I took her to India. I had wanted so badly for her to experience India as I had my Fulbright year: a whole society that viewed Spirit as the One Reality. Now it has led to this. Our life together henceforth is going to be a challenge. But hasn't it always?

So, coinciding with my imminent retirement, my wife has a new life-orientation. Geeta Jyothi was Swami Hamsananda's suggestion, and the "Song of the Inner Light" has become Shiva's devotee. Her meditation, scripture reading and general *sadhana* now take several hours a day, beginning at five a.m. More ominous, she wants to stop having sex. She is seriously contemplating taking *sannyas* (vows of renunciation), suggesting that I join her in this path.

This is not what I have in mind at all. The best I can do was to negotiate a rule: *Only on Sunday*. She will play the dutiful wife, following scriptural injunction. But she will keep before me other injunctions to gradually retire from the sense world as well as worldly obligations. "It is time to enter *vanaprastha*," she reminds me: the Vedic asrama where a Hindu couple retire to the forest and subsist on roots and herbs.

Along with this steep change in what had finally become a satisfying physical relationship during our Minnesota exile, Geeta announces she wants to spend half of each year in India, doing intense spiritual work at Sivananda Ashram branches under Hamsananda's and Premanand's guidance, alternating with *sadhana* as physician-consultant for a Garhwali women's health network near Tehri. During the previous year, she had reclaimed and strengthened her Hindi; she can actually understand enough now to do make diagnoses. "You can come with me," she says sweetly

"But I thought you told Sunderlal you couldn't practice without a medical infrastructure." I am truly befuddled.

"That's true, but I've been thinking I'd like to explore the possibilities some more. Would you be interested in coming back to the hills and writing about Sunderlal while I did a women's health project?"

I shake my head. "No, I just find the North too depressing. And you can't depend on the power being available for the laptop. I would be very frustrated."

"What if we built a nice little bungalow with a view of the mountains and installed solar power?" She always thought of more possibilities than I could consider.

"Look, the ashram that interests me is the one we might create in Celo, an Appalachian one focused on sustainable life-skills and ecology."

"And we could have a spiritual context for it all, combining the resources of the (Friends) Meeting with Vedanta. ... But I feel called to work with the hill women, and it needs to be about six months each year to create enough continuity so it will stick."

"You're asking a lot—too much. I need to focus my energy, and feel my talents are better suited to awakening middle-class Westerners to what we can do to alleviate the pressures in the developing world." I had begun the process of training with the Buddhist deep ecologist Joanna Macy to teach folks to work through despair over impending global ecological collapse to a sense of empowerment. Going to India as a couple would again derail my life-direction just as it was taking shape.

The tables have turned. Now Geeta is the one swept off her feet by India, and I the reluctant spouse. I have infected her with my passion, then cured into something else, no longer Puer the Hinduphile. We have a lot to work through as we return to Appalachia at the end of May 2000, eleven years after our Northern Plains exile began. As for that bungalow, she does have it built, not at Sunderlal's, but at Swami Premanand's, after he requests help for his rapidly growing ashram on the banks of the Bhagirathi.

Forest Hermitage

"When a householder sees (his skin) wrinkled and (his hair) white, and the sons of his sons, then he may resort to the forest."—*Laws of Manu*

"Your wife is your guru." —Maurice Frydman

"You are Geeta Jyothi. Therefore you have to do *satsang* with *Gita* itself. In the first hour you have to weep like that of Arjuna. In the second hour you have to get up like that of Arjuna with bow and arrow in hands. In third hour you have to be active with your body. In fourth hour you have to renounce the fruit of action. In fifth hour you have to acquire Self Knowledge. In sixth hour self control has to be practiced. ..."

—Swami Hamsananda, 1999

Fourth hour, eight a.m., time to renounce the fruits of action. ...

"Why do you want to go inside this body? It's just a bag of bones, falling skin, swirls of bowel, dying flesh. I am rotting. You want to unite with this?"

"Yeah." The devotee is undeterred.

My playmate-wife is a yogi ... my guru. Is there a conflict of interest here?

My hair is rapidly turning from brindled to white and wrinkles are furrowing their way apace. But my sons seem far from reproducing themselves. We are back in the Southern Mountains, in Celo, where our house *is* in the forest, as I keep reminding Geeta, though we certainly aren't subsisting on roots, berries and alms. So are we still householders, or now forest-hermits? This remains a question for me, but Geeta is eager to move to the hermit stage and beyond. Where will we put the swami when he visits? Instead of building a gallery for the art we had collected in Minnesota—her suggestion during the yuppy years—the charge now is to convert the shed to a guest house.

Our homelife now becomes regulated as if it were an ashram. While we were still in Moorhead, Geeta's coolness towards the marital couch was offset by her remarkable serenity, grace, and an unaccustomed gentleness. Others noticed it, too. She seemed to have undergone remarkable, genuine change. Now she is back in her planning mode, with several life-scenarios running at once. When I mention this shift, she answers "I had nothing to do but wait for you to finish teaching. It was really difficult." So the *sattwic* personality of those two months was a persona after all, maintained by an effort hidden to me. And, since she still accepted her wife station, her efforts at significant lifestyle-change were tentative, probing, experimental.

Back at our forest ashram in North Carolina Geeta sets up a tightly controlled regime for herself, including daily periods of silence. At first I mainly work on rebuilding rotting decks and the long-neglected garden soil. Then I move gradually into writing and teaching deep ecology workshops inspired by my new mentor, Joanna Macy. Typically, Geeta proceeds at a more energetic pace. She enrolls in a distant learning course, a Masters in Public Health at Chapel Hill. She also starts working with the Yancey County Health Initiative, trains as a HIP facilitator (Help Increase the Peace), and becomes active with both national and regional Quaker committees—in addition to her role as board member of Right

Sharing (to be fair, I also clerk our yearly meeting's Ministry and Care Committee and chair the Arthur Morgan School Board, often a time-consuming position).

But what Geeta really wants is to work in India, especially to sit as much as possible at the Swamis' feet, alternating with medical social work under Sunderlal's guidance. She requests a clearness committee from Celo Meeting, on which I agree to serve. After two sessions, we have clearness. She will go to India for four months next winter. This is her best shot at determining whether a health network can really get off the ground and become cohesive enough to continue during her yearly absences. I join the consensus with some reluctance. She's passionate about it, though it is a compromise from the six months she preferred. But I have premonitions.

35 Geeta of Garhwal

January 2001

Lying in bed late at night as the January winds howl, I picture Geeta Jyothi sitting in half-lotus, bundled up, wrapped in a sari, vermillion vibhuti smeared on her forehead. Here in Celo she often smears it askew, looking charmingly peasant-like. There, in the foothills of the Garhwal Himalayas, I see her wrapped against the cold, navy-blue silken long underwear, woolen shawl, rapt in the early morning darkness. My image molts into a Japanese doll with rouged ivory cheeks, dressed in traditional kimono, also tightly wrapped. The Japanese doll is a bride, my bride, Jehudith the flower of Judaea, now Geeta of Garhwal, the doll recast as a Garhwali Shaivite. I want my middle American Jewish peasant back, not the doll I created by dragging that deep spiritual longing of hers to its new Hindu abode in Rishikesh and Garhwal almost thirty years ago. But I know as I lie here that I will miss her even when she is home, whenever she wears this doll-mask.

At first, I enjoy all the time to myself, the deep winter writing retreat which I relish. I knew it would be so. I become more focused on my meditation practice, slowly tracing Ramana Maharshi's memorized face from neck to the top of his head, then cycling back to the neck again. My main problem with this practice is that by the time I get to his Aryan nose, it has a tendency to turn into my more fleshy one. But the deep pools of his eyes are a dip into a reality which awakens, sometimes frightens me.

Answering a flyer promising a discount if you start before the deadline, about a month later I begin sessions with a therapist who reads the body using Chinese acupressure points, a system worked out by a Jungian analyst working in Portland, Arnold Mindell. At the Friends Conference on Psychology and Religion many years before, Marion Woodman introduced me to a Jungian approach which brought the body into the dialogue, and the preliminary results were dramatic, as I writhed on the floor, a fiery sunball coursing through my veins.

When Alicia asks me what the main problem is, I answer, "None. I am pretty balanced. I'm just interested in finding out how you operate." Curious answer from a guy who knew from experience that analysis is interminable. The work turns out to be rich, powerful and integrative. Hearing the invitation, my dreams, which have been mute for months, flood back:

Behind Gaga's [my father's mother], Geeta and I discuss building a new house. I wonder why we would need a new house, but then I remember, and it finally sinks in, that she had said we could rent out Gaga's house for a handsome income. I think it will cost a lot to build the new one, so all that income would just offset the cost of the new building: Zero Sum. Meanwhile, I am clipping around the foundation and new stairs to the new dwelling. I am cutting out diseased shrub tips and discarding them. I've made a new set of deck stairs, wide and well-built. On ground floor level is a stone floor, nice workmanship, already laid.

We need to build a new marital "house," but we have a foundation.

Alicia begins each session by hearing a quick review of my somatic history since the previous session, along with any major life-events. I sit facing her, then stand with my back to her, as she takes notes from this body-reading on a pad diagramming acupressure points. It's like sitting for a brief portrait. Then I mount the massage table, and she elicits images and responses by manipulating the pressure points. The idea is to take the images and memories which come and free associate to their limit. I love it. So does she.

At the first session, I get in touch with a male fetus strangling in his cord. I get the sense that it's not me, feeling no fear. It feels more like a male forebear. What follows are my father's nightmares of being chased by a woman, and his mother's (Gaga's) icy rigidity with respect to sexuality, severely punishing his early adolescent self-experiments. Then comes this stuck feeling accompanying tucking my head towards my left shoulder, which feels like Mallarmé's swan, frozen in the ice, unable to fly (Mallarmé-as-Orpheus was the principal subject of my book, *The Orphic Moment*).

At the second session, asked to have a dialogue between the "stern" father, the rule maker, and the young playful Krishna figure, I see an image of [Blake's] Nobodaddy growing out of a block of ice, tears flowing from blind eyes down his cheeks, long white beard and hair, writing the book of *Urizen* two-handed. As Alicia massages my temples and scalp, I'm back with Mother stroking my scalp as a baby, and then the Earth Mother, a fellow trainee at the Joanna Macy intensive in California the previous fall, "cradling" me in an exercise until I can hardly stand the caresses. *This is what I'm not getting*, I had written.

In the bodywork, Alicia zeroes in on a tender spot behind my heart, saying "This is the place where the wings would attach." Then we move to the taskmaster, the heavy head, leading down to troglodytes and imprisoned titans, all in chains: arms, legs, neck. Again, the image of Nobodaddy writing two-fisted, blind with tears flowing, realizing that he is all head, knees scrunched up to his chin. Then the image molts to gargoyles, Quasimodo climbing the bell cables. I realize that these underworld energies are in the bell tower next to the ringing bells clamoring heavenward. The troglodytes and titans are liberated, bringing their deep-body earth energies up into the steeple, the head. Wow.

"What if you were to imagine writing with this dragon-energy?" I flash back to a midnight scene in Delhi, feeling it from within the body of one of those workers, my sweat gleaming in the streetlights. At the end of the session Alicia concludes, "Cradle the iceman."

The therapy moves rapidly into deeper and deeper levels. And then, as happened in Dallas in my Jungian analysis with Pat Berry, the energies triangulate. In early March, almost eight weeks after Geeta left, I attend a Celo Contradance. Community dances were one of the things which originally drew us to Celo, still a monthly highlight. It is a clear cool night, and I feel alive. I miss my favorite dancing-partner, but a spirit of celebration is upon me, and as I enter the warmth of the hall with the familiar music of Band X, I quickly realize that I am here to give every woman I dance with a great time—and to dance with as many as I can manage. This includes the older single women, for whom this is a rare evening of animation and physical contact.

Thus occupied, I dance with the Girl Next Door, kindling a wild joy. I continue with my plan, feeling more and more joy as I dance with most of the women in attendance. Joy given is joy received. I dance with my neighbor a couple of more times that evening, including a fast polka in place of the waltz at the break. Our wedding dance had been a polka, and my polka expertise reached back to prevailing in the last-couple-standing-wins in eighth grade, a hilarious combination of football and awakening hormones. As we whirl around, I start to tire, not being in eighth-grade football shape. "Lean back," she says. For rest, I simply twirl her while she polkas for both of us. She is younger than I, but soon tires as well, laughing when she catches my game.

Up to now, Geeta has been absent. But with this polka, she's right there, halfway across the world in another set of mountains, yet under the same stars. *Though far apart, dancing new dances with different partners, we are tethered. When I lean back, I feel your weight tugging at the other end, sweeping the other dancers into the rhythm of our wide arc.* (Dallas, 1982)

Ah, but too late. I am hooked.

Ensconced in those mountains, Geeta is trying to figure out for herself what "Shiva has stolen my heart" means, as she weighs the decision to become a *sannyasin* and take vows to renounce the world—possessions, relations, and me. Shortly after this contradance, I receive an e-mail reaffirming that, at least for now, her life is as a householder, not a monk. I really don't know what this means, given her behavior over the previous year. Still, I record in my journal: *And Shiva wept.*

This householder Shiva, revered god of our marriage, weeps with joy. A week or so later I receive a Valentine card, depicting Krishna and Radha, much easier to relate to as amorous couple than Shiva and Parvati, whose postures require yogic training beyond this beginner's body. The resplendently colorful gold-embossed card depicts Radha with one leg wrapped around Krishna from behind, arms around his neck, and one hand on his flute, helping to finger the notes. The card is accompanied by "love and kisses." It reciprocates the Holi-Valentine card filled with red powder (*vibhuti*) that I sent Geeta at Sivananda Ashram from Dewas in early 1974. *Shiva wept* with relief, but still I have a question about the relation of yogic love to this commonplace remark. I e-mail back, "What does that mean, love and kisses? A kiss on the forehead? A metaphor? If so, then it is a cruel one."

Since I cannot deny the power of my feelings for my new dance partner, I send Geeta a letter telling her what is going on.

"In the midst of this, dear one, as [James] Hillman says, 'when the soul awakes, we fall in love.' I have developed a strong romantic interest in someone who is practically the girl next door. ... I am still a man, not a yogi, and my self-energies include a strong sexual current." I continue, saying that I want that current to be integrated in our relationship. If not, we need to explore "alternatives."

Geeta's response is an e-mail: "You deserve romance." We accept our longstanding bond, the power of our friendship, and start talking in the most specific and serious terms ever about the "junior wife" we have co-fantasized almost as long as we have been married. Maybe we should be a threesome up on Snake Ridge, I fantasize.

At my third session with Alicia, the Sacred Whore in white nightclothes is delivered to a god in my intestines: first Shiva, then a figure more like Vulcan, busily stoking the roaring intestinal fires. As we explore the base chakra, I find Shiva lying erect, a Pleasure Garden of intestines growing up around him, turning to a maze of walls. Later, I see shit streaming underneath, and the more solid form of the walls is crusted dung over fresher stuff.

Then, working around the heart again, Shiva walks down a country road arm-in-arm with Krishna. Krishna keeps molting with the image of Hanuman, and finally Hanuman is a third, between the other two. The three are closely bonded, energy flowing between them. I send the image to Geeta along with an interpretation: "Shiva is in the position of the Father, the king, the rule-maker, but he is not rigid ... Krishna is the playful trickster, the figure expressed with my new friend. Hanuman [Ram's monkey-king devotee] is the image of loyalty, and he cements the bond between the older-younger figures and their energies. This loyalty may also be loyalty to the marriage. Like I said, the life-energies are moving into a good place, but Krishna and his amorous interests need a life. ..." In the journal: *What about loyalty to the Self?*

When I confess my feelings to the Girl Next Door at the end of March, her response is "I'm honored"—hardly passionate. But in the next sentence, she acknowledges mutual attraction. This is the way it is the rest of the spring. Every time I feel my passion rebuffed, she says something that reopens the door just a little. And from then on, we discuss what it would be like for the three of us to live on the ridge together. Having been pulled into an affair with a married man once before who lied to her about his marital status, she wants to talk directly with Geeta. Fair enough. Geeta and I have always been honest with each other in these matters. So we agree to be affectionate, nothing more.

The following week, Jacob, Jesse and I join my friend Jerry at a performance of *A Winter's Tale* in Asheville. When Hermione comes back to life, I start to cry. The unfreezing of the cold statue, gone from her husband's bed for so long, dramatizes my deepest hopes. It is like watching a mystery play about my own marriage.

I write Geeta about this, and the letter which crosses mine speaks of my being her best friend. Now it is I who is "honored," but, dammit, I want cradling and loving as well.

The budding of spring, the intro chapter of Barbara Kingsolver's Prodigal Summer *and its eroticism, the whole forest in sympathy with the heroine ... and Geeta of Garhwal is far away. No crows today, only sweet chirping. I turn and twist like a sausage on the fire, and write Geeta-Love to release me to my Friend:*

> The swelling hickory buds each a tiny phallus
> raising its ripe springing head to spring.
> I ache like the sap of spring unable to flow.
> "But mark me, no sap flows until your return."

"You are a ripe peach," says my Friend. "A ripe peach afraid of becoming a rotten peach."

I cook a seductive fish, which my Neighbor feeds me (I want to lick her fingers, hand, arm and more). I also prepare cannabis-spiced greens before we go hear live Indian music. On the way home from the concert we visit the "saddhu," perhaps her romantic friend, and he stones her some more. They walk me home, and the three of us sit under the stars on our glorious upstairs deck. The swollen hickory buds are shrouded in darkness.

The ache of longing, going back as long as I can remember into adolescence. Off in the woods at Springs, the suburban landscape in Pittsburgh, blocked from expressing these feelings to a woman. Now I press my suit, get intimate loving friendship, thrown back upon my own desire.

The progress of spring, so achingly beautiful, and the contrast with those who would ruin the earth and spring's freshness—especially the purveyors of fossil fuel and the giant Ag firms who are re-splicing plants into new genomic patterns. So spring aches for herself, for union with her natural pattern, her own nature. The yearning can never have been greater, not since the Big Bang swelled into time.

Waking, surrounded by birdsong, I think that I am in a nest, lullabied. But if that's true, then I'm a catbird, and I've stolen their nest. Still attached to my conveniences and lifestyle, I am the species which apprehends it all as mine. Repent. *Turn back, oh Man!*

When Geeta sends a letter confirming the death of sexual desire on her part, I want to go ahead and consummate the affair. But my Friend still wants to wait. Mocking up an old spread on me that she would cut to create a lungi, (I delight to have her at my feet, my personal tailor), she says that this consummation will "never happen."

I write Geeta, "I am very happy that things have worked out at Uttar Kashi [Premanand's]. One option is obviously for you to spend more time there, to follow your heart. It's dishonest in a way to stay tethered here out of "duty," merely. On the other hand, I am committed to keeping a home for you here on Snake Ridge, Dharma Way."

Huge, yawning gulf of need, lovesickness, achiness. Banging around of ghosts this afternoon, spirits flying through upstairs (former lovers?). ... Mostly, just wanting to get it on with my Friend, or have a true miracle with my yogi-wife. I feel like I have decades, if not lifetimes, of need.

I write one last time, close to despair, saying that "yogic friendship" is not enough, that I need "total intimacy, a caring nest." "I can see you moving already to make it all better, your mind quickly figuring how to appease me and still get what you want. But I'm not optimistic that either of us can have our cake and eat it too." I feel alone and abandoned. Geeta has gotten the message, though I'm not confident a response is possible that can right our situation.

That same night I attempt to visit my Friend. My friend Nancy is out front. "Oh, she's off with that guy."

I go over to my Friend's house. The car's in the drive, but she doesn't answer my knock. I'm certain they are in bed together, and flee the scene in consternation, throat knotted, stomach sore, as if pummeled. I have lost my Spring Song, her fantasy for him replacing mine for her. It is Friday, Freitag, Freiya's night, the Hebrew love-night.

I can't sleep, and at three a.m. go outside, almost convulsed with crying. Desperate, I catapult a prayer out through the stars asking for Geeta to respond somehow. The next morning, she calls me from Garhwal, the first time she has ever phoned from India. My prayer is answered. We are connected, tethered across the globe. Still, on the phone, we have different interpretations of what our love-life has been over the previous year, and therefore how much change might be needed when she returns. *It will not be easy*, but the body will have its needs met, in some way, with care, intimacy and mutuality. Then comes Geeta's last e-mail: "Love, it's not all that serious. This *lila* [divine play] that we're *apart* of"—her slip confirming my complaint.

On May Day, the creature from my sessions with Alicia, my dream-saddhu, will go to meet Geeta of Garhwal. He is naked, dark skin framing glaring yellow-stoned eyes, smeared with white ash, crowned with dreadlocks, his gyroscope a long, cloaked penis. He is the aboriginal Shaivite, not the tamed Vedic Victorian. Thus burns the creature who greets the saddak, this Mataji returning from attempted *moksha* to *swadharma*—the dharma of this Appalachian life, mountain mama-wife.

The Sacred Whore

Each time I go into therapy I fall in love, and the transference goes to the lover, not the therapist. But it is all of a piece: the beloved, the therapist, and the self in triangle. Falling in love is the forward growth of triangles.

The good thing about all this is that the Girl Next Door played the "game," a ritual we created out of love and friendship as it went along. The container was my marriage, and the "no sex" pact served the marriage—and both of us—well. So why did she "lead me on" gentle and subtle as it was, if not for the sake of my soul-initiation and clarifying so acutely what Geeta and I need to work on? The ritual sequence was in fact the encounter of Everyman with the Sacred Whore. My Friend does it quite well. Once again I was reminded that my work involves something more than being a good teacher and writer or saving the earth—what Thomas Berry, mirroring the alchemists, calls the "Great Work." Whatever else that work is, it is also soul work. The key to the work with the Sacred Whore was putting me in touch with my deepest longing: my extreme discontent with the status quo in our marriage, pushing me to voice that.

Awakened to my need, needing to fulfill the central love relation of my life, I focus on "mutual sex" with Geeta, now compromised by her yearning for monkhood. But I have a long history of being content just being to myself. Masturbation is actually quite satisfying, and I love cooking for myself, especially since I'm a creative cook. I've always been a homebody, and convenience foods just don't do it for me. I am pleased to putter at my own pace, answerable to nobody else's schedule.

> Leaving the Sacred Whore Intact
> I wake with a fierceness burning
> like a diamond center.
> Breezes of spring, infinite longing, pure desire
> untouched by seed-flow into pictures of babes;
> leaving the sacred whore intact.
> Restored to myself.

Looking out the window, I see the cherry tree I planted in honor of Doc Armstrong when he died. Beneath it, a carpet of pink petals coating the Honda, reminding me of a wedding. Hell, if there's a wedding here, then I marry myself.

Return of Geeta Jyothi

On the day of Geeta's long-awaited return that May, watching her walk towards me down the aisle in the Greenville Airport in ordinary travel clothes with a warm, natural smile, I feel a tremendous relief. "It feels so ordinary, you seem normal, just you." She smiles. "Of course, who else would I be?" I have feared the cool yogic smile after this long spell at the ashram, remembering the previous spring in Saint Paul. Not now. Two days later, we work together with an army of South Toe Valley volunteers combating the woolly adelgid—a Japanese import which has attacked our beloved hemlocks with mortal intent—spraying soap from firetrucks and pick-ups. Our re-grounding has begun in earnest. But ever-active Geeta the energizer bunny has scheduled herself at out-of-town meetings for much of May and June.

Continued bickering, out-of-sync. For me this is a "revolution"; Geeta Jyothi sees it merely as moving from one "play" to another. At Friends' Meeting, a friend urges, "*Smile*, your wife's back." But I struggle during Meeting with the previous night's dream: *my wedding band is broken, right at the enlargement crease.* Geeta reads it as my fear. I fear it's more straightforward. More likely the meaning eludes my thick ego: grow, enlarge the band again, or the marriage will die.

Geeta's first nine days of meetings away, which I grumpily endure, are followed by a meeting of her clearness committee. As we drive to the meeting, it becomes clear to me that she has no intention of addressing our relationship, just to ask for the committee's blessing to move forward with her work in India. I am flabbergasted.

During the meeting, after Geeta gives a business-like report on her work with the Garhwali women, I speak about the shift in our relationship ever since Geeta said, "Shiva has stolen my heart," on the eve of our move back to Celo. The group balks at giving Geeta its blessing, urging marriage counseling before moving any further with a project that has severely unsettled our marriage.

Afterwards, we visit our plot in the adjacent community garden. I start weeding.

"I was upset with what you reported," I said. "Shiva is not a figure of romantic desire. You should know that."

I feel like a little boy, a bad student, and a chastened husband spreading false rumors. I read "Shiva has stolen my heart" as a bhakta, not a jnani. Oh, the shame of it. "I guess I did. I wanted to share the full emotional effect. But you *are* talking about a movement of the heart, and it's away from me. I agree with the committee. I think we need marriage counseling."

Her face darkens into a black cloud. "Marriage counselors break up marriages. The only thing they can do is help couples *hear* when they are unable to hear each other. We don't have that problem. We communicate. In our case I don't think it'll do any good."

"Susan knows us well. And she's good. Is this a control thing?" They have been professional partners in Asheville.

"No, it's not that. If we went to a counselor, they would push us to get all our feelings out, and I'd end up feeling resentment. I don't want to go down that road."

Resentment especially over my re-instating our longstanding rule of not being apart more than three months a year. The second part of my new "bottom line," more delicately, is asking for "mutual sex"—nigh-impossible in the context of our previous year. But something has changed. Rather than a set of rules compelling "wifely duty," Swami Premanand at Uttar Kashi told Geeta she had it all wrong, trying to enforce her yogic ways by rules. "The way you accomplish these things is by love," said Krishna's devotee. It takes the full four months for this message to get through. We don't do the counseling.

As the summer grows fat, Geeta does her best to adjust to our new order. Conjugally, I feel like I have my wife back. As for the enforced geographic limitations, ever the proponent of "Plan B," she starts thinking of things to do with her life other than spending up to half her time networking in Garhwal. Finally, as I drive her to the airport for yet another Friends committee, she says, "I think I am going to need a ritual putting to death my dreams for the women's work in Garhwal." She's not emotional, just matter-of-fact.

Put this way, I realize how much I am asking her to give up. This feels wrong, because she is so suited to the work. My needs feel like an insufficient reason for her to enact this death-rite. "Do you think the marriage—and the family—is worth such a sacrifice?"

"So you don't?" Geeta replies.

By early fall, during another of her longish trips, this time to three different meetings, I reach resolution. If she can't decide between her work and the family, I'll decide for her. The work is just too important to sacrifice to our middling marriage. My rational analysis of the situation is reinforced by an extraordinary waking image I receive after praying for Psyche to give me a sign about our marriage. Judith appears larger than life, long black tresses framing her angular face, only with yellow eyes, vertically slit pupils. She gets right up in my face and hisses, "Get back!"

Well damn, there you have it. This is my answer. I am deeply shaken, but how can I deny the message? First the broken marriage ring, now this. Those Lamias I had felt dripping down, reaching for my heart at midnight in placid Moorhead, now reduced to one yellow-eyed serpent. Okay, her essence is the eternal *atman*, but the last tough core surrounding it is a natural raging power, a snake waiting to be transformed into Shiva's servant-mistress. I wish her well in that final transmutation. I won't be around to witness it.

And Shiva wept again. This time, releasing her to the work in India, I cry tears of loss, not Leontian tears of restoration. Hermione/Jyothi *is* going to a nunnery. Of course, Shiva never weeps, and he will embrace her into the cool rigors of his worship as I let her go.

The sari-slip, powder-blue on the greenhouse clothesline, treasuring Geeta Jyothi even as I know I am losing her. Getting together her things, the dancing dress and black spaghetti-strap top (oh, the lavender delta of veins at her neck!) to take her at the Black Mountain Festival directly across the mountains, so we can play-pretend one more time as partners in the old way.

At the festival, where love and tolerance and fine music and delectable street-food set the tone, we step right back into the family play. Jacob meets us shortly after lunch. No longer an adolescent, he chooses to hang out with his parents for the rest of the day rather than with his many friends. This was the place we had come to celebrate as a family since he was eight or nine. We still have the same old canvas car tent. We share food. We sit in camp chairs listening to string bands and soul music like a confirmed old couple. We dance and Jacob dances with his mother. This is a family ritual, and we play our parts.

The precious time at Black Mountain is a brief encounter before Geeta is off again to another meeting. Yet clearly the emotional tone has shifted, and it's going to be hard to stay with my plan of sending her off to Garhwal with my blessings. But when she returns, this is precisely what I set out to do.

One night while Geeta is at a community meeting, a small group of us sit around drinking wine and discussing our marriage. Geeta's sister Layne's husband Michael is so critical of Geeta that I'm getting uncomfortable. Independent-minded Nancy (she who shunned Moorhead) doesn't buy it. "I just keep trying to get inside Judi's head. What's it like from *her* perspective?" Indeed, not many Americans have sympathy for the Hindu view of sex, especially the idea that it's something from which you wean yourself from midlife on. I understand where the Hindus are coming from, and in some ways feel their views are healthier than our obsessive ones, refusing the natural diminishment of potency, and the falling away of desire with age. Instead in the brave new world of the West we have heroic Viagra and a hormone-replacement regimen.

As for the geographic restrictions I have been insisting upon, Nancy turns to me. "How would you like it if Judi restricted where you worked?" I take the point, and realize that my unilateral rule, even if it is something we had agreed upon in years past, has created an asymmetry that will eat away at our unity with a power at least equal to Robert Bly's insistence on my following "economic necessity."

So it isn't really mine to "decide for" Geeta. She has been unwilling to decide between family and India-work, and this "having her cake and eating it too" has been part of her "fantasies of omnipotence," as our friend Jerry said (another member of the clearness committee). There is still a decision on the table, but it's hers, not mine.

One afternoon as we drink tea on our deck, fall resplendent around us, Geeta speaks wistfully of her wish to go to a Divine Life Congress in Orissa, scheduled over the New Year. "But I can't go, since it's our anniversary." Part of our negotiations had initially been that she wouldn't go to India for a long sojourn this winter, her pattern for the last three.

"Why should that stop you? It's not a landmark year or anything."

The next week, we have a marriage co-counseling session with old friends, a couple who have gotten back together again after seven years apart.

They're struggling again. When he shares his continuing fantasies about other women, something clicks in Geeta. The next day, she realizes that she *has* been resenting my restrictions, precisely what she hadn't wanted a marriage counselor to encourage her to feel. I feel the energy shift as what she *really* wants comes into play. We are reciprocating again. This is a mutual decision. She makes reservations to go to Orissa after Christmas and stay the remainder of the time in Rishikesh, a total of four weeks in India.

While Geeta is away yet again, this time at the American Public Health convention in Atlanta, I have another encounter with her Lamia-self. After a desultory morning working on this manuscript, I start out the front door, planning without much enthusiasm to plant cover crop in my garden beds. But I lose interest, and turn to the next task queued among the "Ten Thousand Things" I attend at the homestead. But with each task I envision, I stop in my tracks, totally without desire or will to act. Having a bad morning at the writing desk sometimes robs me of my joy for the tasks of the afternoon, but this is much deeper. The next thing I know, I 'm spiraling down what feels like the same whirlpool of despair that had caused my breakdown many years before. For a moment, I feel helpless, then say aloud, "NO!"

I go inside, make tea, then go out to the porch. Immediately, I feel such peace that I enter into meditation. I still don't want to *do anything*, and nothing I can do will *save* me. But instead of fearing this, I accept it fully. Musing thus, moving gently in and out of a meditative state, I hear the phone ring. For some reason, I answer. It's Geeta's travel agent Diane, saying that she has twenty-four hours to confirm her India-reservation. I jump into action. Though I have no idea where she is staying, I guess that the conference would be at the Westin downtown. It is, but she's not a registered guest. However, the clerk informs me that many guests are staying across the street at the Marriott. I get through, leave a message, and head straight to my desk. Galvanized into action, I immediately know what I must do: contact the Lamia. It was *she* who had stopped me cold earlier that afternoon, forcing me to face what I had been avoiding.

Utilizing Jung's remarkable technique called "active imagination," I sit down and invite the Lamia to a frank talk. As always, I ask, "What do you want from me?" Stupid question. "Get back!" she hisses. But as we talk, I learn that I had completely misinterpreted the original image. It was not Judith, Geeta Jyothi, that I needed to back off from, but my embrace this negative self. And that self is not necessarily Geeta's at all, but *my own projection*. Sure, she is a tough lady with some sharp edges—"Goddess of

Angular Momentum" read her award at our joint fortieth birthday party. But that doesn't mean that she and this venomous snake-woman are one. Once I pull back from this over-determined image, Lamia starts shrinking. I focus on the possibility of the figure actually drawing strength from my wife: "Can the lamia survive without the resentment, without negative energy towards me?" Lamia gives me one last parting shot before leaving. "You don't have the power to control me."

"Yeah, I know that damn well. But God does, thus Geeta works her utmost to be God-led." I sneeze as I say it, experiencing a chill from shoulders to toes. Immediately, I think of the ancient gods' punctuating numinous moments with a sign. I see Lamia one last time: shrunk, looking like one of Odilon Redon's starfish creatures, phosphorescent green, rising into the sky.

Then a subtle awareness from the previous hour, seated on the deck marveling at the sudden peace after near-panic, returns. Dakshinamurthi, Shiva's silent son, has spread his peepul-shaded form behind my head as we both face South. He is my protector. O merciful Shiva, destroyer of illusion!

Geeta gets my message. When she returns from the conference, two letters from Swami Hamsananda await. He writes in very clear terms that her first duty is to her family, that she needs to be *home* in the West: "*Sevaya* (Service) is possible by doing service in the home itself.... Leaving the house is not at all possible as long as you live in the House of God." She could always ask questions through letters, and she could come to India periodically for spiritual guidance, but her place and her work were in America with her family, her original culture. She accepts this, and I am stunned. Life is opening for us, step by step.

A few days later after her morning meditation she announces that she has had a revelation of her true motives in wanting to organize the women's health project. It was "ego-aggrandizing," she says; furthermore, "rationalization, so my friends don't think I'm going to India just for spiritual growth."

So it's not mine to "decide for us," as I bravely told Jerry when I thought we were at endgame. Nor is Robert Bly's vaunted toughness towards uppity women—"bottom line" demands—required. I have let go of both, though with a heartfelt prayer for mercy from the Power behind the universe. Geeta has done the same in her different way. Later, she says she is convinced that what has caused her desire for the India-project to "drop away completely" is "the Guru's grace, *shakti*. There is no other possible explanation."

36 Turn and Turn Again

It's been a year since Geeta's desire for the medical project in Tehri-Garhwal "dropped away completely." The infrastructure problems were just too unworkable, and as Sunderlal insisted, she would need to live in a village to be truly effective. But she continues to leave the house, living a full life away from Dharma Way attending her Committee Dharma. The medical project no longer hides her real focus, an annual retreat in India for as long as she can negotiate.

Now I understand. She returns on her best behavior, bolstered by regular contact with holy men, the vibes of chanting Sanskrit every day, and a sheltered life without the stresses of home: doctor, wife, mother. Experiencing Geeta at her best, I drop my resentment. Yet inevitably we fall into bickering or worse. So she goes back to India to escape me. There, Shiva's tireless helpers in this "yogic marriage" support her in restoring her quiet, forgiveness, and affection.

Going to the ashram every winter reinforces her strong urge to take vows of *sannyas*. She is invariably there for Sivratri (our favorite Hindu holiday, celebrated the dark moon in February-March), present for the young monks' annual ceremony of renunciation. All told, she has witnessed the rite five or six times. "I sit on the promontory above the Ganga, watching as they throw all their remaining possessions into the river: clothes, books, letters from home. It makes me feel such longing to join them. You know it's dry season, but half the time it lightnings on that day."

Jacob's new wife Bevin, Geeta and I sit at their dining table in Asheville. We have no grandchildren yet, but hearing Geeta's plans for *sannyas* and making India her base, Bevin anxiously asks, "But what about the grandkids? When will you be part of their lives?"

"When they are older, they can visit me in India. It will be a whole experience for them."

Bevin looks at me.

"But it'll be years before they could make such a trip on their own. And we can't count on the airline fares making us kings forever," I respond.

Geeta shrugs her shoulders. "It'll all work out."

This past year in India, she met a woman householder who had taken *sannyas* at seventy. She was lying in her sickbed overlooking the ghats at Sivananda Ashram, Geeta standing at her bedside. The old woman impressed Geeta with her bearing and dispassion. Geeta-ma, as they call her at the ashram, was excited, for here was her model, someone who had accomplished what she herself longed for.

"So when I'm seventy, I can take sannyas."

"O my dear, I wouldn't cause that hardship again. I was trying to simplify things and follow the Vedas, but it has been a disaster. It has immensely complicated everyone's lives, and the resentments are too many to count. That was the worst decision I ever made."

We are back at Jacob's, trying to understand how our joint family will function, as Geeta relates this incident. "Isn't this good to know? I will not be a sannyasin, that much is clear."

Bevin, Jacob and I all breathe a sigh of relief. Jacob in particular has been hugely concerned about his mother's plans to be a distant grandmother—and mother, as well.

And me? I've been trying to figure out "retirement." Ever since my training with Joanna Macy, it has been clear that my work post-university prof is listening to the Earth and training others to join me. The invocation for one of Joanna's rituals teaches me that our work is to speak for mute and silenced voices. As a teacher and writer, I will give Earth a voice. Though a born pessimist, I will do what I can to "save" her. Wary of the Celo Paradise trap of my youth, I plan to work in Asheville with the churches.

March 2002. *I'm at the beach, going into a kind of amusement house. I approach an oracular figure, Orpheus in half-lotus, head bowed under a canvas or light blanket covering. He is tall—Bob, my Earth Team mentor. Recognizing the figure, I joke about his paradoxical nature, and he answers in effect "Since you get it, it's your turn to be Orpheus." I am shown the seat and take it. The blanket, this mantle, falls over me, and I instantly feel the strange energy of entering an alien being.*

I am anointed, the dream seems to say. *Strange energy, alien being* ... the teacher-scholar will try on the unfamiliar cloak of activism.

In early summer at Southern Appalachian Yearly Meeting at nearby Warren Wilson College, a brilliant therapist leads a workshop for us mountain Quakers on getting in touch with our callings. He asks us to look at the "shoulds" which block those calls. A huge one comes up immediately. *I want to justify my existence by teaching others how to save the earth.* Justification by works, my perennial unuttered goad. The impossible bind is obvious. If I can't get others to act to save the planet, then my own existence is unredeemed. Orpheus sits, mute and forgotten, head bowed under his shroud.

But every now and then I realize that I am loved, justified, saved, okay just as I am. Even if *Amerika* and the developed world are going to hell with my complicity. On those days I do not need a wife to tend me or a university paycheck to tell me that I am worthy, a contributing capitalist citizen. I putter contentedly in the garden. I gather firewood. I start dinner in the morning, returning to the kitchen for a relaxed leisurely final prep as afternoon runs down. I write a poem, not worrying whether it will be published. Best of all, I run in the woods with the dog.

In the midst of all these transitions, in late July, I host my second annual retreat at Arthur Morgan School. My old friend Betsy, who now calls herself Elizabeth, has agreed to assist me. She's a clinical psychologist, Buddhist-Quaker, poet, and singer. We work well together. A good group has gathered, thirteen folks, close to optimum for our intimate format. Some of my closest friends are here, as well as a fellow board member of the North Carolina Council of Churches Ecojustice Committee, boosting the work and deepening our friendships. We will dance, read poetry, and engage in Joanna's exercises and rituals. A friend calls this time "the dark night of the World-soul," giving me our theme: "Nourishing Sacred Ground in a Dark Night." As I write in the brochure, "Our country is at war with a series of enemies, real and imagined, and our economic system is at war with the earth herself. ... At such times, spiritual energies for those who are awake become intensified by the very forces that undermine soul. In this awakening, as the poet Anna Akhmatova writes, 'the miraculous comes so close.'"

We begin Friday night, and will end Sunday afternoon, with Joanna's signature, the Elm Dance. It's a simple circle dance set to a Latvian mother's war lament, where we dance to regenerate the elm forest hardest hit after Chernobyl, and any other earthly being requiring healing in these trying times. The music is haunting, and the faces around me show it. I doubt I will host many retreats where I do not lead this dance.

The next morning, I lead the exercise Joanna calls the Double Circle, where wordless future beings a hundred years hence thank denizens of our present crisis for the work we have done to preserve the earth. The hope in folks' hearts afterwards is palpable. As with the Elm Dance, several participants are in tears.

On Saturday, the heart of the retreat, we enter into both of Joanna's major rituals, the Truth Mandala and the Council of All Beings. Either one of these can be the focus of an entire retreat. But these people are ripe for the work, and we are going to go as deeply as we can. Grief, rage, fear and expressions of deadness and apathy fill the Arthur Morgan School meeting room, a safe cocoon for us to confess our deepest feelings to each other. Wisely, Joanna roots the expression of these feelings in concrete objects: dead leaves for sadness, a stone for fear, a stick for anger (we don't wave it around, but grasp it as tightly as we can), an empty bowl for apathy.

Afterward, we have a solid meal from local produce and a long rest with journaling until a lively session in the garden with the AMS summer interns. The balance is right. After we make masks for creatures whose voices we will represent in the evening, we are ready for the nervous humans to witness the pain we are causing all the other earth tribes. As we gather in our masks and costumes, a couple of folks have brought guitars. I may not get to bed as early as I had hoped.

Sunday morning after a meeting for worship on behalf of the Earth, Elizabeth leads an exercise to strengthen us against doubt, using Mara, the embodiment of sin and death, as the Accuser. When Gautama sat beneath the bodhi tree for days and days, waiting for an answer to *why suffering?* Mara was infuriated, and called forth all kinds of distractions, both pleasurable and painful, to stop him from invading her domain. Buddha was steadfast. Mara challenged him, saying "By what authority do you resist my power?" Buddha said nothing, only reached his hand to touch the earth. As Elizabeth speaks, she leans slightly to the left, reaches down and touches the floor of the AMS dining hall. The gesture unexpectedly and instantly becomes a lightning rod, connecting to my own witness. And it connects me to the more innocent time when Judi and I visited that bodhi tree in Bodh Gaya. In the lifetime since then, Kali Yuga has grown to terrifying ripeness.

Here at the retreat, we go through the dialogues with Mara, dredging doubt and fear, and touching the earth for witness to our resolve to do this work. That mudra of touching Earth is my mature experience of the bodhi tree in North India, and a deeper balancing. Integrating this realization, connecting to Earth as my witness on bad days, is going to be a continuing balancing act. As we leave after lunch, Elizabeth and I reflect on the retreat, agreeing that it has gone well. As we part, she says, "We should take this show on the road." I'm more than ready.

In the fall, Geeta away in Hindustan, I realize I am in a *book-bind*. The Lamia, the reptilian wife exiled as a ghoulish green star, is banished, while the real wife takes another step towards recognizing her humanity. But this is a temporary plateau. The marriage is still troubled; she calls it a "battlefield." I feel like a yoyo, rebounding from a growing contentedness sufficient to myself each winter to a reactive, jealous husband fighting for turf when she's home. *If the marriage fails, does the book?*

"We are together throughout time and space," Geeta writes from Rishikesh. She brings me up short with this. My devotion to the marriage mysteries is imperfect, because I try to forget her when she's gone, make the best of things, live my own life. What does she mean, and why her excitement about this?

When she returns, she explains that she's inspired by a story in the *Yoga Vashishta*, the text she's been reading with Swami Hamsananda. I agree for her to read it to me as a bedtime story, like we sometimes do with poetry. But even the abridged version contains too much late-night philosophy, and I regularly fall asleep. Eventually, the story emerges.

Once there was a royal couple, Chudala the Queen and King Sikhidhvaja, scriptural exemplars of beauty and kingship. Chudala yearns for enlightenment, making remarkable progress, and before long attains her goal. When she tells her husband, he laughs and says to get back to her queenly duties.

After a while, though, he becomes infected by her desire and decides to seek enlightenment himself. The King retires to the forest, leaving his wife the enlightened sage to rule the kingdom alone. He forges ever more deeply into asceticism. Finally, he is on the verge of burning his little cottage as the ultimate act of renunciation. Disguised as a young sage, she intervenes, pointing him away from outward renunciation.

Chudala speaks directly to our ongoing tension: "What does the knower of the truth, the sage of self-knowledge, gain by abandoning that which is obtained without effort? I should make it possible for my husband to enjoy conjugal pleasures with me." *Yoga Vashishta* gives Geeta permission to be conjugal with me, not shunning natural desire, acting only out of wifely duty. And since the transmission comes via Swami Hamsananda, she implicitly has the guru's permission as well.

She expects me to be really pleased. But I am hurt, angry and shamed that she has to enlist text and teacher to accept the honest passion of our youth. Swami Hamsananda is the same teacher who once looked her straight in the eye and said, "If you really understand *Gita*, you *will not want* to drink wine with your husband," robbing me of yet another shared pleasure.

I absorb all this in silence. I feel less and less physically connected to the woman I married. Being a man, lust continues to drive me to consummation. But the doubts I have long harbored join, bit by bit, with a shift in how it feels to share bodies.

Like the Hindu king, I am not in accord with her withdrawal from the world, especially when it feels like withdrawal from me. "Day by day, the queen grew more introverted, rejoicing more and more in the bliss of the Self." But Vashishta also writes, "A good housewife does not obstruct her husband's wishes."

"Bob, I appreciate that you no longer criticize my India travels my in front of friends and family. But I still don't feel supported in my sadhana."

"I guess it's just that I feel abandoned each time you go. I try to put myself in your shoes, but yeah, there's resentment, especially the feeling that you try to push your India time to the max."

When I suggest to Jerry, my closest male friend, something like the reciprocal rule, "A good husband does not obstruct his wife's wishes," he balks.

"Watch it, Bob, you're caving in. Geeta always wants to have her cake and eat it too. You have to decide what you want from the relationship and tell her." Here again, *Yoga Vashishta* is in her corner: "You will enjoy the pleasures of the world and attain final liberation too." She has the bull by the nose-ring.

We need something like courtly love, one focus of "Love in the West," which I taught at Moorhead State. Genuine love engenders respect, and neither partner enforces anything against the other's wishes. It's so sweet to experience couples who follow this reciprocal courtly law. But they are rare, and we are not among them

I am out of tune with myself and out of sorts. Geeta, playing the respected ashram matron, "Mataji," free of all entanglements, back on Ganga's banks where I dragged her thirty years ago, is loving it, but not loving me—not in the way I want. She writes from India, "You are my best friend. ... I love you, but I don't desire you. Why should you want to be desired?" The India honeymoon refrain echoes all over again.

Back home that fall, our wrangles continue. The last day of November, standing on Hannah Branch Road in front of our dear friend Don's house, we're yelling at each other about no-sex and housework. Don's hospice chaplain suddenly appears to tell us our dear friend has just died. At the end, our tall, craggy mountain man, preeminent expert on Southern Appalachian highland flora, listens to Robert Frost read by a circle of family and friends, propped up watching the sun set over his beloved Black Mountains one last time. But we aren't there. The chaplain's message brings us to silence. We hear the South Toe River rush by.

"I'm leaving. I'm fed up with thirty years of name calling and put-downs. I won't take it anymore," Geeta says with an air of finality.

"This sounds like the first of the three *I divorce you*'s of Islam. We've got two more," I answer.

After her extensive Committee Dharma that fall, when Geeta returns I tell her what I really want as a homecoming present is for her to go with me to the first Friday Celo Contradance in January. In December, she'll be at a board meeting; by February, back in India. When the night arrives, she's tight-lipped, driven to clean the house, which is a mess. The dance is almost upon us, so I throw myself into cleaning the kitchen with her. A half hour after the dance begins, I decide we've reached a beachhead. "Let's go. We can finish the rest later."

She is unmoved. "I'm not going until the house is straight."

"But I asked you two months ago to come with me to this dance, our only one before you'll be gone for God knows how many dances!" I am really angry, feeling betrayed. But damn if I'm going to miss the dance just because she's playing Sergeant Bitch. I walk down to AMS in the bracing January air. I dance hard, but I can't forget her absence and the unkept promise.

After dinner the next month, shortly before going on her annual trip to Hindustan, Geeta's wearing her super-serious look, undergirded with compassion. Something difficult is coming. "Bob, I'm disassociating to be able to be with you in bed."

"Then you're just like a whore. I don't want to sleep with a whore. Never have."

"I suppose that's not a bad analogy," she admits.

The next day, having digested this, owning a sense of disconnection over a long time, I make a decision.

"I'm not going to ask you to have sex with me anymore. If things change for you, let me know. But I won't expect you to disassociate any longer. It would be living a lie for both of us." We are back to the rules of courtly love—something freely given.

After this, we get along better. I no longer set myself up for disappointment—bitter when she says no, more subtle but actually worse when we assent to the dull lust of the flesh. On the eve of her annual winter in India, I feel relief.

February 16, 2004. I am in a doctor's office to have my staples removed from the previous week's "procedure." The doctor's in his forties, trim with close-cropped receding hair. I lie on a table and he takes out a gun which clips staples. It looks like one of those spark-guns for lighting a gas range. He says don't worry about it, it won't nick the skin. I avert my gaze as he cuts the staples one by one. I start to peek, but fear he's going to grab the hairy flesh on my chest, so I close them again. As I look down, I see the shaved rough hide of a tawny animal, a rectilinear shape going from beneath my nipples to below my navel. The procedure was "minor"—"successful" according to the doctor. "As this will be"—he added, removing the staples. It had something to do with regulatory function of some kind in the gut. But I am surprised at the size of the territory under the incision.

I can never forget the dream moment of looking down at my transplanted tawny hide. It feels like I'm the Cowardly Lion with a new lion heart. And there's the splendid detail of lighting my gut-fire with the spark gun. Searching my Greek texts, I see my memory is correct, the *thymos* is the organ of action in Homeric times. "It is the thymos which rouses a man to action." But by Socrates' time, it is increasingly supplanted by *noos*, the mind as organ of discrimination: idea, image, receiver of action. The *thymos* is instinctual knowing, *animal soul*. As a function, rather than organ, it is will, character.

No wife, no therapist, all staples removed successfully. I no longer need my staple, which the *OED* defines as "post, provider." Support is the key meaning of staple—the things you count on, your staple dependencies, emotional and material. Then comes another meaning: raw wool, closer to the animal hide graft.

Fill yourself up with yourself, Puer had mused, callow *hippy-saddhu* in Hindustan, fly-ash streaking his face and lily-white pyjamas. But the kid had no idea, no stirrings yet, of an animal soul.

When my Buddhist friend Janey's teacher Tara comes to Asheville, I decide to attend her workshop. Geeta's in India on her annual retreat. Tara invite us to imagine a healing with a significant person close to us, conjuring whatever figure of Higher Power we are comfortable with. Immediately, I imagine Geeta and me in the old goat barn that is Celo Meetinghouse. We sit opposite the red door on a wormy chestnut bench. Ramana Maharshi sits between us. Reaching out, he joins our hands in his lap. He radiates love and acceptance, and we bathe in it. Judi is wearing her wedding dress. Bhagavan is his old, saggy-fleshed self, dressed in diapers.

The place where we sit is exactly where I was a few years ago when I had the arresting experience of a taproot growing out of my anus, down through the bench, and into the mottled cement slab which the men of the meeting troweled over the goaty soil. From my arms and shoulders sprouted vines, climbing over the bench and down its sides. As this happened, I spoke to my fellow worshippers about the experience, ending with, "I am rooted to this meetinghouse and this Meeting." This doubling of my rooting with my home meeting feels almost like a vision, figuring a blessed renewal. But we are still a long way from actualizing it. Before the winter ends, I write:

Geeta my love and dear friend,
> ...I feel we are shifting from a marriage relationship to being good friends.... I have no agenda or timetable, I think that's just the way it is.... I have no resentment, no anger, but the dynamic is the same as if you had said you had fallen in love with another man.... What is important to me now is that we treat each other with the utmost respect.

The next year, with Geeta away again in Garhwal, at the Celo contradance I dance with a woman who has been giving me looks I haven't gotten in decades. Taking those looks as promise of something more, I call and ask her to go to an Asheville contradance with me. Acknowledging our chemistry, she says, "I'll dance with you all you want in Celo, but I won't go to Asheville with you. You're a married man; I won't be your mistress." I thank her for her forthrightness. She adds, "There's a sadness about you. It's so great to see you smile when you dance."

I hang up, gut churning. It's not her refusal so much as the sadness remark. I look in the mirror and see the sad self she described. Within a couple of days, I admit the source. I am unhappy with my marriage.

I go to talk it over with a good friend, a retired Jungian counselor. In one afternoon it all comes together—finally owning the feelings about being the recipient of Geeta's conjugal favors thanks to a yogic text and feeling like the dull, grasping, King who obstructs her desire for liberation. Most of all, seeing myself as a *consort*.

"How do you feel about this?" Karin asks.

"I find it very interesting."

"Interesting? Is that a feeling?"

I analyze the *Yoga Vashishta* text some more, grasping for what I feel.

"That's Geeta's story," she says after I tell her about Chudala and her chauvinistic King. "But what is *your story*?"

When I get home, I realize that my recurrent image of the consort is a default story, a complementary stance. Both my Uncle Pierce and my friend Jerry have long said that our marriage is a classic role reversal, but I've fought against being pinned into that box. Now, with Karin's question about *my story*, I realize that, being unclear about mine, I've been living Geeta's story because it's so clear and compelling. And my reactiveness and lack of support for her spiritual trip, has come from my vulnerability due to that lack of clarity.

I write Geeta a fateful letter. It feels huge, bringing fits of bottomless regret and sadness. These alternate with a restoration of my resolve, tawny lionhide girding my tender gut.

Feb 28, 2005

Dearest Geeta—

…What I realized was that I was unhappy in our marriage, and have been denying that, out of loyalty, out of dependency, out of wanting as always to be a "good boy." I pushed it down, saying my personal happiness was not important, that it was the work and the family that mattered.

The story that I have been a character in is the one that you have written ever since you said to me, 'Shiva has stolen my heart.' At that moment I knew our life together was irrevocably changed. What I did not notice was that I started virtually immediately to accommodate, to be the dutiful husband and dutiful character in your story, taken up anew after our long-ago India pilgrimage, in order to delay indefinitely dealing with that sense of loss.

So all the modifications to your reborn wish for God-union as a Shaivite that you have sincerely tried to make, even your sacrifices, each time that you shift to accommodate the Old King in his castle back in Celo, have happened from the perspective of your life-story, embedded in Vedanta and the Hindu asramas, rewritten from that moment of the stolen heart. This was a story we wove together as a young couple on pilgrimage, and, whatever modifications we made as a couple raising a family in the West, we made together, more or less. …

A really good example of being woven into your story is your breakthrough with the story of the King and Queen and their quest for enlightenment, followed by returning to the marriage [bower]. … You were so excited to find mythic support for being conjugal with me. … [I] found it "interesting" as I analyzed it, denying what it meant emotionally. … And again, I was a character in that myth. No question here of what your heart said, or on my dutiful part, what my heart said. Your heart remains with Shiva, and mine doesn't buy in. But I allowed myself to be a willing pawn in this mythic game, needy and evasive of my heart's truth.

I didn't understand what Bud (an Asheville Jungian therapist) meant when he said "the trouble with you is you don't have a myth." Now I do. I was living your myth of a marriage where both of us, admittedly at varying rates, would let go of worldly desires and prepare for the fourth asrama. I went along with the rewritten story without reaching for what my myth was, and pretended to both of us that I was still the young Hindu wannabe you married. Once again, as I was during the long unhappy youthful Celo years, I became your consort. It certainly didn't help that as usual you knew exactly what you wanted and configured your life to get that as much as possible, whereas I was feeling my way, and have only recently been clear about my work-vision, seeing it start to manifest. ...

There have been signs and images along the way, starting way back in '96 with the dream that I told at that final party for us in Breach Candy Udayan's students gave for us. There's a lot to the dream, but the part that I didn't get until about a year ago was that the Nazi matron jailer who came to check on me just as I finished masturbating, and who was cutting off inmates' 'sick parts' was you. So we've each experienced the other in recent Celo years as a jailer. My dream-fear was that you would cut off my hands.

Right after your return in 2001 I had the dream of my wedding ring breaking. I was alarmed, you pooh-poohed it, and I interpreted it as meaning the ring needed upsizing to accommodate growth in the union. That same spring, while you were in Himalaya, I had a powerful nightmare image of you as a hissing lamia who said "Get away!" I worked the image through active imagination, and it dissolved in the energy of divine love.

The consort I felt distinctly one night when I came to join you in meditation beside your raised *asan*. As I looked at the statue of Shiva and Parvati, I felt with a deep pang that the mirror image in front of the meditation table was of Parvati taking the lead, and Shiva at her side. You once asked why I meditated, an excellent question which I could not answer at the time. Now I know. It has been to please you: wife, master, Mother.

During my recent illness I had a couple of afternoon waking images. In one, you were the mother, growing huge as a tree, and I was the baby. 'He stwong' you said repeatedly as I split wood this winter. The second image was even more powerful. You were lying in our bed, and I was like an organ on your right side—a baby-growth. Again, it is not only a Mother-baby image, but a reversal of the Genesis story: I am Adam being formed out of your rib. That one at least shows movement, as I am moving towards a birth, towards being on my own. As the poem ended during Carol spring 2001, "I marry myself."

That would be quite a different ending than the one I have been sadly and privately weaving: whenever I've thought of wanting marital fulfillment, I've just imagined myself old and tired and impotent in my late seventies. Ah, if I could only just skip over to that stage, I would imagine. ... What I want in love is a partner who not only loves me in a familiar old-shoe sort of way, but who wants me. More than that, someone with whom I can play, can express my joie de vivre without apology. Someone who will laugh with me and at my jokes. Someone who still sees life as a dance worth dancing, rather than being dominated by a withdrawal of the senses, judging ego-desires as foolish and misguided. 'What do you mean by play?' you asked.

I do not experience these deep desires as immature or inappropriate. I know that all of this *will* wane soon enough. But I'm not willing to hang it up prematurely by being strung along by a story, a life-history that is not deeply my own. ... I may be consigning myself to loneliness, but if that's true, at least it will have been on my own terms. I will continue to make the wager of life, rather than cowering behind the false front of your Vedanta. ...

Though we both may be deeply sad, you have the chance, now more than ever, to pursue your deepest desires beyond Bob and family.

A deeply sad old romantic partner,

Bob

After sending the letter, I continue to swing wildly from grief to exhilaration. Grief over what is ending, exhilaration for the New Life I have proclaimed for myself, weekly reinforced by the powerful Artist's Way class, where the touchstone is always, "What is your heart's desire?" I feel like I've launched a guided missile, headed inexorably for its target.

The eve before my missile should hit—I've mailed the ashram enough to know that it takes eight days—I pick up the *tanpura*. Two years ago, I finally got over my fear of the high strings breaking under the tension of restringing, and restored the instrument. Then, several months back, the fifth, a thicker string, unexpectedly broke, a loud "pop" in the night. Now I pluck the strings, a casual caress of a forgotten friend. Immediately I'm surrounded by a perfect series of overtones. One of the high *sa*'s has slid to the *pa*, the fifth. I am in tune, soul-strung again.

I wait expectantly for her reply. It arrives a month later.

Dear Bob,

It saddens me that you became trapped in the 'Shiva has stolen my heart' story. Because for me that story has changed and deepened and it is not anything that I would say now. It is like someone who has been given a delicious treat and thinks that it will forever be the favorite, and then finds that the variety of foods is the real joy. When the *lila* of the world is so glorious and varied and the inner light is barely becoming visible—how can a single manifestation capture anything?"

The trouble may stem from the fact that you were a Hindu wannabe when we got together and I found the fountain to quench a childhood spiritual thirst in Vedanta, which made great sense as a way to permanent joy and happiness. It is not as you call it a "wish for enlightenment," the foolish thought of youth, but it is an aspiration to be in touch with the inner depth that keeps the heart ever full of joy and singing.

The Chudala story was not "an excuse" to be with you conjugally, it was an opening to know I had been denying us, out of false understanding, the joy of expressing our love together. You are trying to write my story—it is mine to do—if your happiness comes from living your own story, isn't creating one for me that you 'find yourself trapped in' the same as when you returned from the Bly workshop and said that I was your problem because you had no economic necessity?

...*I will go where you send me, where shall you send me?*

Each time you have lashed out at me with your anger that 'Geeta was the problem, Her control was the problem. Bob would be happy without Geeta,' I have asked you if you wanted me to leave. Now, in a time of deep inwardness, I guess you have found the courage to say, 'Yes, please go.'

I am crying as I ask you to please help me figure out where. You are my closest Friend, perhaps my only Friend. ...

I guess my story is that we have been on a journey together for 33 years. It has been a journey where I have grown and learned and cared and felt great comfort even though many times the path was covered by prickly brambles and sometimes getting part way to somewhere it was the wrong place. It's with great sadness that "I am now free" to go alone. Maybe also part of it is fear. On the other hand, the journey will continue and I have a lot of deep guidebooks and several trusted guides. So whatever happens, I will put on my knee bandages and walk forward.

Love, Geeta Jyothi

"I can't go on with this." By phone, Geeta has talked me into going to see Susan, the marriage counselor she refused four years before. We would see if we could "fix" things. But when I speak hopefully of those prospects at Artist's Way check-in, I hear my voice growing hollow, and as I finish, a leaden feeling of having lied to my core. My energy sapped, I spiral into depression. Falling out of tune, I am unstrung from my resolve.

I go for an editing session with Mendy, our Artist's Way leader. I'm annoyed that she wants to hear how things are going with my incipient separation. I am paying for her time as an editor, not a therapist.

"Do you feel free?" she wants to know.

I hedge. "Sometimes. But I know things are still not resolved until I can look her in the eye and say it all again."

That evening, my knees start to shake. I feel the pre-quake symptoms of a panic attack. I call our friend Peggy and go to see her as soon as she can meet with me the next day.

"What is it you fear?"

"That Mommy is going to be hurt and angry and won't forgive me." Bingo. The panic reaction does not return. Geeta's return imminent, I start sleeping in the shed, soon to be my write-shed and lair. Anticipating next steps, I write:

Trout House
I will banish Mother from this house
though we will cook dinners together for a while.
Will I stop her from weeding the lawn?
I will build her a little house on the ridge.

When my lover sees candlelight through night
branches, I'll answer her question truly:
Oh, that's just my sometime wife, doing her evening devotional.
If you like she can come to dinner tomorrow.

Then I remember running through the woods,
Mother-Wife in faraway Hindustan.

Suddenly I am struggling to emerge from the
lips of a large trout, hands bloodied by its tiny teeth.

Below me is the net, one ragged end around my ankle,
suspended between this fishmaw and the vast womb of Jocasta
yawning in the blackness beneath. Vagina dentata,
this teacher of myth imagines, panting up another steep hill.

So we continue, she in the marriage bed, I in the write-shed
drinking coffee over my morning journal in the Pouthouse.
Tonight she cooks Indian in the Big House, I her guest.
Tomorrow I start my own bank account, like when I was fifteen.

When Geeta gets back, we agree to separate for a year, splitting time in the house. Since she has a three-month stint as locums doc at the Celo Health Center coming up this summer, she gets first occupancy, and I get the car. I work out a summer rental, then some house-sits for traveling friends. I move around a lot, but love the independence. It's all very amicable, and we get together every couple of weeks to share a meal. We also share the garden. It's strange visiting at "her" house to tend it. Since I have the car, I help with her shopping. She bikes to work.

We go see Susan. Until the first appointment, Geeta doesn't fully take me seriously. The professional she refused when we clearly needed help four years ago is now necessary to give this work the stamp of reality. Geeta straightens up and takes notice.

With great deliberation and care, I start seeing the woman who gave me those looks at the dance. I'm not going to jump into bed with her. This is about repossessing myself. She understands and supports this, which also protects her while I sort things out with Geeta. She is reclaiming her potting career after a hiatus. I am a writer. We artists will support each other.

At a baby blessing during this realignment, I find myself seated in a large circle precisely in the middle of Geeta and the Potter, who are opposite each other. I look within to observe where my energy is pulled. It is steady, dead center upon my own gyroscope. *I marry myself.*

A few weeks later, the three of us are in an intimate circle, Dances of Universal Peace led by a stunningly beautiful young Sufi nursing mother. Before it begins, Geeta and I skinny-dip in Dewing Pond like the olden days. As I swim towards the dock, she glides up from behind, swimming on top of me. How perverse to be seductive *now*. In the midst of a dance, the young leader starts lactating, staining her blouse, highlighting the nipple in relief. She smiles serenely and continues dancing. I dance between my two women, feeling the same kind of steady serene love the dance leader radiates. Wearing my Indian whites again, bare feet in the mossy grass, I feel blessed, my cup overflowing.

After seeing the Potter a few times, she invites me to dinner. All day long, I fight the impulse to have sex with her. How long am I supposed to be a monk, restricted by a cell of my own making? Am I not a man? I cast the *I Ching*, a rare act. The oracle answers, "Ten years."

Running late as usual, I suddenly hear a great fluttering in the blueberries. A raven has flown underneath the netting and is ensnared. He fights furiously, then rests, hanging ponderously in the black net. I feel sympathy, but decide I'll just let this berry thief hang. After all, I'm late. But I can't ignore my thief and decide to cut the poor bird loose. It isn't easy, so entangled he has become. He's huge, with thick, glistening black feathers and a hard, shiny black beak, full of a sinuous power now mostly spent on his futile effort to free himself. As I work with the scissors, I realize that piercing black eyes closely observe my every move, looking right into their liberator.

Finally, I free the raven and rush off to my tryst. Driving into her garage, I hear a crunch, and realize that I have cargo on the roof. I get out and find that the bike is fine, the seat neatly wedged against the garage door frame. The roof of the Honda is dimpled, some paint scratched. The bike rack took the brunt of the force, now bent beyond repair.

At supper, I tell the Potter about how liberating the raven has resolved my struggle with desire. For the moment I cut the bird free, my own desire fled as well. I feel clean, fresh, and the sympathetic spring to my step is no longer a carbuncular late-middle-aged itch.

She is riveted. "You see, the Raven is my totem. You weren't the only one being protected."

Standing in our library while Geeta is at work, I turn to a passage from Thomas Merton: "It is not that someone else is preventing you from living happily; you yourself do not know what you want." But maybe I do now.

At the Dewing Pond dock, by the house where we house-parented for four years and Geeta bore our two sons, the dock where Jacob proposed to Bevin two years ago, I tell Geeta that we don't need a year, because it's over. But the next day, I propose an experiment. We have reserved some appointments with Susan just in case we wanted to work on the relationship. Since we might see her, why not move back into the house, staying in separate bedrooms, carefully observing our interactions. She can help us sort out whatever comes up. It is a chance to grow, whether we stay together or not.

One part of this plan makes me hesitate. I want Geeta to move her meditation room, an extension of the master bedroom. I have essentially slept in it ever since building the house on Snake Ridge, since it's right at the foot of our bed. We once hung curtains, but I struck them long ago, preferring the cathedral ceiling and its exposed half-round poplar rafters. That meant seeing her kitschy posters of the gods and the perennially overflowing altar, crammed as any Hindu household. Back at Kudzoo Kastle, our first shared bedroom, we at least had a framed wall and open doorway between the bed and the tiny yoga-meditation room. A boundary.

Before I mention it, Geeta says, "I'm going to move the meditation room."

"Great. I was going to ask you to, but thought you might be offended."

"Swami Nirliptananda (the new Sivananda Ashram head) told me to move it a year ago, but I thought you didn't like change."

Just like that, we accomplish the hardest part about the move. No longer do I feel like an encumbrance, an imposter in her meditation room. And no longer do I feel her in my space, compromised by graven images.

When we see Susan a fortnight later, she takes one look at us and says, "It looks like things have definitely shifted."

July 2005. *I get back home after a storm and find total mayhem. A large hickory has broken off and is lying atop the chimney, which is now on the east side of house, no apparent damage. The chimney, the lingam, saved the house. In front, a massive beech tree lies across the yard, it's topmost tiny branches just touching the greenhouse glazing. There is debris everywhere, whole trees are on all sides of the house, trunks crossing up in the air. I think I will call the Shufords; they'll get a lot of lumber from this. In the middle of this mayhem lies a large dog, white and yellow, lying there calmly, at home. He lifts his head in recognition, then lays it back down. I look to the South and see a tall squarish structure, dull yellow. I go to check it out and find that the huge beech tree was cut by the construction crew renovating the place.*

As I mull over the dream, I realize the color of the edifice to the south is precisely that of buildings at Sivananda Ashram. The saffron Tower of Vedanta has almost beeched my Tree of Life. But the lingam-chimney itself, the pillar of the personal ashram I built, protects my home, where I am reunited with my comfortable, loyal dog-soul, presiding familiar spirit of this site. I will survive the storm.

Love and Work. Both have been sick, eaten by the Invisible Worm of Doubt. In two successive periods of counseling, I wanted to bracket love, and get on with work. Now, love is vigorous and steady. My wife, unlike many her age, is responsive, her cup overflowing. There, at least, I am content. But work?

I have chosen to work to awaken others to the escalating global ecocrisis as the final chapter in my life's work. The more climate science I read and understand, the more worried I become. I teach Joanna's Deep Ecology workshops, where folks go deeply into sympathy with the earth. They seem to get that we are daily crucifying the Earth, as Matthew Fox says. But this is within the nest of a protected retreat. Later I see the same folks carrying on their lives as if nothing had happened, materially acquisitive, eating from every corner of the industrial food empire, jet-setting around the world, spewing CO2. *Father, forgive them, for they know not what they do.* But what if we do know, and do it anyway out of habit, greed, and apathy? An extinct species, a collapsed ecosystem, has no resources with which to forgive.

And am I so different from my wayward students? I read to Geeta from a hard-hitting piece on the eco-sins of the middle class, precisely those who have the material means, potentially the time and energy, to do something about the crisis. She returns a withering barrage of facts about my own excesses—and hers as well. "Don't talk about the middle class as if you were somehow separate from them." *Your wife is your guru.* So be it.

It's hard not to see my work within the frame of the End Time—not of the Earth, certainly, but of our species and so much that we love. So when a swami, supposedly a realized being, comes to speak at the Celo Community Center, I am prepared with my question. It's the same I asked Sunderlal in Tehri ten years earlier.

"Swamiji, what happens to the Creator's desire for Creation to know him through attaining self-realization as human beings if an irreversible wave of climate change leads to the extinction of our species on this planet?"

Audible gasps ripple through the full hall of listeners. It is a good question.

Swami Parmanand responds, "Do you know creation?"

Chastened by the knowledge of all that I don't know, I reply, "Sounds like what Yahweh said to Job out of the whirlwind."

Swami Parmanand mimes a stalk of wheat. "What happens when the stalk ripens to maturity?" he asks.

"It is harvested," Job replies.

The Swami nods. Just so the world when it has run its course, and thus our species when it's race is run, whether the divine *lila*—the game that God plays by hiding Himself in all creation, as the *Upanishad* playfully details— is fulfilled or not.

As Swami Parmanand holds his forearm up to the sky, I am struck by the homology with the Eleusinian mysteries, where the priest held up a blade of wheat to be sacrificed, Demeter sacrificing her daughter Persephone, to be reborn as spring. Both the Dionysian and Christian mysteries replay this ritual. The swami is extending our local imagery— local to the West and the planet—to the universal dance of death and rebirth, universe after universe.

The swami isn't finished. "Do you know the purpose for which you were born?"

Damn. They always get to this, these teachers. Even the casual Hindu fellow traveler on the train would ask, "And what is your purpose, my goodsirrh?" My purpose, from the standpoint of Vedanta and a line of sages stretching back five thousand years is the Hindu version of *know thyself.* Become realized yourself, and stop worrying about creation.

"Swamiji, I understand what you are saying. But I don't accept this with the same equanimity as a realized being."

Swami Parmanand nods again, smiling. At least the aspirant knows where things stand.

On a bright crystal-clear afternoon in October, Geeta comes into my bedroom, once our marriage bed, dressed in the skimpy multicolored bra and G-string she once modeled for me in the dressing room at Victoria's Secret in Fargo. Pushing sixty, she still looks damn good. On the corner of the bed, I seat her on my lap and we have our own private lap-dance, without the constraining rules of gentlemen's clubs. Pingala has come home to Shiva, come home to roost.

THE PLATFORM OF THE HEART

When Jesse and I accompanied Geeta on site visits for Right Sharing in 1999, we visited a very old temple near Madurai, not far from our quarters at the Gandhi Peace Center. It was a Shiva-temple, but more specifically the temple honored his son Dakshinamurthi, the silent south-facing god so central to the teaching of Ramana Maharshi. If Ramana was an incarnation of Shiva, this is the aspect he embodied.

My interest was first drawn by the unusual quality of the sculptures in the pillared front hall, exquisite renderings in black stone of the Shaivite pantheon with incredibly detailed gestures of hand and face. One statue showed Shiva as hunter, an affectionate Nandi (his bull-servant) curled about his legs, licking his hand. At a focal pillar depicting Shiva-Parvati, the priest showed us the deeply hollowed stone at the foot of the statue created by generations of devotees' foreheads in prostration. We followed suit, even skeptical Jesse. I felt grasped by the familiar from the moment I came into this temple. Everything but the hollowed ritual stone was covered with a layer of dust. Looking around at all the cobwebs on the statues, I was reminded of home in North Carolina, where the spiders we protect re-spin webs as soon as we remove them.

"I wish we could donate money to clean the place up," Geeta said.

As we proceeded to the heart of the temple, we approached a beautiful life-sized black stone statue of Dakshinamurthi, rendering all of his silent dignity. The ever-silent youthful son of Shiva sits under a peepul tree, its canopy stylized as two cobra hoods. The first snake graces one of his right hands; the second supports his left knee. He is kingly, bearing a magnificent Mayan-looking headdress, his right foot planted on the back of the toddler ego, as in Shiva Nataraj statues. The hands in his lap inscribe the peace mudra of the Buddha. We turned from this exquisite statue to enter the central sanctuary, where instead of a lingam astride its *yoni* platform, we found only an empty platform. Its import readily struck me, almost a gasp of wonder. But to make sure we got it, our priest motioned us over for an explanation.

The priest was burly, yet with a dignified, gentle manner. He was dressed only in a white dhoti, his twice-born red string a carpenter's chalkline strung diagonally from waist to shoulder. He gave an eloquent little prologue about the matter-of-fact tolerance of the Hindu religion, then centered his homily on the platform. He explained very carefully the usual cult depictions of the *ars sacra*: the lingam, representing the cosmic power, occupied this "platform" in most Shiva temples. "Here, however, you notice there is no lingam. So what is the meaning? The meaning is that this is the platform of the heart, and we each must pray within to find what is the divinity belonging on this platform. It is whatever your heart deeply desires. But I suggest sincere purification to help you find what is on your platform, and Lord Dakshinamurthi can assist you in this sacred act."

We all listened intently. I recalled Joseph Campbell: "God is your ultimate concern." For a deep moment I didn't want to leave. But we had women's associations to visit, and in the context of the day's *dharma*, there was no point in lingering. As we left Jesse commented, "It sounds like Quakerism to me. I can live with that." Father, mother and son walked slowly and thoughtfully together back to their taxi.

This experience was a gift, a profound restoration of the old Hindu mystery. The temple, the statue, the empty platform, and the words of the presiding priest, whom I thanked warmly, all brought me back to where I began, Puer's initial awakening passage. Then the river of life swept me up again in its current.

Almost ten years after visiting that funky temple near Madurai, Ramana-Dakshinamurthi has come back into my life, whose whole panoply and drama I see as preparing the heart platform. Yesterday I was out splitting wood, and suddenly, right behind my head, I felt Dakshinamurthi rise, straight up, out to the edge of the enfolded universe. It reminded me of Shiva manifesting as an infinite lingam of light, outstripping the power shows of Brahma and Vishnu, who bowed in recognition of his preeminence. Right there, the South Indian brahmins say, at Arunachala. Back on Cambridge Street at Harvard Ed, Puer hung a wall poster of Ram and Lakshman sacrificing to Vishnu as Shiva looked down benevolently from heaven, trident in hand, young moon on his brow. Shiva presided over Vishnu and his avatar Rama from heaven, essentially the same idea.

Dakshinamurthi has hovered about ever since my first visit to Tiruvanamalai on our honeymoon, where I purchased a little soapstone statue for eight rupees. He has quietly journeyed through drawers, boxes and desk-nooks, now nestling in our river rock chimney-lingam in the meditation room, facing south. On the altar sits a portrait of Ramana Maharshi, the photo Maurice Frydman gave me in Bombay in 1968. It has not always graced the altar. Sometimes the master's face felt accusing, reminding me that I was a wayward devotee. I would return it to the little clothbound folder in which Maurice had presented it, bound and hidden, like Maurice folded into a tiny mantis skeleton in my matchbox dream.

A few years ago, Dakshinamurthi rose almost imperceptibly behind me, warding off a panic reaction, banishing the Lamia figure who had usurped the image of my beloved Geeta Jyothi, embodied feminine manifestation of Shiva's light-lingam. This happened only a few feet from where I was now splitting wood, directly below the upstairs meditation room. No need to go to South India to bathe in that light.

When we first moved to Celo more than thirty-five years ago, I dreamt of the red-clay bank of a great river, and looking closely, saw the emergent big toe, then the ankle of a great god embedded in the riverbank. I immediately knew it was the foot of Ramana. The rivers sustaining our lives, whether the Mississippi of Geeta's youth, the Mobile River of mine, now the pure, clear South Toe of our adult home in these mountains, have all been watched over, channeled by Bhagavan Ramana.

The guided meditation at the Asheville workshop with Tara, Bhagavan tenderly holding our hands within his, was the perfect counter to my dream of the broken wedding ring a few years ago. He radiated love and acceptance, and we bathed in it. Here was the sacrament we needed, a couple of old married warriors, too tired, too close to allowing the happiness that is our birthright, to fight any more for the first-born's illusory assurance of being right and in control.

AHAM and A. Ramana

The AHAM ashram is in Asheboro, NC, about three hours southeast of us. When we learn of it from two trusted friends, Geeta and I go for a weekend exploration. The acronym is for Association for the Happiness of all Mankind. I like the Sanskrit, *I AM*. But I'm embarrassed by its promise of happiness, not something I have considered the highest goal in life, and certainly not attainable for everyone.

The AHAM campus is a collection of trailers, prefab houses, and some rustic cabins loosely arrayed around one central brick house. Trucks rumble by on the state highway, but the ashram is deeply quiet. In the carport sits a Cadillac bearing the license plate, "AHAM 1." The office trailer is painted green and brown camouflage, resembling a little jungle army outpost. But the main hall is spacious and light-filled, surrounded by glass doors. Entering, I am struck by the twin portraits gracing the focal wall to either side of the teacher's big armchair on a raised platform. Stage left, Jesus, a familiar rendering with handsome beatific gaze, heavily lidded eyes looking slightly down. Stage right, Ramana Maharshi, the very photo I have known so long, left eye total compassion, right eye, cool and penetrating. They are the presiding Masters at AHAM.

The spiritual director of AHAM is A. Ramana, a large, balding man, now past eighty. He wears glasses, shorts and plain white t-shirt, a prominent tattoo of Texas on his left forearm. Since his stroke a few years ago, he moves less well and needs help eating, wearing a bib. According to his followers, he is a realized being. But he is no-nonsense, and roughly rejects any gestures of guru-worship.

Our first conversation is pleasant. We tell him about our honeymoon to India. I speak of Maurice Frydman's sending me to the Maharshi's ashram at Tiruvanamalai. "Maurice Frydman, I've heard of him. There are good reports of Maurice. You know, we have an ashram in Tiruvanamalai."

Suddenly I remember. We had just arrived outside Ramanasramam during our family visit in 1999. As we got out of the taxi, a man approached to tell us about a teacher "also named Ramana," recommending his ashram for satsang. Standing in the busy thoroughfare in front of what had been our bucolic home base in South India during our honeymoon, I was in shock at all the traffic and development right up to the slopes of the sacred Hill. My worst fears were realized. No way was I going to visit some American imposter, when I already had to share my precious time here with visits to women's microcredit associations.

So this is that man, and this his American ashram. At the long dining table, Geeta speaks of Sivananda Ashram and our long association with Swami Chidananda. "Yes, we know these people. Our ashrams recognize each other. They do good work there." The conversation continues for ten minutes, all very pleasant, all on the level of spiritual gossip.

Early the next morning, when I enter the meditation hall, from his perch on a large comfortable chair on a raised dais, hands folded about his midriff, A. Ramana lifts his huge head from its downward incline, shooting me a glance. Quick, sly as a cat, piercing my depths. I feel a definite jolt of energy. Is this a silent initiation of the sort that devotees of Bhagavan Ramana Maharshi spoke about? Who is this guy?

Around the time of my initial immersion in India, a Texan climbing the ladder of the sales motivation movement, while passing a bookstore in Dallas, was prompted to enter. He walked to a shelf in the spirituality section, pulled down a book and opened it to the same photo of Ramana Maharshi that Maurice Frydman gave me, cutting it out of another book at his dining table in Bombay with a razor pen. Gazing at the photo, the man entered a place of profound awareness. When he brought it to the bookstore owner to ask who this teacher was, the owner said he didn't have the book in his inventory and had never seen it before. Dee Trammel left with the book, and set about discovering the Maharshi's self-inquiry for himself. The process deepened until he began to experience a continual awareness that the Self, Brahman, the Ground of Being, was all that existed.

After a couple of years, Trammel started to develop a training course in practicing self-inquiry. He would integrate the Hindu vichara with motivational material and the Twelve-Step program. The result was AHAM. When Trammel met the popular Hindu teacher Muktananda, the swami gave him the name Arunachala Ramana. Students call him A. Ramana to distinguish him from Ramana Maharshi.

Dee Trammell began his journey as a working-class West Texan. As a small child, he had a mysterious experience overseen by a local shaman, healing a terrible burn that covered most of his body. This gave him a deep sense of inner happiness and detachment from the world until age ten, when he lost the blessing. After three marriages and a motley career giving motivational lectures as the chief disciple of Napoleon Hill, his long search ended in that Dallas bookstore.

The next morning at breakfast, we encounter a different A. Ramana. He sits at the head of the long hardwood table, hands folded over his belly as he leans back, looking at each of us in turn. His manner reminds me of Doc Armstrong when he confronted me about my co-habitation with Judi Goldman at Indian Springs: towering man, long table, moment of truth. Eyes keen, he gives the group a koan: "The function of the mind is to supplant Being and all that Being has become identified with. Therefore, if Being has become identified with the mind—meaning it now thinks it is the mind—then what has become the purpose of the mind?"

Deep silence. Ramana repeats the query.

One woman says, "To achieve Realization."

Ramana shakes his head.

A man says, "To maximize pleasure and minimize pain."

Ramana laughs. "And how long were you in analysis?"

Another woman: "To undo its own knots and confused pathways. To get back to a desireless state."

Ramana: "That is our purpose here, but not the mind's."

Geeta then cites impeccable Vedanta. "The purpose of the mind is to create the world."

"Nope." This is not what he's looking for, either. We are all in deep puzzlement. Geeta and exchange a long quizzical look.

When we reassemble for lunch, none of us can go any further. After the meal, Ramana reveals the answer: "The mind's purpose is to survive itself." Many confused looks. "See how the mind obfuscates? It's so simple, and yet we can't see what's right in front of our noses."

Stan, one of the trainers, tries to help, pointing to the language of the obituary: "X is survived by y and z. He's using the term in an archaic way."

OK, the mind wants to perpetuate itself, never to die. It supplants the deathless Self, an imposter. I realize Ramana's word-choice is perfect. "Survive itself" definitely works for me. This guy is no slouch.

After this first taste, we decide to return for the eight-day intensive training. I attend first, and Geeta will follow, since couples undertake the plunge separately to avoid psychic contamination. The second night of the intensive, A. Ramana stares intently through his dark-rimmed glasses as he studies our faces. "Would you rather be right or happy?"

Chanting in chorus like a group of kindergarteners, most of the others immediately say they want to be happy. I hesitate. This sounds a lot like the personality test where you must answer whether you'd rather be smart and mean or dumb and happy. I always opted for smart at any cost. But I realize I have not come to challenge. I know from friends I respect that AHAM has transformed lives. Maybe I'll give happiness a chance. So when Ramana turns in the direction of my hesitation, I answer, "Happy... at least for now," feeling doubts crowd in immediately.

Ramana's eyes widen. He leans forward. "Now? And what moment is it as we speak? Is there any other existence than now?"

Embarrassed, I realize I've fallen into one of the legion of traps that await us all at this table.

At midweek we meet with A. Ramana again. I have been wondering about integrating my passion for healing the earth with this fundamental process whose end result is to recognize the world's unreality. We each take a turn querying the master. As he levels his implacable gaze at me, I am disturbed by the annual travel back-and-forth to the ashram in South India undertaken by staff and students. Ramana himself glories in the mild weather, being able to stay barefoot and shirtless.

"Bhagavan Ramana Maharshi lived in a more innocent time, before we realized that our actions were causing Global Warming. Nevertheless, he lived the simplest of lives. If one were a realized being today, wouldn't his life be virtually carbon-neutral?"

Ramana stiffens and gives a long harangue, ending with "Don't tell us how to run our program!"

I am bewildered. But I've been here before, severely chastened by a holy man. As we leave, one of the women in our group, another thinking type, bolsters me. "Thanks for asking your question."

The next time we gather at lunch, Ramana is conciliatory. "I was too hard on you all last time," acknowledging the rude intrusion of personality. But shock and awe is his method. "I just had a really good shit. That shit is worth more than all the concepts of the world's scientists and philosophers."

Some of the staff and regular visitors chuckle knowingly. I stiffen in resistance. Dee Trammell is simply a crude redneck Texan trying to shock us spiritual wannabees. But this is too much. I immediately think of the climate scientists and their elegant models, coming closer and closer to replicating the world inexorably melting around us.

"I mean it," Ramana says. "This is no metaphor. These theories are concepts, no better than dreams, which are concepts of another order. Concepts have no reality."

Folks at AHAM do not think much of dreams, following this teacher and Bhagavan Ramana as well. I muse about the whole symbolic world this method leaves out, the middle realm of metaphor, approaching reality by indirection. A future question begins to form.

But the method of self-inquiry, repeated over and over, interspersed by exercises and Socratic interrogation, starts to take hold. When Geeta and I were first there, I briefly experienced dropping identification with this body, but it didn't last. This time, a profound morning meditation sends me to a place that deepens and deepens. I am in a kind of trance. All my senses are hyper-alert, but I don't identify with the information they relay. I carefully observe this state during an entire silent lunch and into the afternoon before it wears off. A couple of evenings later I read Bhagavan Ramana's comment, answering a question put by my own Maurice Frydman. The Master distinguishes between *manolaya*, a kind of self-hypnosis, and *manonasa*, permanent extinction of thoughts. *Manolaya* is a temporary state, a momentary abeyance. I'm still wading in the baby pool.

At our last *satsang* with A. Ramana, I steel myself to repeat the question about earthcare, emphasizing my efforts with the churches. I speak calmly, without accusation in my voice or heart.

"Fine. Hell, start a movement. But you'd better do the inquiry, because it may be too late."

So this guy does know something about climate science after all. And yes, I have to agree that, having discovered a method which takes away the burden of fear and guilt over wrecking the planet, I need to make the practice regular.

Towards the end of my intensive, we learn of the Venkataraman family's insistence, backed by the brahmin priests, that nobody be allowed to teach Ramana Maharshi's *vichara* at Sri Ramanasramam. Hearing this feels like being struck by a glacier that has been moving towards me all my life. *Of course, we received no instruction.* Hugo Maier, the leader of the Euro-American contingent in the early Seventies, had started his own ashram, filled with Germans, surrounded by high walls. A. Ramana started his, as well, right in my backyard. Back at Ramanasramam, the priests chant the Vedas while devotees circle the mahasamadhi tomb with the odd black statue of the master, no palpable expression in the eyes. We would sit in the hall, each in our private devotions, and joyfully climb the Hill. But no instruction in yoga, meditation, learning Sanskrit, or interpreting texts, like at Sivananda Ashram. And I preferred it that way. Sivananda Ashram felt so busy, echoing the master who founded it. But my freedom at the foot of Arunachala left me too much at the mercy of moods, hankering to experience the special lingering vibes. It was not *practice*.

Practice. With AHAM, retreats are followed by buddy-pairings and weekly group calls, reinforcing and deepening the self-inquiry practice taught at the center. After several training events, I match with a "sponsor," a senior student in the process. As with AA, this person is a mentor, a spiritual friend, inviting a relationship that progresses indefinitely. The goal is to end one's addiction to thinking, working through ten principles, echoing Alcoholics Anonymous. Though progress often feels slow, Ron, my sponsor, has become my lifeline, calmly and persistently reminding me that the mind's agenda is irrelevant to the heart's current.

In addition to the trainings, Geeta has gone several times to the Asheboro ashram to do *seva*, sacred service, while others undergo training. She's there now. With a skeletal staff and only three trainers, they sorely need volunteers. Her sponsor is the director of AHAM's ashram in Tiruvanamalai, and she and Jan seem to have a genuinely mutual relationship. Many of the AHAM folks benefit from Geeta's thorough knowledge of Vedanta as practiced in India, and her knowledge of Sanskrit. Her practice, which used to rely heavily on the Divine Life swamis in India, from my perspective has blossomed, seamlessly weaving East and West. No longer seeking the special protection of *sannyas*, she now has support for her Advaita Vedanta practice without the necessity of going to India. That support comes from the AHAM community of seekers and now, at long last, from me.

After all our struggles, what seemed a common bond when we first met is truly so. More and more, we are "conscious company" for one another, *gurubhai* as well as husband and wife. Through a rough Texan and his motley crew in rural North Carolina, that which we sought forty years ago has borne fruit, with continuing access to careful, honest pruning.

In our youth, we traveled halfway around the world so I could show Geeta that the real teachers were in India. I had already met Maurice Frydman in Bombay, and she found Swami Chidananda in Rishikesh. But in Tiruvanamalai, we encountered only the silent teaching of Dakshinamurthi, born in this age as Venkataraman Iyer, Ramana Maharshi. Though there was no outward master, no formal instruction in Bhagavan Ramana's *vichara*, the silent inner teacher has stayed with us henceforward, waiting to unfold in our lives and practice.

So who rests on the platform of *this* heart? At my best moments it is the unnamable God Itself, and at these moments I am a true servant-minister to my Quaker Meeting, workshop students, friends, family and wife. At others, it is merely myself as the little god, Prince Puer, this ego filling the space because it *appears* empty. The key is to hold the space, to allow it to be available to the god of the moment, incarnate in a child, lover, mother, father, sister, son, daughter-in-love. Sometimes it's an earthly place or one of her exquisite beings. I am enough of an advaitist to accept that ultimately, to *marry myself* means to marry the Self, the Being who is the Sole Actor underneath this panoply of multifarious play. I AM is the author of my life, writing the script that allows me to practice cleaning the altar, to perfect the waiting for the Self. Quakers call it "waiting worship."

Who is Shiva, Lord? Now I have my answer. Prince Puer, husband, father, seeker, teacher, are all his masks. But as the nirguni masters of Dewas insisted, the divine ultimately is without name or form. Behind the immensely powerful mythic figure named Shiva is the silent Self waiting within the Platform of the Heart: maker, sustainer and destroyer of worlds.

Glossary

adiwasi tribal, pre-Aryan dweller of Indian subcontinent
Advaita Vedanta non-dual path of Hindu religion: "not two"
andolan movement, campaign, protest
artha gaining material wealth, one of the four goals of life
arthi worship form involving waving of lights/incense in front of honoree, divine or human
asrama a monastery; also a stage of life
ayya maid (Tamil)
baksheesh gift, alms, tip
bandish short song used in khyal, two to eight lines
bedi thin hand-rolled cigarette from crude tobacco
betel nut mildly psychoactive nut chewed alone or mixed with other ingredients and rolled in leaf as paan
bhakta devotee
Bhagavan god personified, Lord
bhajan devotional song, hymn
bhang spiced concoction made with cannabis, used for religious festivals
Bhudan Andolan Vinoba Bhave's movement persuading village landowners to give land to the landless
brahmacharin celibate youth, student
bhava habitual or emotional tendencies
bhavana contemplation, spiritual cultivation in general
bus enough
chai, garam milk tea, hot
darshan viewing, seeing, showing of divine persona
dharma right order, law duty. Used for nature, society and persons.
dharamsala hostel for pilgrims
dhobi laundry person
dhoti long cloth wrapped around the waist and groin; a man's "sari"
diksha initiation, giving of teaching
dood milk
gharana a school or "house" of classical music, lineage carrying forward a particular musical style
gopi female cowherd, beloved(s) of Krishna

grhastha householder, second of four stages (asrama) of life
gunas: satwas, rajas, tamas the fundamental moods governing human behavior: purity, desire, inertia
gurubhai brother (or sister) by way of having the same teacher
harmonium portable hand-organ with bellows
Hinduism western scholars'(19th c) name for the various religious traditions endemic to South Asia; particularly those stemming from the Vedas
hoven sacrificial/ceremonial fire-pit
hridiyam the heart as spiritual organ
ishta devata chosen deity: Krishna, Hanuman, Shiva, Kali etc.
japa practice of prayer by repetition of mantra or name of god
jauhar ritual suicide of a married woman: suttee
jayanthi anniversary celebration
jnana path to the divine involving continual discrimination of real from unreal
jnani a practitioner of jnana. More often, one who is adept at the practice
juldi quickly
jyothi the inner feminine light
karma, parabdha residual karma which may govern behavior even after realization
karma yogi one following the path of service
khyal modern North Indian classical singing, representing influence of Moghul musicians on indigenous classical form. Provides great scope for improvisation.
kitchari rice, dal, and vegetables cooked together with mild spices. One-dish meal.
kutir hut, simple dwelling
lingam outer physical form, usually a stone, of Shiva, with phallic overtones.
lukri wood
mahasamadhi final absorption into Brahman
mandir temple
moksha deliverance, the final aim of life
mouni a silent devotee; *moun:* keeping silence
nadi the sound-essence of the material world.
paan betel nut and spices wrapped in betel leaf, chewed for refreshment
PCV Peace Corps Volunteer

prasad blessed food offering
puja worship, often elaborate ritual of bathing and chanting over images
pujari priest who performs puja
rajas fiery, extroverted guna (tendency)
rudraksha large seeds of plant sacred to Shiva, especially used in necklaces
sardar Sikh
saddhu wandering ascetic
samadhi, mahasamadhi state of absorption in the divine; the "great" or final absorption
samskaras the marks or scarring of the karmic body from past actions
sannyas renunciation, the final stage of life. Sannyasin: renunciate.
sarangi bowed stringed instrument derived from folk instruments, widely used to accompany khyal.
Satchidananda truth, knowledge, bliss; also swami who presided over Woodstock
Satguru the inner teacher
satsang gathering of devotees
sattwa, sattwic guna of goodness, constructive, harmonious
Shankara Shaivite medieval reformer of Hinduism
shakti feminine spiritual energy and power
shishya disciple, (not spiritual)
siddhis paranormal yogic powers
swadharma one's own particular path
taan rapid rendering of running notes in Hindustani khyal, requiring great vocal suppleness and control
tala rhythm
tanpura drone instrument providing continuo for Indian classical music, fashioned from a gourd
tapas, tapasya performance of austerity
thali "plate" consisting of a complete Indian meal
tilaka red dot on forehead, indicating a married Hindu woman
vanaprastha forest dweller, retiree from grihastha, family stage of life
Vedanta Upanishadic teachings, conclusion (danta) of the Vedas
vichara self-inquiry: Ramana Maharshi's method for Self-realization
yatra pilgrimage
yoni that in which the lingam sits, the female principle

About the Author

Robert McGahey is a retired humanities teacher, working that fertile field at settings in junior high, high school and college. He is a graduate of Harvard College, with an EdM from Harvard Graduate School of Education, following his Fulbright year in India. He earned a PhD in myth studies at Emory University's Graduate Institute of the Liberal Arts in 1989, afterwards teaching integrative humanities at Moorhead State University (MN). After retiring from full-time college teaching in 2000, he trained with Joanna Macy to facilitate deep ecology groups (*The Work that Reconnects*). He is past board member of NC Interfaith Power and Light, and past board chair of Arthur Morgan School. He and his wife Geeta have lived in the North Carolina mountains within Celo Community, the oldest non-sectarian community land trust in the US, for 45 years. He has a long history with Quaker Earthcare Witness, giving many workshops on the global ecocrisis at Friends General Conference, and is now presiding clerk of Southern Appalachian Yearly Meeting. Robert continues to be active with choral singing and hosts a contradance in Celo. He loves to hike, garden, and spend time with his four grandchildren.

Robert is the author of *The Orphic Moment* (Albany: State University of New York Press, 1994), and most recently, an essay in *Dark Mountain 17*, "The Blade of Wheat at the End of the World." He blogs at ecospirit.blogspot.com.